The British Migrant Experience, 1700–2000

The British Migrant Experience, 1700–2000

An Anthology

Edited and Introduced by
P. J. Leese
B. Piątek
I. Curyłło-Klag

Foreword by
C. K. Steedman

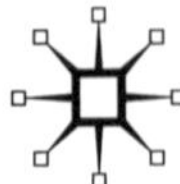

First published 2002 by
PALGRAVE MACMILLAN
Houndmills, Basingstoke, Hampshire RG21 6XS and
175 Fifth Avenue, New York, N. Y. 10010
Companies and representatives throughout the world

PALGRAVE MACMILLAN is the global academic imprint of the Palgrave Macmillan division of St. Martin's Press, LLC and of Palgrave Macmillan Ltd. Macmillan® is a registered trademark in the United States, United Kingdom and other countries. Palgrave is a registered trademark in the European Union and other countries.

ISBN 0–333–99863–4

This book is printed on paper suitable for recycling and made from fully managed and sustained forest sources.

A catalogue record for this book is available from the British Library.

Library of Congress Cataloging-in-Publication Data

The British migrant experience 1700–2000 : an anthology / edited and introduced by P. J. Leese, B. Piątek and I. Curyłło-Klag.
p. cm.
Includes bibliographical references and index.
ISBN 0-333-99863-4
1. Great Britain – Emigration and immigration – History – Sources. 2. Great Britain – Ethnic relations – Sources. 3. Great Britain – Race relations – Sources. 4. Immigrants – Great Britain – Biography. 5. Minorities – Great Britain – Biography. I. Leese, Peter. II. Piatek, B. (Beata) III. Curyllo-Klag, I. (Izabela)

DA125.A1 B755 2002
304.8′41 – dc21 2002072301

10 9 8 7 6 5 4 3 2 1
11 10 09 08 07 06 05 04 03 02

Printed and bound in Great Britain by
Antony Rowe Ltd, Chippenham and Eastbourne

Contents*

* Extracts marked [M.] relate to cases of migrancy; extracts marked [I.] to immigrancy. See General Introduction for further explanation.

Acknowledgements

Many thanks to the following: Susan Maingay and Trevor Jones of the British Council, Warsaw, who agreed to establish and continue the research funding for the project; Ros Lucas and Christine Wiskin, of the University of Warwick Department of History, who smoothed the way in making practical arrangements and obtaining copyright permissions; staff and students at the Jagiellonian University Department of English for listening to and commenting on our collective work in progress during conferences and classes; Elżbieta Wójcik-Leese for her unsparing, constructive criticism; Carolyn Steedman, for her wise council.

The editors and publishers also wish to thank the following who have kindly given permission to print extracts and copyright material in this anthology:

BEDFORDSHIRE AND LUTON ARCHIVES AND RECORDS SERVICE: for extracts from Settlement Examinations (Settlement Papers, overseers of the poor). J. BROWN: for extracts from *The Un-Melting Pot* (London: Macmillan – now Palgrave Macmillan, 1970) reproduced with the permission of Palgrave Macmillan. R. BURMAN: for extracts from 'The Jewish woman as breadwinner: the changing value of women's work in a Manchester immigrant community', *Oral History*, 10 (1982) 27–39. J. BURNETT: for extracts from *Useful Toil* (London: Routledge, 1994). CALIBAN BOOKS: for extracts from H. Mayhew, *The Morning Chronicle Survey of Labour and the Poor: The Metropolitan Districts* (Horsham: Caliban, 1981). CITY OF BRADFORD METROPOLITAN COUNCIL ARTS, MUSUEMS AND LIBRARIES DIVISION: for extracts from *Destination Bradford: A Century of Immigration* (Bradford: Heritage Recording Unit, 1987). K. E. COLLINS: for extracts from *Second City Jewry: the Jews of Glasgow in the Age of Expansion, 1790–1919* (Glasgow: Scottish Jewish Archive 1990) reproduced with the permission of the Scottish Jewish Archive Centre. T. EDENSOR, and M. KELLY: for extracts from *Moving Worlds: Personal Recollections of Twenty-one Immigrants to Edinburgh* (Edinburgh: Polygon, n.d). P. EDWARDS and D. DABYDEEN: for extracts from *Black Writers in Britain 1760–1890* (Edinburgh: Edinburgh University Press, 1991). N. EVANS: for extracts from 'Immigrants and minorities in Wales, 1880–1940: a comparative perspective', in Holmes, C. (ed.) *Migration in European Society, vol. 2* (Cheltenham: Edward Elgar, 1996). F. FINNEGAN: for extracts from *Poverty and Prejudice, A Study of Irish Immigrants in York 1840–1875* (Cork: Cork University Press, 1982). Copyright © Cork University Press, 1982. Reproduced by permission of Cork University Press, Crawford Business Park, Crosses Green, Cork, Ireland. T. GALLAGHER: for extracts from *Glasgow: The Uneasy Peace. Religious Tension in Modern Scotland* (Manchester: Manchester University Press, 1987).

H. GOULBOURNE: for extracts from 'Oral history and black labour in Britain: an overview', *Oral History*, 8 (1980) 24–34. J. GREEN: for extracts from *Them* (London: Secker and Warburg, 1990). HAMBLEDON AND LONDON: for extracts from H. HEINRICK, *A Survey of the Irish in England*, (1872), ed. O'Day, A. (London: Hambledon, 1990). M. JONES: for extracts from 'Welsh immigrants in the cities of North-West England, 1880–1930: some oral testimony', *Oral History*, 9 (1981) 33–41. B. KAY: for extracts from *The Complete Odyssey: Voices from Scotland's Recent Past* (Edinburgh: Polygon, 1996). R. I. LAWLESS: for extracts from *From Ta'izz to Tyneside* (Exeter: Exeter University Press, 1995). D. MAC AMHLAIGH: from *An Irish Navvy: the Diary of an Exile* (London: Routledge, 1964). INSTITUTE OF RACE RELATIONS: for extracts from K. C. Ng, *The Chinese in London* (Oxford: Oxford University Press, 1968). A. OSLER: for extracts from *Speaking Out: Black Girls in Britain* (London: Virago Upstarts, 1989). C. M. V. TRIPP: for extracts from K. Gershon, *We Came as Children: A Collective Autobiography* (London: Gollancz, 1966). P. MOHANTI: for extracts from *Through Brown Eyes* (Oxford: Oxford University Press, 1985). R. PERKS: for extracts from '"You're different: you're one of us": the making of a British Asian', *Oral History*, 15 (1987) 67–74. N. M. C. SINCLAIR: for extracts from *The Tiger Bay Story* (Treforest: Zenith, 1993). D. SINGH TATLA: for extracts from 'This is our home now: reminiscences of a Punjabi migrant in Coventry', *Oral History*, 21 (1993) 68–74. B. TEMPLE: for extracts from 'Telling tales: accounts and selves in the journeys of British Poles', *Oral History*, 23 (1995) 60–4. UNIVERSITY OF LEICESTER PRESS: for extracts from L. Sponza, *Italian Immigrants in Nineteenth-Century Britain: Realities and Images* (Leicester: Leicester University Press, 1998). WARWICKSHIRE COUNTY COUNCIL RECORD OFFICE: for extracts from Settlement Examinations (Settlement Papers, Overseers of the Poor), Warwickshire Record Office, Bedworth. J. L. WATSON: for extracts from *Between Two Cultures: Migrants and Minorities in Britain* (Oxford: Blackwell, 1977). B. WILLIAMS: for extracts from 'The Jewish immigrant in Manchester: the contribution of oral history', *Oral History*, 7 (1979) 43–53. J. ZUBRZYCKI: for extracts from *Polish Immigrants in Britain: a Study of Adjustment* (The Hague: Nijhoff, 1956) with kind permission of Kluwer Academic Publishers.

Every effort has been made to trace all copyright holders, but if any have been inadvertently overlooked, the publisher will be pleased to make the necessary arrangements at the first opportunity. In the following cases no copyright holder could be traced:

T. J. COTTLE, *Black Testimony: The Voices of Britain's West Indians* (London: Wildwood House, 1978). A. G. DENT, (ed.) *The Family Records of Benjamin Shaw Mechanic of Dent, Dolphinholme and Preston, 1772–1841* (n.p: Record Society of Lancashire and Cheshire, 1991). E. FERRON, *'Man, You've Mixed': A Jamaican Comes to Britain* (London: Whiting & Birch, 1995). R. GLASS, *Newcomers: The West Indians in London* (London: Centre for Urban Studies/George Allen & Unwin, 1960). M. SHINWELL: for extracts from *Lead with the Left: My First*

Ninety-six Years (London: Cassell, 1981). H. THOROGOOD, *East of Aldgate* (London: George Allen and Unwin, 1935). M. LEVINSON, *The Trouble with Yesterday* (Bath: Cedric Chivers, 1973). A. LEVY, *History of the Sunderland Jewish Community* (London: Macdonald, 1956). K. LUNN, (ed.) *Hosts, Immigrants and Minorities: Historical Responses to Newcomers in British Society* (London: Dawson, 1980). B. MAAN, *The New Scots: The Story of Asians in Scotland* (Edinburgh: John Donald, 1992). N. MORRISON, *My Story* (Inverness: Highland News Office, 1937). C. ROTH, *The Rise of Provincial Jewry* (London: Jewish Monthly, 1950). Settlement Examinations (Settlement Papers, Overseers of the Poor), Bradford Record Office, Sharp Bridges. U. SHARMA, *Rampal and His Family* (London: Collins, 1971).

Foreword

Professor C. K. Steedman

What is it we know, then, about movement and stories, about journeys and narrative? Perhaps, that the journey provides the paradigmatic structure of Western literature (and perhaps of life, if we take 'life' to mean the enormous variety of ways in which people have understood what it is they're *in*, and what it is they're *doing* by existing). All the founding narratives of Western society are to do with this kind of movement, from one place to another, in order to become some other kind of person, some other sort of thing. It does not matter that in the Biblical variant of this paradigm, the actors are *forced* to do what it is they do; what matters is that they *walk out* of Eden:

> Some natural tears they dropt, but wiped them soon;
> The world was all before them, where to choose
> Their place of rest and Providence their guide:
> They, hand in hand, with wand'ring steps and slow,
> Through Eden took their solitary way.
> (Milton, *Paradise Lost*, XII. 645–9)

Without those steps, there is nothing: no story at all. Why then, in the accounts that follow in this book, do so few people pay attention to the steps, the walking, the details of the journey (dusty road, canal barge, railway line, jet plane); why so little attention to the means of *getting there*?

The answer to that question must have something to do with what lies at the end of that journey, or what happens during that journey, in some other dimension of time and space, some other place of being, separate from the journey itself. Here, the walking, the movement, one foot in front of the other, is the means by which *something else* happens, and the hero, the character, the traveller, is made into something new and strange.

Ulysses did it, and Odysseus too; but the story is always also about the lower orders. The narratives of movement and identity reproduced in this book begin in the eighteenth century, as if providing historical evidence for Franco Moretti's literary propositions concerning the great move in representation from spatiality to temporality in the modern period, and that provides the framework to his discussion of novels about relatively ordinary human lives that are the focus of *The Way of the World*. In the world and in the text, we must reckon up innumerable stories of movement, made under the impulse of the many revolutions (political, philosophical, economic) that Moretti uses as the context of the *Bildungsroman* he discusses. That the journey was made by the unimportant, the low, the 'mob', is exemplified in a simple proposition of, say, Henry Fielding, writing *Joseph Andrews* (1742) and the way in which he was able to make his hero a common man – a servant no less – and even to spend long stretches of the novel exploring the question of whether or not his hero was fit to be one. An attractive (though 'low') hero goes on a journey: he *travels* through a landscape that is both a 'real' geographical landscape; and also through a moral landscape, something in the manner of the knight of the courtly romance, more like his popular derivative, the chapbook of Guy of Warwick or Bevis of Southampton. In this new form of writing, that we have come to call the novel, the protagonists *change*: they are altered by happening and circumstance; the journey plays a part in what it is they have become, in the story their inventor tells about them. This capacity to change, to undergo a psychological process, is what makes them *characters*, in the literary sense, and *subjects* in the philosophical sense. But over the last thirty years many have observed that female characters in the eighteenth-century novel stay indoors, do not go on journeys, in the same way as men do.

Traditions of writing, theories of criticism, and implicit understandings on the part of the reader as to what a hero is, what a heroine is, have a bearing on literature concerning women writers in the second half of the eighteenth century as well. In fact, we need to think of both literary history *and* of fairly new ideals of feminine propriety if we are to consider the problems of constructing a heroine in this period. Public morality and public taste demanded that female characters be models of a kind of perfection, models of domestic happiness and duty, in much of the way that Richardson depicted Pamela in 1740. Pamela is a richly conceived character, but at the same time, she just *is*, or rather her goodness just *is*. She does not acquire it, through a progress in life. As Jane Spencer says in *The Rise of the Woman Novelist* (1986), a mixed character was all very well for the depiction of a young man, but it was difficult for readers to get to grips with the idea of a woman who was lovably fallible, for fallibility in a woman had much more serious implications than it did for a man. A heroine could not be allowed the experience that shaped a hero, for experience would involve sexual encounters, and those were unthinkable in a respectable young woman. Faced with the problem of depicting change – character change – in young women, writers like Fanny Burney and Jane Austen resolved the difficulty by making the landscape smaller and the journey quieter for their heroines: in fact, by making the landscape and the struggle an *interior* one, that largely takes place in the heroine's mind, and in her heart. And in this way, an extraordinary richness of *insideness*, of *interiority* in characters, the reason why we read novels, and why we find them so pleasurable still, was born. Very soon, at the end of the eighteenth century, and at the beginning of the nineteenth, male novelists were going to be able to do the same for their heroes: Goethe in Germany and Stendhal in France, were going to be able to give depth and interiority to young male characters like Wilhelm Meister and Julien Sorel. They learned a trick perhaps, a device, a set of textual procedures, that had been worked out for the main part by women writers faced with the difficulties of showing change in young female characters who (outside the realm of pornography) were scarcely allowed any experience at all.

Joseph Andrews is about a journey, a farcical, funny, Hogarthian journey through sordid inns and the unpleasantness of social relations in eighteenth-century England. Fielding sets the journey in real time, in a real society. Early on, Parson Adams tells his audience, and Fielding's slow-witted readers, something very useful about the journey we are on as readers, which is not a journey through a real world, nor even its simulacrum, but a journey through a text, in which other texts, and characters and ideas from other texts surface: 'Since thou art so dull to misunderstand me still . . . I will inform thee; the travelling I mean is in books, the only way of travelling by which any knowledge may be acquired . . .'

There are Franco Moretti's important points about the *Bildungsroman* to note here. First, that under conditions of modernity, when high value came to be placed on youth, the *Bildungsroman* emerged as a symbolic form. Moretti argues that from the mid-eighteenth century onwards, Western society came to see youth as the most meaningful part of life. He suggests that what makes heroes and heroines like Julien Sorel and Elizabeth Bennett interesting, is youth itself, 'or rather,' as he says 'the European novel's numerous versions of youth, become for our modern culture the age which holds the "meaning of life".' The *Bildungsroman* was the symbolic form developed in order to explore and underline this perception of youth as the most significant part of human life. The topic of the *Bildungsroman* is the protagonist's life and character as he or she grows from childhood through various experiences – often through a spiritual crisis or internal struggle – to maturity, and to a recognition and acceptance of his or her place in the world. Moretti explains this form, and the significance attached to Youth within it, by considering the social processes that gave rise to capitalism in the West. He discusses the collapse of status society (society organized hierarchically by rank), and the processes of urbanization and industrialization. Old forms of socializing the young into preordained position were eroded; ideas of apprenticeship, of 'growing up', of becoming 'mature' no longer meant a slow and predictable progress towards a father's or a mother's work and role. Capitalism (particularly the kind of early industrialization experienced in Northern Europe, and its seeking out of new sources and new markets in the colonized contact zones) imposed mobility, and dismantled the continuity between the generations. The written forms of the society began to explore these questions through tales of travel and adventure; tales of wandering and getting lost; stories that end with finding a home, and 'finding yourself', at one and the same time. Literature explores these questions through what Moretti terms 'an exploration of social space': the self is found through exploring this space.

The fictional journey resolves a dilemma of modernity, and of modern capitalism. The dilemma was that 'It is not enough that the social order is legal; it must also appear symbolically legitimate.' This is to say that 'free individuals must perceive social norms as [their] own, fusing external compulsion and internal impulses, until the former is no longer distinguishable from the latter'. Moretti's thesis then, is about learning (all of us learning, given the state we're in) to want to do – to *really* want to do – what you have to do anyway. Such a reading of the novel eschews all notions that a literary form is, or can be, a *reflection* of social reality. Moretti reads the eighteenth and nineteenth century novel as a social practice, or as an *activity* within modern capitalist society, a practice or activity which is formative of the individual human subject. Thus the *Bildungsroman* 'works' by bringing the hero or heroine, and the reader, to the point of understanding that happiness is to be found at home, by giving up freedom; and by recognizing that the true self is the socialized self (the self that has learned a lesson, on its journey through the social world). The individual then, *finds herself or himself* in society, not in freedom. In this argument marriage is an unique institution in that it offers the most private of emotional satisfactions, and that is also a cornerstone of the state. In the *Bildungsroman* it offers a solution: the finding of a home which is simultaneously the finding of a self. In Moretti's analysis, marriage is the social bond which is freely entered into, chosen, and in which happiness may be realized at last.

What Moretti does *not* observe, but which is implied in his argument is that the position of men and women within this symbolic form were different, for men and women make different kinds of journey. In the realist novel, women cannot realistically explore social space, and most kinds of adventures and exploits are not available to them. So the common form of symbolic journey taken by a heroine is a journey to the interior, to discover the true self, and its needs. We should add to this observation the recent discussion by historians of the separation of public and private spheres, and speculate that in the late eighteenth and early nineteenth centuries, young bourgeois women (unlike young men) became *more* (not less) certain of the life work that was expected of them: marriage, the life of Domestic Woman. The feminine 'quest' in the *Bildungsroman* is for a partner; the discovery of the true 'inner self' is the discovery of a self that desires love and domesticity. The hero is educated in the novel to recognize and desire his inner self; the heroine's lessons are about discerning the true hero. These are the differing tasks that domestic fiction sets its heroes and heroines. Where the social self thus constructed must conceal as much as it reveals, reading the signs correctly becomes a necessity, a major preoccupation for men and women, whose comfort and future security depend on their ability to do so. The novel is a literary form which lent itself to the exploration of the relationship between appearance and reality, between 'outside' and 'inside', and was an ideal forum for exploring the disparity between them.

Moretti's account allows us to speculate about the invention of 'interiority' and its relationship to the depiction of the feminine in the realist novel. The great social changes that Moretti alludes to (industrialization, urbanization, the breaking of kinship ties) promote not only mobility, but also *interiority*. That is to say that the movement through new and strange circumstances generates new hopes: a richer and deeper sense of ones hopes and of oneself. The creation of a feminine self – indeed, like that of a man, but in a different way – has not been done under conditions that women themselves have controlled. We need to adapt Marx's famous observation, at the beginning of *The Eighteenth Brumaire* (1852), that 'men make their own history, but not of their own free will; not under circumstances they themselves have chosen but under the given and inherited circumstances with which they are directly confronted . . .' Women have made themselves, told themselves, and sometimes written themselves, but not of their own free will; not under circumstances they themselves have chosen . . .

Freedom and happiness have both been understood as the bedrock of modern Western culture. As Moretti says, 'our world calls for their coexistence . . . and it therefore calls for a cultural mechanism capable of representing, exploring and testing that coexistence'. He found that cultural mechanism in the novel of development; but his work gives us space to imagine the multiplicity of ways in which the interiorization of this kind of contradiction might have been achieved in the multiplicity of unrecorded, or only-half-recorded selves made throughout the process of European modernization.

Moretti's thesis emerged during the same period of academic activity that saw historians of literacy and culture reinforce the connection between the development of modern autobiography and modern selfhood. Any historian of the Early Modern and Modern periods in Europe and the Americas works with the heavy freight of a historiography that charts the rise of individualism and individuality in the West. This insistent 'background' stresses the role of writing and reading in the making of modern social and political persons. From two ends of the twentieth century, two examples make the point: in Max Weber's *The Protestant Ethic and the Spirit of Capitalism* (1904–5), spiritual journals, confessional tales, Bunyan's first-person narratives and a whole range of literary texts of the seventeenth and eighteenth centuries are used to inscribe Economic Man or (less figuratively and more prosaically) the relationship between Protestant selfhood and the structures of early capitalist development. In a major publishing enterprise of the 1980s, *The History of Private Life* (1989), the volume dealing with the seventeenth and eighteenth centuries elaborates, refines and *illustrates*, in charming and compelling detail all the categories of modernity, so that we might see the things and feelings that proliferate around reading and writing (novels, pens, writing manuals, chairs for reading in and *peignoirs* to read whilst sitting in them, libraries, closets; romantic love and love for children, privacy, intimacy) as the modern subject makes him or herself. Such techniques of feeling, connected to the practices of reading and writing, have been even more recently celebrated in John Brewer's *Pleasures of the Imagination* (1997).

Outside the fields of literary studies, the question of autobiography – telling or writing yourself – has been moved away from exclusive concentration on the written word, and into the more general terrain of narrative. In *Modernity and Self-Identity*, Anthony Giddens describes a three-hundred-year development in the West, by which personhood and self-identity have come to be understood as 'the self . . . reflexively understood by the person in terms of his or her biography'. He understands 'autobiography' not so much as a form of writing, nor as a literary genre, but rather as a way of thinking and feeling: as a mode of cognition. According to Giddens, actually writing an autobiography, getting it published and having it read is a very minor variant of a much more general 'autobiographical thinking'. He says that in this 'broad sense of an interpretive self-history produced by the individual concerned, [autobiography] whether written down or not . . . is actually the core of self-identity in modern life'.

Over the last twenty years, self-narration (meaning 'interpretive self-history' *and* the formal written autobiography) has come to be emphasized again and again as formative, constitutive and descriptive of the subject of modernity. The understanding is refined by – for example – Charles Taylor, in his *Sources of the Self. The Making of the Modern Identity* (1989). Here he surveys the whole of Western philosophy, and the great sweep of its cultural history (Renaissance humanism, urbanization, Reformation, Protestantism, capitalism, individualism), in order to claim that *the thing that has happened* since the end of the fifteenth century is the move of the self from outside to inside. He describes the emergence of a 'disengaged, particular self, whose identity is constituted in memory'. This identity is expressed in self-narration: 'the life at any moment is the causal consequence of what has transpired earlier . . . [and] since the life to be lived has also to be *told*, its meaning is seen as something that unfolds through the events'.

For Taylor these developments are important because of the questions they force about the *form* of the life-stories people tell. He asks whether the narrated story of the self is simply 'the *result* of the happenings as they accumulate', or whether the form of the life is there already, is somehow 'already latent', waiting to be expressed though an account of what came to pass in any individual life. In these deliberations, the self is conceived of as a remembered thing as well as a narrated thing.

This book would not exist if some handful of journeys to some other place and to some other kind of self, had not been recorded in writing. A small number of the testimonies that follow were extracted narratives, autobiographies that were demanded, and written down by an interlocutor (a justice of the peace, or his clerk). The examples here show the English administrative state, in its statutory requirement that an applicant for poor relief *must* tell it *how it was*, from the beginning of the tale, in chronological sequence (parents' names, their place of settlement; when put to work and where; where the last place that service was done and wages paid for a whole year . . .), in order to gain a dole, or a settlement in a parish then obliged to provide relief in times of hardship and penury. In the injunction to tell a journey story, rather than the upswelling *desire* to tell it or write it, might be found an answer to the question: why, in these multifarious stories of movement and identity, does the *journey itself* count for so little? Applicants for relief under the English Poor Laws like Ann Linford [No. 15] told a story that was highly prescribed, in response to legally-required questions, and in which there was no interest at all in dusty roads, highways made seas of mud in February, and the lesser discomforts of the parish cart. But puzzling absence of the journey remains, in the majority of these testimonies. And yet: it is not as if that kind of testimony does not exist. In editing John Pearman's – the 'Radical Soldier's' – Memoirs, some years ago now, I was intrigued by the autobiographical writing of the mid nineteenth-century common soldier, whose interest in the exotic landscapes they traversed, their emotional investment in the detail of Tegus or Ganges River, in the villas and temples, vineyards, olive or mango grove on the banks they passed, stupefied with heat and the remembered descriptions of their childhood fairy-tales – sprang from the page. The Vagrant Boy below [No. 40] uses the chapbook shipwreck and pirate stories of his childhood, in order to see himself as the hero of his own life, in something of the way that English working-class soldiers of the 1840s mapped a woodcut Arabia onto the scene that unfolded before their eyes, as the transport ship moved them upriver, to the scene of battle. Even a route-march from prosaic Brighton to prosaic Birmingham in 1832 might produce the same – certainly textual, perhaps experiential – effect. In 1848, in his *Autobiography of a Working Man*, Alexander Somerville wrote an account in which it is impossible to tell who is watching the soldier's passing:

> I . . . can at will, sitting by the hearth, looking dreamily into the fire or vacantly upon a book, draw out the whole line of country before me: the villages, road-side inns, half-way houses where we halted to rest, swinging sign-boards, village greens, broad commons, cross-roads, finger posts, travellers journeying with us, telling us where a gibbet once was . . .

The soldier moved – along a road, up the Tegus, up the Ganges – through a landscape made strange certainly by his childhood reading in the chapbook *Arabian Nights* – but also by his presence in the scene, and his gaze upon it, so that in the passage above, it becomes impossible to tell who are actually the spectators – the marchers or those who watch them. There is perhaps enough here to lay the foundations of an explanation for Somervillle's concentration on the journey itself – one foot in front of another – and the relative absence of roads, railways and airplanes from the accounts presented here. We must assume for the time being, that this absence is an acknowledgement that to make a journey, to start to *move*, is already to have made an identity, or at least to have begun its story, so that the gaze turns inwards, towards the self that is becoming. Evidence then perhaps, that the great changes in consciousness and self understanding in modernity, that Moretti accounts for in the European novel of development, *did* in fact take place, in ordinary lives and on journeys undertaken for material purposes, even though we must remain as uncertain as ever about how this process took place, in one society, over a three-hundred-year span.

Migrants know, and have known about these questions of identities in radical transition. Cindy Blake [No. 159] points out that something happens to time for the immigrant. Simple duration, perpetuity and chronology implode, or drain away. 'You can't say to the person you're with, remember something we did together five years ago, or look at that building, that's where I used to live. You can't refer back . . . you're . . . cut off . . .'

If we gather enough evidence of this kind, we may soon be able to write the history of movement and identity in the modern period. We might even begin to work out how literary forms came to shape quite ordinary people's perceptions of what it was that was happening to them; what it was they were on the way to becoming.

C. K. STEEDMAN

General Introduction: Movement, Place and Memory – Migration and the British Isles

Peter Leese

Mapping migration stories

The experience of migration is an experience of doubleness: a new country maps onto the old country, a new landscape maps onto the old landscape, a new self maps onto the old self. The experience of migration is also an experience of storytelling. Migrants tell stories to fit the past into the present, and later, to fit the present into the past; to fix themselves into a landscape of newly discovered features; to take measure of the distance between the old and the new. Storytelling tries to dissolve the doubleness. Like telling a national history, telling a personal history helps imagine a community of shared values and experiences.

Migrants most certainly dwell on their places of departure and arrival, scrutinize the landscapes they move between, even though few have tried to record their experience. Occasionally they write down their own stories, and their purpose is to answer that most natural of all migrant questions: 'who am I now?' Journalists, social reformers and historians collect such accounts too, posing a related question: 'what does this make us now?' Some of the many and varied replies to these questions are brought together in *The British Migrant Experience*, an anthology of personal accounts as well as related commentaries on the movement of peoples within and into mainland Britain from the eighteenth century onwards. My answer to these questions is both professional and personal.

As a British historian living and working in Poland, I have noticed that the subject of migration always catches the imagination of my students, perhaps because the migrant's perspective – that of an outsider looking into a foreign culture – is close to their own. I have also long wanted to compile a thematic anthology of primary sources to use in the classroom to help students develop their skills of historical text analysis and interpretation. Personally, I wished to put my own migrant experience into a wider perspective: to understand how women and men in the past coped with the shift from one culture and locality to another, how their historical experience altered through time, how they were changed by leaving behind all that was most familiar and cherished. Looking at Britain from the far side of continental Europe through the 1990s, I noted too the growing debates on national identity. It seems to me that one way to comprehend British society is through reports on the specific, workaday lived experience of those participants who are distanced observers yet have a personal investment in the country.

The British Migrant Experience has three parts, each of which cross references and informs the others. Part I, 'Migrant Life Stories in the 18th and 19th Centuries', and Part II, 'Migrant Life Stories in the 20th Century', contains accounts of arrival, settlement and integration (or its failure). These two parts are divided into six thematic categories: (1) Transition, (2) Settlement and Work, (3) Childhood and Home Life, (4) Community, (5) Another Culture, (6) Searching for a Place. Part III, 'Migrant Place Stories from the 18th to the 20th Centuries', includes accounts of place settlement and community, and is divided into six regional categories: (1) the South, (2) the Midlands and East Anglia, (3) North West England (4) North East England, (5) Scotland, (6) Wales.

The extracts for the anthology were chosen primarily on the principle that migrants describe their own experiences in their own words. Second was the attempt to illustrate long-term changes in migration patterns not just as demographic statistics but as personal experience and as collective cultural upheaval. Hence the inclusion of more general commentaries by a number of historians, whose presence is not meant to indicate that the editors are drawing a comprehensive picture of population movements over the last three hundred years – we are not – but is meant to give glimpses of larger patterns of movement, and of changing perceptions among commentators across a significant time span. Our final selection criterion was the requirement to present stories of both international as well as internal migration. Surprisingly, as our research progressed, we found that international migrant accounts are easier to locate, perhaps because the experiences they record appear more dramatic, thereby attracting greater attention. Although internal migration has much the same psychological impact as movement from one country to another, it is not as well documented.

Whatever further details are available accompany each extract, for example, migrants who sought permanent settlement and integration (immigrancy = [I.]) or those whose purpose was to keep moving, often in cyclical or seasonal patterns, for reasons of employment, remuneration or personal preference (migrancy = [M.]). Similarly, we have included available biographical details on the author/speaker together with comments on the type of account: autobiography, journalism, oral history interview, historical gloss, for example, and the details of its production. Readers should also refer to the index for lists of extracts related to particular themes: genres, ethnic groups, occupation, cities among others. The concepts of immigrancy and migrancy require a further word of explanantion. The distinction between the two as the editors have interpreted it lies in the fact that the former journey into a new locality, often but not always a new country, has behind it the intention of settlement; there is an awareness of transfer as a permanent shift. In the case of migrancy, by contrast, movement might be a way of life, as it was for some tramps, gypsies or those engaged in 'cadging' for a living; seasonal, as with agricultural labourers; or a matter of seeking out better wages and conditions, as was often the case with skilled craftsmen such as stonemasons. Migrancy has an air of impermanence about it. Of course, seasonal labourers could settle and overseas immigrants could move on or return home, so the barriers dividing these groups are permeable: the position of the Irish may be said to change with alternations of political opinion and legal partition as well as personal preference.

In addition to the varied types of account, there are also a number of extracts which run to several pages, while others are no more than a few lines or a paragraph long. The inclusion of shorter extracts was a point of principle in that the inarticulate and illiterate were for the greater part of the last three hundred years precisely that section of the population most likely to engage in varied forms of migration. Furthermore, in some cases the original source quotation was very brief; in others there was no longer or more expressive source to document a particular idea or theme. Even including relatively brief comments, the variety of first-hand accounts is nevertheless limited, and many an 'authentic' voice is filtered by her or his court clerk, oral historian or editor. (This is also why, when an especially articulate or illuminating account was available, we have sometimes quoted from it more than once.) Hence the need to turn to another view of migrant lives, that of near-contemporary observers: historians who extensively quote otherwise unavailable primary sources; journalists who distill the moods and thoughts of the moment; and academics with an eye for local detail. Introducing these accounts serves a second purpose: to register the multiplicity of voices debating the movement of peoples into and within the British Isles as well as its effects on the social fabric, cultural mores and self-perception of the nation, and to record the dialogue between immigrant and host community. Moreover, given the long timespan and the variety of approaches and experiences that might be represented in *The British Migrant Experience* our criteria have always included the wish to be suggestive rather than comprehensive: hence not all groups could be included, though we have tried to include many of the most significant as well as some of the less known. Likewise, in the introductory essays comments are confined to a select group of texts which were chosen to indicate how further research might be carried out, what further lines of enquiry, as Professor Steedman implies in her Foreword, might be opened up. The thematic bibliography provides a broader review of research on related themes.

The British Migrant Experience was compiled, then, to describe: first, the changing traffic of migrants as they travel around and settle within the

Britain Isles; second, the communities formed by migrants as well as their experience of new landscapes; third, remembering and telling the past as well as the conditions that shape telling. The individual stories presented in the anthology may be more fully understood after a brief review of the wider historical context which shaped them.

Patterns of movement and place: (1) the 18th century

In the late 17th and early 18th centuries only a few internal migrants moved to the bigger cities such as London – most travelled relatively short distances.[1] These short-distance migrants are difficult to count, since their activity is inadequately documented, yet the fact of mobility is demonstrated in Parish settlement testimonials and, for example, in movement certificates issued by the Scottish church. Recent evidence also shows that through the eighteenth and nineteenth centuries local mobility was far more common than inter-regional movement.[2] Though such evidence cannot be generalized too far, it does appear that individuals had strong attachments to particular locations as well as communities, and that if they moved out of a settlement or neighbourhood within a town, they would often return to the same district later.[3] Poor labourers at this time had relatively few possessions, they rented rather than owned their homes – circumstances which encouraged ease of mobility. If local movement was logistically straightforward, and the means of transportation, either on foot or on horse and cart, available to everyone, as Benjamin Shaw's comments indicate, such movement involved material and psychological disruption as well as readjustment. As age increased and family ties grew stronger, movement became all the harder.[4] The young and unattached – apprentices, domestic servants and farm workers – were therefore the most mobile in the pre-industrial Britain of the later seventeenth and early eighteenth centuries. During the proto-industrial age of the later eighteenth century the pull of larger towns and cities prompted mobility by drawing workers labour from within a 30–40 mile radius. Partly as a result of this many cities doubled in size between 1750 and 1780: London reached 750,000, Manchester 42,821, Birmingham 50,000, Glasgow 36,000, Liverpool 34,000 all in the second half of the eighteenth century, while the most rapid increases were between 1780–1820.[5]

Among the migrant populations of the 18th century, the Huguenots were industrious, in some part prosperous, and well established by 1718 with 35 churches and a flourishing community in Spitalfields, East London. Small white colonial and West Indian born populations also existed; while it is impossible to precisely quantify immigrants arriving in the larger towns and cities in the 18th and early 19th centuries, the presence of small numbers of Palatinate refugees was noted early in the 18th century, and the slave trade ensured a black presence in ports like Bristol and Liverpool, if not as slaves, then as domestic servants, sportsmen, or musical entertainers.[6] Non-British European immigrants constituted a large group too: confectioners might be Italian, valets French, but the Irish were by far the largest, poorest group, and tended to live in the worst slum districts and by casual labour, often as porters or prostitutes.[7] For economic necessity the Irish also tended to travel widely, assimilate rapidly, and settle either permanently or cyclically in England, Scotland and Wales.[8]

Patterns of movement and place: (2) the 19th century

The fact of growing inward migration might seem to support the influential argument put forward by Zelinski in the early 1970s: that there is a shift through the 19th century from limited to longer distance movement, that the pace of mobility change accelerates, and that these developments take place alongside industrial modernization. However, this understanding has been challenged in recent years.[9] Among others Lawton and Pooley have argued that in the Victorian period supposed in-migration accounts less for rapid urban population growth in cities than natural increase.[10] Nevertheless, with caveats for rural, inter-urban and inter-suburban movements, this period is marked by widespread rural depopulation and rising urban population. Cities continued to draw rural inhabitants from a surrounding radius, while larger movements over distance and in number had particular causes, such as the depopulation of the Highlands (most dramatically during the Clearances from the 1790s) or of Ireland (again most memorably during the famine crisis of the mid-1840s). On grounds of religion, work practice and living conditions the Irish were viewed with suspicion, nevertheless, the social geography of Glasgow and Liverpool and many smaller settlements was permanently changed by their presence. Both Scots and Irish laboured to bring England's worldwide industrial ascendancy during the 19th century. Naturally then, Welsh and Irish labour gangs, such as the navvies moving from Merthyr Tydfil to Middlesborough, travelled widely and settled in new districts.[11] Populations were also consolidated in the later 19th century due to suburban growth and commuting as well as higher wages, greater job security and better housing.[12] Once again later large scale movements had direct, sometimes dramatic, causes: 22 per cent of the population moved in the armed forces because of the Great War of 1914–18.[13]

Such mass movements did not lessen the fright of individual encounters with a new locality. Travelling in 1889 from Shawbost, Isle of Lewis – in the outer Hebrides – to Glasgow, for instance, N. Morrison was distressed by his initial encounter with big city life while patrolling as a duty officer policeman.[14] Beyond individual experiences of culture shock, much greater collective detail on the movement of populations becomes available in the mid-19th century when the first census figures appear. Industrial and urban development meant that by 1851, for example, internal mobility was far greater: over half of the population, both rural and urban, now living two kilometres or more away from their place of birth.[15] In other cases movement was frequent but over very short distances. In a study of one small district in Liverpool 40 per cent moved within a year, but the majority of these stayed within the same area, transporting themselves perhaps only a few hundred yards. Internal mobility peaked between 1840–90. Trains made it easier to go longer distances; later, bicycles made it easier to go short distances. Irish, Welsh and Scottish Highland labourers went in search of farm work; others went to London, or to the new boomtowns like Middlesborough, St Helens or Bradford, but by the inter-war period council housing and rent controlled areas discouraged many people from moving.[16] This stabilization of living conditions began earlier though, in the second half of the 19th century, when transport and communications encouraged commuter travel and new roads, while buildings and suburbs started to spread across the country.

The high point of Irish immigration was 1861: 602,000 in England and Wales, with a further 204,000 in Scotland; in Paisley, Glasgow, Kilmarnock and Dundee, 10 per cent of the population was Irish-born in 1861.[17] Among the newly arriving groups, a German minority, mainly industrial capitalists, settled in the second half of the 19th century in such northern industrial centres as Bradford, Liverpool and Manchester.

Nineteenth-century Scotland offers one variant on the pattern of arrival and settlement through the century. The Irish began to arrive in Scotland in the early 18th century: a private census of Glasgow in 1818–19 shows 10.3 per cent of the population as Irish born. With the establishment of the Belfast–Greenock ferry service in 1821 concentrations increased still further. By 1841 the highest percentages were in the south west: Dumbarton 11 per cent, Renfrew 13.2 per cent, Wigton 14.7 per cent.[18] The second large immigration movement into Scotland occurred in the later 19th and early 20th centuries: from 1870 to 1914, when the inward movement of peoples was mainly from the east, so that by 1911 there were 285,000 'aliens' in England and Wales, and another 25,000 in Scotland. Most were Russians, Poles and Germans, many fleeing anti-Semitic restrictions after the assassination of Tsar Alexander II in 1881.[19] Italians constituted about half the immigrant arrivals between 1891 and 1901; almost all the rest were Russian and Polish Jews settling in the western Lowlands, a third in Glasgow, the remainder mostly in Edinburgh, Fife and Stirling. By 1911 almost half the miners and about 12 per cent of the tailors came from the new immigrant groups, while there were also significant numbers in shipping, iron and steel, cabinet making and commercial travelling; Italians controlled 58 per cent of the wholesale and retail restaurant business in 1911.[20]

Patterns of movement and place: (3) the 20th century

Turning finally to more recent patterns of movement, if long-distance moves are defined as over 50km, such journeys were unlikely, difficult, and numerically insignificant before mass motor car ownership arrived between the wars. Furthermore, it is only since the mid-20th century that journeys of 100 km or more have become practical and comfortable.[21] It seems that if inter-regional mobility did not change drastically through the 20th century, neither did the social or psychological disturbance involved in a short or a long distance move much alter. Long-distance moves are mostly the result of kinship or employment contacts; moreover, few migrants have followed the example of Rhonda Little, who moved from Londonderry to London in 1938 and later on went back to her community of origin.[22] However, the growth of urban centres and the depopulation of rural centres is confirmed by population growth statistics that show the lowest percentage increase between 1891 and 1981 – 36.7 per cent – was in Orkney, while the highest percentage increase – 362.7 per cent – was south of London in the county of Surrey.[23] Council house residence can also be taken as a sign of population stability as well as lessening mobility; these increased steadily between the end of the Great War and the Housing Act of 1980.

Between the wars migrants arrived from Ireland, because of the partition and new entry restrictions in America, and from central Europe as fascism forced Jews and political dissidents into exile. A smaller group of ex-servicemen, students, writers and political activists came from the colonies, for example the West Indies. After World War Two a much larger post-colonial migration began: West Indians, Indians and Pakistanis formed the largest groups.[24] Additionally 100,000 members of the Polish forces remained in Britain, some permanently, after 1945; 20,000 Hungarians came after the 1956 failed Uprising; the largest rise in Irish immigration since the 19th century took place between 1951–61.[25]

From the latter part of the 19th century the movement of migrants into mainland Britain is a more noticeable trend than increased mobility in the native population. It may be useful to additionally note two points. First, for most of the 20th century emigration has exceeded immigration, tailing off since the 1960s, creating, as one historian of Britain has put it, 'an enormous worldwide community of communities who in one way or another had maintained ties with their original homelands in the Isles'.[26] Second, the often painful history of immigrant communities and their acceptance within Britain does show that the country is becoming a remarkably integrated multi-cultural society which, despite its serious failures, still appears the most harmonious within Europe. The redefinition of British identity is consequently never finalized, but always evolving and always the outcome not of aggregate experiences reduced to common factors, but of individual perceptions of local communities.

Patterns of memory

The mental patterning of migrant place relates first of all to the old country: to the routines of the working day and the patterns of movement it encompasses, to the different sights and sounds of street and field. Away from home, the migrant imagines the look and feels of home; missing the lived experience, the migrant imagines it as an abstraction. Past and present leach into one another as the constant routines of daily life are recreated in a new surrounding. Thereafter, attitudes to the home country and to the host country vary, depending, for example, on the migrant's stimulus (financial or ideological), on the extent of contact with fellow migrants or host community, and on the receptivity of the new society. Internal migration, by contrast, expands the migrant's view of his country, but there is nevertheless a comparison between the home community and the host community. Village, friends and family give way to wider circles at work and in the city; fields and cottages are replaced by a landscape of factory and terrace. And in this new, expanded version of the self, nations are also re-imagined.

For both the international and internal migrant the immediate business is survival, and survival means pooling resources and knowledge: in the second half of the 19th century Irish speakers gathering on Sunday evening at 'Connacht Square' in the Carlton district of Glasgow to swap news and gossip; in the 1900s Russian Jews finding each other work in Strangeways or Redbank, Manchester; in the 1950s West Indians buying houses collectively in Notting Hill, London.[27] The earliest of these communities looked towards the sea because their members had sea-related trades. This is how the small black enclaves of Liverpool and Bristol formed in the late 18th century.[28] The Butetown district of Cardiff in Wales was a lively dockside area until the post-Second World War redevelopment. Tyneside had a more self-contained group of Arabs, also in the first half of the 20th century, sailors from the British Protectorate of Aden: some settled, most returned home.[29] The seaport communities moved inland during the Second World War, adding to the long-established immigrant districts of big cities such as Manchester.[30] Here, before the Great War, Ancoats was known as 'Little Italy', and here too, in the same part of the city, generations of Irish Catholics, either by birth or by culture, were raised before the post-World War Two slum clearances destroyed the area.[31] After 1945, just as the new Jewish immigrants were arriving, the older community was moving into the suburbs, especially Cheetham Hill, while Moss Side changed from a 'Victorian bourgeois stronghold' into the centre for another new immigrant community, and thereafter was known as the 'black belt'.[32]

In districts such as these, international and internal travellers, immigrants and migrants joined and faced the same problems of finding homes and jobs. In the larger migrant communities, they also benefited from the same cultural background: a common knowledge of the mother tongue, a common history and tradition to keep alive. In this space between past and present migrants form impressions of the new landscape, the 'look' of the new country reveals itself here first. For migrants, looking, observing and interpreting without fully understanding is the first condition of the new life. Before the host language there is the migrant's memory and the host's landscape.

Migrant memory has a special urgency, because deprived of the familiar surroundings that shape identity, it becomes all the harder to imagine the shape of the future. To begin with, the migrant occupies a blank, pastless place and therefore has to remember his way into the future. Patterns of migrant memory are themselves shaped through time. The shift from traditional to modern social order – which unfolds through time, but which may additionally occur within the life of an individual – is also a shift from external to internal referentiality.[33] In 1770 the author of a slave narrative (Ukawsaw Gronniosaw) says, 'Let it go, my God is in Heaven', thereby giving an external version of the self based on authority and intercession between man and God. In 1970 the British-born son of post-war Ukrainian immigrants (Jaroslav Madylus) says in an interview, 'I began to find . . . that to be Ukrainian, there was much more interest, more meaning', thereby giving an internal version of the self based on choice and personal conscience.[34] Migrant accounts reflect, therefore, a rise in what Giddens calls the 'reflexive project of the self', which shows itself in a heightened sensitivity to place, and personal as well as national identity.[35]

Like all memory patterns, migrant memory is also re-shaped according to the expectations and needs of the teller and audience.[36] This process is all the more important because minorities have a sharpened sense of group identity. Their right to have a place in the host country, and their belief that they belong to the host country, are constantly challenged. Migrants must reaffirm themselves by retelling themselves. So, one genre of migrant memory tells the 'supportive' history of a chosen people, with its set pieces, heroes and symbols. Autobiographies can also be 'supportive' by bearing witness to certain events or embodying in one person the story of the whole group. Here, initiates, fellow countrymen and supporters need the teller of the history to evoke communal values, common beliefs and individual incidents that illustrate the wider story. A second genre of migrant memory refers more to life in the host community and the migrant's experience there. These accounts take migrants as their first audience, but also address the wider host community. These are dramas of arrival and survival, of dashed hopes and disillusion, of the struggle for dignity and secured identity.

The role of the teller complicates still further the patterns of migrant memory. In the social act of articulating, the teller is author, as well as one who seeks authorization, and one who speaks with authority. Moreover, the teller creates a persona – a presentation of the self that empowers the individual as well as the group, the 'we', but also the 'I'. The telling of the past shows personal identity is inseparable from social identity. The last of the audiences for migrant narrative is the teller.

To migrate is to take on a new self-identity, and by telling their stories of past and present, migrants try to overcome the duality of their new lives. It is this new self, partly or wholly remade, that enters, experiences and imagines the new nation. It is this new self that reworks national and personal identities in subjective experience and in memory.

How to use this anthology

There are many ways to analyse and interpret the material presented here – students and teachers will certainly develop their own approaches, however the following lines of analysis and interpretation may provide a useful starting point:

Thematic: by focusing on particular groups, such as navvies, beggars, or individual ethnic communities, or by reference to one place or region, such as Glasgow or the north west.

Chronological: by observing the changes in migration patterns over time, or shifts in personal perception and expression.

Dialogic: by contrasting accounts of participants and observers that work out the negotiation of identities from the perspectives of nation, region or individual.

Contextual: by considering the type and extent of knowledge imparted by reference to external sources and considering the reasons for calques and silences, prejudices and merits.

Textual: by examining how events are expressed, spoken and recorded in the text in its range of vocabulary, grammatical, rhetorical narrative genre choices.

Objective/subjective: by distinguishing between what reflects external events, subjective interpretation or emotion, and how these combine within any given document.

Notes

1. M. Anderson, 'The social implications of demographic change', in F. M. L. Thompson (ed.) *The Cambridge Social History of Britain, 1750–1950, vol. 2, People and their Environment* (Cambridge: Cambridge University Press, 1990) 10. See also: P. Clark, 'Migration in England during the late seventeenth and early eighteenth centuries', in Clark, P. and Souden, D. (eds) *Migration and Society in Early Modern England* (London: Hutchinson, 1987), 213–52.

2. C. Pooley and J. Turnbull, *Migration and Mobility in Britain Since the 18th Century* (London: UCL Press, 1998) 300–3.
3. Dent, A. G. (ed.) *The Family Records of Benjamin Shaw Mechanic of Dent, Dolphinholme and Preston, 1772–1841* (n.p: Record Society of Lancashire and Cheshire, 1991) 25.
4. Pooley and Turnbull, *Migration and Mobility*, 302–3.
5. R. Lawton and C. Pooley, *Britain 1740–1950: An Historical Geography* (London: Edward Arnold, 1992) 30–1.
6. C. Holmes, *John Bull's Island: Immigration and British Society 1871–1971* (London: Macmillan – now Palgrave Macmillan, 1988) 81; P. Fryer, *Staying Power: The History of Black People in Britain* (London: Pluto, 1984) 38–44.
7. V. G. Kiernan, 'Britons Old and New', in Holmes, C. *Immigrants and Minorities in British Society* (London: George Allen and Unwin, 1978) 38–42.
8. See, for example L. M. Cullen, 'Scotland and Ireland, 1600–1800: their role in the evolution of British society', in Houston, R. A. and White, I. D. *Scottish Society 1500–1800* (Cambridge: Cambridge University Press, 1989), 226–44.
9. Pooley and Turnbull, *Migration and Mobility*, 321–3.
10. Lawton and Pooley, *Britain 1740–1950*, 127.
11. Lawton and Pooley, *Britain 1740–1950*, 32. See also N. Evans, 'Immigrants and minorities in Wales 1840–1940: a comparative perspective', in Holmes, C. (ed.) *Migration in European Society, vol. 2* (Cheltenham: Edward Elgar, 1996) 293–314.
12. M. Anderson, 'The social implications of demographic change', in Thompson, (ed.) *Cambridge Social History*, 12.
13. Lawton and Pooley, *Britain 1740–1950*, 236.
14. N. Morrison, *My Story* (Inverness: Highland News Office, 1937) 18–19.
15. M. Anderson, 'The social implications of demographic change', in Thompson, (ed.) *Cambridge Social History*, 12.
16. M. J. Daunton, 'Housing', in Thompson, ibid., 248–9.
17. P. Joyce, 'Work', in Thompson, ibid., 142.
18. M. Flinn, *Scottish Population History: from the 17th century to the 1930s* (Cambridge: Cambridge University Press, 1977) 455–7.
19. C. Holmes, 'The Promised Land? Immigration into Britain 1870–1980', in Coleman, D. A. (ed.) *Demography of Immigrants and Minority Groups in the United Kingdom* (London: Academic Press, 1992) 2. See also J. Klier, *Imperial Russia's Jewish Question, 1855–1881* (Cambridge: Cambridge University Press, 1995).
20. M. Flinn, *Scottish Population History*, 457–8.
21. Pooley and Turnbull, *Migration and Mobility*, 303.
22. Ibid., 306.
23. N. Davies, *The Isles: A History* (London: Macmillan – now Palgrave Macmillan, 2000) 807.
24. C. Holmes, *John Bull's Island*, 17–23.
25. C. Holmes, 'The Promised Land?', 6.
26. N. Davies, *The Isles*, 806.
27. C. Holmes, *John Bull's Island*, 40; B. Williams, 'The Jewish immigrant in Manchester: the contribution of oral history', *Oral History*, 7 (1979) 47; M. and T. Phillips, *Windrush: The Irresistible Rise of Multi-Racial Britain* (London: HarperCollins, 1998) 135–6.
28. P. Fryer, *Staying Power*, 60.
29. R. I. Lawless, *From Ta'izz to Tyneside: An Arab Community in the North-East of*

England during the Early Twentieth Century (Exeter: Exeter University Press, 1995); N. M. C. Sinclair, *The Tiger Bay Story* (Treforest: Zenith, 1993).

30. C. Holmes, *John Bull's Island*, 285.
31. Ibid., 26; also S. Fielding, 'A separate culture? Irish Catholics in Working Class Manchester and Salford, *c.*1890–1939', in Fielding, S. and Davies, A. (eds) *Workers' World: Cultures and Communities in Manchester and Salford, 1880–1939* (Manchester: Manchester University Press, 1993) 42–3.
32. C. Holmes, *John Bull's Island*, 234, 242.
33. A. Giddens, *Modernity and Self-Identity: Self and Society in the Late Modern Age* (London: Polity, 1997) 144–9; C. Hay, M. O'Brien, and S. Penna, 'Giddens, modernity and self-identity: the "hollowing out" of social theory', in Bryant, C. and Jary, D. *Anthony Giddens: Critical Assessments* (London: Routledge, 1997) 85.
34. Ukawsaw Gronniosaw, *Narrative* [1770] in Phillips, C. (ed.) *Extravagant Strangers: A Literature of Belonging* (London: Faber and Faber, 1997) 4; Jaroslav Madylus, Interview, 1970, in J. Brown, *The Un-Melting Pot: An English Town and Its Immigrants* (London: Macmillan – now Palgrave Macmillan, 1970) 63–4.
35. A. Giddens, *Modernity and Self-Identity*, 52–5.
36. E. Tonkin, *Narrating our Pasts: The Social Construction of Oral History* (Cambridge: Cambridge University Press, 1998).

Part I
Migrant Life Stories in the 18th and 19th Centuries

Introduction to Part I: Migrant Life Stories in the 18th and 19th Centuries

Beata Piątek

All migrant experience, seemingly irrespective of time and place, has certain common characteristics: one is the need to move away, be it for reasons of war, religious persecution, poverty or the hope of betterment; another is the initial encounter with a new locality, a new landscape for an internal migrant, a new culture for an international sojourner. The migrant competes too in the search for work so as to provide for the family that has been left behind, or has also travelled, or has yet to arrive. Competition in a new labour market as well as such noticeable marks of a foreign origin as language, religion and customs will very likely, sooner or later, arouse some degree of suspicion if not open hostility. If these elements are common, however, over the span of two hundred years covered by Part I of *The British Migrant Experience* they appear in a variety of hues, they are related in a medley of voices. The earliest eighteenth-century accounts, for example, pertain mostly to the lives of local migrants as recorded in settlement examinations and court proceedings, which reduce both teller and tale to barest details; later on in the same century the autobiographical writings of educated former-slaves provide rich, elegantly stylized, often moving accounts. The spread of literacy enabled some members of the hitherto obscure class of travelling labourers to produce their own written accounts. In the nineteenth century these are accompanied by the official reports of government clerks, historians and journalists who ventured into the districts populated by both obscure foreigner and penniless native tramp.

Among eighteenth-century testimonials, those written by educated Africans stand out in length and complexity. The purchase and import of African slaves was already practised in the sixteenth century.[1] By the eighteenth century owning a black slave had acquired its own fashionable cachet among the wealthy, so that they were favoured over other servants, and a few were privileged with an education.[2] In some instances too, it was possible for slaves to buy their freedom. Thus equipped, they might transcend social barriers to achieve celebrity status in fashionable society, as in the case of Ignatius Sancho (1729–80), who enjoyed the friendship of David Garrick,

Samuel Johnson and Laurence Sterne. In his lifetime, Sancho wrote poetry, plays and musical pieces; his *Letters* (1792) were in such demand that they required five reprints. *The British Migrant Experience* also includes the accounts of less prominent black writers: Olaudah Equiano (1745–97) and Ottobah Cugoano (b. 1757), both campaigners who wrote pamphlets, organized meetings and secured the support of numerous radical organizations towards the abolition of slave trade. The autobiography of Ukawsaw Gronniosaw (b. 1710) is a less didactic account which focuses on family life; he married an English woman and received assistance from his protector, yet, despite his industriousness, the family suffered poverty and starvation.[3] All of these writers produced complex narratives, engaged in self-reflection and looked critically at British society; their self-confidence leaves no doubt that they were writing with an intention to publish, unlike their uneducated, native British contemporaries.

The 'star performances' of the African writers appear side by side with other kinds of testimony: the accounts of domestic servants, craftsmen, apprentices, farm labourers and vagrants recorded in settlement examinations and early working-class autobiographies (see Case Study 1 pp. 19–23). These documents are in many respects impersonal and uninformative; they seldom allow access to opinion or emotion. Instead they provide us with factual detail on the kind of employment available, its duration, wages, and distances travelled. Such accounts give anecdotal evidence, supported by later research, that between approximately 1660 and 1730 migration was the norm, not the exception.[4] Farm labourers, among the most mobile members of the population, would walk from farm to farm in search of work and cover relatively short distances; similarly, domestic servants tended not to move far unless they travelled with their employer.

One of the more extensive eye-witness accounts included here is Benjamin Shaw's *The Family Records of Benjamin Shaw Mechanic of Dent, Dolphinholme and Preston 1772–1841* (written in 1836), which documents the movements of the Shaw family around Cumbria and North Yorkshire and into Lancashire while various members search for work, and which, much like a settlement examination, is impersonal and factual. More personal, but also more stylized, is the autobiography of Godfried Leschinsky, who left Riga on an English ship in 1776, changed his name to one that would be easier to pronounce for the English, and in 1810 published *The Life of John Thompson, Mariner Written By Himself*. Didacticism of a religious kind shades the long pamphlet of Samuel Harris, who at the age of thirteen converted to Christianity and then set out from Warsaw for London: he wrote *The History and Conversion of Samuel Harris a Polish Jew* in 1833.

Before the nineteenth century foreigners did come to Britain in larger groups, yet these earlier migrant groups, excepting the Irish, were usually either wealthy, like the Sephardim Jews, well-organized, like the Huguenots, or highly skilled, like the German engineers.[5] Their nineteenth-century counterparts were mostly poor and unskilled, subjected to exploitation and ghettoization. They often featured in the numerous nineteenth-century parliamentary investigations into the condition of the poor: on the situation of women and children in factories (1832), the workings of the poor relief system (1834), the conditions in mines (1842) and the potteries (1843) among others. These accounts together with the activities of the Society for the Suppression of Mendacity, which was founded in London (1818) and which investigated the circumstances of beggars, signal the continuing preoccupation of the nineteenth century with the condition of the poor, which in turn contributed to the emergence and growth of investigative journalism.[6] Though if Henry Mayhew's 'Survey of Labour and the Poor' (1849–50) helps define the genre, it is one which gains greater popularity only in the twentieth century.[7]

Overview of Part I

Transition covers the experience in both the old land (motivation to migrate) and the new (first encounters). The motives for migration vary, but it was seldom a premeditated decision or pre-planned journey. The most frequent underlying stimulus was economic (3, 9, 12, 13); another reason to move was religion: Samuel Harris's father rejected his son when he converted to Christianity (8), Mrs Braverman's parents decided to flee Lithuania to avoid conscription in the army which did not allow Jews to practise their religion. Equiano and Cugoano were compelled by dint of trickery and on pain of death to travel (1, 2). Cugoano's account of his kidnapping in Fanti (in modern Ghana) and the voyage across the Atlantic on a slave ship is strikingly naturalistic. Equiano exercises his literary talent in a highly artistic representation of his first encounters with the cold climate and the artefacts of white man's culture: 'I had often seen my master and Dick employed in reading; and I had a great curiosity to talk to the books, as I thought they did; and so to learn how all things had a beginning: for that purpose I have often taken up a book, and have talked to it, and then put my ears to it, when alone, in hopes it would answer me . . .' (1). Among the few first-hand accounts of the internal migrants in the eighteenth century *The Family Records of Benjamin Shaw* stands out as an invaluable source of factual detail concerning distances covered and working conditions of the mechanic and his family (3). Extracts 5 and 7 testify that not all the internal migrants moved in search of work; the former is a brief excerpt from the diary of Mrs Piozzi (Hester Lynch Thrale, 1776–1821), who expresses her exasperation with those who talked about 'their Excursions . . . from the Metropolis' (5). Unlike the well-travelled Mrs Piozzi, the poet John Clare seems paralysed by the prospect of moving to a village three miles away from his native Helpston; however overstated his reaction, it highlights the role of native locality and landscape (7). Tramping and vagrancy are two more important variations of internal migration (9, 10); vagrancy on the one hand was perceived as an antisocial act and was regulated by the state, but on the other it was romanticized by journalism and literature.

Settlement and Work documents, for example, the movement of illiterate domestic servants in the eighteenth century as recorded in the interviews conducted by the Poor Law officers (15, 16, 17, 18), and one of the dominant themes throughout this section is material, mental and familial insecurity. Migrant workers were most vulnerable and therefore commonly subject to exploitation in sweatshops (27, 32). The Irish were 'not so much given to combine' as the English workforce (24), which, together with their alleged superhuman strength (29), won them the appreciation of their employers. The Irish dominate the scene in the nineteenth century as the largest group of international migrants and, consequently, chief competition for the English workforce on the labour market. The responses to their willingness to accept lower wages and ability to survive on very little are polarized between praise for their hard work and physical strength (21, 24, 25, 29) and blame for their 'demoralisation and depression of the English working class' (23). The other conspicuous group of international migrants, the Jews, seemed to benefit from a well-organized network of mutual support (33). The Italian ice-cream seller (34) and street performer (28) both show great determination and resourcefulness, the traits that ensure survival.

Most of the extracts in **Childhood and Home Life** are related indirectly via the institutions that were in charge of, or attempting to assist, the poor. Eighteenth-century court proceedings, for example, illustrate the disruptions of migrant family life; thus the criminal record of the 16-year-old Jeffrey Morat (36) appears to corroborate the theories of some opponents of the importation of slaves (19). Most of the accounts of migrant childhood resonate with the mood of instability and insecurity (40, 41, 42, 43). Against this austere background Gronniosaw's familial affections seem almost sentimental: 'I did all in my power to keep my dear partner's spirits from sinking' (38). In the second half of the nineteenth century education became an important part of even the poorest childhood: the Irish children in York attend a Catholic school despite their 'state of semi-barbarism' (42), whereas for a Jewish boy at the end of the century school becomes daily routine.

Community juxtaposes the migrants' point of view with the perspective of the British. The former stress the consolidating role of custom, celebrations (62), music (48), crime and trade (49), religion (50, 51, 61) and sport (63). Denvir's accounts of the Irish in London in the late nineteenth century highlight the economic and professional success of several of his compatriots (57, 58), George provides a bleaker view in **Another Culture** (64). Here the two accounts in which outsiders, the English, report on their encounters with foreigners, evince an alarmed incomprehension. Salter, a missionary about to enter the maze of Chinatown uses the discourse of a gothic story or crime fiction to build suspense, thus revealing his impression of this settlement: 'Let us enter the first house of this colony of evil spirits' (52). The fact that Salter does not speak Chinese does not stop him from interpreting the gestures of the gamblers: 'The flashing eye, the rapid and excited accent of the tongue, tell us that things are becoming desperate.' The journalist reviewing a variety hall show in 1874 was dissatisfied with the authenticity of the 'niggers' performing on stage as they were: 'jolly well-fed; and play and no-work darkies, whose sole business in life appeared to be to sleep away the morning, and throughout the afternoon play upon the banjo . . .' (53).

Another Culture opens with some wonderfully vivid descriptions of first encounters by the Black writers (65, 68). This section continues the theme of mutual incomprehension: when Besant observes the busy Jewish market in London, he describes it as an exotic and mysterious place ridden with deception and dishonesty (69). George's account of the Irish community in London in the eighteenth century famously sums up their position: 'The Irish in London were a police problem, a poor-law problem and an industrial problem' (64).

Searching for a Place shows various aspects of migrant failure or success. Court proceedings from 1735 point to John Torlton's predilection for movement as a weakness and one of the causes of his destruction, for in London he 'lost all Credit and Character, and became utterly contemptible and infamous . . .' (70). George reports on how 'Jew-baiting became a sport' in the eighteenth century and how the young Jews took to boxing in self-defence after Daniel Mendoza set up boxing school in 1787 (72). The advice on the consecration of the new synagogue in Glasgow (80) presents education, especially acquiring a good command of English, hard work and religion as the recipe for success of a migrant community.

Case study 1: personal identity as narrative

As Peter Leese states in the General Introduction, the documents in *The British Migrant Experience* can be interpreted in varied ways and for diverse purposes. While there are clearly certain factual points which can be surmised in these documents, how they fit together and what themes assume prominence is a matter of individual readers' predilection and purpose. The editors would like to create a collage of accounts rather than a jigsaw puzzle: a cubist depiction of Britain's migrant past rather than an ultimate reproduction. The following examination of three documents from Part I (3, 35, 40) uses the theme of narrative as one of the available lay-out techniques.

The affinity between narrative and identity is recognized by philosophers, sociologists, psychologists and literary theorists alike. For Paul Ricoeur the temporal character of narrative renders it particularly suitable for the expression of life story.[8] Anthony Giddens maintains that '[a] person's identity is not to be found in behaviour, nor – important though this is – in the reactions of others, but in the capacity to keep a particular narrative going.'[9] Paul John Eakin takes this idea even further in his study of autobiography when he argues that 'narrative plays a central, structuring role in the formation and maintenance of our sense of identity'.[10] He cites the findings of developmental psychologists who demonstrate that between the ages of three and four, a child learns to express her autobiographical memories arranged in narrative form. A cognitive psychologist, Robyn Fivush, sees direct links between autobiographical memory and the sense of self of an individual.[11] These findings lead Eakin to formulate a claim that in autobiography narrative and identity shape and inform each other.

Here the significance of narration as a social act should be highlighted: the circumstances in which the process of storytelling takes place, the audience who may be addressed by the narrator, and her motives for telling the story.[12] Not only in literature but also in life the act of narrating determines the structure of the narrative, the selection of facts and the style of their presentation.

In the eighteenth century written autobiography was a genre of self-expression inaccessible to the majority of migrants, who came from the lowest echelons of society and were individually, if not collectively, illiterate.[13] We have turned to the archives of parish records in order to trace the life stories of those who did not record them themselves. For example, 'Sarah Cheatham and her daughter' (35) is a settlement examination from the parish of Dunstable recorded in 1718. Settlement was a permanent right to take the benefit of the poor laws in a particular parish. The first Elizabethan Poor Law held the parish responsible for their poor; their upkeep was financed from the rates paid by the local population. The first Poor Law was immediately followed by the Vagabonds Act (1603) which made vagrancy a criminal offence and stated that those in need of relief outside their parish 'were to be sent to the place of their dwelling, if they had any; if not, to the place where they had last dwelt by the space of one year.'[14] Settlement passed from parents to children and from husband to wife; one could acquire the right to settlement by working in a parish (receiving wages) for a period of over a year.[15] Hence settlement examinations, that is, the questioning of the poor applying for relief, by which means the poor law officers tried to establish the history of employment and movement of the applicant so as to decide whether they should be given relief in this parish or be removed to another one. This history shapes the story that Sarah Cheatham is allowed to tell about herself and her daughter, and is one of the determinants in her act of narrating as well as in the record surviving till the present. Hence explicit in the document is information on where Sarah Cheatham went, how long she stayed there, whether she was employed or not, whether she received wages.

We do not know the name of Sarah's daughter; her name is not relevant to the poor law officers, whereas the fact that she is a bastard is relevant, because the right to settlement can be acquired through marriage and passes from father to his legitimate children. Sarah's identity and her narrative are thus veiled; to know them we have to reconstruct them for ourselves. In the hands of a Richardson this might become a *Clarissa*, but the institution of the eighteenth-century poor law casts a grid of very formal questions on Sarah Cheatham. Even if these questions do not completely erase her voice, they stifle it effectively for the answers are reported to us in the formal language of the courtroom, which, we can only guess, does not bear much relation to Sarah's language. In her work on the social construction of oral history, Elizabeth Tonkin argues that memory, cognition and identity are mutually dependent; she also demonstrates how social milieu and status contribute to the identity building processes by forging cognitive ability.[16] The record of Sarah Cheatham's case, and the events that produced the document, provide a vivid illustration of how these processes function, not because she has no personal identity, but because her status is so low that her identity is manifest (once) in the documentation of her name, and thereafter she becomes 'the examined'. The name is, in fact, the only indication that we are dealing with a human being and a woman. In the document the focus is on her biological needs, on 'victuals and drink'. Similarly a phrase such as 'the said Stubbs had Carnal Knowledge of her body' lays emphasis on the physiological while the event itself might have been a passionate love affair or brutal harassment. Not just in the administrative record, but in the social relations between examiner and examinee Sarah's status is that of an object or an animal: her memory is reduced to what the institution of the poor law requires her to recall, as for her cognition we know nothing.

Let us compare the settlement examination record with an early autobiographic document: *The Family Records of Benjamin Shaw Mechanic of Dent, Dolphinholme and Preston, 1772–1841* (3, 20, 73). On the one hand there seems to be an enormous divide between Sarah Cheatham and Benjamin Shaw since, being literate, he has higher social status and therefore the authority that enables him to become an author.[17] But on the other hand, although his *Records* is narrated in the first person, the choice of events and the style resemble those in the previous document. Benjamin Shaw lists the places where his family lived, the kind of employment they found and the wages they received. Extract 73, in which he relates the life story of his wife, Betty, bears a striking resemblance to settlement examination records. Extract 3 has a more candid, personal quality, mostly due to the opening remark about Benjamin Shaw's mother's distress at leaving her native town to which she 'was greatly atached'. The expression of personal emotions creates an intimacy between the narrator and the reader entirely absent from the first document. It is, however, apparent that in those early days of working-class autobiography the authors were looking for models, 'channels of expression' as Tonkin would call them, and a sense of formality and factuality, parallel to that which guided the settlement examination process, shapes Benjamin Shaw's account of himself.[18]

Another variation on this now familiar model, though evolved almost beyond recognition, is an interview with 'a vagrant boy who travels as a beggar throughout England' (40); one of many that Henry Mayhew conducted with workers in various trades: street sellers, entertainers and paupers when he worked for the *Morning Chronicle* (1849–50). His *London Labour and the London Poor* published in 1851 by that paper, sold 13,000 copies weekly.[19] Mayhew's interviews might be taken as early examples of investigative journalism, a genre with a lineage that may be traced back to interviews with beggars conducted by the Society for Suppression of Mendacity, or even to settlement interviews. Mayhew's achievement lies in his method, which combined objectivity and distance, yet seemed to provoke his interviewees to deeply personal statements. Although this interview, like much of Mayhew's work, appeared in print as a monologue, the journalist introduced the speaker with details of age, occupation, if any, and appearance. Each interviewee was asked about their parents, place of birth, while those in employment or some other profitable activity were asked about their trade, working hours, conditions and income. The inquiries were, however, erased from the text, and the readers were presented with a flow of first-person narrative. Apart from his questions, which must have born some similarity to those Sarah Cheatham was asked, Mayhew engaged in a dialogue with his subjects, using supplementary prompts relevant to the story he recorded. So, when the vagrant boy (40) says that he ran away from the tailor, and embarks on the story of his travels, Mayhew must have asked about reasons for his escape because the boy replies: 'My reason for running off was . . .' and returns to the story of his apprenticeship. The journalist helped his interlocutors open up and volunteer information by interacting; he showed interest and concern, also by allowing extended commentary even if they strayed off the subject.

That the vagrant boy read avidly and borrowed books from a library may have been of passing interest to a sociological survey of the 1850s; however, this detail directs a modern reader to some of the sources that shaped this account. The boy knew of *Robinson Crusoe* and had actually borrowed from a library and read Clark's *Lives of Pirates*. As Franco Moretti notes in *Atlas of the European Novel 1800–1900*, a survey of the titles available in circulating libraries shows the flourishing of lowbrow historical novels, war stories and nautical stories around the mid-nineteenth century.[20] Moretti's research contextualizes the boy's comment: 'My father had no books but religious books' – if there was only one book in the house, it was a religious book. Furthermore, Moretti confirms what we might suspect anyway: that when the poor reached for a book, it was not a classic (*Robinson Crusoe*), but a cheap, penny number, and that these novels contributed greatly to the spread of literacy in nineteenth century Britain long before the Education Act of 1871.[21] They almost certainly fed the boy's dreams of going to sea. Moreover, they probably affected his decision to become a vagrant; also, they helped to shape his description, as Mayhew records it, by providing a template and rhetorical motifs within which the interviewee could place his own experience. It is worth noting too that while both Sarah Cheatham and Benjamin Shaw were forced to migrate in search of work, the vagrant boy seems closest to having chosen migrant labouring as a way of life. He admits that he ran away from home, gave up a trade and decided to follow his fancy, he mentions the 'sort of pleasure' he derived from watching ships.

In these three documents the personal identity of the migrant emerges gradually, with a shift from the third-person to first-person narration accompanied by a shift of focus, from basic facts of life to emotions, feelings and choices. In our search for personal identity in the narrative we will inevitably look for such intimate detail. Therefore we may perceive as most revealing the narrative that contains the subjective accounts of processes which do not lend themselves easily to historical scrutiny and verification. It would be naïve to assume that a life story is a reliable account of the past because the narrator claims to have lived through it. In modern times the narrative of identity, especially the autobiography, has evolved into a highly self-conscious genre. Raphael Samuel points out that autobiographies are patterned; would-be autobiographers have models to follow and frequently try to shape the representations of their lives morally.[22] Jean Peneff develops the point in an essay on myths in life stories by defining myth as 'the pre-established framework, within which individuals explain their personal history', and listing the most common distortions that occur in the life stories of the Algerian entrepreneurs.[23] The characteristic feature of these distortions is the application of a familiar model of a life story, for example, of a self-made man, which not only helps the narrator organize the events into a coherent narrative, but also presents him in a better light. Rather than disqualify autobiographical narratives as unreliable, these studies of self-fashioning open up new possibilities for analysis of such documents. One of the purposes of *The British Migrant Experience* is to suggest that the models chosen by the authors may be as informative about their world and identity as the events described. As Tonkin has noted, much of our life 'is taken for granted and unreflexive'. Yet, she continues, 'Reflection and questionings are themselves guided by underlying expectations and already-provided channels of expression.'[24]

Notes

1. P. Fryer, *Staying Power: The History of Black People in Britain* (London: Pluto Press, 1984) 1–13.

2. V. G. Kiernan, 'Britons old and new', in Holmes, C. (ed.) *Immigrants and Minorities in British Society* (London: George Allen and Unwin, 1978) 31, 42.
3. Fryer's *Staying Power* also details the lives of the 18th and 19th century African writers and celebrities.
4. See General Introduction and, for example, P. Clark, 'Migration during the late seventeenth and early eighteenth centuries', in Clark, P. and Souden, D. (eds) *Migration and Society in Early Modern England* (London: Hutchinson, 1987) 213–52.
5. The literature on individual groups is too vast to cite here, but for two local studies see: M. Cox, *Life and Death in Spitalfields* (York: British Council for Archaeology, 1996), and A. Palmer, *The East End: Four Centuries of London Life* (London: John Murray, 2000).
6. M. A. Crowther, 'The Tramp', in Porter, R. (ed.) *Myths of the English* (Cambridge: Polity Press, 1992) 91–113, 101.
7. V. Neuberg, 'Introduction', in Mayhew, H. *London Labour and the London Poor* [1851] (Harmondsworth: Penguin, 1985) xiii–xxiii; see also S. Dentith, *Society and Cultural Forms in Nineteenth Century England* (London: Macmillan – now Palgrave Macmillan, 1998) 119–23.
8. P. Ricoeur, *Time and Narrative*, (Chicago: Chicago University Press, 1984–8).
9. A. Giddens, *Modernity and Self-Identity. Self and Society in the Late Modern Age*, (Cambridge: Polity Press, 1997) 54.
10. P. J. Eakin, *How Our Lives Become Stories: Making Selves* (London: Cornell University Press, 1999) 123.
11. Ibid., 111.
12. G. Genette, *Narrative Discourse* trans. J. E. Lewin (Oxford: Blackwell, 1980) 26.
13. For a suggestive account of how reading might have functioned socially in the later eighteenth century, and of the debates on what might have constituted literacy at this time, see: R. Darnton, 'History of reading', in Burke, P. (ed.) *New Perspectives in Historical Writing* (Cambridge: Polity Press, 1997) 140–67.
14. H. Davey, *Poor Law Settlement and Removal* (London: Stevens, 1925) 2.
15. The requirement that the person must receive wages for a year to be entitled to settlement excluded those imported as slaves.
16. E. Tonkin, *Narrating Our Pasts; The Social Construction of Oral History* (Cambridge: Cambridge University Press, 1998) 38–49, 97–136.
17. Ibid., 39.
18. Ibid., 107.
19. A. Humphreys, *Travels into the Poor Man's Country; The Work of Henry Mayhew*, (Horsham: Caliban, 1977) 19.
20. F. Moretti, *Atlas of the European Novel 1800–1900* (London: Verso, 1999) 143–64.
21. See especially D. Mitch, *The Rise of Popular Literacy in Victorian England* (Philadelphia: University of Pennsylvania Press, 1992).
22. R. Samuel, cited in E. Tonkin, *Narrating Our Pasts*, 57–8.
23. J. Peneff, 'Myths in life stories', in Samuel, R. and Thompson, P. (eds), *Myths We Live By* (London: Routledge, 1990) 36–48.
24. E. Tonkin, *Narrating Our Pasts*, 107.

Transition 1

1) Olaudah Equiano's first encounter with England, 1757 [I.]

Born in Essaka (modern day Nigeria) in 1745, Olaudah Equiano was kidnapped, shipped across the Atlantic to the West Indies, then to America, and eventually sold to an English naval officer. Later Equiano bought his freedom, married an Englishwoman and went on to became an abolitionist campaigner. The Interesting Narrative of the Life of Olaudah Equiano, or Gustavus Vassa the African, written by himself *(1789) founded the slave narrative genre and is regarded as a major work of African and Black American literature.*

> . . . all my alarms began to subside when we got sight of land; and at last the ship arrived at Falmouth, after a passage of thirteen weeks. Every heart on board seemed gladdened on our reaching the shore, and none more than mine. The captain immediately went on shore, and sent on board some fresh provisions, which we wanted very much: we made good use of them, and our famine was soon turned into feasting, almost without ending. It was about the beginning of the spring 1757 when I arrived in England, and I was near twelve years of age at that time. I was very much struck with the buildings and the pavement of the streets in Falmouth; and, indeed, any object I saw filled me with new surprise. One morning, when I got upon deck, I saw it covered all over with the snow that fell over-night: as I had never seen any thing of the kind before, I thought it was salt; so I immediately ran down to the mate and desired him, as well as I could, to come and see how somebody in the night had thrown salt all over the deck. He, knowing what it was, desired me to bring some of it down to him: accordingly I took up a handful of it, which I found very cold indeed; and when I brought it to him he desired me to taste it. I did so, and I was surprised beyond measure. I then asked him what it was; he told me it was snow: but I could not in anywise understand him. He asked me if we had no such thing in my country; and I told him, No. I then asked him the use of it, and who made it; he told me a great man in the heavens, called God: but here again I was to all intents and purposes at a loss to understand him; and the more so, when a little after I saw

> the air filled with it, in a heavy shower, which fell down on the same day. After this I went to church; and having never been at such a place before, I was again amazed at seeing and hearing the service. I asked all I could about it; and they gave me to understand it was worshipping God, who made us and all things. I was still at a great loss, and soon got into an endless field of inquiries, as well as I was able to speak and ask about things. However, my little friend Dick used to be my best interpreter; for I could make free with him, and he always instructed me with pleasure: and from what I could understand by him of this God, and in seeing these white people did not sell one another, as we did, I was much pleased; and in this I thought they were much happier than we Africans. I was astonished at the wisdom of the white people in all things I saw; but was amazed at their not sacrificing; or making any offerings, and eating with unwashed hands, and touching the dead. I likewise could not help remarking the particular slenderness of their women, which I did not at first like; and I thought they were not so modest and shamefaced as the African women.
>
> I had often seen my master and Dick employed in reading; and I had a great curiosity to talk to the books, as I thought they did; and so to learn how all things had a beginning: for that purpose I have often taken up a book, and have talked to it, and then put my ears to it, when alone, in hopes it would answer me; and I have been very much concerned when I found it remained silent.

P. Edwards and D. Dabydeen, (eds) *Black Writers in Britain 1760–1890* (Edinburgh: Edinburgh University Press, 1991) 61–6.

2) Ottobah Cugoano kidnapped and taken to England, *c.*1770 [I.]

Born in Aqimaque (Adjumako, modern day Ghana) c.1757, Ottobah Cugoano was enslaved and transported to England around 1770. Eighteen years later he was free and had entered English society as a personal servant and court painter to the Prince of Wales. On the evidence of a surviving letter his Thoughts and Sentiments on the Evil and Wicked Traffic of the Slaver and Commerce of the Human Species *(1787) was extensively revised from a first draft, possibly by Equiano.*

> I was born in the city of Agimaque, on the coast of Fantyn; my father was a companion to the chief in that part of the country of Fantee, and when the old king died I was left in his house with his family; soon after I was sent for by his nephew, Ambro Accasa, who succeeded the old king in the chiefdom of that part of Fantee known by the name of Agimaque and Assinee. I lived with his children, enjoying peace and tranquillity, about twenty moons, which, according to their way of reckoning time, is two years. I was sent for to visit an uncle, who lived at a considerable distance from Agimaque. The first day after we set out we arrived at Assinee, and the third day at my uncle's

habitation, where I lived about three months, and was then thinking of returning to my father and young companion at Agimaque; but by this time I had got well acquainted with some of the children of my uncle's hundreds of relations, and we were some days too ventursome in going into the woods to gather fruit and catch birds, and such amusements as pleased us. One day I refused to go with the rest, being rather apprehensive that something might happen to us; till one of my play-fellows said to me, because you belong to the great men, you are afraid to venture your carcase, or else of the *bounsam*, which is the devil. This enraged me so much, that I set a resolution to join the rest, and we went into the woods as usual; but we had not been above two hours before our troubles began, when several great ruffians came upon us suddenly, and said we had committed a fault against their lord, and we must go and answer for it ourselves before him.

Some of us attempted in vain to run away, but pistols and cutlasses were soon introduced, threatening, that if we offered to stir we should all lie dead on the spot. One of them pretended to be more friendly than the rest, and said, that he would speak to their lord to get us clear, and desired that we should follow him; we were then immediately divided into different parties, and drove after him. We were soon led out of the way which we knew, and towards the evening, as we came in sight of a town, they told us that this great man of theirs lived there, but pretended it was too late to go and see him that night. Next morning there came three other men, whose language differed from ours, and spoke to some of those who watched us all the night, but he that pretended to be our friend with the great man, and some others, were gone away. We asked our keepers what these men had been saying to them, and they answered, that they had been asking them, and us together, to go and feast with them that day, and that we must put off seeing the great man till after; little thinking that our doom was so nigh, or that these villains meant to feast on us as their prey. We went with them again about half a day's journey, and came to a great multitude of people, having different music playing; and all the day after we got there, we were very merry with the music, dancing and singing. Towards the evening, we were again persuaded that we could not get back to where the great man lived till next day; and when bedtime came, we were separated into different houses with different people. When the next morning came, I asked for the men that brought me there, and for the rest of my companions; and I was told that they were gone to the sea side to bring home some rum, guns and powder, and that some of my companions were gone with them, and that some were gone to the fields to do something or other. This gave me strong suspicion that there was some treachery in the case, and I began to think that my hopes of returning home again were all over. I soon became very uneasy, not knowing what to do, and refused to eat or drink for whole days together, till the man of the house told me that he would do all in his power to get me back to my uncle; then I eat a little fruit with him, and had some thoughts that I should be sought after, as I would be then missing at home about five or six days. I enquired every day if the men had come back, and for the rest of my companions, but could get no answer of any satisfaction. I was kept about six days at this man's house, and in the evening there was another man came and talked with him a good while, and I heard the one say to the other he must go, and the other said the sooner the better; that man came out and told me that he knew my relations at Agimaque, and that we must set out to-morrow morning, and he would convey me there. Accordingly we set out next day, and travelled till dark, when we came to a place where we had some supper and slept. He carried a large bag with some gold dust, which he said he had to buy some goods at the sea side to take with him to Agimaque. Next day we travelled on, and in the evening came to a town, where I saw several white people, which made me afraid that they would eat me, according to our notion as children in the inland parts of the country. This made me rest very uneasy all the night, and next morning I had some victuals brought, desiring me to eat and make haste, as my guide and kidnapper told me that he had to go to the castle with some company that were going there, as he had told me before, to get some goods. After I was ordered out, the horrors I soon saw and felt, cannot be well described; I saw many of my miserable countrymen chained two and two, some hand-cuffed, and some with their hands tied behind. We were conducted along by a guard, and when we arrived at the castle, I asked my guide what I was brought there for, he told me to learn the ways of the *browfow*, that is the white faced people. I saw him take a gun, a piece of cloth, and some lead for me, and then he told me that he must now leave me there, and went off. This made me cry bitterly, but I was soon conducted to a prison, for three days, where I heard the groans and cries of many, and saw some of my fellow-captives. But when a vessel arrived to conduct us away to the ship, it was a most horrible scene; there was nothing to be heard but rattling of chains, smacking of whips, and the groans and cries of our fellow-men. Some would not stir from the ground, when they were lashed and beat in the most horrible manner. I have forgot the name of this infernal fort; but we were taken in the ship that came for us, to another that was ready to sail from Cape Coast. When we were put into the ship, we saw several black merchants coming on board, but we were all drove into our holes, and not suffered to speak to any of them. In this situation we continued several days in sight of our native land; but I could find no good person to give any information of my situation to Accasa at Agimaque. And when we found ourselves at last taken away, death was more preferable than life, and a plan was concerted amongst us, that we might burn and blow up the ship, and to perish all together in the flames; but we were betrayed by one of our own countrywomen, who slept with some of the head men of the ship, for it was common for the dirty filthy sailors to take the African women and lie upon their bodies; but the men were chained and pent up in holes. It was the women and boys which were to burn the ship, with the approbation and groans of the rest; though that was prevented, the discovery was likewise a cruel bloody scene.

But it would be needless to give a description of all the horrible scenes which we saw, and the base treatment which we met with in this dreadful captive situation, as the similar cases of thousands, which suffer by this infernal traffic, are well known. Let it suffice to say, that I was thus lost to my dear indulgent parents and relations, and they to me. All my help was cries and tears, and these could not avail; nor suffered long, till one succeeding woe, and dread, swelled up another. Brought from a state of innocence and freedom, and, in a barbarous and cruel manner, conveyed to a state of horror and slavery: This abandoned situation may be easier conceived than described. From the time that I was kidnapped and conducted to a factory, and from thence in the brutish, base, but fashionable way of traffic, consigned to Grenada, the grievous thoughts which I then felt, still pant in my heart; though my fears and tears have long since subsided. And yet it is still grievous to think that thousands more have suffered in similar and greater distress, under the hands of barbarous robbers, and merciless task-masters; and that many even now are suffering in all the extreme bitterness of grief and woe, that no language can describe. The cries of some, and the sight of their misery, may be seen and heard afar; but the deep sounding groans of thousands, and the great sadness of their misery and woe, under the heavy load of oppressions and calamities inflicted upon them, are such as can only be distinctly known to the ears of Jehovah Sabaoth.

This Lord of Hosts, in his great Providence, and in great mercy to me, made a way for my deliverance from Grenada. – Being in this dreadful captivity and horrible slavery, without any hope of deliverance, for about eight or nine months, beholding the most dreadful scenes of misery and cruelty, and seeing my miserable companions often cruelly lashed, and as it were cut to pieces, for the most trifling faults; this made me often tremble and weep, but I escaped better than many of them. For eating a piece of sugarcane, some were cruelly lashed, or struck over the face to knock their teeth out. Some of the stouter ones, I suppose often reproved, and grown hardened and stupid with many cruel beatings and lashings, or perhaps faint and pressed with hunger and hard labour, were often committing trespasses of this kind, and when detected, they met with exemplary punishment. Some told me they had their teeth pulled out to deter others, and to prevent them from eating any cane in future. Thus seeing my miserable companions and countrymen in this pitiful, distressed and horrible situation, with all the brutish baseness and barbarity attending it, could not but fill my little mind with horror and indignation. But I must own, to the shame, of my own countrymen, that I was first kid-napped and betrayed by some of my own complexion, who were the first cause of my exile and, slavery; but if there were no buyers there would be no sellers. So far as I can remember, some of the Africans in my country keep slaves, which they take in war, or for debt; but those which they keep are well fed, and good care taken of them, and treated well; and, as to their cloathing, they differ according to the custom of the country. But I may safely say, that all the poverty and misery that any of the inhabitants of Africa meet with among themselves, is far inferior to those inhospitable regions of misery which they meet with in the West-Indies, where their hard-hearted overseers have neither regard to the laws of God, nor the life of their fellow-men.

Thanks be to God, I was delivered from Grenada, and that horrid brutal slavery. – A gentleman coming to England, took me for his servant, and brought me away, where I soon found my situation become more agreeable. After coming to England, and seeing others write and read, I had a strong desire to learn, and getting what assistance I could, I applied myself to learn reading and writing, which soon became my recreation, pleasure, and delight; and when my master perceived that I could write some, he sent me to a proper school for that purpose to learn. Since, I have endeavoured to improve my mind in reading, and have sought to get all the intelligence I could, in my situation of life, towards the state of my brethren and countrymen in complexion, and of the miserable situation of those who are barbarously sold into captivity, and unlawfully held in slavery.

P. Edwards and D. Dabydeen, (eds) *Black Writers in Britain 1760–1890* (Edinburgh: Edinburgh University Press, 1991) 40–5.

3) Benjamin Shaw travels North West England for work, 1791 [M.]

Born in north-west England c.1782, Benjamin Shaw describes in his Family History *the details of movement among his extended family of thirty-nine members in the years from 1766 to around 1830. The family travelled within a relatively restricted area between Kendal (Cumbria) and Preston (Lancashire), and in all they moved 167 times, circulating between urban and rural areas. The account, written in Preston in 1836 and not intended for publication, was based on the authors' memory as well as on earlier notes.*

this leaving our own Countery was a great cross to my mother, for she was greatly atached to her Native town, & had she known what would follow, I am sure that she never would have left her relations & countery on any account. I think this was the most troublesome part of my Parents Life, for at the end of first Pay (for they only Paid once a 3 weeks) the master & my father disagreed about wages, & my father and all his family was discharged – however the children were employed again soon after, my father went into the north where he was known, a Clock dresser – soon after this my master sent for me, & told me that I would go apprintice he would ingage me for 3 years, as I could work well at the Vice – I consented to be bound for 8 shilling per week for the first 2 years, & 9s for the third, we set our hands to an agreement august the 4th 1791, and I began work again, we wrought from 6 o'clock in the morning, to 6 in the evening, had 1 hour at noon, and went to our drinking &c, Sometimes after this, may father got work again at the factory, to piece rovings, & we settled here, & thing went smoothly for a time.

A. G. Dent, (ed.) *The Family Records of Benjamin Shaw Mechanic of Dent, Dolphinholme and Preston, 1772–1841* (n.p: Record Society of Lancashire and Cheshire, 1991) 26.

4) Godfried Leschinsky sails to England, 1796 [I.]

Born in Riga, Latvia, in 1762, Godfried Leschinsky travelled to England by ship in 1796. His autobiography was published in 1810.

On the 4th, May 1796, I was regularly bound to the owners of the Formosa, for the return of five years, and three days after that, I took a sorrowful, and as it pleased God to make it, a last farewell of my indulgent parents, my friends and acquaintances: we spread our sails towards England, whose shores we reached in about five weeks after our departure from Riga. The vessel brought up at Newcastle, where I was treated in the most affectionate manner by Captain Strachen, who frequently had me to his house, and at all times attended to me with almost paternal solicitude.

About this time I thought proper to alter my name to John Thompson, my shipmates never being able to recollect the name of Godfried, and as to Leschinsky, not one in a hundred could pronounce it.

J. Thompson, *The Life of John Thompson, Mariner, Written By Himself* (Newcastle: J. Catnach, 1810) xvi.

5) Hester Piozzi returns from Italy, 1808 [M.]

Born in 1784, Hester Piozzi (formerly Hester Lynch Thrale) was an aristocratic, literary lady whose diaries record her movements between country and city according to season and mood. As well as being a diarist she was a prolific, witty letter writer. Her accounts register, on occasion, both distaste for London and kinship with Wales.

11th August 1808: People now make a point of having to tell how remote their Excursions have been from the Metropolis. Comical Enough!

Hester Piozzi in: K. C. Balderston (ed.) *Thraliana. The Diary of Mrs Hester Lynch Thrale Later Mrs Piozzi 1776–1809*, vol. 2 (Oxford: Clarendon 1951) 1095.

6) Indians arriving in London, 1809 [I.]

An anonymous, official report on the 'Lascar Problem'.

> . . . the natives of India who came to this country are mostly of bad constituents. Numbers are landed from these ships where they have been ill a great part of the voyage . . . Those who are landed healthy are of course exposed to the same dangers of climate and season; and in addition almost all of them give way to every excess in drinking, debauchery and contract to a violent degree those diseases (particularly venereal) which such liberties are calculated to produce.

India Office Records L/MAR/C902 vol. 1 (1809).

7) John Clare moves from Helpston to Northborough, 1831 [M.]

Born at Helpston, Northamptonshire, in 1793, John Clare became a celebrated 'natural poet' in the 1820s with the publication of Poems Descriptive of Rural Life. *Though he did make a trip to London at the height of his fame, he spent most of his life in Northamptonshire. The letter quoted here, from Clare to John Taylor, dates from October 1831. The poet died in 1864.*

> I have had some difficulties to leave the woods and heaths and favourite spots that have known me so long for the very molehills on the heath and the old trees in the hedges seem bidding me farewell – other associations of friendships I have few or none to regret – for my father and my mother will be often with me – and altho my flitting is not above three miles off – there is neither wood nor heath furze bush molehill or oak tree about it.

J. W. and A. Tibble (eds) *The Letters of John Clare* (London: Routledge and Kegan Paul, 1951) 174.

8) Samuel Harris travels from Warsaw, *c.*1820s [I.]

Born in Warsaw, Poland in 1807 Harris' account is a religious tract tracing the author's conversion to Christianity and simultaneously his move to England. Strongly didactic in tone, it nevertheless gives a detailed account of westward bound, early 19th century immigration.

> About this time, two Missionaries came to Warsaw from the London Society for promoting Christianity among the Jews. Having learned that they gave away books gratis, I ran to them and asked one of them to give me one of their books, I wished to have one of the pretty bound books, viz. a Testament, but he gave me a tract, and said, if you read this tract, and let me know what you have read when you come again, I will then give you one of these pretty books. I received the tract with joy, and the moment I came out of the house, I opened it and cast my eyes on the following words, or such like, 'How long will the children of the house of Israel refuse to believe the truth as it is in Jesus Christ?' I was quite astonished, and I repeated in my mind; believe in Jesus the Messiah! I never heard of him: who can this mean?

I could not read any further, but thought who Jesus was. While I was thus musing, I arrived at home, where I found my father just sitting down to dinner, and I ran up to him with a degree of pleasure, with the tract in my hand. 'See, father,' I said, 'a gentleman gave me this as a present. Who is Jesus Christ it speaks about?' I looked earnestly into his face, expecting to hear who Jesus was; but, oh! how can I express my sorrow to say that my dear father was so ignorant, and so much blinded with prejudice, that he tore and burned the tract in my sight, and after punishing me very severely, he ordered me to inquire no more after this name, on pain of being turned out of the house. I pleaded my ignorance, and told him I thought it was a good book, because it was written in the holy language: yet he would make no allowance for me, he repeated his threatenings. This appeared a very severe treatment to me then, but seeing now that was an instrument on the hands of the all-wise God, to bring me among the witnesses of the Saviour, I cannot help exclaiming with the Apostle, 'How unsearchable are his judgements, and his ways past finding out!'

I concluded that my father did not punish me for inquiring after Jesus, but that he did not like me so well as my brothers and sisters, and therefore treated me badly in order to get me out of the house. I had not this long in mind before I began to think of leaving home, and having heard of a gentleman that was in want of an errand-boy, I went and engaged myself to him, although in my father's house there was bread enough and to spare, even for hired servants. With this gentleman I lived about two years, during which period I attempted several times to go home and see my mother, but my father never welcomed me, and sometimes ordered me out of the house, saying to my mother, 'He will turn out a Meshomet, or an apostate, you'll see.' Rather than be thus mortified by living in the vicinity of my relations and not be permitted to see them, and by seeing my brothers and sisters idolized, and myself hated, I determined to beg my bread from door to door in a foreign land, where, if I should meet with bad usage, I should know it was from strangers. I said, summer is coming. I'll take out a passport, and leave my father's house, my kindred, and my native land, and go where God in mercy may direct me. These thoughts I soon put into action; and though my parents put obstacles in my way at first, yet when they found they could not hinder me, they consented. Leipsic fair was now approaching, and many merchants were setting out for it from Warsaw. I agreed with some of them to make their beds on the way,* and clean their shoes, and do any other thing they wished me to do, if they would let me ride in their waggon. The day for setting out having arrived, as is customary among the Jews, the waggon went about a mile out of town, and the relations accompanied the travellers to take leave of them, and pronounced a blessing upon them. My mother walked with me, and gave me much good advice, and as I stepped into the waggon, she said, go '*Bishom elohy yisriole*,' in the name of the God of Israel.

* It is common in Poland for travellers to carry their beds with them.

Having got quite sat down in the waggon, I began to employ my leisure in meditating on my journey's end. A thousand difficulties appeared to me. I was aware I should soon have to leave the waggon, and what must I begin at then, said I, the twenty shillings that I have will soon be spent, and how shall I get to London, a distance of sixteen hundred miles? When I get there, to whom shall I go? for whom shall I enquire? I know nobody, and nobody knows me. When I want any thing, how shall I speak? I do not know a word of English. Such thoughts as these perplexed my mind for the first two or three days; but then the merchants engaged me to wait upon them at Leipsic, my mind became eased, and I hoped that Israel's God would help me yet. In ten days we performed our journey to Leipsic, and the merchants with whom I came, behaved kindly to me at the time they remained here, which was about three weeks. When they left the fair, they made me a present of a little money, so that I was able to keep up my twenty shillings, I now began to think of proceeding to Hamburg, and sought for an opportunity, which I found with less trouble than I expected, as there was a waggoner there who had fled from the vigour of the Polish laws for selling contraband goods. He did not think himself safe even here, and determined to take his waggon to Hamburg with passengers and afterwards to sell his waggon, and proceed to England. He promised to take me for nothing.

S. Harris, *The History and Conversion of Samuel Harris, a Polish Jew* (Bradford: n.p., 1833) 14–17.

9) A labourer begins 'tramping', 1840s [M.]

Born c.1820 in Winibush (Essex, near Saffron Walden) this unnamed navvy travelled widely as a harvester and tunnel constructor to Sussex, Derbyshire, Yorkshire, Hertfordshire, Oxfordshire as well as (modern day) Hereford and Worcestershire. He eventually settled in London. According to the editor of this account, which first appeared in Macmillan's Magazine *(1861–2), the 'Autobiography of a Navvy' was 'taken down from his own narration, facts and sentiments together, just as they came'.*

After I left home, I started on the road 'tramping' about the country, looking for work. Sometimes I'd stop a few weeks with one master and then go on again, travelling about; never long at a time in one place. I soon got into bad company and bad ways, and at times it would come over my mind that I thought more about the devil than I thought about my Saviour; but I still kept wandering on in that long lane and feared no end to it.

J. Burnett, *Useful Toil* (Harmondsworth: Penguin, 1974) 58.

10) A vagrant boy travels from Kent to London, 1850 [M.]

Born c.1837, the only biographical details, as was usually the case with Mayhew's interviewees, are contained within the speaker's account. Henry Mayhew (1817–87) was a journalist and social investator whose four volumes of London Labour and the London Poor *(1st edition, 1851–2; 2nd enlarged edition, 1861–2) – a unique, rich collection of first hand testimonies – grew from a series of articles in the* Morning Chronicle. *Mayhew's working notes have not survived, but he clearly conducted many interviews both at his newspaper offices and in the streets of the capital, often using a template question and answer sheet. The final accounts were edited into monologues with the help of assistants. See also Introduction to Part I.*

The last statement I took was that of a boy of thirteen. I can hardly say that he was clothed at all. He had no shirt and no waistcoat – all his neck and great part of his chest being bare. A ragged cloth jacket hung about him, and was tied, so as to keep it together, with bits of tape. What he had wrapped round his trowsers did not cover one of his legs, while one of his thighs was bare. He wore two odd shoes – one tied to his foot with an old ribbon, the other a woman's old boot. He had an old cloth cap. His features were distorted somewhat from being swollen through the cold.

'I was born (he said) at a place called Hadley, in Kent. My father died when I was three days old, I've heard my mother say. He was married to her, I believe, but I don't know what he was. She had only me. My mother went about begging – sometimes taking me with her; at other times she left me at the lodging-house in Hadley. She went in the country round about Tonbridge and there, begging. Sometimes she had a day's work. We had plenty to eat then, but I haven't had much lately. My mother died at Hadley a year ago. I don't know how she was buried. She was ill a long time, and I was out begging; for she sent me out to beg by myself a good while before that, and when I got back to the lodging-house they told me she was dead. I had 6d. in my pocket, but I couldn't help crying to think I'd lost my mother. I cry about it still. I didn't wait to see her buried, but I started on my own account. I met two navvies in Bromley, and they paid my first night's lodging; and there was a man passing, going to London with potatoes, and the navvies gave the man a pot of beer to take me up to London in the van, and they went that way with me. I came to London to beg, but sometimes wouldn't get a farthing in a day, often walking about the streets all night. I have been begging about all the time until now. I am very weak – starving to death. I never stole anything. I always kept my hands to myself. A boy wanted me to go with him to pick a gentleman's pocket. We was mates for two days, and then he asked me to go picking pockets; but I wouldn't. I know it's wrong, though I can neither read nor write. The boy asked me to do it to get into prison, as that would be better than the streets. He picked pockets to get into prison. He was starving about the streets like me. I never slept in a bed once I've been in London. I'm sure I haven't. I generally slept under the dry arches in West-street, where they are building houses – I mean the arches for the cellars. I begged chiefly from the Jews about Petticoat-lane, for they all give away bread that their children leave – pieces of crust and such like. I would do anything to be out of this misery.'

H. Mayhew, *The Morning Chronicle Survey of Labour and the Poor: The Metropolitan Districts vol. 2*, (Horsham: Caliban, 1981) 40–1.

11) Harriet Jacobs travels from New York to London, mid-19th c. [M.]

Born c.1815, Harriet Jacobs' (alias Linda Brent) Incidents in the Life of a Slave Girl *(1861) was only the second slave narrative (after Mary Prince's* History *of 1831) written by a woman. Although mostly concerned with her life in America she visited Britian where she had been offered work as a governess.* Incidents *is thought to be Jacobs' own work, though an advisorial and editorial role was claimed by the abolitionist campaigner L. Maria Child. The author died in 1880.*

In the spring, sad news came to me. Mrs. Bruce was dead. Never again, in the world, should I see her gentle face, or hear her sympathizing voice. I had lost an excellent friend, and little Mary had lost a tender mother. Mr. Bruce wished the child to visit some of her mother's relatives in England, and he was desirous that I should take charge of her. The little motherless one was accustomed to me, and attached to me, and I thought she would be happier in my care than in that of a stranger. I could also earn more in this way than I could by my needle. So I put Benny to a trade, and left Ellen to remain in the house with my friend and go to school.

We sailed from New York, and arrived in Liverpool after a pleasant voyage of twelve days. We proceeded directly to London, and took lodgings at the Adelaide Hotel. The supper seemed to me less luxurious than those I had seen in American hotels; but my situation was indescribably more pleasant. For the first time in my life I was in a place where I was treated according to my deportment, without reference to my complexion. I felt as if a great millstone had been lifted from my breast. Ensconced in a pleasant room, with my dear little charge, I laid my head on my pillow, for the first time, with the delightful consciousness of pure, unadulterated freedom.

P. Edwards and D. Dabydeen, (eds) *Black Writers in Britain 1760–1890* (Edinburgh: Edinburgh University Press, 1991) 181–2.

12) Russian Jews arrive in Leeds, 1852 [I.]

An anonymous recollection recorded by S. Manham for his article in the Yorkshire Evening Post *(1852).*

All of those I remember in my early days in Leeds came here as single men. Later on men came with their wives from Russia, but the early ones were single and either made wives in this country or sent Russia for his sister and I married her. It was a usual thing for young fellows, when they had settled here, to send to Russia for their parents and brothers and sisters and that is how the Jewish people made a home in Leeds.

E. Krausz, *Leeds Jewry: Its History and Social Structure* (Cambridge: Heffer, 1964) 4–5.

13) Irish workers arrive in Greenock, *c.*1880s [M.]

The incident descibed here is attributed to oral evidence from a descendant of Billie Conn and other workers in sugar refineries.

As the tide of migration from Ireland rose to continually higher levels, the proportion of Irish workers in certain industries such as sugar refining became even larger until they came almost to dominate them. This factor of occupational dominance was itself an important determinant of occupational choice. New immigrants would be introduced by their friends and relatives, and as the refiners came to be staffed almost entirely by Irish men, then they could ensure that only their fellow countrymen were employed. One sugar refinery in Greenock, for instance, was known as 'Bille Conn's sugar hoose' after a well-known Irish foreman. A new Irish immigrant landing in the town would often have been given instructions to ask for Bille Conn's sugar house, and when at length he arrived there and was able to proclaim his proper origins and religious affiliations, he would be given employment if there was any work available.

R. D. Lobban, 'The Irish community in Greenock in the nineteenth century', *Irish Geography* (1961) 274.

14) Mr Stone's parents travel from Suwalki to Glasgow, 1880 [I.]

Mr Stone's parents were born in Lithuania c.1860. His recollections were recorded c.1980 for the BBC Radio Scotland documentary series Odyssey.

My folks were married in Suwalki, that's in Lithuania. They were penniless. Round about 1880 it was enacted that all Jews were liable for military service. Well, there was the difficulty with the dietary laws bein' infringed and they wanted time for worshippin', so they decided to get out. The problem was how to get over the border. My mother related that the young girls would chat to the border guards while the rest of the Jews skipped over. Once you had a foot over the border that was you safe, you were in Prussia. They hitch-hiked tae Hamburg and the main thing tae notice, they'd practically no food.

> Water, herring, and black bread, that sustained them. It was pure chance whether the ship arrived in Leith, Cardiff or Liverpool.

M. Rodgers, 'Glasgow Jewry', in B. Kay (ed.) *The Complete Odyssey: Voices from Scotland's Recent Past* (Edinburgh: Polygon, 1996) 227.

Settlement and Work 1

15) Ann Linford in the Bedford area, 1750s [M.]

Born in Risley, Bedfordshire c.1735, Ann Linford worked as a domestic servant in and around Bedford. Her account was taken down during an official settlement examination in 1760. See also Introduction to Part I.

The examinant Ann Linford upon her oath saith that she was born in the Parish of Riseley in the County of Bedford that her father Alexander Linford a mason was loyally settled in the sd Parish of Risley. That she was 18 years of age before she went from Risley and from thence she went to hire with Abraham Little a butcher at Milton [Ernest] with whom she lived one year, and from there she came back to Risley and there lived with one Mrs Dawson of Risley for two years, from thence she went . . . to Wile^{m} Poppierts victualler at Sharnbrook with whom she lived two years, from thence in service with Mrs Bittray in the town of Bedford for Six or Nine Months, from thence she went and hired with John Whitehouse victualler at the Green Dragon on whom she lived there three months, and from thence she was let to Rich Colley at the —— Inn in Bedford . . .

Taken before us this 7th day of January – 1760.

Settlement Examinations (Settlement Papers, Overseers of the Poor), Parish of Bedford St Paul (1768) Bedfordshire and Luton Archives, Bedford, P 1/13/4.

16) Eleanor Perkin in Coventry and Oakham, 1760s–70s [M.]

Born c.1740 in Withybrooke, Eleanor Perkin worked as a domestic servant in and around Coventry. Her account was taken down during an official settlement examination in 1780. See also note on extract No.15.

c.40 years. b. parish of Withybrooke 'that when she arrived at the proper age she went to service. Hired in several places: that about fourteen years ago she hired herself to a year to Mrs Chambers of y Parish of St Trinity in the

> City of Coventry wch term she served & received her full wages: that without any fresh hiring she continued with y said Mrs Chambers in said Parish as a servant two years longer & received y same Wages as for ye first year: that leaving Mrs Chambers she went to Oakham in y Country of Rutland & lived a Servant with John turner of said Parish Innkeeper & for three years or thereabout but never was hired for a year or any other stated Term, nor was any sum stipulated for wages till she left her said Master & this examinent further said she hath done no act to gain a settlement except as above' [10 August 1780]

Settlement Examinations (Settlement Papers, Overseers of the Poor), Warwickshire Record Office, Bedworth (1780) DR 225/327/88–132.

17) William Vollum in England, Ireland and Scotland, 1770s–80s [M.]

Born in Bedford in 1741, William Vollum was a professional soldier who travelled extensively in Britain and Ireland. His account was taken down during an official settlement examination in 1788. See also note on extract No.15.

> Who on his oath saith that he is the Son of William Vollum and Mary his Wife that his father was a Private Soldier in the Third Regiment on Foot and was Quartered in the said town of Bedford in the year 1741 that his said Mother on his said Father on his march and that on the twenty fifth Day of November 1741 his said mother was delivered him of this . . . in the Parish of Saint Paul in the said town that his father was a Scotsman and born in or near the town Brochin in Scotland as his said father hath informed him And this . . . further saith that he hath been in the Army all his lifetime and . . . that about fourteen years ago he was legally married in the Kingdom of Ireland to his late wife Ann by whom he hath one Child born in Wedlock now in Scotland viz. . . . about Nine years

Settlement Examinations (Settlement Papers, Overseers of the Poor), Parish of Bedford St Paul (1788) Bedfordshire and Luton Archives, Bedford, P 1/13/4.

18) Thomas Hollings in southern England, 1787 [M.]

Born in Coventry c.1765, Thomas Hollings travelled through southern England as a servant in the 1770s and 1780s. His account was taken down during an official settlement examination in 1787. See also note on extract No.15.

> b. Parish St Michael in Coventry 'and served an apprenticeship in the same Parish' . . . 'that about ten years ago he was hired for a year to George Bond Esq of Clapham in the County of Surrey and served him there about one month and then went with his Master to Bath Ford there his said Master had

> a House and Served him there about Four Months, then went with his master to Little Hampton in the County of Sussex where his Master went for the purpose of Sea Bathing and served him there about Five Months, then went with his Master to Bath where he had Lodgings and served there about Three months and returned again to Clapham and served about three weeks and then quitted the said Masters service that he hath a Wife now with him named Elizabeth'

Settlement Examinations (Settlement Papers, Overseers of the Poor), Warwickshire Record Office, Bedworth (1787) DR 225/327/88–132.

19) Sir John Fielding protests against West Indians slaves in England, late 18th c. [I.]

Half brother to the novelist Henry Fielding (1707–54), Sir John Fielding was known as the 'Blind Beak' magistrate, and as the most interesting 'hostile' witness against the 18th century black community in London, most notably in An Account of the Origin and Effects of a Police Plan *(1753) and* Penal Laws relating to the Metropolis *(1768).*

> 'The immense confusion that has arose in the families of merchants and other gentlemen who have estates in the West Indies from the great number of negro slaves they have brought into this kingdom . . . deserves the most serious attention. Many of these gentlemen have either at a vast expence caused some of their blacks to be instructed in the necessary qualifications of a domestic servant or else have purchased them after they have been instructed; they then bring them to England as cheap servants having no right to wages; they no sooner arrive here than they put themselves on a footing with other servants, become intoxicated with liberty, grow refractory, and either by persuasion of others or from their own inclinations, begin to expect wages according to their own opinion of their merits; and as there are already a great number of black men and women who have made themselves so troublesome and dangerous to the families who brought them over as to get themselves discharged, these enter into societies and make it their business to corrupt and dissatisfy the mind of every black servant that comes to England; first, by getting them christened or married, which, they inform them, makes them free . . . Though it has been decided otherwise by the judges. However it so far answers their purpose that it gets the mob on their side, and makes it not only difficult but dangerous . . . to recover possession of them, when once they are spirited away ; and indeed, it is the less evil of the two to let them go about their business, for there is great reason to fear that those blacks who have been sent back to the Plantations. . . . have been the occasion of those . . . recent insurrections in the . . . West Indies. It is a species of inhumanity to the blacks themselves, to bring them to a free country.'

J. Fielding, *Penal Laws* (1768) in M. Dorothy George, *London Life in the XVIIIth Century* (London: Kegan Paul, Trench, Trubner, 1925) 135.

20) The Shaw family moves from Dent to Dolphinholme, 1791 [M.]

See note on extract No.3.

> . . . some people were come to a factory at dolphinhome in wiresdale 3 miles from golgate, Lancashire – from our town – there was a man named Miles Burton, a carter, this man was a native of dent and employed at this factory, and there happenend to be a want of hands there, this miles informed the master that he could get them hands at dent, so he was authorised to come over to dent to hire hands, & trades being bad, some families went thither & seemed to Like [it] well, & being in want of more hands, Mr Edmondson the managing master came over to dent to engage hands, several more families hired, & among the rest my father and family – we were 7 children, & they liked large families the Best, for the Childrens sake – my father engaged for him & me to work in the mechanic shop, at our trade &c – so my father sold the greater part of his goods, and some he left unsold, and came to Dolphinholme with some others . . . [in July 1791 this year there]

A. G. Dent, *The Family Records of Benjamin Shaw Mechanic of Dent, Dolphinholme and Preston, 1772–1841* (n.p: Record Society of Lancashire and Cheshire, 1991) 25–6.

21) The Irish in London, early 19th *c.* [M.]

An historical gloss by the early 20th century historian M. D. George. London Life in the XVIIIth century *(1925) is described by its author as 'an attempt to give a picture of the conditions of life and work of the poorer classes'. George stresses too the use of quotations to give some impression of the contemporary point of view. However, she also notes that 'The conditions under which they [the poorer classes] lived are hard to come by, and are chiefly to be gathered from the incidental information of trials, depositions of witnesses, petitions to Quarter Sessions, reports of coroner's inquests, settlement cases, the publications of charities and the pamphlets of reformers'.*

> While Irish ruffianism in London decreased, the number of 'industrious Irish' increased. In the middle of the eighteenth century it was held (by the employing classes) that these were an economic necessity, but after 1815 at least they were an economic danger. Till 1819 the law gave the Irish an advantage over the English poor in allowing them to apply for poor relief without fear of being sent back to their parishes. They had a special gift for relating stories of distress, 'you never can believe one word they say,' said Burgoyne, 'they have so much ingenuity and so much imagination. . . .' The pressure of the Irish poor threatened to break down the poor-law machinery in some of

the London parishes as well as in Liverpool and Manchester, and made the administration of the vagrancy laws more defective than ever. Peace brought poverty and unemployment to England, and in Ireland, without a poor law, distress reached such a point that emigration to England was forced upon the people. The effects of this immigration in London is illustrated by the experiences of the Mendicity Society which offered work at stone-breaking to the poorest able-bodied men who came to their office at which they earned from a shilling to eighteenpence a day. The Irish however undertook the work at a rate which gave them only sixpence or eightpence a day. 'The most destitute of the English would not work for those wages, yet, the Irish did it cheerfully and regretted when they could not have the work to do. . . . The news of their being thus employed reached Ireland, the natives came over in large numbers, men, women and children, and sat themselves down in the street near the office – their numbers caused great alarm.'

The Irish had other qualities besides a low standard of living which gave them an advantage in the London labour market. They had greater physical strength than Londoners, and some of them (those of St. Giles always excepted) were perhaps thriftier than the English of a corresponding class. Mayhew found that this was the case in the nineteenth century, and it was probably equally true in the eighteenth. It might be expected from their peasant origin and their habit of saving money for the rent of their land and cabin in Ireland. Two characteristically Irish occupations, that of the chairman and the milk-seller (milk-walks were bought and sold by the milk-sellers) both needed some small amount of capital as well as physical strength.

M. D. George, *London Life in the XVIIIth Century* (London: Kegan Paul, Trench, Trubner, 1925) 124–5.

22) Travelling beggars in Scotland and Yorkshire, 1820s–30s [M.]

William Cameron was a widely known storyteller and beggar-wit in Glasgow and West Scotland in the first half of the nineteenth century. He travelled extensively in Scotland and England. His autobiography was written between 1840 and 1850 when he was in Glasgow Town Hospital.

I crossed the country to Lawrencekirk, and met the other party to whom I communicated the 'pulling match'. We then went to Blairgaurie stopping at Lochee, and next day crossed to Broughty Ferry, we landed at Portencraigs. As this was the party that went by Stirling they were not known in Fife. We went by Cupar, crossing Fife to Queensferry, and at the south ferry each took their own road. I took one of them in company, and travelled for England, we entered Brampton in Cumberland; the woman with me was a bred tinker, and could turn her hand to anything in travelling.

She started the southering (soldiering), it took well in that country, and some days we could make 20s; we travelled together till we reached

> Manchester, where we fell in with another corps of 'routers' on their way to Galway in Ireland; she had travelled with them before, and wished to do so again; she proposed it to me in an anxious manner, but I told them I would never join such a gang; they then wished me to fill up their schedules but I was aware of their treachery, and would not do it.
>
> The next morning she started with them for Liverpool and left me 'skirling' for my loss.
>
> I then went to Leeds and stayed some time in Yorkshire; this is the land of the cadger; it is the most charitable country in the three kingdoms, if not in the world. I estimate the number of vagrants in Yorkshire at 15,000, and the expense of their support, taking them by the lump of £25 a-year, would break the contractor in nine months.

W. Cameron, *Hawkie: The Autobiography of a Gangrel* (Glasgow: D. Robertson, 1888) 19–20.

23) Irish migration to Manchester, 1832 [M.]

J. P. Kay (1804–77), doctor, reformer and educationalist, was among the first 'hostile' witnesses of the Irish in England. The Moral and Physical Condition of the Working Classes *(1833) attacked the Irish as a destructive influence on native working class morals and standards of living.*

> The great and sudden fluctuations to which trade is liable, are often the sources of severe embarrassment. Sometimes the demand for labour diminishes, and its price consequently falls in a corresponding ratio. On the other hand, the existing population has often been totally inadequate to the required production; and capitalists have eagerly invited a supply of labour from distant colonies, and the sister kingdom. The colonisation of the Irish was the first encouraged; and has proven one chief source of the demoralisation, and consequent physical depression of the people.

J. P. Kay, *The Moral and Physical Condition of the Working Classes, Employed in the Cotton Manufacture in Manchester* (London: J. Ridgeway, 1832) 80.

24) Irish miners in England, 1836 [M.]

Evidence of William Dixon to the Select Committee on the State of the Irish Poor in Great Britain.

> The Irish in the coal mines with us bear a good character; we have nothing to complain of them on that score; they are fully more obedient and tractable than the native, and are not so much given to combine; they are lively, and sometimes, when they get drink among them, they are a little excited, but not to any extent worth speaking of . . . We find them very useful labourers, and their services are of considerable use to us; at present we could not do without them.

K. Lunn (ed.) *Hosts, Immigrants and Minorities: Historical Responses to Newcomers in British Society* (London: Dawson, 1980) 330.

25) The Irish in Greenock, 1836 [M.]

A government report on the 'Irish problem'.

> Not only did the Irish workers possess many useful skills, but they also had many fine qualities as workers. Time and again local employers declared how important their Irish employees were to the success of their enterprises. The Irish workers, for example, proved much more adaptable than the Scottish labourers to the conditions of work and the excessive heat of the sugar refineries. One sugar refiner observed that 'if it were not for the Irish we should be forced to give up trades', and the same applies to every sugar house in the town. 'We decidedly prefer the Irish as labourers either to the English or Scotch,' he declared. 'They work with more heart and good will, and are more civil and attentive. Highlanders could be got in sufficient numbers, but we do not like them so well, they are not so willing and obedient, nor so hardworking and industrious.'

Report of the Royal Commission on the State of the Irish Poor in Great Britain, 1836, (London: Parliamentary Papers, 1836) 41.

26) The Irish in England, 1841 [M.]

John Denvir (1834–1916), a leading Liverpool Irish nationalist campaigner, published his census on The Irish in Britain *(1892) to stress the achievements of his fellow countrymen on the mainland, the creation of a middle class in Liverpool, Manchester and Glasgow, and their continued low status elsewhere. Based on first hand knowledge and eyewitness accounts he also intended* The Irish in Britain *to promote the cause of Home Rule.*

> It might be expected, from the Irish coming in such large numbers, year after year, for over a century, to reap the harvests in England, that a considerable number of them would be found settled in the agricultural counties: It was precisely in these that the smallest proportion of Irish were to be found, according to the census of 1841 showing that the labourers, as a rule, either returned to Ireland each year, or found employment in the mining and manufacturing districts, and the seaports of Great Britain. Thus there were, at this time, in Lincolnshire, a county much visited by Irish reapers, but 1244 Irish-born, or a percentage of 0.3 of the general population, while in Lancashire the Irish-born were 105,916, a percentage of 6.3 of the entire population, constituting more than one-third of the whole Irish-born of England. The great mass of these were in the large towns, particularly Liverpool, where, at this time, nearly all the dock labourers were Irish, who formed, indeed, nearly one-third of the population of the great seaport.

Up till now the typical collier was always an Englishman, and considered to be about the lowest type of a Briton – morally and intellectually. The Irish at this time, however, began to be employed in the collieries. Now they are numerous in the pits all over the country, and, whether they can claim any credit for the change for the better or not, it is an undoubted fact that the mining population of Great Britain are among the foremost in political intelligence, and in every respect, compare favourably with any other class.

In all the ironworking districts the Irish were now beginning to get employment, which accounts for their being numerous in Cumberland, Durham, Northumberland, Monmouthshire, and Glamorganshire. But it was in the larger cities and towns that they were to be found in the greatest numbers. London – as might be expected – had the largest population of Irish-born. They formed, as we have seen, as far back as the middle of the last century, a considerable element in the river-side population, and had been making their way in every walk of life. The same could be said of the other principal towns of Great Britain. In the great seaports they were employed largely in connection with the shipping, while they were gradually gaining a footing in the various industries of the manufacturing towns, particularly in Lancashire and Yorkshire.

J. Denvir, *The Irish in Britain From the Earliest Times to the Fall and Death of Parnell* (London: Kegan Paul, Trench, Trubner, 1892) 115–6.

27) The recruitment of Irish tailors for sweatshops, 1850 [M.]

See note on extract No.10.

My informant tells me that the wives of many sweaters make a practice of being continually on the lookout to entrap young and inexperienced hands from the country. If they see a youth whom they know to be a tailor by the peculiarity of his walk, and he appears to be a stranger in London, they stop him, and inquire if he has come to town for work. If he answers in the affirmative, they tell him that their husband will give him as much as he wants – that if he chooses to come and live and lodge with them he shall be very comfortable, and may earn as much as 16s. a week. The youth is generally inveigled by what he hears, is taken home to the sweater's house, and once in there it is impossible to extricate himself. His coat is soon pledged, and he is forced to remain working with the sweater for the merest pittance, living on the worst food and inhabiting the foulest rooms for months, and perhaps years. My informant assures me that he knows many such cases, and indeed this, he says, has now become so general a practice, that even the old hands in the trade are frequently, stopped in the street, and accosted by these women. He himself has had such overtures made to him several times. The system of importing cheap Irish and foreign labour is also very extensively carried on. Letters are sent to Ireland to the friends of the London sweaters, telling them that they are in want of hands, and then a supply is shipped off to the sweater on the promise of good wages.

H. Mayhew, *The Morning Chronicle Survey of Labour and the Poor: The Metropolitan Districts vol. 2* (London: Caliban, 1981) 115–16.

28) An Italian street performer, 1850 [I.]

See note on extract No.10, and Introduction to Part I.

I received the following narrative from the old man who has been so long known about the streets of London with a troop of performing dogs. He was especially picturesque in his appearance. His hair, which was grizzled rather than grey, was parted down the middle, and hung long and straight over his shoulders. He was dressed in a coachman's blue great coat, with many capes. His left hand was in a sling, made out of a dirty cotton pocket handkerchief; and in his other he held a stick, by means of which he could just manage to hobble along. He was very ill, and very poor, not having been out with his dogs for nearly two months. He appeared to speak in great pain. The civility, if not politeness, of his manner threw an air of refinement about him that struck me the more forcibly from its contrast to the manners of the English belonging to the same class. He began:

'I have de dansing dogs for de street – now I have noting else. I have tree dogs, von is called Finette, anoder von Favorite, that is her nomme, and de udder von Ozore. Ah,' he said with a shrug of the shoulders, in answer to my inquiry as to what the dog did, 'On dance, on valtz, on jomp a de stick, and troo de hoop – non, nothing else. Sometime I had de four dogs – I did lose de von. Ah, she had beaucoup d'esprit – plenty of vit you say – she did jomp a de hoop better dan all. Her nomme was Taborine. Taborine – she is dead dare is long time. All ma dogs have des habillements – de dress, and de leetel hat. Dey have a leetel jackette in divers couleures en etoffe – some de red, and some de green, some de bleu. Dare hats is de rouge et noir – red and black, wid a leetel plume – fedder you say. Dare is some ten or eleven year I have been in dis country. I come from Italie – Italie! Oui, monsieur, oui. I did live in a little ville trente miglia, dirty miles de Parma. Je travaille dan le campagne. I vork out in de countree, je ne scais comment vous appellez le campagne. There is no commairce in de montagne. I am come in dis country here – I have leetel business to come. I thought to gaigner ma vie – to gain my life – wid ma leetel dogs in dis countree. I have dem deja when I am come here from Parma. J'en avait dix. I did have de ten dogs. Je les ai porte – I have carried all de ten from Italie. I did learn, yes – yes, de dogs to danse in ma own countree. It did make de cold in de montagne in vinter, and I had not no work dere, and I must look for to gain my life some oder place. Apres ca I have instruit ma dogs to danse. Ils learn to danse, I play de moosic, and dey do jomp. Non, non! pas de tout! I did not never beat ma dogs; dare is a way to learn de dogs widout no vip. Premierement ven I can come here I have gained a leetel monnaie – plus que now – beaucoup d'avantage – plenty more. I am left ma logement – my lodging, you say – at nine hours in de morning, and I am stay avay vid ma dogs till seven or eight hours in de evening. Oh, I cannot count how many time de leetel dogs have danse in de day – twenty – dirty – forty – peut-etre – all depend. Sometime I vould gain de tree shilling, sometime de couple, sometime not nothing – all depend. Ven it did make bad time I could not vork – de lectel dogs could not danse. I could not gain my life den. If it make cold, de dogs are ill – like tout le monde. I did pay plenty for de nourriture of de dogs. Sometime dey did get du pain (de bread) in de street – sometime I give dem de meat, and make de soup for dem. Ma dogs danse comme les chiens, mais dey valtz comme les dames, and dey stand on dare back legs like des gentilhommes. After I come here to dis countree two day, I am terreeble malade. I am gone to hospital – to Sainte Bartolome – the veek before the Jour de Noel (Christmas-day). In dat moment dere I have de fievre. I have rested in l'hopital quatre sernaine – four veek. Ma dogs vere at liberte all de time. Von compagnon of mine have promised me to take de care of ma dogs, and he have lose dem all – tout les dix. After dat I have bought tree oder dogs – one espanol, anoder qu'on appelle 'grifon,' and de oder was de dog ordinaire – non! non! not one 'pull-dog' – he no good. I must have one month, or six semaine, to instruite ma dogs. I have rested in a logement Italien at Saffron-hill, ven I am come here to London. Dare vas not much vant of Italians dare. It vas tout plein – quite full of etrangers. All come dare – dey are come from France, from Germany, from Italy. I have paid two shillan par semaine each veek – only peur le lit – for de bed. Every von make de kitchen for himself. Vot number dare vas dare, you say? Sometime dere vas twenty person dare, and sometime dere vas dirty persons in de logement – sometime more dan dat. It vas a very petite maison. Dare vas von dozen beds, dat is all; and two sleep demselves in each bed. Sometimes, ven dere arrive plenty, dey sleep demselves tree in von bed, but ordinairement dere vas only two. Dey vas all musicians dare – on play de organ – de piano – de guitar – de flute – yes dare vas some vot played it – and de viol too. De great part vas Italians. Some of dem have des monkeys, de oders des mice, white, and des pigs d'Indes (guinea pigs), and encore oders have des dolls vid de two heads, and des puppets vot danse vit de foot on de board. Des animals are in an apartment apart vit de moosek. Dare vas sometime tree monkeys, von dozen of mice, five or six pigs d'Indes, and ma dogs altogether, vid de moosek by demselves. Dare is all de actors vot vas there. Ma tree dogs gained me sometime two shillan, sometinre von shillan, and sometime I vould rest on my feet all day and not gain two sous. Sometime de boys would ensoolt ma dogs vid de stones. Dare is long time I am rested in London. Dare is short time I vas in de campagne – de countree here – not much. London is better dan de campagne for ma dogs – dare is always de world in London – de city is large. Yes I am always rested at Saffron-hill for ten, eleven, years. I am malade at present – since the l5th of Mars. In ma arms, ma legs, ma tighs, I have de douleur. I have plenty of pains to march. Ma dogs are in de logement now. It is since the l5th of Mars dat I have not vent out vid ma dogs – yes, since de l5th of Mars I have net done no vork. Since dat time I have not pay no money for ma logement – it is due encore. Non, non. I have not gained ma life since the l5th of Mars. Plenty of time I have been vitout noting to eat. Des Italiens at de logement have give to me de pieces of bread and bouilli. Ah, it is very miserable to be poor like me. I have sixty and dirteen years. I cannot march now but with plenty of pains. Von doctor have give to me a letter for to present to de poor-house. He did give me my medicine for noting – grattis. He is obliged. He is de doctor of de paroisse. He is very brave and honest man dat doctor dare. At de poor-house dey have give to me a bread and six sous on Friday of de week dat is passed, and told to me to come de Vednesday next. But I am arrive dare too late, and dey give to me noting, and tell to me to come de Vednesday next encore. Ma dogs dey march now in de street, and eat someting dare. Oh, ma God non! dey eat noting but vot dey find in de street ven it makes good times; but ven it makes bad times, dey have noting at all, poor dogs. Ven I have it dey have it – but ven dare is noting for me to eat dare is noting for dem, and dey must go out in de street and get de nourriture for demselves. Des infants vot know ma dogs will give to dem to eat sometime. Oh yes, if I had de means I would return to Italie – ma countree. But I have not no silver, and not no legs to walk. Vat can I do? Oh yes, I am very sick at present. All my limbs have great douleur – oh yes, oh yes, plenty of pain.'

H. Mayhew, *The Morning Chronicle Survey of Labour and the Poor: The Metropolitan Districts vol. 4* (London: Caliban, 1981) 235–8.

29) Irish labourers in London, 1883 [M.]

J. T. Smith's volume of informative social reportage, which combines eye-witness accounts, personal opinion and speculative commentary rather than direct interview, also includes portrait engravings of each subject.

Of all people the poor Irish are the most anxious to gain employment, and are truly valuable examples of industry. They sleep less than other labourers; for at the dawn of day they assemble in flocks at their usual stands for hire, – namely, Whitechapel, Queen Street, Cheapside, and on the spot formerly occupied by St Giles's pound, at the ends of Oxford Street and Tottenham Court Road. The most laborious of them are chairmen, paviers, bricklayers' labourers, potato-gatherers, and basket-men; and to the eternal disgrace of the commonality of the English, these people, as well as the Scotch and Welsh, are guilty of very few excesses, particularly in that odious practice of drinking, a vice so much increased by the accommodation of seats in gin-shops, which are the first open and last shut in London.

> The Irish carry immense loads. A hod of bricks, weighing one hundred and ten pounds, is carried one hundred and twenty times at least in the course of the day, and sometimes up a ladder of the height of five stories, and all for two shillings and ninepence per day. The pavier's rammer, of more than half a hundred weight, is raised not fewer than two thousand times in the course of a day. *What Englishman could do that?* With respect to loads on the head, the Irish surpass all others. Leary makes nothing of carrying two hundred weight from Fox under the Hill, near the Adelphin, to Covent Garden, many times on a market morning; and yet, extraordinary as it may appear, his feats have been more or less equalled by a female. A man by the name Englesfield, who has sold flowers in Covent Garden for the last thirty-six years, knows an Irish girl who would often walk under the weight of two hundred pounds. He declares that she brought a load of one hundred and a half from Newgate Market to Covent Garden on her head, without once pitching, though it must be observed that this was not potato-weight, which has always one hundred and twenty-six pounds to the hundred.

J. T. Smith, *Mendicant Wanderers through the Streets of London* (Edinburgh: William P. Nimmo, 1883) 26–7.

30) Scottish, Welsh and Irish merchants in London, 1883 [M.]

See note on extract No.29.

> Of Scottish, Welsh and Irish merchants there are now very few in London; perhaps their full number does not exceed fifty, unless by including that lower order of street musicians who so frequently distract the harmonious ear with their droning bag-pipes, screaming clarinets, and crazy harps. These people, with their match, tooth pick, and cotton-ball venders, may be considered but as one remove from beggary.
>
> The lowest class of the Scotch are bakers' men; the women are laundresses. The Welshmen, of whom London never had many, are principally employed by the potters of Lambeth, at which place they have an old established house of worship. It is a cheerful sight to behold their women, who are remarkable for their cleanliness, and, like the Scotch, are generally pictures of vigorous health. These will go in trains of twenty or thirty persons, from Hammersmith to Covent Garden, joining in one national melody, and perfuming the air with their baskets of ripe strawberries.

J. T. Smith, *Mendicant Wanderers through the Streets of London* (Edinburgh: William P. Nimmo, 1883) 26.

31) London and Leeds sweatshops, 1888 [I.]

From the Report of the Board of Trade on the Sweating System in Leeds *(1888).*

> . . . the chief difference between the London and Leeds systems is to be found in the fact the work is chiefly carried out in workshops of fair size, fairly cleanly, well ventilated, and under the supervision of the Factory Inspectors . . . This state of things has brought with it not only a better sanitary and moral condition of the workers, but also shorter hours of labour. In these facts . . . is to be found the reason why the Jewish tailors of Leeds are far in advance of those of the east end of London. It is also said that the Leeds attempts at organisation among the men have been more successful than those in London.

E. Krausz, *Leeds Jewry: Its History and Social Structure* (Cambridge: Heffer, 1964) 30.

32) Jewish tailors in Leeds, 1897 [I.]

R. H. Sherard's The White Slaves of England *(1897) was first published in 1896 as a series of reports in* Pearson's Magazine *on 'the worst paid and most murderous trades in England'. The author visited six manufacturing centres in the Midlands and the North of England and examined the activities of alkali workers, nailmakers, slipper-makers, woolcombers, white-lead workers and chainmakers as well as the tailors described here.*

> But from what I saw in the sweating dens in the Leylands, I am convinced that their circumstances are, at least, as bad as those of the sweated tailors in London. They all work, on a weekly wage, and from twelve to seventeen hours a day. Here may be seen, in some filthy room in an old dilapidated factory in the Leylands, fifty people (men, women, boys, and girls), all huddled together, sewing as though for dear life. A girl may be earning 6*s* a week, a man from 22*s* to 30*s*. The stench in the room, its uncleanliness, surpass description. The finished garments are lying pell-mell on the floor in the filth and the vermin.
>
> They are 'flogged into their work', as one said, 'for all the time the gaunt sweater stalks about, scolding, inspecting; while now and then he will snatch a garment from some worker's hand, and set himself to work upon it, whilst a stream of vituperation pours from his lips'. He is usually a haggard and starveling man, himself a victim of inhuman competition. There are weeks when he does not earn a penny for himself. In a good week he may earn 10*l*. The Jews work almost exclusively on men's and youth's coats. They do no cutting, and they seem unable to make 'juveniles' and 'trouserings'.

P. Panayi, *Immigration, Ethnicity and Racism in Britain: 1815–1945* (Manchester: Manchester University Press, 1994) 144–5.

33) Mr Tobias on Jewish labouring in Glasgow, *c.*1890 [I.]

Mr Tobias's recollections were recorded c.1980 for the BBC Radio Scotland documentary series Odyssey.

> They had a hard, hard life at the beginning. Ma father told us that he used to get up at maybe three or four o'clock in the morning and rush down to the Gorbals to see it he'd missed the time to go to his work. They'd no clock, nothing! The poverty was absolutely diabolical. He had a trade, he was a blacksmith and he worked for twelve years for this company and the boss was a real slave driver! . . . Well, he went to a firm in Glasgow, a Jewish company of merchants called Shaunfield & Co., Hope Street and they supplied him with an anvil and bellows and equipment to start up on his own. They supplied him with steel to do the work and some of the merchants give him a little credit. He started his own business in 1900 in MacFarlane Street in the Gallowgate and many a week he'd come home with hardly a penny in his pocket after he'd paid one or two bills. It wasn't easy going.

M. Rodgers, 'Glasgow Jewry', in B. Kay (ed.) *The Complete Odyssey: Voices from Scotland's Recent Past* (Edinburgh: Polygon, 1996) 228–9.

34) Frederico Pontierio, an Italian ice-cream seller, on work in Cambuslang, *c.*1900 [I.]

Frederico Pontierio arrived in Cambuslang around the turn of the century. His recollections were recorded c.1980 for the BBC Radio Scotland documentary series Odyssey.

> At the beginning I mean I stood a lot o' abuse, yes, kids especially, because you couldnae speak. Many's the time though you'd get some o' the young boys, they were very good. I gave them 'pokey-hats' and they gave you a hand to shove it [the barrow] up the hill. Some o' the hills you couldnae really shove it up the way and the barrow was pushing down the way. I even pushed the barrow up the Cathkin Braes one morning and you know how much I made? Two pence! Aye, it was heavy, heavy work and it was quite a wee bit hard life tae build up the business. When I did come here the day start seven in the mornin', didna finish till one o'clock, maybe two o'clock in the mornin' and that was for eight solid years. There were one night we went to the pictures, and three o' us and when we went back home, they told us, 'No more pictures!' We hadna a night off nor nothing. I mind o' Mr Ranaldi, I think he was the first Italian settled in Cambuslang, he used to go down the Clyde there and cut the ice. They cut the ice in the Clyde at that time so it must have been an awfu' number of years ago because I never seen a Clyde frozen since! (laughs) It was breakin' ice off for the ice-cream. Aye it was a struggle, you know, it wasna money made easy I assure you.

M. Rodgers, 'Italiani in Scozzia', in B. Kay (ed.) *The Complete Odyssey: Voices from Scotland's Recent Past* (Edinburgh: Polygon, 1996) 130.

Childhood and Home Life 1

35) Sarah Cheatham and her daughter, 1718 [M.]

Sarah Cheatham was born c.1700. Her place of birth and occupation remain obscure, but because of her affair with Samuel Stubbs she travelled from the north to the Midlands and southern England. Her account was taken down during an official settlement examination in 1718. See also Introduction to Part I.

> Who saith that about a week or fortnight after midsumer . . . delivered of a female Bastard Child at a farmers house in Dunstable in the County of Bedford whose name she since hears is John Purton where she stayed from Sunday until the Wednesday following when she came forw^ds^ towards Ches-shire and was four or five days a roaming to Towcster in the County of Northampton where she left the said female bastard Child about Eleven of the Clock in the night in the Door of the Poor Woman house in Towcster aforesaid and then went forwards to Holmes Chappel in Ches-hire aforesaid where she stayed sometime then to . . . Staffordshire where she stayed awhile ab^t^ a fortnight since at which time she came into this County again with designs to take her child again; And this examinant further saith that Purtons wife gave and found her victuals and Drink while she stayed at Dunstable aforesaid and whom she . . . gave her eighteen pounds in Money towards Carrying her home, And this examt further saith that one Samuel Stubbs of Holmes Chappel aforesaid Husbandman is the Real father of the said Bastard Child and saith that she lived with the said Stubbs a quarter of a year . . . During which time the said Stubbs had Carnal Knowledge of her body several tymes and when she went from him . . . he paid her her wages and gave her twenty shilling and half a crown to carry her to London that nobody might know she was with Child and promised to send her money to defray her charges of laying in

Settlement Examinations (Settlement Papers, Overseers of the Poor), Parish of Dunstable (1718) Bedfordshire and Luton Archives, Bedford, P 72/13/4.

36) Jeffrey Morat's trial and death, 1736 [I.]

Born in Guinea c.1719, Jeffrey Morat, or Murat, was brought to England in his infancy, apparently separated from his parents and intended for slavery or domestic service. He died of unknown causes in his prison cell in 1736. Morat's testimony was noted down during his trial for the latest of a succession of assaults on Hannah Emberton.

Jeffrey Morat alias *Murat*, (a Negro) of St. *George's Hanover-Square*, for breaking and entering the houfe of *Peregrine Bertie*, Efq; commonly call'd Marquis of *Lindfey*, about the Hour of Two in the Night, and ftealing thence 2 Pairs of Silver Breaft-Buckles, value 20s. and 2 Guineas in Money, the Property of the faid Peregrine Bertie &c. *Feb.* 1.

He was a fecond Time indicted for affaulting *Hannah Emberton*, in the Houfe of Peregrine Bertie, Efq; commonly call'd Marquif of Lindfey, putting her in Fear, and taking from her a Staff and Silk Pocket, value 2 *d.* a Silver Thimble, value 6 *d.* and Three-pence Half-penny in Money, *Feb.* 2.

He was a Third Time indicted for felonioufly breaking and entering the faid Houfe with an Intent the said *Hannah Emberton* to kill and murther, againft the Peace of our Lord the King, &c. *Feb* 1.

12. Jeffrey Morat alias Murat, about 16 or 17 Years of Age was a Black born in *Guinea*, and could give no Account of his Country nor Parentage, only that he was brought very young to *England*, and happen'd to fall into a noble Family, who took good Care of him, had him educated at School, and infructed in Christianity, but he feem'd to be of a perverfe unthinking difpofition, naturally vicious, and extremely wicked; for altho' he was liberally allow'd, well kept, and wanted for nothing, yet he kept the vileft Company, went to bad Houfes, and lately (as he himfelf confefs'd) abus'd and robb'd a Gentleman of a Guinea, after he had dragg'd him into an ill Houfe, and the Gentleman was forc'd to make the beft of his Way, fearing he fhould be murther'd. The Account he gave of the Fact for which he was condemned was, that upon the firft of *Feb.* Laft, he fpoked to a Shoe-boy whom he called *Thomas*, and they ftaid together 'till late at Night, having agreed to break into the Houfe, by opening up a back Window, and hid themfelves till 8 or 9 o'Clock in the Morning, and then looking about, they got into fome of the Rooms, and ftole 2 Guineas; then the Houfe-keeper coming in, was aftonished to fee fome of the Doors open, fee went to the Kitchen, where *Morat* the black affaulted and endeavour'd to murder her, fhe ftruggl'd 'till they got to the Top of the Kitchen Stairs, and then he with a Poker knock'd her down, and cut her Throat with a Knife, wounding her in feveral Places befides, 'till at laft he left her for dead; after the Gentlewoman had made moft earneft Prayers and Intreaties to fpare her life, Mrs *Emberton* gave this in Evidence againft him, and this he did notwithftanding fhe knew him feveral Years paft, the Marquif of *Lindsey's* Houfe being within a Door or two of the Houfe of that Noble Family in which the Black ferved. Upon the Trial, *Murat* had

nothing to fay in his Defence, but hanging down his Head, denying nothing, and looking confounded, having confeffed all before the Right Honourable the Lord *Carpenter*.

While under Sentence, he was fick all the Time, did not come often to Prayers, and at laft he was fo carelefs of himfelf, and grew fo nafty, that fcarce any body could go into the Cell. He knew little of Religion, and when I vifited and exhorted him in the Cell, he acknowledged his great Sin, and that he was heartily grieved, having committed this Fact without any manner of Neceffity, but merely out of a wicked devilifh Temper. He declared that he was a Chriftian, cried to God for Mercy, and was in Peace with all Men.

On *Tuefday* Morning of 1ft of *March*, when the Keepers opened the Doors, he was found dead in the cell.

Proceedings at Sessions of Peace. City of London and County of Middlesex, vol. 2, 1735–1740, 167–8.

37) A servant girl in North West England, 1768 [M.]

Born c.1720, Tabitha was a domestic servant who lived and worked in the West Riding of Yorkshire and in Staffordshire. Her account was taken down during an official settlement examination in 1768.

The Case appears to be

That Tabitha the Pauper abt. The year 1742, when she was a Spinster, was hired for a year with Wm Poskett of Mathley, & served such year Service, whereby she became then legally settled there –

That abt. 7 years afterwards she intermarried with one Joseph Turner ar Garforth, but where his legal Settlement was she never knew for a Certainty, or otherwise than as she has heard him say yt it was at Hepelstone or some such like Place in Staffordshire. That Turner havg. run away from her, She was removed with one or two Children she had by him by virtue of an Order on the Complaint of the Officers of Garforth some time abt. the year 1752 to this Parish or Place in Staffordshire. That the Officers of the Place, to wch she had been so removed agreed with the Officer, who conducted her thither, to bring to Methley, which he did accordingly, and that she was received at Methley . . .

That the Pauper, havg. been informed of Turner's Death, some Time afterwards, vizt, in June 1755 intermarried with Jonathan Reynolds (who was sometime a Boatman, and some time a Porter at Leeds) at Coley Chapel in Parish of Halifax, by who she had the 3 Children mentioned in the Order, who were all born in the Township of Leeds.

That in May 1764 Joseph Turner returned to Leeds, & findg. the Pauper in the Possession of Reynolds as his Wife, demanded her of him, but at last Turner & Reynolds came to an Agreement touching, her whereby the former pretended to sell, and the latter to buy her, & so Reynolds still continued in

Possion, till he ran away & left her some 20 or 30 Weeks ago. What is become of Turner is not known, nor can it be found that either he or Reynolds did any Act whereby to gain a Settlement at Leeds.

From the above State it does appear that either the legal Settlemt of the Pauper on her own Right, or the Settlement of Joseph Turner or Jonathan Reynolds is at Leeds – & consequently there cd. be no Pretence for removing her to Leeds – And altho' the Children mentioned in the Order may, possibly, be Bastards, & the Place of their legal settlement may be there as being the Place of their Birth – yet they are not removed hither as such, or if they were, cod. they be bastardised by the Justices Order, but must be deemed legitimate, as Attess will be presumed, till contarary Sentence in the proper Court, & even aditting them Bastards, for Argument sake, yet are they supposed to be inseparable from their Mother, being all Nurse Children under the Age of 7 years, & ought to have been removed with her to her Place of Settlemt. as a necessary Appendage of hers, & not she with them. The Respondts. have given Notice / See it annexed / to produce the Pauper to be examd. before the Justices in Sessions – So we apprehend they will rely almost, if not altogether, on her single Evidence –

The Pauper being removed by the Order as the Wife of Reynold

To prove that Jonathan Reynold about 18 or 19 years ago being then unmarried was hired for a year with Jas Garnet Miller of Castleford Mills [which is either in the Township of Castleford, or in the Township of Ollerton otherwise Water Ollerton] & served him for such year – tis said Reynolds served Garnet for sevl years successively as his hired Servt for a year

*Call James Garnett

The Pauper will prove, if necessary; her Settlement at Metley in her own Right, & the Removal by Officers of Garforth to a parish in Staffordshire, & her being conveyed from thence to Methley as mentd. in stating, & Case. Please to move for Cots & Damages pursuant to 8 & 9 W.3 c.30. & 9 Geo c.7 s.9 if Appeal determined in Favour of Appellants. NB the Pauper & her 3 Children were removed to Leeds 29 Decr. Last.

Settlement Examinations (Settlement Papers, Overseers of the Poor), Sharp Bridges Archive (1768), Bradford Record Office, 16D86/1150.

38) Ukawsaw Gronniosaw describes family life after his marriage to an Englishwoman, *c.*1770 [I.]

Born in Borno (west of Lake Chad in modern day Nigeria) c.1710 Ukawsaw Gronniosaw was kidnapped as a teenager, became a house slave in America, a soldier in the British Army and eventually a resident in England. A Narrative of the Remarkable Particulars in the Life of James Albert Ukasaw Gronniosaw, An African Prince, related by Himself (*c.*1770) *relates how in these latter years he lived in extreme poverty with his English wife Betty. Though often religious in tone, perhaps because the account was 'taken from his own mouth, and commit-*

ted to paper by the elegant pen of a young lady of the town of Leominster', the Narrative *is nevertheless at times both ironic and bitter.*

The boundless goodness of God to me has been so very great, that with the most humble gratitude I desire to prostrate myself before him; for I have been wonderfully supported in every affliction. My God never left me.

My dear wife and I were now both unemployed, and we could get nothing to do. The winter proved remarkably severe, and we were reduced to the greatest distress imaginable. I was always very shy at asking for anything, and could never beg; neither did I choose to make known our wants to any person, for fear of offending, as we were entire strangers; but our last bit of bread was gone, and I was obliged to think of something to do for our support. I did not mind for myself at all, but to see my dear wife and children in want, pierced me to the heart. I now blamed myself for bringing her from London, as, doubtless, had we continued there, we might have found friends to have kept us from starving. The snow was at this season remarkably deep, so that we could see no prospect of being relieved. In this melancholy situation, not knowing what step to pursue, I resolved to make my case known to a gentleman's gardener that lived near us, and entreat him to employ me; but when I came to him my courage failed me, and I was ashamed to make known our real situation. I endeavoured all that I could to prevail on him to set me to work, but to no purpose, for he assured me that it was not in his power. But just when I was about to leave him, he asked me if I would accept of some carrots. I took them with great thankfulness, and carried them home. He gave me four, and they were very large and fine. We had nothing to make a fire with, consequently we could not boil them, but we were glad to have them to eat raw. Our youngest child was then an infant, so that my wife was obliged to chew it, and feed her in that manner for several days. We allowed ourselves but one every day, lest they should not last till we could get some other supply. I was unwilling to eat at all myself, nor would I take any the last day that we continued in this situation, as I could not bear the thought that my wife and children should be in want of the means of support. We lived in this manner till our carrots were gone, and then my wife began to lament because of our poor babes. I comforted her all that I could, still hoping and believing that my God would not let us die, but that it would please him to relieve us, which he did almost by a miracle. We went to bed as usual, before it was quite dark, as we had neither fire nor candle; but we had not been there long before some person knocked at the door and inquired if James Albert lived there. I answered in the affirmative, and rose immediately. As soon as I opened the door, I found that it was the servant of an eminent attorney who resided at Colchester. He asked how it was with me, and if I was almost starved. I burst out into crying, and told him that I was indeed. He said that his master supposed so, and that he wanted to speak with me, and I must return with him. This gentleman's name was Danniel. When I came to his house, he told me that he had thought a great deal about me of late, and was apprehensive that I must be in want, and could not be satisfied till he had sent to inquire after me. I made known my distress to him, at which he was greatly affected, and generously gave me a guinea, and promised to be kind to me in future. I could not help exclaiming, 'O the boundless mercies of my God! I prayed unto him, and he has heard me. I trusted in him, and he has preserved me. Where shall I begin to praise him, or how shall I love him enough?'

I immediately went and bought some bread and cheese, and some coal, and carried them home. My dear wife was rejoiced to see me return with something to eat. She instantly got up and dressed our babes, whilst I made a fire; and the first nobility in the land never made a better meal. We did not forget to thank the Lord for all his goodness to us. Soon after this, as the spring came on, Mr. Peter Danniel employed me in helping to pull down a house, and to rebuild it. I had then very good work, and full employ. He sent for my wife and children to Colchester, and provided a house for us, where we lived very comfortably. I worked at his house for more than a year, till it was finished, and after that I was employed by several successively.

I had at this time an offer made me of going to Norwich, and having constant employ. My wife seemed pleased with this proposal, as she supposed that she might get work there in the weaving manufactory; that being the business she was brought up to, and more likely to succeed there than in any other place; and we thought as we had an opportunity of moving to a town where we might both be employed, it was most advisable to do so, and that probably we might settle there for our lives. When this step was resolved upon, I went first alone, to see how it would answer, which I afterwards very much repented; for it was not in my power immediately to send my wife any supply, as I fell into the hands of a master that was neither kind nor considerate. She was reduced to great distress, so that she was obliged to sell the few goods that we had; and when I sent for her, she was under the necessity of parting with our bed.

When she came to Norwich, I hired a room ready furnished. I experienced a great deal of difference in the carriage of my master from what I had been accustomed to from some of my other masters, and he was very irregular in his payments to me. My wife hired a loom, and wove all the leisure time that she had, and we began to do very well, till we were overtaken by fresh misfortunes. Our three poor children fell ill of the smallpox, which was a great trial to us; but still I was persuaded in myself that we should not be forsaken. I did all in my power to keep my dear partner's spirits from sinking. As her whole attention was now taken up by the children, she could mind nothing else, and all that I could get was but little to support a family in such a situation, besides paying for the hire of our room, which I was obliged to omit doing for several weeks; but the woman to whom we were indebted threatened that if we did not pay her immediately, she would turn us all into the street. The apprehension of this plunged me into the deepest distress, considering the situation of my poor babes. But my God, still faithful to his promise, raised me up a friend. Mr. Henry Gurdney, a Quaker, heard of our distress, and sent a servant to the woman we hired our room from, who paid our rent, and bought all the goods, with my wife's loom, and gave us them all.

Some other gentlemen hearing of his design, were pleased to assist him in these generous acts, for which we can never be sufficiently thankful. After this my children soon came about, and we began to do pretty well again. My dear wife worked hard and constantly when she could get work, but it was very disagreeable, her employ being so uncertain. I was far from being happy with my master, as he did not use me well. I could scarcely ever get my money from him; yet I continued patient till it pleased God to alter my situation.

P. Edwards and D. Dabydeen (eds) *Black Writers in Britain 1760–1890* (Edinburgh: Edinburgh University Press, 1991) 19–21.

39) The marriage of Hart Samuel's daughter, 1792 [I.]

An historical gloss, by a mid-20th century historian, on 18th century Jewish community.

In 1790, the daughter of Hart Samuel, a single young woman, was sent to Amsterdam, Holland, with instructions to ask the local communal leaders to assist in selecting a suitable 'Shochet and Chazan' [slaughterer and Precantor/synagogue leader] for Sunderland. Jacob Joseph was selected for the post and came to Sunderland the same year. Two years later he married the very Miss Samuel who had been sent to Holland to find a shochet-chazan.

Most people will agree that this romance was not altogether a coincidence. The brothers, Adam and Hart Samuel, the first Jews to settle in Sunderland, were either native Dutch, or had sojourned in Holland for some considerable time on their way from Bohemia or Germany.

Hart Samuel, the younger of the brothers, it will be recalled, came to Sunderland later than did Abraham; incidentally, he was the more successful in business. In Amsterdam, Hart doubtless had many close friends with whom he was in constant touch, and to whom he probably addressed himself when a shochet-chazan was required for Sunderland; also, he had a marriageable daughter.

It is not unlikely therefore, that when Jacob Joseph was recommended as a candidate for the post of chazzan-shochet, his Amsterdam friends, knowing the circumstances, probably hinted that this handsome man might well suit as a prospective son-in-law.

With a hint of that sort it was natural that Hart Samuel should take his daughter into his confidence, and, being a sensible young woman, she very properly expressed a desire to see the young man, a desire that was promptly fulfilled by sending her to Amsterdam. The couple had no children; they were happily married for more than sixty years.

A. Levy, *History of the Sunderland Jewish Community* (Edinburgh: Macdonald, 1956) 36–8.

40) A vagrant boy travels through England, 1850 [I.]

See note on extract No.10. See also Introduction to Part I.

An intelligent boy, of 16 years of age, whose dress was a series of ragged coats, three in number – as if one was to obviate the deficiency of another, since one could not button and another, was almost sleeveless – gave me the following statement. He had long and rather fair hair, and spoke quietly. He said: – 'I'm a native of Wisbech, in Cambridgeshire, and I am sixteen. My father was a shoemaker, and my mother died when I was five years old, and my father married again. I was sent to school, and can read and write well. My father and stepmother were kind enough to me. I was apprenticed to a tailor three years ago, but I wasn't long with him. I runned away; I think it was three months I was with him when I first runned away – it was in August. I got as far as Boston, in Lincolnshire, and was away a fortnight. I had 4s. 6d. of my own money when I started, and that lasted two or three days. I stopped in lodging-houses until my money was gone, and then I slept anywhere – under the hedges or anywhere. I didn't see so much of life then, but I've seen plenty of it since. I had to beg my way back from Boston, but was very awkward as first. I lived on turnips mainly. My reason for running off was because my master ill-used me so; he beat me, and kept me from my meals, and made me sit up working late at nights for a punishment. He pretended, anyhow, that it was for a punishment; but it was more to his good than to punish me. I hated to be confined to a tailor's shopboard, but I would rather do that sort of work now than hunger about like this. But, you see, sir, God punishes you when you don't think of it. When I went back my father was glad to see me, and he wouldn't have me go back again to my master, and my indentures were cancelled. I stayed at home seven months, doing odd jobs, in driving sheep, or any country work, but I always wanted to be off to sea. I liked the thoughts of going to sea far better than tailoring. I determined to go to sea if I could. When a dog's determined to have a bone, it's not easy to hinder him. I didn't read stories about the the sea then – not even 'Robinson Crusoe' – indeed, I haven't read that still, but I know very well there is such a book. My father had no books but religious books; they were all of a religious turn, and what people might think dull, but they never made me dull. I read Wesley's and Watt's hymns, and religious magazines of different connexions. I had a natural inclination for the sea, and would like to get to it now. I've read a good deal about it since – Clark's 'Lives of Pirates,'

'Tales of Shipwrecks,' and other things in penny numbers (Clark's I got out of a library though). I was what people called a deep boy for a book, and am still. Whenever I had a penny after I'd got a bellyful of victuals, I went for a book, but I haven't bought many lately. I did buy one yesterday – the Family Herald – one I often reads when I can get it. There's good reading in it; it elevates your mind – anybody that has a mind for studying. It has good tales in it. I never read 'Jack Sheppard' – that is, I haven't read the big book that's written about him; but I've often heard the boys and men talk about it at the lodging houses and other places. When they haven't their bellies and money to think about, they sometimes talk about books; but for such books as them – that's as 'Jack' – I haven't a partiality. I've read 'Windsor Castle' and 'The Tower' – they're by the same man. I liked 'Windsor Castle,' and all about Henry VIII, and Herne the hunter. It's a book that's connected with history, and that's a good thing in it. I like adventurous tales. I know very little about theatres, as I was never in one. Well, after that seven months I was kindly treated all the time. I runned away again to get to sea, and hearing so much talk about this big London. I comed to it. I couldn't settle down to anything but the sea. I often watched the ships at Wisbech. I had no particular motive, but a sort of pleasure in it. I was aboard some ships too, just looking about as lads will. I started without a farthing, but I couldn't help it. I felt I must come. I forgot all the suffering before – at least the impression had died off my mind. I came up by the unions where they would take me in. When I started, I didn't know where to sleep any more than the dead; I learned from other travellers on the road. It was two winters ago, and very cold weather. Sometimes I slept in barns, and I begged my way as well as I could. I never stole anything then or since, except turnips; but I've been often tempted. At last I got to London and was by myself. I travelled sometimes with others as I came up, but not as mates – not as friends. I came to London for one purpose just by myself. I was a weeks in London before I knew where I was. I didn't know where to go. I slept on door-steps or anywhere. I used often to stand on London Bridge, but I didn't know where to go to get to sea, or anything of that kind. I was sadly hungered, regularly starved, and I saw so many policemen I daren't beg – and I dare not now, in London. I got crusts, but I can hardly tell how I lived. One night I was sleeping under a railway arch somewhere about Bishopsgate-street, and a policeman came and asked me what I was up to? I told him that I had no place to go, so he said I must go along with him. In the morning he took me and four or five others to a big house in a big street. I didn't know where; and a man – a magistrate, I suppose he was – heard what the policeman had to say, and he said there was always a lot of lads there about the arches, young thieves, that gave him a great deal of trouble, and I was one associated with them. I declared I didn't know any of the other boys, nor any boys in London – not a soul; and I was under the arch by myself, and only that night. I never saw the policeman himself before that I know of. I got fourteen days of it, and they took me in an omnibus, but I don't know to what prison. I was committed for being a rogue and something else. I didn't very well hear what other things I was, but 'rogue' I know was one. They were very strict in prison, and I wasn't allowed to speak. I was put to oakum some days, and others on a wheel. That's the only time I was ever in prison, and I hope it will always be the only time. Something may turn up – there's nobody knows. When I was turned out I hadn't a farthing given to me. And so I was again in the streets, without knowing a creature and without a farthing in my pocket, and nothing to get one with but my tongue. I set off that day for the country. I didn't try to get a ship, because I didn't know where to go to ask, and I had got ragged, and they wouldn't hear me out if I asked any questions of people about the bridges. I took the first road that offered, and got to Greenwich. I couldn't still think of going back home. I would if I had had clothes, but they were rags, and I had no shoes but a pair of old slippers. I was sometimes sorry I left home, but then I began to get used to travelling, and to beg a bit in the villages. I had no regular mate to travel with, and no sweetheart. I slept in the unions whenever I could get in – that's in the country. I didn't ever sleep in the London workhouses till afterwards. In some places there were as many as 40 in the casual wards – men, women, and children; in some only two or three. They used to be part boys like myself, but far more bigger than I was; they were generally from 18 to 23; London chaps chiefly, I believe. They were a jolly set; they used to sing and dance a part of the nights and mornings in the wards, and I got to sing and dance with them. . . .

. . . Sometimes there was fighting in the casual wards. Sometimes I was in it. I was like the rest. We jawed each other often, calling names, and coming to fight at last. At Romsey a lot of young chaps broke all the windows they could get at, because they were too late to be admitted. They broke them from the outside – we couldn't get at them from inside. I've carried on begging and going from union to union to sleep until now. Once I got work in Northampton with a drover, and kept working, when he'd a job, from August last to the week before Christmas. I always tried to get a ship in a seaport, but couldn't. I have been to Portsmouth, Plymouth, Bristol, Southampton, Ipswich, Liverpool, Dover, Brighton, Shoreham, Hastings, and all through Lincolnshire, Nottinghamshire, Cambridgeshire, and Suffolk – not in Norfolk, they wouldn't let you go there. I don't know why. All this time I used to meet boys like myself, but mostly bigger and older; plenty of them could read and write, some were gentlemen's sons, they said. Some had their young women with them that they'd taken up with, but I never was much with them. I often wished I were at home again, and do now, but I can't think of going back in these rags; and I don't know if my father's dead or alive (his voice trembled), but I'd like to be there and have it over. I can't face meeting them in these rags, and I've seldom had better, I make so little money. I'm unhappy at times, but get over it better than I used, as I get accustomed to this life. I never heard anything about home since I left. I have applied at the Marine Society here, but it's no use. If I could only get to sea, I'd be happy, and I'd be happy if I could get home, and would, but for the reasons I've told you.'

H. Mayhew, *The Morning Chronicle Survey of Labour and the Poor: The Metropolitan Districts, vol. 3* (London: Caliban, 1981) 33–7.

41) Irish families in Dundee, 1850 [I.]

From the Dundee, Perth and Cupar Advertiser, *18 January 1850.*

Since Friday last four Irish parents have left their families to the care of the parochial authorities. One of these consists of three children, and another of two, while two are illegitimate. A mother of one of the illegitimate infants, conscience-stricken, has returned and taken possession of her infant. None of these individuals have the slightest claim on parochial relief; and instead of availing themselves of the opportunity of being sent home to their native country, they have adopted the alternative of abandoning their offspring to the charge of the public.

W. M. Walker, *Juteopolis* (Edinburgh: Scottish Academic Press, 1979) 115.

42) The 'children of the famine', 1866 [M.]

Comments, by an Irish nun, on the condition of the Irish in York.

On the first day of general admissions January 1852 only two out of 50 or 60 girls from 8–13 years old who presented themselves, could spell a few words of three letters, these same children too, were the only possessors of shoes or bonnets, the others were enveloped from head to floor in their mothers' old gowns or in a large shawl, or had the skirt of their own frocks turned up over their heads, and few or none out of the whole assembly could boast of even any pretensions to cleanliness. Their hair nearly stood on end or was so matted as to defy the power of brush or comb. This state of semi-barbarism may be judged from the following, for they appeared not to comprehend what was said and had no notion of control. Their favourite seats (and on which they shelved themselves if the sister's eye was withdrawn a minute) was the large projecting chimneypiece, while their feet hung dangling over the fire. Others who could not find room as above seated themselves on the stone fender around the fire, but as close to it as they could thrust themselves in Turkish posture on the writing desks, not one having the least idea of sitting on a form or stool, although the room was well supplied with both.

Three or four times an attempt was made to classify them, but no sooner were they divided and placed in separate parts of the room, than with a simultaneous rush they scampered off and in less than a minute were again in their original places.

As words were unavailing the influence of music was tried and proved most effectual. The sister taught them a hymn to the Blessed Virgin and they seemed completely softened down. They were then well exercised in marching time and in less than a week they were models of order . . .

Many more children could come to school, if their parents would take the trouble of requiring them to do so. From the extreme poverty of the great majority of the parents and from the gross negligence of a large number of these poor people, it is feared that very few of the children will remain sufficiently long at school to admit of their passing even in the 4th standard . . . Many parents consider their children have 'got sufficient schooling' when they have mastered the rudiments of reading and writing and made their first communion.

F. Finnegan, *Poverty and Prejudice, A Study of Irish Immigrants in York 1840–1875* (Cork: Cork University Press, 1982) 124–5, 130.

43) The Padroni system in South Wales, 1892 [I.]

From W. H. Wilkins' essay The Italian Aspect.

The traffic was carried out in this wise: the children were brought over from their natural country by men who obtained them from their parents for a very small sum, for a few ducats annually.

The *padroni*, that is the master, having obtained the possession of the children, then brings them by circuitous routes to England. How the slavedrivers – for they are little better – manage to evade the new Italian law against their traffic is not easy to say, but when they have got clear of the frontier their plan is plain. Some travel by railway, but many of them actually journey by foot, from town to town and village to village, all the way up to Dieppe or Calais, from thence crossing over to our shore.

The *padroni* are cruel and pitiless masters, and treat their children just like slaves. If the little ones do not bring home a sufficient sum they are cruelly beaten and ill-treated, kept without food or nourishment and sent hungry to bed.

A. White (ed.) *The Destitute Alien in Great Britain* (London: Edward Arnold, 1892) 51.

44) Mr Grossman on Jewish schoolchildren in Glasgow, 1890s [I.]

Born 1885 Mr Grossman was a first generation east European immigrant who lived in the Gorbals, Glasgow's inner city immigrant district. Her recollections were originally recorded c.1980 for the BBC Radio Scotland series Odyssey.

> I went to Rose Street School. They were nearly all Jewish children and we used to come in half-an-hour later than the rest o' them because they said their prayers at that time. In those days we didn't say any prayers to my knowledge – I might be wrong, mind ye, maybe I was too late in getting' into school! We had teachers to teach us the various things and we went to little *chedarim* [small, traditional, religious schools] and they maybe had some pupils. Other times you might have a teacher come to the house to teach you, you were lucky if it was a twenty-minute lesson and then he dashed away to another house. That was quite common in my day and I was born in Glasgow in 1885.

M. Rodgers, 'Glasgow Jewry', in B. Kay (ed.) *The Complete Odyssey: Voices from Scotland's Recent Past* (Edinburgh: Polygon, 1996) 231.

Community 1

45) Advice for servant girls travelling to London, 1776 [M.]

From the London guide book A Brief Description of London and Westminster *(1776)*.

> a word of advice to such young women as may arrive strangers in town . . . Immediately on their arrival . . . and sometimes sooner, even upon the road to it, there are miscreants of both sexes on the watch to seduce the fresh country maiden, with infinite protestations of friendship, service, love and pity, to prostitution. For this reason, the very carriages which convey them are hunted and examined; the inns where they alight are beset by these infernal hirelings who . . . put on the demure show of modesty and sanctity for their deception. If she applies to an office of intelligence, 'tis odds but she falls into the hands of some procuress . . .

M. D. George, *London Life in the XVIIIth Century* (London: Kegan Paul, Trench, Trubner, 1925) 113.

46) William Davidson's view of other black Londoners, 1820 [I.]

Born in 1786, William Davidson was the acknowledged son of a black woman and the then Attorney General of Jamaica. Davidson gained notoriety in the early years of the 19th century as a radical who together with co-conspirators planned in 1820 to blow up the Cabinet. He was indicted and executed on charges of conspiracy in 1820. The following comments were recorded by H. B. Howell in his volume State Trials *(1826).*

> . . . he said 'Mr. Davidson, if you have no objection to going for this blunderbuss, you had better go as you pledged it, lest the man should object to my having it.' I did not think he intended to forfeit my life; he told me where to meet him the next morning in Oxford-street, and I took the blunderbuss under a gateway in Oxford-street to him; he said, 'will not you walk in, and have a glass with a countryman of your's?' I said, 'what do you mean by a

countryman?' I was not much acquainted with him; he says, 'a man of colour.' I had an objection to going in, for though I am a man of colour, I have never associated with any of them. I was very well brought up. I found them all very ignorant; who this man of colour was I do not know. Mr. Edwards promised to meet me the next day, but that night I was apprehended.

P. Edwards and D. Dabydeen, (eds) *Black Writers in Britain 1760–1890*, (Edinburgh: Edinburgh University Press, 1991) 131.

47) A German band member performing in London, 1850 [I.]

See note on extract No.10.

Next come the German Bands. I had the following statement concerning these from a young flaxen-haired and fresh coloured German, who spoke English very fairly:

'I am German, and have been six year in zis country. I was nearly fourteen when I come. I come from Oberfeld, eighteen miles from Hanover. I come because I would like to see how it was here. I heard zat London was a goot place for foreign music. London is as goot a place as I expect to find him. There was other six come over with me, boys and men. We come to Hull and play in ze country about half a year; we do middling, and zen we come to London. I didn't make money at first when I come; I had much to learn, but ze band, oh! it did well, We was seven. I play ze clarionet, and so did two others; two play French horns, one ze trombone, and one ze saxhorn. Sometime we make 7s. or 8s. a piece in a day now, but the business is not so goot. I reckon 6s. a day is goot now. We never play at fairs, not for caravans. We play at private parties or public ball-rooms, and are paid so much a dance – sixpence a dance for ze seven of us. If zare is many dances it is goot; if not it is bad. We play sheaper zan ze English, and we don't spend so much. Ze English players insult us, but we don't care about that. Zey abuse us for playing sheap. I don't know what zeir terms for dances are. I have saved money in zis country, but very little of it. I want to save enough to take me back to Hanover. We all live togezer, ze seven of us. We have three rooms to sleep in, and one to eat in. We are all single men but one; and his wife, a German woman, lives wis us, and cooks for us. She and her husband have a bedroom to zemselves. Anysing does for us to eat. We all join in housekeeping and lodging and pay alike. Our lodging costs 2s. a week each; our board costs us about 15s. a week each; sometime rather less. But zat includes beer, and ze London beer is very goot, and sometime we drink a goot deal of it. We drink very little gin, but we live very well, and have goot meals every day. We play in ze streets, and I sink most places are alike to us. Ladies and gentlemen are our best frients; ze working people give us very little. We play opera tunes chiefly. We don't associate with any Englishmen. Zare are three public-houses kept by Germans, where we Germans meet. Sugar bakers and other trades are of ze number. There are now five German brass-bands, with thirty-seven performers in zem, reckoning our own, in London. Our band lives near Whitechapel. I sink zare is one or two more German bands in the country. I sink my countrymen, some of them, save money; but I have not saved much yet.'

H. Mayhew, *The Morning Chronicle Survey of Labour and the Poor: The Metropolitan Districts vol. 5* (London: Caliban, 1982) 3.

48) A Highlander playing the bagpipes in London, 1850 [M.]

See note on extract No.10.

The Highlanders, with their bagpipes, are next in order. A well-looking young man, dressed in full Highland costume, with modest manners, and of slow speech, as if translating his words from the Gaelic before he uttered them, gave me these details:

'I am a native of Inverness, and a Grant. My father was a soldier and a piper in the 42d. In my youth I was shepherd in the hills until my father was unable to support me any longer. He had 9d. a day pension for 17 years service, and had been thrice wounded. He taught me and my brither the pipes; he was too poor to have us taught any trade, so we started on our own accounts. We travelled up to London, having only our pipes to depend upon. We came in full Highland dress. The tartan is cheap there, and we make it up oursels. My dress as I sit here, without my pipes, would cost about £4 in London. Our mithers spin the tartan in Inverness-shire, and the dress comes to maybe 30s., and is better than the London. My pipes cost me 3 guineas new. It is between five and six years since I first come to London and I was twenty-four last November. When I started I thought of making a fortune in London, there was such great talk of it in Inverness-shire, as a fine place with plenty of money; but when I came I found the difference. I was rather a novelty at first, and did pretty well. I could make £1 a week then; but now I can't make 2s. a day, not even in summer. There are so many Irishmen going about London and dressed as Scotch Highlanders, that I really think I could do better as a piper even in Scotland. A Scotch family will sometimes give me a shilling or two when they find out I am a Scotchman. Chelsea is my best place, where there are many Scotchmen. There are now only five real Scotch Highlanders playing the bagpipes in the streets of London, and seven or eight Irishmen that I know of. The Irishmen do better than I do because they have more face. We have our own rooms. I pay 4s. a week for an empty room, and have my ain furniture. We are all married men, and have no connection with any other street musicians. 'Tullochgorum,' are among the performances best liked in London. I'm very seldom insulted in the streets; and then mostly by being called an Irishman, which I don't like; but I pass it off just as well as I can.'

H. Mayhew, *The Morning Chronicle Survey of Labour and the Poor: The Metropolitan Districts vol. 5* (London: Caliban, 1982) 4.

49) A gypsy in southern England, 1865 [M.]

See note on extract No.10.

We give the following brief autobiography of a person who has recently returned from one of our penal settlements, having been transported for life. In character he is very different from the generality of our London thieves, having hot African blood in his veins and being a man of passionate, unbridled character. He was formerly a daring highway robber. He was introduced to us accidentally in Drury-lane, by a Bow-street police officer, who occasionally acts as a detective. On this occasion the latter displayed very little tact and discretion, which made it exceedingly difficult for us to get from him even the following brief tale:

'I was born in a tent at Southampton, on the skirts of a forest, among the gipsies, my father and mother being of that stock of people. We had generally about seven or eight tents in our encampment, and were frequently in the forest between Surrey and Southampton. The chief of our gang, termed the gipsey king, had great influence among us. He was then a very old, silver-headed man, and had a great number of children. I learned when a boy to play the violin, and was tolerably expert at it. I went to the public-houses and other dwellings in the neighbourhood, with three or four other gipsey boys, who played the triangle and drum, as some of the Italian minstrels do. We went during the day and often in the evening. At other times we had amusement beside the tents, jumping, running, and single-stick, and begged from the people passing by in the vehicles or on foot.

'During the day some of the men of our tribe went about the district, and looked out over the fields for horses which would suit them, and came during the night and stole them away. They never carried away horses from the stables. They generally got their booty along the by-roads, and took them to the fairs in the neighbourhood and sold them, usually for about 10*l*. or 12*l*. The horses they sold were generally light and nimble, such as might be useful to themselves. They disfigured them by putting a false mark on them, and by clipping their mane and tail. When a horse is in good order they keep it for a time till it becomes more thin and lank, to make it look older. They let the horse generally go loose on the side of the road at a distance from their encampment, till they have an opportunity to sell it; and it is generally placed alongside one or two other horses, so that it is not so much observed. The same person who steals it frequently takes it to the fair to be sold.

'The gipsies are not so much addicted to stealing from farms as is generally supposed. They are assisted in gaining a livelihood by their wives and other women going over the district telling fortunes. Some of them take to hawking for a livelihood. This is done by boys and girls, as well as old men and women. They sell baskets, brushes, brooms, and other articles.

'I spent my early years wandering among the gipsies till I was thirteen years of age, and was generally employed going about the country with my violin, along with some of my brothers.

'My father died when I was about six years of age. A lady in Southampton, of the Methodist connexion, took an interest in my brothers and me, and we settled there with our mother, and afterwards learned coachmaking. I lived with my mother in Southampton for five or six years. My brothers were well-behaved, industrious boys, but I was wild and disobedient.

'The first depredation I committed was when thirteen years old. I robbed my mother of a box of old-fashioned coins and other articles, and went to Canterbury, where I got into company with prostitutes and thieves. The little money I had was soon spent.

'After this I broke the window of a pawnbroker's shop as a cart was passing by, put my hand through the broken pane of glass, and carried off a bowl of gold and silver coins, and ran off with them and made my way to Chatham.

'Some time after this I was, one day at noon, in the highway between Chatham and Woolwich, when I saw a carriage come up. The postillion was driving the horses smartly along. A gentleman and lady were inside, and the butler and a female servant were on the seat behind. I leaped on the back of the conveyance as it was driving past, and took away the portmanteau with the butler's clothes, and carried it off to the adjoining woods. I sold them to a Jew at Southampton of 3*l*. or 4*l*.

'Shortly after I came up to London, and became acquainted with a gang of young thieves in Ratcliffe Highway. I lived in a coffee-house there for about eighteen months. The boys gained their livelihood picking gentlemen's pockets, at which I soon became expert. After this I joined a gang of men, and picked ladies' pockets, and resided for some time at Whitechapel.

'Several years after I engaged with some other men in highway robbery, I recollect on one occasion we learned that a person was in the habit of going to one of the City banks once a week for a large sum of money – possibly to pay his workmen. He was generally in the habit of calling at other places in town on business, and carried the money with him in a blue serge bag. We followed him from the bank to several places where he made calls, until he came to a quiet by-street, near London bridge. It was a dark wintry night, and very stormy. I rushed upon him and garotted him, while one of my companions plundered him of his bag. He was a stout old man, dressed like a farmer. I was then about twenty-two years of age.

'At this time I went to music and dancing saloons, and played on my violin.

'Soon after I went to a fair in Maidstone with several thieves, all young men like myself. One of us saw a farmer in the market, a robust middle-aged man, take out his purse with a large sum of money. We followed him from the market. I went a little in advance of my companions for a distance of sixteen miles, till we came to a lonely cross turning surrounded with woods. The night happened to be dark. I went up to him and seized him by the leg, and pulled him violently off his horse, and my companions came up to assist me. While he lay on the ground we rifled his pockets of a purse containing about 500*l*. and some silver money. He did not make very much resistance and we did not injure him. We came back to London and shared the booty among us.

'About the time of the great gathering of the Chartists on Kennington Common, in 1848, I broke into a pawnbroker's shop in the metropolis, and stole jewellery to the amount of 2,000*l*., consisting of watches, rings, &c., and also carried off some money. I sold the jewels to a Jewish receiver for about 500*l*. I was arrested some time after, and tried for this offence, and sentenced to transportation for life.

'I returned from one of the penal settlements about a year ago, and have since led an honest life.'

J. Binney, 'Thieves', in H. Mayhew, *London Labour and the London Poor*, vol. 4 (London: C. Griffin, 1865), 376–7.

50) The Greek Orthodox community in London, 1863 [I.]

An article entitled 'The King of the Greeks attending Divine Service at the Greek Church', in the Illustrated London News, *24 October 1863.*

The small but important community of Greek merchants in London manifested their fidelity to George I, the newly-elected King of the Greeks, by causing a grand 'Te Deum' to be sung, on Sunday week, in honour of his Majesty, at the Greek Church, on London-wall, on which occasion the King honoured his subjects dwelling in London by his presence.

The church is a small but well-built edifice in the Byzantine style, having a high vaulted roof. It was erected about twenty years ago, by the Greek residents of London, who bought the ground and expended altogether about £20,000 on the work.

P. Panayi, *Immigration, Ethnicity and Racism in Britain: 1815–1945* (Manchester: Manchester University Press, 1994) 148.

51) The Irish Catholic community in Liverpool, 1872 [M.]

Hugh Heinrick was 'special correspondent' for The Nation, *which sent him to survey the political influence of the Irish communities throughout England. His letters, first published in instalments, and then as* A Survey of the Irish in England *(1872), note poor registration of Irish voters and the tendency to drunkenness in some quarters, but also signs of prosperity among the same groups in northern England: a contradiction of the predominant images of the Irish.*

> The religious and educational requirements of the Irish in Liverpool are very well attended to, and all that zeal and labour can effect for the safety and preservation of the people is done on their behalf. Here the Irish people have, in nearly every instance, furnished the means, and Irish priests and Irish teachers, following in the footsteps of the people, have been mainly instrumental in fostering the intelligence and preserving the faith of their countrymen. But whether furnished from English or Irish sources, the evidences that the Faith is vital and progressive, and that the means for the education of the people are not wanting, meet the eye at every turn. There are twenty-three Catholic churches, ten convents, and seven monasteries in Liverpool.
>
> These have all, or nearly all, been built, and are now supported, by the zealous charity of the Irish people. The rich contribute their pound; the poor, their pence; and so churches and schools have risen in evidence of the constancy in faith and the loving thirst for mental cultivation which had ever distinguished the Irish people. The church accommodation – one church to 8,000 population – can scarcely be deemed sufficient; but the school accommodation is almost, if not entirely, equal to the requirements of the time. A careful examination of the School Board statistics will show that the Catholic population of Liverpool have provided school accommodation in elementary schools, industrial schools, and reformatories, for 22,369 children; or for about one in eight of the Catholic population – a proportion which in a community such as this, where a larger proportion of the people remain unmarried than in most other towns – is found to be ample for present requirements. These statistics only supply information in reference to schools within the borough. Outside this boundary there are several large schools, public and private. There is probably school accommodation in and around Liverpool for 25,000 children – certainly for a larger number, if we include Birkenhead and the smaller places on the other side of the Mersey.

P. Panayi, *Immigration, Ethnicity and Racism in Britain: 1815–1945* (Manchester: Manchester University Press, 1994) 146–7.

52) A description of London's Chinatown, 1873 [I.]

The Reverend Salter here applies his extensive knowledge of customs and language in Asia to survey the 'Oriental' immigrant communities within Britian. Salter's account is prefaced by Henry Venn, Honourable Secretary of the Church Missionary Society.

> We are now in the Oriental quarter; there are several houses devoted to Asiatics, presided over by Chinese, Malays, and Indians, according to the country of the Asiatic seeking championship. Each of the proprietors is assisted by an English mistress, some of whom have lived so long in this element, that they use the Oriental vernacular, and have even been known

to act as interpreters at the Police-courts when the oft-repeated quarrels of Asiatics have brought them into trouble. We have indications here of their position in the names which the women bear; names, indeed, which they have earned for themselves, such as Mrs Mohammed, Mrs Peeroo, Mrs Janoo, oriental names derived from the proprietors of the houses above referred to; or Chinese Emma, Calcutta Louisa, and Lascar Sally, names which in themselves may justly be considered to suggest the mode of life adopted. Let us enter the first house on this colony of evil spirits. It is a house of three rooms and is kept by a stalward Chinese, aided by Emma. This is a Chinese gambling-house, and these celestials are so earnest in their dangerous play, that they are by no means troubled by our presence. At one end of the table they are gambling with dice, which they cast with much energy into a glass, whirl it violently round, and toss the dice out again with fevered excitement. The money is rapidly changing hands, poverty and destitution will soon be the heritage of the gamblers. At the other end of the table they are equally in earnest, though at a different, still quite as dangerous a game. Here they are playing with Chinese cards: these are about three inches long and three-quarters of an inch broad, embellished with Chinese pictures and reading. The flashing eye, the rapid and excited accent of the tongue, tell us that things are becoming desperate. It was in this house the poor fellow of whom we spoke lost his £60, and at this very table of sin. Above is the opium room, which serves for fraud and robbery as well as the gambling room. In this house about twenty Chinese are accommodated. The proprietor is a native of Amoy, a very friendly and easy-going Chinese, but, roused to action and out of temper, he is a very desperate man, and his Emma in her drunken fits tries him to the uttermost. Her life, on these occasions, has several times been in imminent danger. Some years past, two speculating Chinese bought her in China at a low price, hoping to make a great gain by her in the metropolis of sight-seers, but they quarrelled over their interests, and one of the speculators stabbed the other, and while one was in the hospital suffering from his wounds, and the other in prison expiating his offence, a servant of Christ snatched the girl from her perilous position. Christian sympathy educated her; the Saviour, who blessed little children, put his hand on her heart, and she returned to China to teach her pagan countrymen the way of eternal life.

J. Salter, *The Asiatic in England: Sketches of Sixteen Years' Work Among Orientals* (London: Seeley, Jackson and Halliday, 1873) 26–8.

53) A variety hall show, 1874 [I.]

James Greenwood (1852–1929) was a journalist who specialized in social reportage. His other works include The Seven Curses of London *(1869) and* Low-life Deeps *(1876), though he was best known for his account of a night spent in disguise as a tramp in a London workhouse.*

> After Miss Maclachlan had sung for the third time, three 'niggers' bounded in, and it augured well for the sympathy of the working men of England with the genuine down-trodden slave that they so kindly tolerated the wretchedly threadbare quips and cranks of these worn-out make-believes. They were funny 'niggers' – jolly, well-fed; all play and no-work darkies, whose sole business in life appeared to be to sleep away the morning, and throughout the afternoon play upon the banjo, and sing of what they had for dinner and what they expected to get for supper, varying the amusements by inventing conundrums. Their jokes as a rule were not original. The majority, as they rolled out of their capacious mouths, were as familiar to the audience as the story of Jack-the-Giant Killer, and when they essayed something new, it were preferable that they once more show Blunderbone, though for the thousandth time. Nor were their doings a bit newer than their sayings. Jumbo artfully withdrew Mumbo's chair, as of old, bringing Mumbo with a crash to the ground, and whereon Jumbo, as of old, promptly delivered himself of an apropos, though not over delicate riddle, concerning the railway engine and the tender behind. Gumbo played the bones over his head, and under his legs, and behind his back; and Jumbo played the banjo over his head, and under his legs, and behind his back; and Mumbo cried, 'Gor 'long, nigger!' several times, and in very effective style; and at the termination of the performance there was a burst of applause provocative of the suspicion that, although by no possibility could Britons voluntarily become slaves, still, if the dire day ever did fall, and a choice were allowed the conquered, they would to a man elect to be slaves on a sugar plantation 'down Souf'.

J. Greenwood, *The Wilds of London* (London: Chatto and Windus, 1874) 92–3.

54) Mutual support among Manchester Jewry, 1887 [I.]

Walter Tomalinson's Bye-ways of Manchester Life *(1887) is a detailed account of social conditions in the mid-Victorian era.*

> Various societies have been formed for special needs and for the relief of special necessities. The United Visitation Committee of Hebrew Congregations of Manchester and Liverpool, was instituted to provide for the proper and systematic visitation of prisons, hospitals and asylums in Lancashire. The prisons are visited periodically by Jewish ministers, and by special permission of the Home Office; and although very few Jews in our part of the country find their way thither, black sheep are not altogether unknown. A few also find their way, through stress of circumstances, into the hospitals and asylums. One special object of these visitations is to discover and bring home any who may chance unfortunately to die there . . .

W. Tomalinson, *Bye-Ways of Manchester Life* (Manchester: Butterworth and Nodal, 1887) 36–7.

55) Anglo-Jewish relations in Manchester, 1880s–90s [I.]

Rickie Burman's contrastive article (published in 1982) on the role of Jewish women as wage earners in late 19th and early 20th century Russia and Poland, and then in Manchester, gives an unusually detailed account of changed community and family relations. The author interviewed three first generation and six second generation immigrants born between 1887 and 1912.

The relation of the established Anglo-Jewish community to their host society in Manchester was very different. This was a more 'open' society, with less formal restrictions: Jews had the legal freedom to live and work where they chose, even if certain clubs and privileges remained closed to them. Furthermore, there was a close identity of interest between the Jewish establishment and the liberal upper middle classes, who saw the established Jews as conforming to and exemplifying their own standards of hard work, sobriety and philanthropy.

This acceptance was, however, perceived as conditional, and rather than being encouraged to maintain their distinctiveness, heavy pressure was exerted on the immigrant Jews to become acculturated as quickly as possible. The institutions established by the elite, such as the Jewish Board of Guardians, the Jewish Ladies' Visiting Association, the Jews' School and Jewish Lads' Brigade, pursued an active, and effective, policy of anglicisation. Their aim was to 'iron out the ghetto bend', to convert the 'slouching children of the ghetto' into erect and self-respecting English gentlemen or ladies. Distinctive marks of Jewishness or foreigness were seen as a threat which would attract adverse attention, falsifying the favourable middle class view of the Jews as respectable and useful English citizens and opening the gates to an indiscriminate antisemitism.

A leader in the Jewish Chronicle, 'the organ of British Jewry', in 1881 emphasised that 'one of the most pressing problems of the future' was 'how best to facilitate the transformation of Polish into English Jews':

> We may not be able to make them rich; but we may hope to render them English in feeling and in conduct . . . By improving their dwellings, attracting them to our synagogues, breaking down their isolation in all directions and educating their children in an English fashion, we can do much to change our foreign poor into brethren who shall not only be Jews but English Jews.

In contrast to the situation in Eastern Europe, therefore, in England the Jews had before them the possibility of tolerance, even acceptance, provided they were prepared to conform to the standards already established by the elite.

The strategy here, then, was to emulate the standards and lifestyle of the Anglo-Jewish establishment, which in turn followed the pattern of the English middle classes. In neither area was the situation static, however, and it is likely that in so far as Eastern Europe itself was undergoing, with considerable time lag, comparable processes of industrialisation and social change, so to some extent parallel but distinct changes in Jewish society were also in progress.

R. Burman, 'The Jewish woman as breadwinner: the changing value of women's work in a Manchester immigrant community', *Oral History*, 10 (1982) 36.

56) Anti-Irish feeling following the Phoenix Park Murders, 1882 [M.]

See note on extract No.26.

Mr Forster having withdrawn himself from the scene, the chief of the permanent officials of Dublin Castle, Mr Burke, was marked as a victim. It was his life that was sought and taken in the Phoenix Park, when Lord Frederick Cavendish, who happened to be with him at the time, in loyally standing up in defence of his comrade, shared his fate.

It was a crushing blow for the Land League, just as it seemed on the point of success. A new reign of coercion was inaugurated. In Great Britain the anti-Irish feeling became roused to fury, and, in several quarters, scenes were enacted like those of the Gordon riots and subsequent outbreaks. Looking back at the history of our people here during the last and present centuries, the steady progress they have been making in numbers, social position, and political power, is from time to time overshadowed by the records of what seem to be struggles against stupendous odds for the mere right to live. Driven forth from their own soil, they have but too often found themselves the Ishmaelites of Great Britain – with every man's hand against them. Although the feeling against the creed and nationality of the Irish has almost always been present, it has generally been when the fierce breath of some strong political or religious excitement has swept over the land that they have felt the full fury of the British mob. So it was at this crisis.

There was an anti-Irish outbreak at Brighouse, in Yorkshire, on Monday, May 8th, when a number of our people were maltreated and their houses nearly demolished, this being accompanied, as usual, by an attack on the Catholic church.

At Stalybridge the low Orange element threatened an attack on the Irish and their church. But as the outrages committed fourteen years previously were still vividly in the minds of the Irish population, they silently and determinedly gathered round the church and schools on the evening of the threatened attack. Some remained on guard the whole night. Needless to say, the Orange rabble, finding the Irish prepared to meet them on equal terms, did not make their appearance.

The most terrible of these riots occurred at Tredegar, in Monmouthshire, just on the South Wales border. The momentary passion against the Irish undoubtedly precipitated the attack, but the feeling against them was of longer standing, and was intensified by other causes.

J. Denvir, *The Irish in Britain from the Earliest Times to the Fall and Death of Parnell* (London: Kegan Paul, Trench, Trubner, 1892) 296–7.

57) On the disappearing 'Irish quarters' and the professional success of the Irish, 1892 [M.]

See note on extract No.26.

It is a mistake, frequently made, both in London and elsewhere, to suppose that the bulk of our fellow-countrymen live in what have been termed the 'Irish quarters'. However it may have been formerly, it is not so now. Those who are compelled by circumstances to live in undesirable surroundings do not, perhaps, constitute one-tenth of the whole. As in other large towns these quarters are gradually disappearing. You find that our people are now spreading all over London, and in much healthier localities than formerly. Although not so numerous among the substantial 'middle-class' traders as one would wish to find them, they are making fair progress, and it is no uncommon thing to find substantial shopkeepers and wholesale traders who have been costers or are the sons of costers; while in every calling and profession you find Irishmen in most responsible positions. In London, as elsewhere throughout Great Britain, you meet with a numerous body who prove that 'with a fair field and no favour' Irishmen are bound to come to the front. These are the Civil Service and Customs Officials. Formerly but few Irishmen could get employment as officials of this kind. In the old days of patronage it was practically 'no Irish need apply'. Since the competitive examination system has been in operation, the native gifts of Irishmen have proved them to be second to none. As a consequence, you now find in the ranks of the Civil Service and in the Customs a greater proportion of them, perhaps, than of the other nationalities of the empire. As a rule, there are no truer Irishmen, and, being men of education, they are often able to render valuable assistance to the cause. In this connection it must not be forgotten that there are a great number of Irishmen in the Government Ordnance Survey, and among the ablest in the various departments.

Irish doctors are numerous in London, and recognised even by those who have no love for their nationality, as among the most skilful in their noble profession.

Of the devoted body of Irish priests, who can speak in sufficient praise? A dignitary of the Church in London has said that had they the same materials to work upon as the clergy at home in Ireland, and were their difficulties not so much greater, such is their zeal and self sacrifice that our people here would be all saints. But the noble work of the clergy is taken so much as a matter of course that it is apt to be forgotten.

To sum up the Irish in London, in the higher social grades, they are far better represented in the various professions than in trade, so that besides Government employes, doctors, and clergymen, there are a large number of men of our nationality who are eminent as lawyers, painters, sculptors, actors, musicians, and in every department of literature.

J. Denvir, *The Irish in Britain from the Earliest Times to the Fall and Death of Parnell* (London: Kegan Paul, Trench, Trubner, 1892) 398–9.

58) The Irish in London, 1892 [M.]

See note on extract No.26.

The Irish are numerous in Clerkenwell . . . South Hackney, Bethnal Green, and Haggerston are noted centres of the boot and shoemaking trade, which gives employment to a portion of the Irish population in these districts. In Marylebone, North Kensington, Chelsea, Fulham and Westminster, these are districts where the Irish and their descendants are largely in evidence. As in other parts of London, while there is a satisfactory proportion who have 'got on', the bulk of these are in the ranks of labour. It is satisfactory to know that many Irish labourers in connection with the building trades have been able to bring up their sons as masons, carpenters, or bricklayers. Among the artisan class you find many who have received a fair education at the schools in connection with the various Catholic churches – men who have never, perhaps, seen Ireland but who are among the staunchest upholders of the national cause, as well as being the keenest and most intelligent politicians to be found in the metropolis.

On the south side of the Thames you find small colonies of our people in Camberwell, Peckham, and other centres. In fact they are everywhere – even in places where you never dream of finding them, as any priest will tell you who has ever opened a mission in London . . .

Perhaps the densest mass of Irish is to be found among the river-side population stretching for miles eastward of London Bridge, on both sides of the Thames. On the north side you meet them in large numbers in Whitechapel, Wapping, Shadwell, Limehouse, Poplar, Millwall, Barking Road and Silvertown, their chief employment being in connection with shipping . . . On the north side of the Thames the Irish population is largest in Southwark, Bermondsey, Rotherhithe, and Deptford, and mostly employed at the docks and the river-side. In and about Bermondsey you find a number of them connected with various branches of the leather trade, for which the district is noted, both as employers and work people.

P. Panayi, *Immigration, Ethnicity and Racism in Britain: 1815–1945* (Manchester: Manchester University Press 1994) 140–1.

59) Marriage between immigrant groups, London, 1890s [I.]

Born in London in 1884, Emmanuel ('Manny') Shinwell was raised in Glasgow, elected as a Labour MP in 1921, and became a prominent left-winger in the government of 1945–51. Early on in his autobiography, published five years before his death in 1986, Lord Shinwell recalls his family origins.

My docker uncle was a native of Portugal. The marriage was not regarded with favour by the family. The Dutch preferred to integrate only with the Dutch. Those who had come from other countries, like the Poles, kept to themselves in other parts of the East End and frowned on marriage with any of Dutch or Russian origin. When my father, whose parents had escaped from persecution in Poland in the early '60s of the last century, married my mother, it caused a sensation in the family. My paternal grandfather, who was a Master Baker in Leeds, and strictly orthodox in religion, regarded marriage with a Dutch person as almost a mortal sin.

E. Shinwell, *Lead with the Left: My First Ninety-six Years* (London: Cassell, 1981) 3–4.

60) Jewish–non-Jewish relations in Leeds, 1890s [I.]

A quotation from a brief memoir, published as a newspaper article in the Yorkshire Evening Post *in January 1925 and recalling community relations in late 19th century Leeds.*

The Ghetto at that period was divided from Mabgate and Quarry Hill districts by a low wall overlooking the beck at the bottom of Templar Street, and the writer has more than vivid recollections of the periodical week-end raids by bands of hooligans who would cross the 'frontier' armed with cudgels and weapons of all descriptions. Spurred on by those who looked forward to these marauding expeditions as good entertainment, they would go through street and alley and molest and assault any Jew who was fated to fall into their hands.

E. Krausz, *Leeds Jewry: Its History and Social Structure* (Cambridge: Heffer, 1964) 5.

61) Jewish holy day celebrations in Leeds and London, 1880s–90s [I.]

See note on extract No.59.

The Dutch were believed to hold liberal views about Judaism. The term 'liberal' has no political connotation in this connection. Although the Dutch adhered to the Five Books of Moses they failed occasionally to practise every line of the civil and canonical law of the Pentateuch, either as respecting ritual or food. They were not strictly orthodox by comparison with the ultra orthodoxy and strict observance of Judaism of my paternal grandfather, whose literal conception of Jewish law, known as the Torah, was the cause of friction between himself and many of his Jewish neighbours. For example, he would not attend, either on the Sabbath day or on the principal feasts, that is, the Jewish New Year and Yom Kippur (the Day of Atonement), at the usual synagogue, but gathered a small congregation of friends who were in agreement with his views, in his large bakehouse in Bridge Street, Leeds, where he conducted the service. As a member of the priestly tribe of Levi he was permitted to conduct the prayers. . . .

In an orthodox Jewish family it is customary, on the eve of Sabbath, to light candles, say prayers and drink wine. My grandparents were unable to afford luxuries, though sometimes my diamond-cutting uncle, who was better able to afford it, would provide the eve of Sabbath dinner. On many Friday afternoons when I returned from school my grandfather was busy concocting a home-made, although for the purpose quite satisfactory, alternative. He cut up a quantity of raisins, pressed them into a bottle, shook it for a few minutes, and there his wine was. A few of the raisins would sometimes come my way. In addition to the lighted candles on the table there was a large loaf of bread under a white cloth. My grandfather at the head of the table would say a prayer, which to me, with my mind on the bread, seemed unduly long; then he removed the cloth, broke the bread, and gave a piece to each of the people round the table. I later learnt that the ceremony was a thanksgiving to the Almighty for our daily bread. Perhaps also it commemorated the provision of 'manna' when Moses organised the departure of his people from Egypt, and they faced famine in the wilderness.

E. Shinwell, *Lead with the Left: My First Ninety-six Years* (London: Cassell, 1981) 4–5.

62) Vince Davidson recalls Lithuanian festivals in Lanarkshire, 1890s [I.]

Mr Davidson's recollections were originally recorded c.1980 for the BBC Radio Scotland documentary series Odyssey.

They worked hard and they lived hard and they always enjoyed themselves you know. They werena' a crowd for savin' at that time, most of it went on booze. Even a christening used to last about three days. They used to buy a barrel of beer and they put it in the corner and if you went to the christening you just helped yourself. . . . As far as weddings were concerned, they carried on their old tradition. A whole week it went on. I played at the weddings in Lithuania, I played the violin. The fiddlers stood at the door and they played something that was really sentimental and everybody, everybody was crying. And then their cart, it was decorated with flowers, the horses, the lot. Beautiful it was. The whole mob went out to the chapel and then when they got married, if you are a fiddler, you are standing at the door to catch them coming back. Well every time you were playing this they were always dropping coins you know in the slit in the violin. You could hardly carry the damned thing. Oh, it was beautiful, a beautiful custom.

M. Rodgers, 'The Lanarkshire Lithuanians', in B. Kay (ed.) *The Complete Odyssey: Voices from Scotland's Recent Past* (Edinburgh: Polygon 1996) 21–2.

63) Mr Latter on religion and sport in Jewish Glasgow, *c.*1900 [I.]

Mr Latter's recollections were originally recorded c.1980 for the BBC Radio Scotland documentary series Odyssey.

I was playing for the Southern Y.M.C.A. at the time and we were in the amateur cup, doing quite well and thinking that possibly we might win it. We'd won our previous round and then some guy produced a protest against me. He dug up this old rule that if you played for the Y.M.C.A. ye had to have two consecutive attendances in the bible Class! Well, I was desperate because I really thought we'd a chance o' winning this cup. I thought about it and decided to go. Surely it canna be all that bad, I'll no' open ma mouth, no' sing any hymns or anything like that. So when I went I sat at the back, kept my mouth shut the whole time, expecting a bolt from heaven to come down and strike me (laughing). I made my two appearances and that meant I could carry in playin' for the Southern Y.M.C.A. Anyway, this guy must have got the needle and thought that he'd have tae try something different. So he sent an anonymous letter to my aunt and this was eventually passed on to my Dad. In the latter it said, 'If you want to find your son on a Saturday afternoon you'll find him in Glasgow Green playin' for the Southern Y.M.C.A. and if ye wonder where he gets to on a Sunday night, he's at the Bible Class!' Ye can imagine, it caused ructions in the family. It would be a fairy-tale end to say that we won the cup but we were knocked out in the next round (laughing).

M. Rodgers, 'Glasgow Jewry', in B. Kay (ed.) *The Complete Odyssey: Voices from Scotland's Recent Past* (Edinburgh: Polygon, 1996) 232.

Another Culture 1

64) English views of the Irish in London, 18th century [M.]

See note on extract No.21.

In the eighteenth century information as to the Irish is chiefly incidental. They appear in accounts of trade disputes and street fights, in the records of the Old Bailey and of the Middlesex Sessions. As elements in the problem of vagrancy and sanitation they were hardly discussed before the Parliamentary reports of the early nineteenth century; but there can be little doubt that the characteristics of the London Irish had been much the same for a hundred years, probably for two, though their numbers progressively increased under the stimulus of building activities and a more liberal distribution of poor relief in London and the pressure of population upon the land in Ireland. Irish vagrants had been a cause of alarm in the sixteenth and seventeenth centuries: 'Whereas this realm hath of late been pestered with a great number of Irish beggars, who live here idly and dangerously, and are of ill-example to the natives of this kingdom,' ran a proclamation of 1629. At this time the Irish seem already to have turned to the occupation of street hawking; Dekker wrote in 1607, 'as Frenchmen love to be bold, Flemings to be drunken . . . and Irish to be costermongers.'

Riots against Irish harvest labour were common in the eighteenth century. Jealousy of Irish labour seems to show itself in an order of the Tin Plate Workers Company in 1724 that all the unskilled Irishmen (were these tinkers?) should be prosecuted for working. There was a violent outburst against the Irish in Spitalfields in July 1736. Irish weavers and builders' labourers were accused of working at under rates. Sir Robert Walpole wrote, 'this complaint against the Irish . . . is founded upon greater numbers than ordinary . . . of Irish being here, and not only working at hay and corn harvest, but letting themselves out to all sorts of ordinary labour considerably cheaper than the English labourers have, and numbers of them being employed by the weavers upon like terms. . . . They are building a new church at Spitalfields where, I am told, the master workmen discharged at once a great number of all sorts of labourers and took in . . . Irishmen who served for above one-third less per day.' According to another account some Irish weavers who were employed as bricklayers' labourers 'offered to work at half the price of the English, this bred the first disgust.' On two successive, days there was a pitched battle. The English cried 'down with the Irishmen,' broke the windows of the houses where they lodged and 'almost demolished' two Irish public-houses. The Riot Act was read without effect, the Tower Hamlets Militia was called out; but the mob was not dispersed till companies of Guards from the Tower appeared. A report had arisen that numbers of Irishmen had recently arrived in London to supplant English workmen by working at low rates. The strength of the anti-Irish feeling is shown by the fact that few days later mobs arose in Southwark, Lambeth, and Tyburn Road and took upon them to interrogate people whether they were for the English or the Irish, but committed no violence.

Faction fights between English and Irish seem to have been common. In 1740 there was a general onslaught by a body of Irish upon the butchers of Clare Market. It seems that it was the custom to burn a 'Taffy' in effigy on St. David's day, and some rash butchers' boys had ventured to burn a 'Paddy' on St. Patrick's day. The Irish were said to be a great body of men of whom over twenty were armed with cutlasses and thirty or forty more with sticks and bludgeons. When three ringleaders were taken before Colonel de Veil, a 'prodigious mob,' it is said, surrounded his office and many persons armed with pistols and cutlasses assembled in Covent Garden. In 1763 there was a pitched battle (one of the many disturbances of a Westminster election) between a party of sailors and a number of Irish chairmen in Covent Garden. A chair man offered to fight the best sailor present and was beaten. This was followed by a general melee in which the sailors demolished every chair they could find. It was an understood thing that the outcome of a street dispute should be a fight for which the bystanders formed a ring, but when one of the combatants was an Irishman, his fellow-countrymen would join in and a general battle was apt to follow.

Though the excesses of the Gordon Riots are to be explained by the effects of drink and a swamping of the forces of order by the inhabitants of the dangerous districts in London who were always ready for pillage, a strong anti-Catholic spirit undoubtedly played its part. Was this partly due to that prejudice against the Irish of which there are so many indications? Defoe, it is true, said that he believed there were 'ten thousand stout fellows that would spend the last drop of their blood against Popery that do not know whether it be a man or a horse,' but by 1780 the sectarian feuds of the early part of the century had subsided. Irish public-houses seem to have been demolished in much the spirit of the riot of 1736. For instance, one Susannah Clark was tried in connection with the destruction of a public-house in Golden Lane kept by a certain Murphy. Evidence was given that she had said 'it was a Roman Catholick's house and there was nothing but Roman Catholicks in it and it must be pulled down and down it should come . . . there had been an Irish wake in the houses, they were Irish Roman Catholicks and the house must come down.'

The Irish in London were a police problem, a sanitary problem, a poor-law problem and an industrial problem. It was the first aspect of the question which first attracted the attention of the authorities. Saunders Welch, the London magistrate, in 1753 divided the Irish immigrants into two classes:

'The Irish imported into this kingdom of the lower class,' he wrote, 'are those who annually come to harvest work and when that is over return with the savings of their labour to their own country. These are useful, faithful, good servants to the farmer and as they are of great use to the kingdom, deserve protection and encouragement. The others are a set of fellows made desperate by their crimes, and whose stay in Ireland being no longer safe, come to London to perpetrate their outrages, and it may be justly asserted that most of the robberies, and the murders consequent upon them, have been committed by these outcasts from Ireland. . . . That London is the asylum of these rogues and vagabonds as well Irish as English who are driven by their rogueries to seek shelter and concealment is a truth beyond dispute. . . .'
He considered that the two great causes of the supply of rogues to London were 'the unlimited wandering of the poor of our own kingdom and the uncontrouled importation of Irish vagabonds.' Except for the two Fieldings there could be no better authority on the underworld of London than Saunders Welch, and the Fieldings were of much the same opinion. Henry Fielding is reported to have said that the greater number of those committed at Bow Street were Irish (this of course would include a number of trivial assault cases). Sir John Fielding in a letter to the Secretary of State (on the subject of Jews) raised the question of Irish immigration. 'If some restraint could be laid on the importation of the abandoned Irish,' he wrote in 1771, 'it would be another means of preventing many robberies in this country. There are certainly a much greater number both of Jews and Irish than can possibly gain subsistence by honest means.'

The evidence of the Old Bailey *Sessions Papers* supports this theory; it appears that Irishmen deserting from the Irish Brigade came to London from the Continent as well as from Ireland to live by plunder. Things seem to have been at their worst in the forties and fifties and towards the end of the century the criminal element among the Irish seems certainly to have diminished. Crime changed its character with the improvements in street lighting and police, and footpads (among whom the Irish had been conspicuous) and highwaymen gave way to burglars. One of the reasons for crime among the London-Irish was certainly the character of the common lodging-houses in St. Giles and Bloomsbury where beds were let at twopence a night and gin sold at a penny a quartern, whose inhabitants, Fielding says, were chiefly Irish. He describes these places in 1751, his authority being Saunders Welch and his own experience.

'If one considers the destruction of all morality, decency and modesty, the swearing, whoredom and drunkenness which is eternally carrying on in these houses on the one hand, and the excessive poverty and misery of most of the inhabitants on the other, it seems doubtful whether they are most the objects of detestation or compassion: for such is the poverty of these wretches, that, upon searching all the above number the money found upon all of them . . . did not amount to one shilling, and I have been credibly informed that a single loaf hath supplied a whole family with their provisions for a week. Lastly, if any of these creatures fall sick (and it is almost a miracle that stench, vermin, and want should ever suffer them to be well) they are turned out into the street by their merciless host or hostess, where, unless some parish officer of extraordinary charity relieves them, they are miserably sure to perish, with the addition of cold and hunger to their disease. This picture, which is taken from the life, will appear strange to many, for the evil here described is, I am confident, very little known, especially to those of the better sort. Indeed, this is the only excuse, I believe the only reason, that it hath been so long tolerated: for when we consider the number of these wretches, which in the outskirts of the town amounts to many thousands, it is a nuisance which will appear to be big with every moral and political mischief.'

M. D. George, *London Life in the XVIIIth Century* (London: Kegan Paul, Trench, Trubner, 1925) 117–20.

65) Ukawsaw Gronniosaw's first encounter with English society, 1770 [I.]

See note on extract No.38.

I never knew how to set a proper value on money. If I had but a little meat and drink to supply the present necessities of life, I never wished for more; and when I had any, I always gave it where I saw an object in distress. If it was not for my dear wife and children, I should pay as little regard to money now as I did at that time. I continued some time with Mr. Dunscum as his servant, and he was very kind to me. But I had a vast inclination to visit England, and wished continually that it would please Providence to make a clear way for me to see this island. I entertained a notion that if I could get to England, I should never more experience either cruelty or ingratitude; so that I was very desirous to get among Christians. I knew Mr. Whitfield very well. I had often heard him preach at New York. In this disposition I enlisted in the 28th regiment of foot, who were designed for Martinico, in the late war. We went in Admiral Pocock's fleet from New York to Barbadoes, and from thence to Martinico. When that was taken, we proceeded to the Havannah, and took that place likewise. There I got discharged. I was at that time worth about thirty pounds, but I never regarded money in the least. I would not tarry for my prize-money, lest I should lose my chance of going to England. I went with the Spanish prisoners to Spain, and came to Old England with the English prisoners. I cannot describe my joy when we arrived within sight of Portsmouth. But I was astonished, when we landed, to hear the inhabitants of that place curse and swear, and be otherwise profane. I expected to find nothing but goodness, gentleness, and meekness in this Christian land, and I suffered great perplexity of mind at seeing so much wickedness.

I inquired if any serious Christian people resided there, and the woman I made the inquiry of answered me in the affirmative, and added that she was one of them. I was heartily glad to hear her say so. I thought I could give her my whole heart. She kept a public house. I deposited with her all the money that I had not an immediate occasion for, as I thought it would be safer with her. I gave her twenty-five guineas, six of which I desired her to lay out to the best advantage, in buying me some shirts, a hat, and some other necessaries. I made her a present of a very handsome large looking glass that I brought with me from Martinico, in order to recompense her for the trouble I had given her. I must do this woman the justice to acknowledge that she did lay out some little for my use but the nineteen guineas, and part of the six guineas, with my watch, she would not return, but denied that I ever gave them to her.

I soon perceived that I had got amongst bad people, who defrauded me of money and watch, and that all my promised happiness was blasted. I had no friend but God, and I prayed to him earnestly. I could scarcely believe it possible that the place where so many eminent Christians had lived and preached could abound with so much wickedness and deceit. I thought it worse than Sodom, considering the great advantage they possessed. I cried like a child, and that almost continually. At length God heard my prayers, and raised me up a friend indeed.

This publican had a brother who lived on Portsmouth Common, whose wife was a very serious, good woman. When she heard of the treatment I had met with, she came and inquired into my real situation, and was greatly troubled at the ill usage I had received, and she took me home to her own house. I now began to rejoice, and my prayer was turned into praise. She made use of all the arguments in her power to prevail upon her who had wronged me to return my watch and money, but it was to no purpose, as she had given me no receipt, and I had nothing to show for it; so that I could not demand it. My good friend was excessively angry with her, and obliged her to give me back four guineas, which she said she gave me out of charity, though, in fact, it was my own, and a great deal more. She would have employed other means to oblige her to give up my money, but I would not suffer her. 'Let it go,' said I; 'my God is in heaven.' I did not mind my loss in the least. All that grieved me was that I had been disappointed in finding some Christian friends, with whom I hoped to enjoy a little sweet and comfortable society.

I thought the best method that I could take now was to go to London, and find out Mr. Whitfield, who was the only living soul that I knew in England, and get him to direct me how to procure a living without being troublesome to any person. I took leave of my Christian friends at Portsmouth, and went in the stage to London. A creditable tradesman in the city, who went up with me in the stage, offered to show me the way to Mr. Whitfield's tabernacle, knowing that I was a perfect stranger. I thought it very kind, and accepted his offer; but he obliged me to give him half-a-crown for going with me, and likewise insisted on my giving him five shillings more for conducting me to Dr. Gifford's meeting.

I began now to entertain a very different idea of the inhabitants of England to what I had figured to myself before I came among them. Mr. Whitfield received me very friendly, was heartily glad to see me, and directed me to a proper place to board and lodge, in Petticoat-lane, till he could think of some way to settle me in, and paid for my lodging, and all my expenses. The morning after I came to my new lodgings, as I was at breakfast with the gentlewoman of the house, I heard the noise of some looms over our heads, and upon inquiring what it was, she told me that a person was weaving silk. I expressed a great desire to see it, and asked if I might. She told me that she would go up with me, for she was sure that I should be very welcome; and she was as good as her word. As soon as we entered the room, the person that was weaving looked about and smiled upon us, and I loved her from that moment. She asked me many questions, and I, in return, talked a great deal to her. I found that she was a member of Mr. Allen's meeting, and I began to entertain a good opinion of her, though I was almost afraid to indulge this inclination, lest she should prove like the rest that I had met with, at Portsmouth, &c., and which had almost given me a dislike to all white women. But after a short acquaintance, I had the happiness to find that she was very different, and quite sincere, and I was not without hopes that she entertained some esteem for me. We often went together to hear Dr. Gifford. As I had always a propensity to relieve every object in distress as far as I was able, I used to give to all that complained to me, sometimes half a guinea at a time, as I did not understand the real value of it. But this good woman took great pains to correct and advise me in that and many other respects.

After I had been in London about six weeks, I was recommended to the notice of some acquaintances of my late master, Mr. Freelandhouse, who had heard him speak frequently of me. I was much persuaded by them to go to Holland, as my master lived there before he bought me, and he used to speak of me so respectfully among his friends there, that it raised in them a curiosity to see me, particularly the gentlemen engaged in the ministry, who expressed a desire to hear my experience and to examine me. I found that it was my good old master's design that I should have gone if he had lived, for which reason I resolved upon going to Holland, and informed my dear friend Mr. Whitfield of my intention. He was much averse to my going at first; but after I gave him my reasons he appeared very well satisfied. I likewise informed my Betty (the good woman that I have just named) of my determination to go to Holland, and told her I believed she was to be my wife; and if it was the Lord's will I desired it, but not else. She made me very little answer, but has since told me that she did not think it at that time.

P. Edwards and D. Dabydeen (eds) *Black Writers in Britain 1760–1890* (Edinburgh: Edinburgh University Press, 1991) 16–19.

66) Anti-catholic riots in Edinburgh and London, 1780 [M.]

See note on extract No.26.

'A Bill relieving His Majesty's Roman Catholic subjects from certain pains and penalties imposed on them by an act of King William.' The *Annual Register*, in explaining the scope of the measure, says – 'By this bill, for the relief of Roman Catholics, the clause in the Act of William III for prosecuting popish bishops, priests, or Jesuits, is to be repealed; also the clause for subjecting papists keeping school for the education of youth, to perpetual imprisonment; also the clause that disables papists to inherit land by descent, and gives to the next-of-kin (being protestant) a right to inherit such lands; also the clause that disables papists from purchasing manors, lands, or hereditaments, in England or Wales; but leaves all lands in possession just as they were, and all causes in litigation as if this act had never been made; and the benefits arising from it are on condition of taking the oath of allegiance within six months after it passes into law.'

The instalment of justice to the oppressed Catholics in England met with violent opposition from the British rabble. The no-Popery movement that followed commenced in Scotland, where the Irish had now settled inconsiderable numbers. There the bigots, fearing that the relaxation granted to the Catholics in England might be extended to Scotland, determined to prevent this if possible, and for a time succeeded. The *Annual Register* describes how the Catholics in Scotland and their property were molested by furious mobs, and thus details the proceedings in the Scottish capital:

'*Edinburgh, Feb. 3rd, 1779.* – On Friday last copies of the following letter were dropped in the different streets and lanes in the city of Edinburgh:

'MEN AND BRETHREN, – Who ever shall find this letter will take it as a warning to meet at Leith Wynd on Wednesday next, in the evening, to pull down that pillar of Popery-lately erected there.

'A PROTESTANT.'

'*Edinburgh, Jan. 29th, 1779.* – P.S. Please to this carefully, keep it clean, and drop it somewhere else – For King and Country

'UNITY.'

'In consequence of this letter (continues the *Register*), a mob last night assembled at a house at the foot of Chalmers' Close, part of which was intended for a Popish chapel, but had not hitherto been occupied, the rest of the building being possessed by clergymen of that persuasion.'

A description is then given of how the mob broke the windows and destroyed and set fire to the furniture, the inside of the house being reduced to ashes. They also attacked the chapel in the Blackfriars Wynd, and destroyed or carried off furniture and valuable books. They then wrecked the houses of Catholics, and intended to pull down the house of Principal Robertson, in the College Court, but the dragoons arrived in time to prevent this. The mob dispersed on being assured that all thoughts of bringing in a bill for the relief of the Catholics of Scotland had been laid aside. There were also no-Popery riots in Glasgow and other parts of Scotland.

The success of the violent outburst of bigotry in Scotland encouraged the 'Protestant Association' to inaugurate a like reign of terror in England, where, owing to the gradually increasing immigration from Ireland, the hated papist seemed again as if becoming a power in the land. On Monday, May 29th, 1780, a meeting of the association was held in the Coachmakers' Hall, to consider the mode of presenting to Parliament a petition to repeal the Act passed for the relief of the Catholics of England and Wales. The notorious Lord George Gordon was the chairman of the meeting.

Following this, on Friday, June 2nd, at ten in the forenoon, several thousands of fanatics whose numbers were increased enormously from the criminal population of London, assembled in St George's Fields. At eleven, Lord George Gordon arrived, and the multitude was set in motion. It was divided into three bodies, each of which crossed to the north side of the Thames by one of the bridges – London, Blackfriars or Westminster – so as to gather strength on their way to the House of Parliament, where they arrived at half past two, with their petition. Lord George Gordon harangued the people from the top of the gallery stairs, and denounced the friends of the Catholics who were opposed to the petition – particularly Edmund Burke, then member for Bristol. There was great rioting and intimidation of members of Parliament on their way to the House, where Lord George was allowed to bring up the petition; but his motion to have it taken into immediate consideration was rejected. The result exasperated the mob, which now dispersed, but only to gather strength for acts of violence.

On the same evening the dreadful rioting and conflagration commenced, which continued, almost without intermission, from that day, Friday, until the following Thursday.

Among the first places attacked and demolished was the Catholic chapel in Duke Street, Lincoln's Inn Fields, founded in the previous century as the chapel of the Sardinian embassy. The old Sardinian chapel was rebuilt after the riots, and still exists, as a reminder of what Catholics and Irishmen had to suffer in those penal days. Like others of our places of worship dating from that period, it is of modest exterior, as if shunning observation. It is plain, almost to ugliness, with its stuccoed front and circular-headed conventicle-like windows. Round it, and spreading westward, what was probably the first Irish colony in London was gradually increasing in 1780, and the fury of the no-Popery rioters was wreaked on their habitations. The Bavarian chapel in Warwick Street, Golden Square, was also attacked and destroyed; and the sky of London was lit up that night by the burning churches and houses of the persecuted 'Papists.'

On Saturday there was a lull in the rioting, but it commenced with renewed vigour on Sunday, when the mob attacked the chapel in Moorfield, and the dwelling houses of the Catholics in the neighbourhood. They stripped the houses of furniture, and the church of the insignia of religion, and burned them and the church, leaving nothing but the bare walls.

On Monday the rioters paraded with the relics of their havoc, and burned them in the fields adjacent to Lord George Gordon's house. They also destroyed the Catholic chapels in Virginia Lane, Wapping, and at Nightingale Lane, East Smithfield. The existence of these chapels – now no longer in the list of London Catholic places of worship – at this time, shews that the Irish population must have been considerable in these localities in 1780.

J. Denvir, *The Irish in Britain from the Earliest Times to the Fall and Death of Parnell* (London: Kegan Paul, Trench, Trubner, 1892) 82–4.

67) Irish living conditions in London, 1810–11 [M.]

See note on extract No.21.

Simond, who visited England in 1810–11, has recorded his impressions of the place. 'We have in our neighbourhood,' he writes, 'one of those no-thoroughfare lanes or courts. . . . This one is inhabited by a colony of Irish labourers who fill every cellar and every garret . . . very poor, very uncleanly and very turbulent. They give each other pitched battles, every Saturday night particularly, when heroes and heroines shew their prowess at fisticuffs and roll together in the kennel, precisely as at Paris in the Faubourg St. Marceau. We should never have known there were such wretches as this in London if we had not happened to reside in Orchard Street, Portman Square, which by the way, is one of the finest parts of the town. The uproar continued all last night from Saturday to Sunday . . . and it was impossible to sleep. . . . A watchman called for assistance with his rattle. One or more of his brethren assembled and I overheard from the window one of them say, 'If I go in, I know I shall have a shower of brickbats.' To which another answered very considerately, 'let them murder each other if they please.'

M. D. George, *London Life in the XVIIIth Century* (London: Kegan Paul, Trench, Trubner, 1925) 116.

68) John E. Ocansey visits London, 1881 [M.]

John Ocansey was from the interior of the the Gold Coast (present day Ghana). Slave to a family of African traders from Addah (Ada) he was adopted, worked in the family business and later married Salome Ocansey. He travelled to Liverpool and London on trader activities, and his account in African Trading; or the Trials of William Narh Ocansey *(1881) gives an acute view of Victorian Britain, though to the modern reader it can also possess an almost ironic naïvety. The author died in 1889.*

The Train to London

On the day following my arrival, I made enquiries about Hickson, Sykes & Co., and then I found they had been declared bankrupt, and that the l7th of June had been appointed for the meeting of their creditors. This was terrible news. I felt my heart sink, and I could not eat for three days. I thought of my dear father and the heavy loss he would sustain of £2,678 11s. 8d., besides all the delay in the enlargement of his business for want of the steam launch, for which he had already paid, and which ought to have been out and in full working order. I now found that I could do nothing but wait and attend the meeting of creditors. But I remembered that I had business in London, and on the 7th June I decided to visit that great city to see some of my firm's agents. At eleven o'clock in the morning we left Lime Street Station, Liverpool, and arrived in Euston Square Station, London, at 3.50 in the afternoon, travelling at some times at the rate of sixty miles in one hour!

When I first went into the railway train, I observed they were like great coaches, mounted on springs, with strong, heavy wheels. Six persons can sit side by side in a row and they are so high that a man can stand upright with his hat on and not touch the top. The seats are cushioned and the carriages have large, strong glass windows at each end, and a lamp at the top to give light when they are rushing through the dark tunnels. Some carriages will carry fifty or more persons, and the carriages can be hooked on, one after the other, according to the number of passengers. A large and powerful engine, with fires burning inside, was fastened to the front of the carriages. The steam was coming out of the top, or chimney, with great force and noise. After I had been inside, and secured my seat, I came out and stood on the platform, near to the door, to look at the large station, and all the people coming and going, and I was greatly astonished to see so large a place. You can walk about for half-an-hour before you can go all round it; and yet this vast place is all covered over with a glass roof, supported and held up by iron beams and pillars. Whilst I was gazing about a gentleman came up, dressed in a blue suit, with silver buttons. I thought he was a soldier; but he shouted out, 'Take your seats, gentlemen; show your tickets.' I immediately jumped inside, and he took my ticket and made a small cut in it, and then shut the door with a loud bang. I then heard a bell ring, and the engine gave a loud screech, or whistle, and began to move very slowly at first, but gradually increased in speed, and we shot into a dark tunnel, which is made under the houses for about two miles, until we came out into the light in the country. I was bewildered with the motion of the carriages, and the great noise they made in rushing through the tunnel. The carriages were certainly very comfortable, and the lamp in the top gave us good light. But it was pleasant to break out into the sunshine again. Then I settled and composed myself to look out of the window on the country, and behold! all the trees of the field seemed to be flying away from us backwards! It was then I saw how swiftly we were going; swifter than a bird can fly through the sky! And thus the engine rushed and pushed away with all its might; and we went dashing along past houses, villages, and through the midst of large towns, and over high bridges, and darted in and out of deep tunnels, with such a loud noise that I could not hear the sound of my own voice. As I looked out on the country it seemed very green and beautiful. There were many cattle in the fields; and all the land is divided by hedges, and long lines of bushes and trees. There were many houses and towns all the way, and large factories with long chimneys.

After we had been flying along in this way for more than four hours, the train began to get quiet and to go slower, until it stopped; and a man, dressed as an officer, came and violently opened the door, and shouted out, 'Tickets, please!' and he took them from us; then I knew I was in the great city of London! But I was not tired of the journey, it was so pleasant, and so short a time in coming such a long distance.

I consider the distance from Liverpool to London to be equal in length as from Addah to Cape Coast Castle, and that journey by land takes us fourteen days, and now I have travelled it in four hours and a half! . . .

The Sights of London

As I passed along the streets, I noticed the people looking at me very earnestly. The small boys especially would stand and stare, and would sometimes call out to me, 'Halloa! blacky, can't you wash your face before you come out in the morning, and make it white?' My companion kindly said, 'You must not take notice of them, because they do not know any better.' The next morning, my kind friend came again for me at my lodgings, and we went to see the Thames embankment, a long, strong wall built alongside the river. We there saw Cleopatra's Needle, a long upright monument made of marble, and lately brought from Egypt. We then went into the Houses of Parliament, but the members were not there; and we crossed the road and went into Westminster Abbey, which is a grand Church, where they bury the Kings and Queens and all the great men of England. Their monuments are all round on the walls; and are very interesting. We also visited Buckingham Palace, one of the residences of the Queen; and Marlborough House, the residence of the Prince of Wales; and closed a heavy day's work by going to

Madame Tussaud's wax-work exhibition. All the figures were dressed up like living men and women. The following day was entirely spent in the Crystal Palace, a very large collection of buildings all covered in by glass roofs. The inside is full of wonders; so many that I am bewildered when I think of them, and I really cannot describe them. There were all kinds of machines working away as if they were in a factory. I stayed all the day looking first at one thing and then another, and yet they said I had not seen half of what there was in. At nine o'clock we all went outside of the building to see the fireworks, which appeared to me very curious, grand, and frightful. Altogether I was eight days in London, and every day I was out seeing some grand thing, until I got as tired as if I had been on a long, weary journey.

London is a very great place; I thought far too big and confusing, and I would not like to stay there. I was glad, therefore, to come back to Liverpool and be quiet.

P. Edwards and D. Dabydeen (eds) *Black Writers in Britain 1760–1890* (Edinburgh: Edinburgh University Press, 1991) 200–4.

69) Walter Besant observes a Sunday market in the Jewish East End, *c.*1900 [I.]

Walter Besant, novelist, philanthropist and journalist, was best known as the author of All Sorts and Conditions of Men *(1882) a three volume fantasy which became a best seller. Despite its questionable literary merits Besant's work led to the opening of the Queen's Hall of the People's Palace which continued to offer cultural entertainment in the East End until the Second World War. Besant's social reportage could appear less generous than this achievement suggests.*

The place and time in which one sees the poorer Jews of London collected together is a Sunday morning in Wentworth Street and Middlesex Street, Aldgate – the old Petticoat Lane. These streets and those to right and left are inhabited entirely by Jews; Sunday is their market-day; all the shops are open; all streets are occupied by a triple line of stalls, on which are exposed for sale all kinds of things, but chiefly garments – coats and trousers. There is a mighty hubbub of those who chaffer and those who offer and those who endeavour to attract attention. You will see a young fellow mounted on a pair of wooden steps, brandishing something to wear; with eloquent convincing, with gesture and with action, he declares and repeats and assures the people of the stoutness of the material and the excellence of the work. The crowd moves slowly, it listens critically; this kind of thing may be monotonous; the very oratory of the salesman, in order to be effective, continually requires new adjectives, new metaphors, new comparisons; among the crowd are the professors of the salesman's rhetoric. They know the tricks, they have learned the art. One wonders how many such fervid speeches this young man has to make before he effects a single sale. We need not pity him, although at

> the close of the market his voice is hoarse with bawling and the results are meagre; he enjoys the thing; it is his one day of glory, and he has admirers; he knows that among the audience there are many who envy his powers and would fain take his place and deceive the people . . .
>
> You observe that the newly arrived Polish Jew is for the most part a man of poor physique; he is a small, narrow chested, pasty faced person. 'Is this,' you ask, 'a descendent of Joshua's valiant captains? Is this the race which followed Judas Maccabaeus? Is this the race which defied the legions of Titus?' 'My friend," replies a kindly scholar of their own people,' these are the children of the Ghetto. For two thousand years they have lived in the worst parts of a crowded city, they have been denied work except of the lowest [order]; they have endured every kind of scorn and contumely. Come again in ten years' time. In the free air of Anglo-Saxon rule they will grow; you will not know them again.'

W. Besant, *East London* (London: Chatto and Windus, 1903) 199–200.

Searching for a Place 1

70) John Torlton moves from Reading to London, 1735 [M.]

Born c.1702, John Torlton worked as a bricklayer in Reading and later in London where he fell into poverty and became a thief, for which he was put on trial in 1735. Torlton's testimony was taken down during his trial.

> 2. John Torlton, about 32 or 33 Years of Age, born at *Reading,* of honest Parents, who educated him at School, and had him infructed in Principles of Religion, but being of an unfettled Temper, he did not much mind fuch Things, for neglecting all Religion and Virtue, he addicted himfelf wholly to his Pleafures and, fatiffying his luftful Appetite. When of Age they put him to a *Bricklayer,* and afterwards lived by his Bufinefs, and fet up Mafter *Bricklayer* at *Reading,* where he had very good Bufinefs, not wanting Friend to advance his intereft; and marrying a Wife, he got a very handfom Maintinance for his Wife and Family, but not loving to be confined to Bufinefs, he went too much abroad, which brought him into feveral Inconveniences, and obliged him to come to *London,* where being expert in his Trade, he was employed by one of the moft eminent *Bricklayer's* about the Town, and had good Encouragement; but taking up with loofe Women, with whom he idled away his Time, and having forfaken his own Wife, he fell into Poverty and went head-long to Deftruction.
>
> He faid he never robbed on the Highway, nor in the Streets, nor breaking open Houfes, or fuch notorious Acts, but being in great need, he took any fmall Thing that come in his Way, pilfer'd and did petty Larcinies, and loft all Credit and Character, and became utterly contemptible and infamous.

Proceedings at Sessions of Peace. City of London and County of Middlesex, 2, 1735–1740, 44.

71) Ukawsaw Gronniosaw on education and religion, 1770 [I.]

See note on extract No.38.

After I had been a little while with my new master, I grew more familiar, and asked him the meaning of prayer. (I could hardly speak English to be understood.) He took great pains with me, and made me understand that he prayed to God, who lived in heaven; that he was my Father and best Friend. I told him that this must be a mistake, that my father lived at Bournou, and that I wanted very much to see him, and likewise my dear mother and sister, and I wished he would be so good as to send me home to them; and I added all that I could think of to induce him to convey me back. I appeared in great trouble, and my good master was so affected, that the tears ran down his face. He told me that God was a great and good Spirit, that he created all the world, and every person and thing in it, in Ethiopia, Africa, and America, and everywhere. I was delighted when I heard this. 'There,' said I, 'I always thought so when I lived at home. Now if I had wings like an eagle, I would fly to tell my dear mother that God is greater than the sun, moon, and stars, and that they were made by him.' I was exceedingly pleased with this information of my master's, because it corresponded so well with my own opinion. I thought, now if I could but get home, I should be wiser than all my country-folks, my grandfather, or father, or mother, or any of them. But though I was somewhat enlightened by this information of my master's, yet I had no other knowledge of God but that he was a good Spirit, and created every body, and every thing. I never was sensible in myself, nor had any one ever told me, that he would punish the wicked and love the just. I was only glad that I had been told there was a God, because I had always thought so.

My dear kind master grew very fond of me, as was his lady. She put me to school, but I was uneasy at that, and did not like to go; but my master and mistress, in the gentlest terms, requested me to learn, and persuaded me to attend my school without any anger at all; so that at last I began to like it better, and learnt to read pretty well. My schoolmaster was a good man, and was very indulgent to me, his name was Vanosdore. I was in this state when, one Sunday, heard my master preach from these words out of the Revelation; 'Behold, he cometh in the clouds, and every eye shall see him, and they that pierced him.' These words affected me excessively. I was in great agony, because I thought my master directed them to me, only; and I fancied that he observed me with unusual earnestness. I was farther confirmed in this belief, as I looked round the church and could see no one person besides myself in such grief and distress as I was. I began to think that my master hated me, and was very desirous to go home to my own country; for I thought that if God did come, as he said, he would certainly be most angry with me, as I did not know what he was, nor had ever heard of him before.

I went home in great trouble, but said nothing to anybody. I was somewhat afraid of my master; for I thought he disliked me. The next text I heard him preach from was, 'Follow peace with all men, and holiness, without which no man shall see the Lord.' He preached the law so severely, that it

> made me tremble. He said that God would judge the whole world, Ethiopia, Asia, Africa, and everywhere. I was now excessively perplexed, and undetermined what to do, as I had now reason to believe that my situation would be equally bad, to go as to stay. I kept these thoughts to myself, and said nothing to any person whatever.

P. Edwards and D. Dabydeen (eds) *Black Writers in Britain 1760–1890* (Edinburgh: Edinburgh University Press, 1991) 12–13.

72) Daniel Mendoza and Jewish assimilation in London, 18th *c.* [I.]

See note on extract No.12.

> All foreigners in London who had an outlandish look were liable to be roughly treated, or at least abused, by the mob. The Jews were very unpopular (Moritz says more so than in Germany), Jew-baiting became a sport, like cock-throwing, or bull-baiting or pelting some poor wretch in the pillory. Place ascribes the special ill treatment of Jews to the robbery and murder in Chelsea (which drew upon them the attention of Sir John Fielding in l771) for which four Jews were hung.
>
> 'Every Jew was in public opinion implicated, and the prejudice, ill will and brutal conduct this brought upon the Jews, even after they had been detected and punished for it, did not cease for many years. "Go to Chelsea" was a common exclamation when a Jew was seen in the streets and was often the signal of assault. I have seen many Jews hooted, hunted, cuffed, pulled by the beard, spat upon, and so barbarously assaulted in the streets, without any protection from the passers-by or the police, as seems when compared with present times, almost impossible to have existed at any time. Dogs could not be used in the streets in the manner many Jews were treated. One circumstance among others put an end to the ill-usage of the Jews . . . About the year 1787 Daniel Mendoza, a Jew, became a celebrated boxer and set up a school to teach the art of boxing as a "science," the art soon spread among the young Jews and they became generally expert at it. The consequence was in a very few years seen and felt too. It was no longer safe to insult a Jew unless he was an old man and alone. . . . But even if the Jews were unable to defend themselves, the few who would [now] be disposed to insult them merely because they are Jews, would be in danger of chastisement from the passers-by and of punishment from the police.' Moreover, Jewish proficiency in the ring gained the sympathies of the mob and much of their unpopularity disappeared. Jewish pugilists introduced a new school of boxing, relying more on science and less on brute strength, whose heroes were Mendoza, Dutch Sam, and Young Dutch Sam.

M. D. George, *London Life in the XVIIIth Century* (London: Kegan Paul, Trench, Trubner, 1925) 132.

73) Betty Shaw's travels around Lancashire, 1790s [M.]

See note on extract No.3.

> . . . her mother [Benjamin Shaw's mother in law, the mother of Betty Shaw and Benjamin Shaw's wife, b 1773] died when she was about 8 years old, leaving 4 Children, & her father following the seafaring life, the children was but in to the Poor house at lancaster. She Stoped hear sometim, the 2 younges children died very young, & Thomas some time after went to Sea, Betty had an Aunt, her mothers sister in wharmer, 3 or 4 miles of, this aunt took her home to her house (her name was agness young wife of John young, shoe maker, here she lived some years, etc,
>
> * her father soon married again, and had more children, she went home again, & hear she stoped some time, but as her father was not able to maintain his family without Parish relief, Betty was put out towns, or Parish apprintice, her lot fell to be with James Scirrah, who kept a Publick house on the green air, in Lancaster (the sign of the Joiners arms &c) this man dealt in wood &c here she lived for some time, But it seems as the master had several daughters, they could spare her, for they often sent her to wrae [Wray], a small village near Hornby, 10 miles from Lancaster, to help them at Busy times, these People were soon relations to her master &c – some time after, She was agreed to go to A M^{rs} dove^{s} her husband was a sea captain, and mostly from home – they lived on the green are, a very Pleasant situation near the River Lune here she lived some time –
>
> * But disagreeing with her Mr^{s} [Mistress] she took a French lieve [absconded] and went to her fathers, who had shifted some time before to dolphinholme, in Ellel, 7 miles from Lancaster, & 6 from Garstang, east of the great road &c – this was in February 1791 She got work in the factory, and lived with her father, she was now 17 year 3 moth [*sic*] old, in the Somer this year, I came to dolphinholme
>
> * we soon became Suters &c, She continued at dolphinholme, until Octob 1792, then another young woman & her came to Preston to live, she got work at the factory in moor lain, & lived sometime in the Shambles, & then near the moss, she stoped in Preston untill July 1793 when she was sent out of the town, being with child, (for we still courted by letters, & I went over to Preston at Shrovetide, &c) She now went to Lancaster, her father was returned thither, here she lived untill she was married, which was on the 21 Sepr 1793 this was the first year of the last French war, which lasted 22 year
>
> * She now came to my Place at dolphinholme, for I had more than 10 month to serve of my time, she Bought me a Son on the 4th of november, (1793), we lived at this place untill, february 1795, she came soon after, at this time we went to Preston, and took a part of a house where we have lived ere since . . .

A. G. Dent, *The Family Records of Benjamin Shaw Mechanic of Dent, Dolphinholme and Preston, 1772–1841* (n.p: Record Society of Lancashire and Cheshire, 1991) 74–5.

74) A Moroccan street trader in London, 1811 onwards [I.]

See note on extract No.27.

From the street-seller whose portrait has already been given I received the following history. He appeared to be a very truthful and kindly-disposed old man:

'I am one native of Mogadore in Morocco. I am an Arab. I left my countree when I was sixteen or eighteen, I tink I was. My fader was like market man, make de people pay de toll – he rent de whole market, you see, from de government, and make de people pay so much for deir stands. I can't tell you what dey call dem dere. I couldn't recollect what my fader pay for de market; but I know some of de people pay him a penny, some a ha'penny, for de stands. Dere everyting sheap, not what dey are here in England. Dey may stop all day for de toll or go when de market is over. My fader was not very rish – not very poor – he keep a family. We have bread, meet, shicken, apples, all de good tings to eat, not like here – tis de sheapest countree in de world. My fader have two wives, not at once you know, he bury de first and marry anoder. I was by second wife. He have seven shildren by her, four sons and tree daughters. By de first I tink dere was five, two sons and tree daughters. Bless you, by de time I was born dere was great many of 'em married and away in de world. I don't know where dey are now. Only one broder I got live for what I know, wheder de oders are dead or where dey are I can't tell. De one broder I speak of is in Algiers now; he is dealer dere. What led me to come away, you say? Like good many I was young and foolish; like all de rest of young people, I like to see foreign countries, but widout you pay so mush, so Gibraltar was de only part I could go to, it was only one twenty miles across de water – close to us. You see you go to Gibraltar like smuggling – you smuggle yourself – you take wid de Captain and he do it for you.

'My fader been dead years and years before I come away, I suppose I was about ten years old when he die. I had been at school till time I was grown up, and after dat I was shoemaker. I make de slippers. Oh yes! my moder was alive den – she was dead when I was here in England. I get about a penny a pair for de slippers in my countree; a penny dere as good as shilling here amost. I could make tree, four, five pair in one day. I could live on my gains den better dan what I do here wid twelve as mush – dat time I could. I don't know what it is now. Yes, my moder give me. She never see me since' (sighing). 'Oh, yes, I love her very mush. I am old man now, but I never forget her yet;' here the old man burst into tears and buried his face in his hankerchief for several minutes. 'No, no! she didn't know when I come dat she never see me again, nor me neider. I tell I go to Gibraltar, and den I tell her I go to Lisbon to see my broder, who was spirit merchant dere. I didn't say noting not at all about coming back to her, but I tought I should come back soon. If I had tought I never see no more, not all de gold in de world take me from here. She was good moder to me. I was de youngest but one. My broders kept my moder, you see. Where I came from it is not like here, if you one of de family well off, de oders never want for noting. In my country, you see, de law is you must maintain your fader and moder before you maintain your own family. You must keep dem in de house.' Here he repeated the law in Hebrew . . .

'Well, you see I leave my poor moder, we kissed one anoder, and cry for half an hour, and come away to Gibraltar. When I got dere, my broder come away from Lisbon to Gibraltar; dat time it was war time, and de French was coming to Lisbon, so everybody run. When I came away from Mogodore, I have about one hundred dollars – some my moder give me, and some I have save. When I got to Gibraltar, I begin to have a little stand in de street wid silk handkerchiefs, cotton handkerchiefs, shop goods you know. I do very well wid dat, so after I get licence to hawk de town, and after dat I keep shop. Altogeder, I stop in Gibraltar about six year. I had den about five or six hundred dollars. I live very well all de time dere. I was wid my broder all de time. After I am six years in Gibraltar, I begin to tink I do better in England. I tink, like good many people, If I go to anoder part dat is risher – 't is de rishest countree in de world – I do better still. So I start off, and I get here I tink in 1811, when de tree shilling pieces first came out. I try to look what I could do, but I was quite stranger you see. I am about fourteen or fifteen month before I begin to do anything. I go to de play house; I see never such tings as I see here before I come. When I come here, I tink I am in heaven altogether – God a'mighty forgive me – such sops (shops) and such beautiful things. I live in Mary Axe Parish when I first come; same parish where I live now. Well, you see some of my countreemen den getting good living by selling de rhubarb and spices in de street. I get to know dem all; and dat time you see was de good time, money was plenty, like de dirt here. Dat time dere was about six or seven Arabians in de streets selling rhubarb and spices, five of 'em was from Mogadore, and two from not far off; and dere is about five more going troo de country. Dey all sell de same tings – after dat dey get de silks and tings beside. I can't tell what first make dem sell de rhubarb and spices; but I tink it is because people like to buy de Turkey rhubarb of de men in de turbans. When I was a shild, I hear talk in Mogadore of de people of my country sell de rhubarb in de streets of London, and make plenty money by it . . .

'When I first come to dis countree me make plenty of money by selling de rhubarb in de street. Five-and-twenty years ago I make a pound a day some time. Take one week wid another, I dare say I clear, after all de cost of living, tirty shillings; and now, God help me, I don't make not twelve shilling a seek, and all my food to pay out of dat. One week wid anoder, when I go out I clear about twelve shilling. Everything is so sheep now, and dere is so many sops (shops), people has no money to buy tings with. I could do better when everyting was dear. I could live better, get more money, and have more of it. I have better food, better lodging, and better clothes. I don't know wat is de cause, as you say I only know dat I am worse, and everybody is worse; dat is all I know. Bread is sheeper, but when it was one and nine-pence de loaf I could get plenty to buy wid it but now it is five pence, I ain't no five pence to have it. If de cow is de penny in de market what is de use of dat, if you can't get no penny to buy him?'

H. Mayhew, *London Labour and the London Poor,* vol. 1 (London: G. Woodfall, 1851) 452–4.

75) Thomas Wood travels from Bingley to Oldham, 1840s [M.]

Born in Bingley (Yorkshire) in 1822, Thomas Wood was apprenticed to a power-loom manufacturer in 1836. After his apprenticeship he was unable to find local employment and went 'on the tramp' into Lancashire. He eventually found work at Platts Brothers, Oldham, where he worked until 1846. Thomas Wood died in 1880. The Autobiography of Thomas Wood, 1822–1880 *was written in 1878, over the period of a fortnight when the author was staying at the Ilkley Convalescent Home, but only published (privately) in 1956.*

Men were out of work or working short time. The roads swarmed with beggars. Families of six or eight persons were on the road together and esteemed themselves fortunate if they could obtain a shelter of an outhouse or a hayride. I saw there was not work at the shop for the hands there were. I expected no favour such as staying and someone else leaving, so I was not surprised to receive my dismissal about two months after. I had only about 14s. per week as my first wage as journeyman, so the loss was small. The weekly wage was as good as 20s. Perhaps I was not a good man, perhaps they wanted me to leave and not accept it. This is just what I would have done had it been possible without starvation for self and curtailing the comforts of mother.

I gave up my wage till I left home except some very small sums for needful purposes. I left home in search of work in the beginning of March and returned at the beginning of April. Having walked through Lancashire in search of work, I saw hundreds out of work and was regarded as an enthusiast in some places for searching work when so many were out who were known to the masters.

I was accompanied by Edward Jackson, of Crossflats, a fellow apprentice whose parents were rather better off and who all along had rather looked down on me. He was older, stronger and wealthier than me, but I derived no benefit from him in any form. He would frequently walk half a mile ahead of me.

When we approached a shop he would be the first to ask for work. The last day, in returning home, we walked over fourty miles in the wet. I resolved never to tramp again with him or one like him. He got married soon after our return, and soon after that died. If I remember aright, it was hinted that he had over-exerted himself when on the road with me . . .

I had been home about a week, when, meeting my old master, he asked me to go and do a piece of work that would take about a week's time. My very nature was glad and grateful for so small a mercy. I went the following morning. This was in April, 1843. Other work came in. I stopped about two years, then left of my own accord. My wages were advanced in the early part of the time, first 1 s. a week, then 2s and after another 2s. until I had 20s. per week. When I gave notice to leave I was asked if it was a wages question. I replied, 'No', but the desire for improvement.

This was just the truth; I thought I was deficient in my trade, though I learned, and long practiced, all I could learn there. But I heard about new tools, new machines, and new ways of working, I could never hope to see them in our shop, and if I was to learn, to improve, I could do so now before I was either married or thought of it.

So one Friday in the summer of 1845 I left my old master for good and ever, and having arranged my little affairs, left home on the Monday following, for Lancashire. I walked to Hebden Bridge and took a train for Rochdale, my first railway ride. We were put into a truck worse and more exposed than cattle trucks now are. There were seats, or forms, to sit on, but they were swimming with rain. Not a bit of shelter from the driving rail, or sparks from the engine chimney, which were very painful, and had a peculiar knack of falling down the back of the neck.

Sleeping at Rochdale I walked to Oldham, got work, started at dinner-time, and worked a half-day in the Tuesday after leaving home. After securing lodgings at night, I wrote home in a very hopeful strain. My wages at first were 28s. per week, increased afterwards at time and time to 32s. My parents shared my good future, particularly my sick mother. My only regret is that more was not given, and, above all, that it was not given more cheerfully.

J. Burnett, *Useful Toil* (Harmondsworth: Penguin, 1974) 309–10.

76) A Scottish sailor compares Britain and America, 1850 [M.]

See note on extract No.10.

A short man, but evidently of very great strength, brawny and muscular, and with a very good frank expression of countenance, gave me the following account as to the treatment on board the American ships:

'I am a Scotchman born, but am now in the American service, and on board a transit (merchant) ship trading from New York; not a liner, which runs only to one place. I have been in the English service, and was brought up in it. I have served on board one of your English ships that was not fit to go to sea, when she started for Callao. Off the Horn she leaked 350 strokes at the pump an hour. We couldn't sleep in the forecastle for the wet. Some of my shipmates were half dead before we got to Callao. We were always in danger in her, and there's no back way out at sea. The captain and his usage of us was very bad, striking men at the wheel; he once gave her up and cried like a child. She was above 800 tons. The English Consul at Callao wouldn't interfere, and told us, when we complained to him of the state of the ship, that he would do nothing for us, and, for anything he cared, we might all die in the streets. The captain had to ship three crews between Callao, the Clinches – that's the guano mountain – and the port of London. The old crew, all but two or three, were left at Callao. Well, sir, when this ship was at last go to the West India Dock she was patched up, and was then thought good enough for an emigrant ship, and was sent out to Australia with emigrants. I have been, off and on, in the American service these last 5 years. It's a far better service than the English – better wages, better meat, and better ships. No half-pounds of meat short there; eat when you're hungry, and the best of grub. What goes into an English ship's cabin goes into an American ship's forecastle. The Americans are fast getting the pick of the English navy. I have now 15 dollars a month, or £3 2s. 6d. No trouble about bonded stores or such like. You take your tobacco with you from any American port, where it costs 3d. or 4d. a pound; and tea, and coffee, and sugar, and rum are found you. The very best tobacco is 20 cents, that's l0d., in America; but that's for chewing. The six cents tobacco, or 3d. a pound, is as good as you pay 3d. an ounce for here; so there's a pound for an ounce, you see. There's a lot of the American tobacco smoked in England; plenty of it puffed away at 3d. a pound all round the Custom-house. For the same sort of service in an English merchant ship I might get £2, or £2 5s., and starving all the time, unless I chance on a good employer, but they are scarce. The sleeping berths are far better in the forecastles of the American than the English ships – more room, and better fitted up. Why, of course, the English seamen flock into the American service as fast as they can, petty officers and all. I see a lot of foreign seamen in London now. I suppose a 'Dutchman' – that's what any foreign lubberly fellow is now called – is shipped for every English seaman driven out of your fine ports. These Dutchmen will put up with anything whatsoever – kicks and hits, and all. As for want of grub, they'll starve before they'll ask for it, and the English captains know that well, and so prefer those fellows; and the English seaman may go to America, or where he will, for what they care. In every respect, both about registry and everything else, the American service is better than the English. The English service is fast coming to be only fit for Dutchmen – that's about it, sir, you may depend. There's very little else but English seamen in the American ships. Our crew is nineteen, and only four are American born; fourteen are British subjects. If a war broke out – I could answer for myself and for hundreds besides – I wouldn't fight for England against America, but for America against England. I'll not fight for a country that starves and cheats you. I'll never fight for short weights and stinting in everything, not I. I left an English ship at Quebec, which is the greatest place in British America for sailors deserting. The living is so bad that men won't put up with it. They can easily hide in Quebec, and so go overland into the States. Nothing will check desertion in the English service but better wages, better treatment, and better food. The discipline is much the same on board the American as on board the English ships. An English seaman is very little thought of in his own country, but he's well thought of in America. He's a man there.'

H. Mayhew, *The Morning Chronicle Survey of Labour and the Poor: The Metropolitan Districts vol. 4* (London: Caliban, 1981) 14–16.

77) A young Irish woman in London, 1851 [M.]

See note on extract No.10.

A young woman, of whose age it was not easy to form a conjecture, her features were so embrowed by exposure to the weather, and perhaps when I saw her a little swollen from cold, gave me the following account as to her living. Her tone and manner betrayed indifference to the future, caused perhaps by ignorance, – for uneducated persons I find are apt to look on the future as if it must needs be but a repetition of the present, while the past in many instances is little more than a blank to them. This young woman said, her brogue being little perceptible, though she spoke thickly:

'I live by keepin' this fruit stall. It's a poor livin' when I see how others live. Yes, the thruth, sir, but it's thankful I am for to be able to live at all; troth it is, in these sore times. My father and mother are both did. God be gracious to their sowls! They was evicted. The family of us was. The thatch of the bit o' home was tuk off our hids, and we were lift to the wide worruld – yis, indeed, sir, and in the open air too. The rint wasn't paid and it couldn't be paid, and so we had to face the wither. It was a sorrowful time. But God was good, and so was the neighbours. And when we saw the praste, he was a frind to us. And we came to this counthry, though I'd always heard it called a black counthry. Sure, an' there's much in it to indhure. There's goin's on it, sir, that the praste, God rewarrud him! wouldn't like to see. There's bad ways. I won't talk about thim, and I'm sure you are too much of a gintlemin sure. It was the eviction that brought us here. I don't know about where wa was just; not in what county; nor parish. I was so young whin we lift the land. I belave I'm now 19, perhaps only 18' (she certainly looked much older, but I have often noticed that of her class). 'I can't be more, I think, for sure an' its only 5 or 6 years since we left Watterford and come to Bristol. I'm sure it was Watterford, and a beautiful place it is, and I know it was Bristol we come to. We walked all the long way to London. My parints died of the cholera, and I live with mysilf, but my aunt lodges me and sees to me. She sills in the sthreets too. I don't make *7d* a day. I may make *6d*. There's a good many young payple I know is now sillin' in the streets becase they was evicted in their own counthry. I suppose they had no where ilse to come to. I'm nivir out of a night. I sleep with my aunt, and we keep to ourselves sure. I very seldom taste mate, but perhaps I do oftener than before we was evicted – glory be to God.'

H. Mayhew, *London Labour and the London Poor,* vol. 1 (London: G. Woodfall, 1851) 115–16.

78) A Lascar found dead in London, 1873 [I.]

See note on extract No.52.

'Found dead!' Who? Where? Has he no friends? How did he die? To these very natural questions, prompted by the common generosity of the English heart, we reply 'We don't know.' But, gazing in the haggard face of the deported stranger, we conclude he has died in a land in which he was a foreigner; for his tattered clothes and swarthy features suggest that his birthplace cannot be far from the banks of the Ganges. The Coroner and his jury, however, have just come to an unsatisfactory verdict, 'Found dead;' after having put off the inquest to the present day, hoping to gain some information of the deceased; but all that is known is, a policeman found him, on a frosty winter night, dead on the pavement in one of the many avenues in High-street, Shadwell. This child of the sunny land must have been dead some time, for he was quite cold. Nothing was found upon him to tell who he was, or what were the hard circumstances of his death. There was a knife at his side, and his horny hands bore evidence of honest labour and hard toil. He must be one of may Lascars who are engaged in bringing the produce of Hindustan to our isle. Poor fellow, he could have found neither help nor sympathy in this land of gold and philanthropy! Strange, indeed, in the midst of so many merchant princes made rich with Indian gold, that the stranger who brought us the precious things of the torrid zone, should die uncared for on a winter night in one of our London streets. But, perhaps, it was a solitary case, and has never occurred before, and may never occur again, What did the coroner say? Alas! He says that no less than eight human beings of the same class have perished with cold and hunger in our streets during the present winter, and he has held nearly forty inquests on the same class of miserable beings during the last few years! Nearly forty sons of India have perished in our London streets with cold and hunger within a limited time, and no good Samaritan to pour in the oil and the wine, to sooth their dying moments with the good news of the sinner's Friend, and point the dying one to the better lands, where

'Sickness and sorrow, pain and death,
Are felt and fear'd no more.'

And this is all the Christian public know of the numerous class of our fellow-creatures who are living in our very midst, and constantly arriving on our coast with the produce of their own land. Tens of thousands of pounds are annually and rightly spent to ameliorate the temporal and spiritual condition of the heathen in their own distant land, but here in the Christian's home, they only attract our notice when our coroner places the verdict of the jury on the record: 'Found dead,' or 'Died of cold and starvation.'

J. Salter, *The Asiatic in England: Sketches of Sixteen Years' Work Among Orientals* (London: Seeley, Jackson and Halliday, 1873) 19–21.

79) A Chinese juggler in London, 1873 [I.]

See note on extract No.52.

Here is a sketch of the history of a Chinese juggler drawn up by a Missionary:

Awa is a native of Macao. He arrived in England in January, 1851, as cook of a vessel. I first discovered him in Blue-gate Fields. On arriving in London he engaged himself at a tea-shop in Whitechapel, where he remained nine months. He was afterwards engaged in other tea-shops at Westminster, Woolwich, and Marlebone. While in the last situation the famous Chinese junk was sold, and taken to Liverpool, and he was solicited to proceed there with it. He went with the junk, and remained in it a year. He passed the following year at a tea-shop in Coventry. At the close of this year he was invited to Paris, where he remained two years at a tea-firm, but came back to England minus a gold watch, which his employer had continued to detain. We find him, after this, again engaged by his old master at Coventry for a short time. From this period he appears to have entered on a new project with two of his countrymen. Most of the public have been attracted by large bills about the streets, on which are figured two Chinese represented in front. One of these two is Awa. He was in the receipt of £2 weekly for this performance. It was at this time I became familiar with him, for he was then residing at Blue-gate Fields. His performance, however, did not pay at last, and the proprietor became indebted to Awa for £10, which he never obtained, and, as the sum continued to increase, Awa declined to perform any more. Since that time he had entered tea-shops at Bermondsey and Woolwich, but is now residing down a miserable court in the back-road, doing nothing. He declares the last winter to have been a winter of privation such as he had never passed through before. The recommendations and characters he has from various places where he has resided, are very good and very interesting.

J. Salter, *The Asiatic in England: Sketches of Sixteen Years' Work Among Orientals* (London: Seeley, Jackson and Halliday, 1873) 214–5.

80) The Revd Simeon Singer on social assimilation, Glasgow, 1892 [I.]

A speech, reported in the Jewish Chronicle *(9 September 1892), on the consecration of a new synagogue.*

> . . . learn as rapidly as possible, and always and everywhere to encourage the use of the language of the country in which you are settled. That is absolutely necessary if you are not to be strangers in a strange land. I can conceive no good whatever by keeping up in Scotland for an hour longer than you can help the use of Yiddish. For a few weeks or months it may be of service; after that is no longer necessary. We who have been cautioned against every 'mixture of diverse kinds', against *shaatnes* [forbidden mixture of wool and cotton] ought to avoid it in our speech too. German is good and Hebrew is good as a mixture of both, especially of bad German and bad Hebrew is not good. The wisest thing is to exchange your language for (your neighbours).

K. E. Collins, *Second City Jewry: the Jews of Glasgow in the Age of Expansion, 1790–1919* (Glasgow: Scottish Jewish Archive, 1990) 80.

Part II
Migrant Life Stories in the 20th Century

Introduction to Part II: Migrant Life Stories in the 20th Century

Izabela Curyłło-Klag

Throughout Britain's twentieth century urbanization and industrial development altered perceptions of the self within society: work patterns and routines changed concepts of time and social interaction; mass communications added national and international information to the first-hand knowledge of daily experience; mass education transformed the thought processes and self-expression of large portions of the population. Increasing ease and speed of mobility allowed a continual ebb and flow of migration and immigration.[1] These mass population movements shaped the character of regions and neighbourhoods across the United Kingdom to the same extent as geography, tradition and historical changes such as deindustrialization.[2] More significantly, the experience of displaced persons, economic migrants, refugees and asylum seekers as they crossed boundaries, learned to live in new languages and negotiated new cultures came to symbolize the experience of the twentieth century.[3]

In the earliest years of the century, for instance, the largest population movement was by the hundreds of thousands of eastern Europeans, many of them Jews, who had left their homelands to travel west, and while the majority were travelling across the Atlantic, tens of thousands stayed on in Britain.[4] At the same time cheap, foreign labour as well as the living conditions of foreigners and native poor alike, caused displays of concern and bigotry – new arrivals threatened the employment prospects of the local population. Restriction or encouragement of entry to Britain, according to the prevailing political mood, became possible with the first Aliens Act (1905).[5] Successive legislation included the Aliens Restriction Act and the British Nationality and Status of Aliens Act (both 1914), the Trading with the Enemy Acts (1914–18), and the Aliens Act (1919). Passed as a result of the anxieties of war, these laws allowed the confiscation of 'alien', and particularly German, businesses, the registration of foreigners with the police and the increase of the Home Secretary's powers to introduce further restrictive measures. In 1920 an additional order was passed to prevent the employment of foreigners without a work permit and to forbid entry to anyone who could not demonstrate financial self-sufficiency. The selective admission or reduction of new arrivals, for example in times of war or economic growth, continued throughout the century: employment schemes in the colonies and commonwealth boosted the workforce during labour shortage; restrictions were phased in as recession arrived. Political unrest and war constituted exceptions to the rule; for example, during the Spanish Civil War or Nazi rule in Germany significant numbers of refugees were allowed into the country on humanitarian grounds.[6]

Despite the restrictions it took little more than one generation for many pre-Great War Jewish immigrants and their children to rise into affluent respectability and move from the inner city districts of London, Manchester and Glasgow to the outer suburbs. This was only one pattern of internal migration during the rapid social, technological and political changes which affected Britain during the first part of the twentieth century.[7] Disruption and increased movement, for example, came with the mass mobilization of the Great War generation: army work for men, factory work for women, the necessity to move because of bomb damage, the search for employment following the postwar boom. All of these forced mobility, which in turn diminished parochialism and loosened attitudes towards migration. During World War Two the same conditions recurred. Dramatic as these patterns of long-distance internal migration may appear, they were mainly temporary and often the only instance of such movement within a lifetime.[8]

After 1945 it is decolonization which most noticeably affects the movement of immigrants into Britain, while internal mobility, which shaped the lives of overseas settlers and the native population alike, is influenced by less spectacular factors. These include: adjustments in employment practices and the job markets, which made greater mobility necessary for continued career development; changes in home ownership and the housing markets, where owner-occupancy came to prevail in later life. Thus mean short distance moves for housing reasons – usually a matter of a few miles – remain stable until 1919, but then double through the twentieth century.[9] Similar short distance movements were caused by the family crisis of old age, troubled health or the death of a close relative.[10] A curious throwback to the nineteenth century occurred in the last two decades of the twentieth century, when several thousand disenfranchised and disaffected youths came to be called 'travellers'. Successors to the counter-cultural movements of the 'baby boom' generation, they were vilified in the press and outlawed by the state. The Public Order Act (1986) and the Criminal Justice Act (1994) responded in a manner worthy of nineteenth century reactions to the tramping labourer, the tinker or the gypsy. Whereas the 'travellers' serve as a reminder of the long tradition of romance and fear associated with tramping, it is worth remembering that many social and cultural aspects of internal migration remained constant through the century.[11]

For immigrants the virtues of British civilization, advertised generously through the colonial education system, were, at least before arrival, not in doubt. This idealized image of the mother country, together with an economic slump, for example in the Caribbean, and the post-1945 labour shortage and consumer boom of the 1950s, were more than enough to draw economic migrants from underdeveloped and decolonizing regions. A composite, relatively inclusive definition of citizenship was now required, and received legal sanction with the Nationality Act (1948). It was not until the 1960s that a new spate of restrictive law making began. The law that aroused greatest controversy and – paradoxically – encouraged immigration from the former colonies in the West Indies, was the Commonwealth Immigrants Act (1962). It restricted entry by a voucher system which guaranteed the right of employment in Britain. In the months before the Act came into force, West Indians arrived in increasing numbers, mostly with the intention of temporary settlement; many subsequently remained for fear of harsher restrictions.[12] The 1962 Act was followed by the Commonwealth Immigrants Act (1968), the Immigration Act (1971) and the British Nationality Act (1981), all of which gradually narrowed down the definition of British citizenship and eventually granted the right of free entry only to passport holders who had close (parental or grandparental) ties to Britain. By this time, though, the question was not how many more immigrants should be allowed into Britain, but how their presence had reconstituted British society.

Overview of Part II

Transition 2 documents some of the motives which led to settlement in the British Isles, the expectations before arrival, and reactions afterwards. Though twentieth century migrants often had a more extensive knowledge of the country than their eighteenth and nineteenth century predecessors, preconceived ideas did not necessarily alleviate the initial trauma of arrival. The first confrontation with a new locality, a new culture, often shattered illusions, whether they were casually put together with the help of migrant compatriots (88, 91) or systematically developed over the years: E. Ferron (85) and P. Mohanti (90), for example, both comment on the burden of misconceptions inherited by Empire and Commonwealth subjects through their colonial education. Motivation appears to have played an important role in shaping expectation, and many accounts in this section show a relatively matter-of-fact approach to movement, especially among economic migrants. Mrs Coll, for instance, who travelled from Ireland to Scotland each summer around harvest time (81); A. Ram, who left his family in India and went to Britain to earn 'better money' as a street vendor (82); and D. Mac Amhlaigh, who arrived in John Bull's Island during a labour shortage in the 1950s (87) – all describe migration as an economic necessity, and are prepared to treat cultural adjustment pragmatically. Other accounts, including memoirs of those who found themselves trapped in various political turmoil, show that unexpected and unwanted displacement could be far more traumatic: a Basque child brought to a refugee camp at the time of Franco's rule (83); a World War Two veteran reluctant to return to communist Poland (84); or a Ukrainian making a desperate choice between exile and the Soviet regime (86).

Settlement and Work 2 concentrates on efforts to ensure survival in a foreign environment. Finding accommodation and employment is the first step towards stability and therefore the migrant's primary concern. One theme here is the necessity to revise expectations of work and housing opportunities: a Polish geography teacher is employed as a laboratory cleaner (96), an Indian architect is given lavatories to design (97), a black school-leaver works in a laundry (103). While in the previous two centuries the low social status of the mass migrant was often taken as inevitable, particularly after World War Two the expectation of acceptance increased. Individuals show varied degrees of adaptability and willingness to conform; some, like the Asian migrant in Bradford (98), are more vulnerable to unfair treatment and exploitation at workplace, others, like J. Hinsman (103), are ready to tolerate even a dissatisfying job if it offers a chance to earn a living. Those with more confidence tend to engage in intercultural negotiation, for example Satya and her family, who bargain about the price of the house they want to buy (102) or E. Ferron, who convinces an unfriendly landlady that she has no right to refuse him a room (97).

Childhood and Home Life 2 describes attempts to sustain family customs and personal convictions, as well as to cope with behaviours filtering in from the foreign environment and the disruption of traditional values. Stories of family reunions, like those of A. Ram (109) or P. George (110), contrast sharply with memoirs of Jewish refugee children separated from their parents and placed in foster homes across Britain as a result of the 'Kindertransport' campaign before the outbreak of World War Two. The story told by Satya, the wife of an Indian immigrant, brings to light the responsibilities towards elderly relatives that many children were incapable of fulfilling, as well as the feelings of remorse towards family members left behind in the home country. Likewise accounts of second generation immigrants reveal the tensions between parents and children resulting from the conflict of cultural influences at home and outside the family circle (112, 118); at the same time they register instances of mutual support that family members are ready to offer to one another (115). Warren Oster's description of the psychological effect of poor housing underlines, finally, how distress and exclusion could intrude into the most intimate aspects of home environment.

Community 2 examines migrant lives within a broader social context, and from the perspective of both specific minority groups and native

Britons. Accounts in this category describe the means by which ethnic and cultural unity were generated and maintained through religion (119, 122, 128), political activity (126), ritual celebration (129), and participation in varied social gatherings and entertainments (124, 125). The mirror image of these efforts to unite communities is to be found in the ethnic tension between different minority groups or between migrant communities (131) and members of the indigenous population. Only a few such instances are recalled here: N. M. C. Sinclair gives a proud description of the Tiger Bay riots of 1919 from the perspective of one who grew up later in the same district (120); R. Glass reports on how the violence in Notting Hill in 1959 disturbed many within British society and marked the beginning of a more assertive attitude among the immigrant community (127).

Another Culture 2 explores the confrontation with 'otherness', both on the part of the new arrival and the receiving community. Among the extracts which illustrate the migrant's perception of Britishness there are the reminiscences of a Ukrainian learning British customs (135), the letter of a Polish domestic servant outraged with the 'pagan' lifestyle of her employers (136), or P. Mohanti's narrative describing his first Christmas spent with the family of his London friend (140). H. Thorogood's portrayal of London's Chinatown in the 1930s is one instance of immigrant community seen through the jaundiced eyes of a local 'explorer' (134), while a police report on the anti-Jewish riots in Leeds in 1917 provides an insight into the official methods of preventing the outbreaks of intercultural violence (133). Other accounts included in this section deal with the relations between different migrant groups (142, 138) and the importance of language and religion in asserting identity (132, 138, 141). Many of these accounts are characterized by a tendency towards self-reflexivity, which perhaps provides the psychological mechanism to cope with an internal sense of 'difference' and the confrontation with an often hostile society. The memoirs of the Welsh migrant in Liverpool (132), J. Madaylus's reflections on double identity (143), C. Hope's reminiscences about his encounters with the British (145) or Mrs Stanowska's comments on self and memory (146) are all attempts to look within in order to examine and internalise the complex-ities of cross-cultural identity.

Searching for a Place 2 is concerned with social and psychological aspects of the process of adjustment to a foreign environment. While there are some stories of successful assimilation into British society, like those of naturalized European refugees (148), there are failures too: East End Jews before World War Two (147) or the despairing Latvians in 1970s Bedford (154). Many extracts included here present the search for identity as a constant shuttle between different cultural traditions (157, 158, 159). Frequently, the initial attempts to suppress difference give way to a gradually developing feeling of pride in one's ethnicity (150, 151). This attitude is particularly manifest in the second part of the twentieth century, when social fragmentation intensifies and multiculturalism becomes more acceptable. Even the second and third generation immigrants turn back to the culture of their origin, and rediscover the values their parents may have tried to discard: S. Bedford gains reassurance and comfort from the search for her African roots (151); Elaine, a black teenager, protests against being referred to as an 'Afro-Caribbean' (156). Unlike their eighteenth or nineteenth century predecessors, those of the twentieth century attempted to both integrate and achieve recognition of their native background. Ethnic shame itself becomes shameful; as the account of Muhammad Ali indicates (157), those who cast off their past can never become assimilated because they lose the sources of their self-identity, at the same time they fail to gain the respect of the local community.

Case study 2: self-definition through language

In his study of autobiographical writing and self-expression, *How Our Lives Become Stories: Making Selves*, the literary critic P. J. Eakin explores the relational aspect of identity. Drawing on the work of various theoreticians of personality development, such as Jessica Benjamin, Ian Burkitt or Rom Harré, Eakin shows how the assertion of our autonomy depends on other people's recognition of it, and how our selfhood is defined through our communication with others.[13] If the individual's primary means of interaction with a social group is language, the question arises as to what manifestation of autonomy and identity is available to the migrant, whose ability to relate in a foreign tongue (English) or to follow the subtleties of regional usage and idiom, is often limited, and whose different cultural background increases the risk of failed or confused communication. To give one example: in a country that is intensely aware of the social implications of accent, register and complexity in spoken language, and that sees the spoken word as an indicator of cultural as well as national allegiances, outsiders are immediately at a disadvantage as they attempt to make status claims and negotiate their status. The extracts in Part II provide many such instances of the important position which language occupies within the experience of all migrants.

Adapting to a new culture or region necessitates communication: the ability to make oneself understood increases the chances of finding accommodation and employment, of avoiding exploitation and defending ones rights, of making a comfortable home and a profitable settlement into the local community. Lack of linguistic competence leads to a sense of isolation and inferiority, as in the case of Maria, the domestic servant who suspects her employer's children of calling her bad names (136), or the Ukrainian refugee, who, having learnt some basic expressions in English, starts making greetings to strangers in the street and is depressed when he receives no response (135). The consequences of inarticulacy are social and economic as well as psychological. Thus the speakers in Part II are well aware of the connection between command of English and higher social status. 'Those who cannot speak English have to work as cooks or dish-washers', comments Tang, a Chinese cook who himself has to rely on his interviewer to report his story (100). Language sets the limit to Tang's employment possibilities: without it there is no hope of a better-paid job.

While inadequate language renders many inarticulate and consequently invisible, those twentieth-century migrants who record their stories are more able to do so without the mediation of a second party. The popularity of English as the world's lingua franca, and – in the case of Commonwealth subjects – the influence of colonial education, have increased the possibilities of self-expression, yet fluency without exposure to attendant mores and values is no guarantee of effective communication. Thus a South African migrant, C. Hope (145), comments upon the ways in which language defines cultural membership: 'The only thing one had in common with the natives here was the English language. That was the only connection . . . So we seemed like them, but the moment you opened your mouth, and the way you reacted to what you found around you, distinguished you immediately . . . To me their foreignness was so profound and disturbing, and was made all the worse by the fact that I spoke the language.' A similar reflection can be found in the account of Cindy Blake (159), who claims that the experience of migration is universal in that the migrant is always deprived of the grid of references shared by the host community.

The speakers in Part II show a heightened awareness of the subtleties of linguistic usage: the choice of appropriate style and register, for example, is the preoccupation of P. Mohanti when he asks a British friend to proofread his application letter (101). Similarly there is a sense of the connection between linguistic and cultural influences, as when a Welsh woman, who as a child was expected to learn her mother tongue despite living in an English-speaking community, describes the associations between the Welsh language, childhood and immaturity (132): 'I think I was rather like someone, you know, whose got a wooden leg – you can't imagine life any differently . . . I don't think it's good for one's character, for one's maturing, I think it puts off many, many years because you learn to be one thing here and another thing there.'

The process of creating an 'objective', external account of experience by writing or talking is not unique to the twentieth century, but it is expressed anew in the trend towards writing personal histories. In order to resolve the cognitive duality created by the experience of moving between regions and countries migrants indulge in introspective analysis, make an attempt to express the uniqueness of their predicament, and thereby define themselves. This is related to a wider phenomenon – the turn towards written or recorded storytelling – evident in the increasing length and complexity of published accounts. One of the most touching, perhaps because of its very simple language (translated by her interviewer), comes from Mrs Stanowska, a Polish woman forced into exile by the events of World War Two (146): 'I often think about the person I might have been . . . Is that young girl me? Is she me? People don't understand that for us it was not a long time ago and it still makes us cry. We mourn for ourselves and for those who loved us and were part of ourselves.'

The drive to tell one's story helps to reduce the sense of alienation, affecting many migrants so acutely. As Carolyn Steedman observes in her essay on 'State-Sponsored Autobiography', constructing personal narratives helps cultivate individuality and develop 'recuperative selfhood'. Steedman notes how introducing autobiographical writing in British state schools after World War Two enhanced the capacity for self-expression in 'the supposedly inarticulate, the dispossessed and the deprived'.[14] The benefits of such education become visible in many Part II accounts, especially those of the second and third generation immigrants who stress the positive aspects of having double cultural identity. Instances of reassurance and comfort gained from the search for one's roots can be found in the accounts of J. Madaylus, who takes pride in his Ukrainian origin (143), S. Bedford, who rediscovers Africa (151) or Y. Alibhai, who wishes to retain Asian values in a western world which she perceives as 'cold' (158).

Some migrants clearly believe that telling stories of the self, making 'otherness' familiar and educating the host society about foreign customs and traditions, should help their audiences to at least acknowledge and at best embrace cultural diversity. Storytelling thus becomes a way to demonstrate one's cultural and national loyalties and to struggle for their recognition. One such story included here comes from a Jewish refugee, Inge, who was brought to Britain before the outbreak of World War Two and adopted by a British family, while her natural parents remained in occupied Austria (107). Written in German, Inge's diary records a complex process of reconciling present with past. The reader may be surprised with the multiple layers of identity to be discovered in a child of twelve: Inge feels Viennese at heart, is homesick for Austria, but she is also deeply aware of her Jewish origin. Like many adult immigrants whose memoirs feature in *The British Migrant Experience,* Inge becomes conscious of her cultural heritage only after she has found herself in a foreign environment. She begins to appreciate her mother tongue and refuses to learn English, despite threats of punishment. In the light of Claire Kramsch's theory presented in *Language and Culture,* Inge's reluctance to speak English can be linked to her rejection of the culture represented by her foster parents. According to Kramsch, problems with mastering a foreign language may in some cases be a manifestation 'not so much of bilingual failure as of monolingual pride'.[15] The girl's insistence on speaking German can be treated as an act of self-defence against that which she perceives as an attempted violation of her identity.

Native language acquires a symbolic value also for other speakers in Part II. Like Inge, the Irishman D. Mac Amhlaigh writes in his mother tongue. One of the fragments from his diary included here describes a situation when Mac Amhlaigh and his young compatriot Nick indulge in a mock-Irish conversation in order to impress their Polish and Ukrainian workmates (138). In the case of Catholic Irish migrants, fluency in English, although obviously an asset that facilitates assimilation, becomes a painful reminder of cultural tradition thwarted by British dominance. 'Members of a group who feel that their political and cultural identity is threatened are likely to attach particular importance to the maintenance or resurrection of "their language",' explains Kramsch.[16] There are indications too that a complete adoption of the language of the host community can be seen as betrayal of national loyalties: Muhammad Ali admits that his Asian schoolmates who spoke perfect English were distrusted both by the members of the same ethnic group and by the British (157). Some, for example J. Hinsman (103), purposefully violate rules of English or switch to their native tongue in order to emphasize their cultural otherness. Language is such a strong indicator of cultural belonging that even the second-generation immigrants, who frequently do not know their parents' mother tongue, may be extremely sensitive to any attempts to deny, undermine or ridicule their linguistic identity – a case in point is the Punjabi boy at school in Bradford, ready to fight his schoolmate who tries to mock the Asian accent (113).

Trapped in the interplay of conflicting cultural and national allegiances, migrants engage in a difficult dialogue with the receiving community, where the success in communication depends not only on both parties' willingness to participate, but also – or perhaps most of all – on their ability to accept and respect their partner in the exchange. Migration is an enforced lesson in sensitivity: transplanted to an alien environment, newcomers rely on their perceptiveness in order to define their position and understand the reactions of others. Constantly confronted with strangeness, and being strangers themselves, migrants undergo a transformation which has been thus summarized by one of Britain's most famous twentieth-century migrants, Salman Rushdie:

> The effect of mass migration has been the creation of radically new types of human being: people who root themselves in ideas rather than places, in memories as much as in material things; people who have been obliged to define themselves – because they are so defined by others – by their otherness; people in whose deepest selves strange fusions occur, unprecedented unions between what they were and where they find themselves. The migrant suspects reality: having experienced several ways of being, he understands their illusory nature. To see things plainly, you have to cross a frontier.[17]

Notes

1. Attempts to produce a synthetic, comprehensive social and cultural history of twentieth century internal and international immigration are relatively few; connections between the two are rarely discussed. The standard works are C. Pooley and J. Turnbull, *Migration and Mobility in Britain Since the 18th Century* (London: UCL, 1998) and C. Holmes, *John Bull's Island: Immigration and British Society, 1871–1971* (London: Macmillan – now Palgrave Macmillan, 1988).
2. See for example D. Matless, *Landscape and Englishness* (London: Reaktion, 1998), and B. Trinder, *The Making of the Industrial Landscape* (London: Phoenix, 1997).
3. See, for instance, C. Taylor, *Sources of the Self: the Making of the Modern Identity* (Cambridge: Cambridge University Press, 1989) 393–493, or P. Conrad, *Modern Times, Modern Places: Life and Art in the 20th Century* (London: Thames and Hudson, 1998).
4. For one local study see J. Buckman, *Immigrants and the Class Struggle: the Jewish Immigration in Leeds 1880–1914* (Manchester: Manchester University Press, 1983). For a parallel study of immigration in twentieth-century America see D. King, *Making Americans: Immigration, Race, and the Origins of the Diverse Democracy* (London: Harvard University Press, 2000).
5. The standard work remains B. Gainer, *The Alien Invasion: the Origins of the Aliens Act of 1905* (London: Heinemann, 1972).
6. For further details see P. Panayi, *Immigration, Ethnicity and Racism in Britain 1815–1945* (Manchester: Manchester University Press, 1994) and I. Spencer, *British Immigration Policy Since 1939: the Making of Multi-racial Britain* (London: Routledge, 1997).
7. A. Kershen, 'The Jewish community in London', in Merrimann, N. (ed.) *The Peopling of London* (London: Museum of London, 1994) 138–47.
8. C. Pooley and J. Turnbull, *Migration and Mobility in Britain Since the 18th Century*, 265–71. And, for example R. Pope, *War and Society in Britain, 1894–1948* (London: Longman, 1991).
9. C. Pooley and J. Turnbull, *Migration and Mobility in Britain Since the 18th Century*, 237, and 147–92, 229–56.
10. Ibid.
11. See especially M. Crowther, 'The Tramp', in Porter, R. (ed.) *Myths of the English* (Cambridge: Polity Press, 1992) 91–113. For one account of 'travelling' in the late twentieth century see C. J. Stone, *Fierce Dancing: Adventures in the Underground* (London: Faber, 1996).
12. I. Spencer, *British Immigration Policy since 1939*, 132.
13. P. J. Eakin, *How Our Lives Become Stories: Making Selves* (London: Cornell University Press, 1999) 43–98.
14. C. Steedman, 'State-sponsored autobiography', in Conekin, B., Mort, F., and Waters, C. (eds) *Moments of Modernity: Reconstructing Britain 1945–1964* (London: Rivers Oram, 1999) 51.
15. C. Kramsch, *Language and Culture* (Oxford: Oxford University Press, 1998) 74.
16. Kramsch, *Language and Culture*, 77.
17. S. Rushdie, 'The location of Brazil', *Imaginary Homelands: Essays and Criticism, 1981–1991* (London: Granta, 1992) 125.

Transition 2

81) Mrs Coll on Irish–Scottish migration, 1908 [I.]

Born c.1887 in Gweedore, Co. Donegal, Mrs Coll first went to Scotland as a harvest labourer in 1908 and eventually settled in Glasgow, where her children and grandchildren were born. She died in 1980. Her recollections were recorded c.1980 for the BBC Radio Scotland documentary series Odyssey.

> I left Donegal in 1908. They all come to Scotland that time and I came over first in May and then I used to go back and come back to the harvest again. They carried it under their oxter their hooks, for to cut the corn. I mind that as well. I come on the – did ye ever hear o' the Gola boat – a boat that used tae leave from where we stayed just and we got the boat there and she left us in Glasgow. We only paid four shillins.

B. Kay, 'From The Gorbals to Gweedore', in B. Kay (ed.) *The Complete Odyssey: Voices from Scotland's Recent Past* (Edinburgh: Polygon, 1996) 1.

82) Anant Ram travels froxm the Punjab to London, 1936 [I.]

Born in the village of Sherpur – within the Jalandhar district of Punjab, India – in 1912, Anant Ram travelled to Britain in 1936. An early member of the Indian Association, the Indian League, and the Indian Workers Association, he became a much-respected political activist against radial discrimination in the 1960s and 1970s. Mr Ram was interviewed by D. Singh Tatla in the early 1990s.

> **How did your family react to your decision to go to England?**
> I was married then. In those days, people were married at a very young age. I was only nine or ten when I was married. By the age of 24, I had four children, two sons and two daughters, the youngest son was 2½ months when I left for England. My wife said 'why do you have to go so far when you can earn a living here.' However, I wanted to get away for better money. I had already some experience of the world, as I had travelled to Bahavalpur State

with my father. So my wife after initial protest, did not prevent me and said nothing more on this subject. Well, in those days you did not take into consideration much of womenfolk advice.

What were travel arrangements like?
The fare for England was a big problem. It was thirty-one pounds for return sea passage. I had already saved this amount by joining my father in Bahavalpur state and working there. From Punjab, one had to travel to Bombay and then catch a ship. I was joined by Sohan Singh from my village, whilst Bawa Singh joined us from Farwala village.

All three of us had prepared a trunk each. I had a new suit, with two shirts and other essential things. I had 500 rupees on me. On the day we departed, there were 10–12 relatives who gathered to see me off at the railway station. We took the train from Bilga instead of Noormahal, as this was in the direction of the rising sun. Those days people had all sorts of omens about which days are auspicious to travel, or when to travel. We paid nineteen rupees for train fare for Bombay, changed the trains at Ludhiana, after two days of train travel reached Bombay . . .

Those days, the passenger ships came from Singapore passing through Bombay to England. We set out again to Bombay, this time without any pomp and ceremony and caught the ship on the night of 19 May 1936. The ship was a new experience for us, however we were lucky as on our ship there were several old hands from our district. They made our journey comfortable, by cooking together and giving help to anyone who felt seasick. We reached Venice and from there caught the train to France. When we arrived at Victoria, London it was midnight.

What were your first impressions of London?
There was no checking of our papers or passports in London, these were checked back in Bombay. All together there were 25 of us, coming from a cluster of villages in Jalandhar district. Four were returning to England for the second time. These four were received by their London friends. Those who knew London already, exchanged addresses with the first timers, and told us to join them later. They promised to help us find jobs and other contacts. I had two addresses on me. One was located at 17 Whitechapel Lane, East End. Our friends told us that this is a shop where pedlars would buy new stock. They advised us to go to the gurdwara in Shepherds Bush. The gurdwara was the usual destination for those without any immediate connections. But I had another address also. This was number four house. I cannot recall the street now, but it was just behind the Spitalfields Market. With four other first timers, I went to this address. Our friends, who were already familiar with London, before leaving us, guided a taxi driver to take us to this address I was carrying. Here we found Vaiyam Singh from Bilga. He welcomed us warmly and treated us extremely well. In those days there was ample hospitality. Vaiyam Singh gave help to others to reach their connections. Two

others, who came with me from Khere village, had their own friends, so Varyam told Lakha, another Punjabi who was staying with him, to drop them there.

He advised me to stay on with him and immediately applied on my behalf for a licence as a vendor. In those days, this was the only profession our people used to do. The fee for this was 5 shillings. You had to be living at an address at least for a month to qualify for the licence. Where I was staying, there were already about 10–12 people. Others came up on particular days and picked up new clothes from suppliers in Aldgate. Then they would go off on weekly rounds in their established localities.

D. Singh Tatla, 'This is our home now: reminiscences of a Punjabi migrant in Coventry', *Oral History*, 21 (1993) 69–70.

83) A Basque refugee child arrives in England, mid-1930s [I.]

These comments were recorded as a part of a community oral history project published in 1991 by Eduardo Martinez.

When we originally came here we were all taken to Southampton, in Eastleigh, near Southampton and we were in camps there. We were all either Nationalists, or Anarchists or Communists or Socialists or whatever. We were all separated into groups. I didn't know anything about this at the time.

It didn't matter how old you were. In fact that was the terrible thing about it. I came with my elder sister, she was 15, and at the beginning they separated you on your parents' belief at the time and that's how you were labelled, in fact we were all separated into different sections like that and as regards my sister and me we were separated because she was a girl and I was a boy. Although I was just six years old that didn't have any bearing at all, we were just put in tents, put outside and that was it.

Well, my father was Communist, had been from the Communist Party, so I was automatically put in that section. But at the time I didn't know anything about it except of course afterwards that we were all either supposed to be Anarchists or Nationalists or Socialists or whatever, you know that's all that really mattered then.

In Southampton, in Eastleigh, I remember queuing for food, and I remember the music that they had to play to wake us up in the morning over the tannoy. That kind of thing is very, very vivid indeed. We lived in tents, the one that I used to be in was about eight or so to a tent. They were reasonably sized tents.

In Southampton there was many people when we first came over, about 5,000, it was really too big and too impersonal. I didn't know anybody, quite frankly. I came with my sister but we were separated immediately we came off the boat, and quite frankly I hardly saw her at all, in fact I don't recall if I ever saw her in Southampton. I don't even know how long we were there but I have a feeling it must have been something like two months.

Some people started leaving earlier than others. Some people stayed much longer. From there we went to what I think must have been a transition camp, I don't know because we were only there for two weeks and it was in army sheds. It must have been somewhere around Surrey because afterwards we were taken to Bray Court, which was the first colony that I really remember at all. Bray Court was near Maidenhead. I do remember we were there for some months. This was quite a biggish colony. We were in a house that used to be at a hotel at one time, with very imposing grounds and all that. It was very, very nice indeed. We were there about six months, in Bray Court. It was a mixed colony and I was there with my sister. We both went to that colony and they used to organise concerts from there and my sister used to be in the dancing group. They used to give concerts in different places and once they went to Belfast and my sister in fact stayed there, in Belfast. She was adopted there and subsequently a little bit later she took me over there and I spent two years in Belfast.

E. Martinez, 'Ethnic communities oral history project, *Ship of Hope*, 1991', in P. Panayi, *Immigration, Ethnicity and Racism in Britain: 1815–1945* (Manchester: Manchester University Press, 1994) 139–40.

84) 'Jan Kowalski', a Polish soldier, settles in Britain, 1940s [I.]

'Jan Kowalski' (pseud.) was born in Russia in 1914. He spent his early years in Kiev, where his father was a civil engineer; in 1917 he moved to Warsaw, where he became a member of the Radical Syndicalist Party. He studied architecture at the University of Warsaw 1934–9. Kowalski took part in the Polish Campaign of 1939, was captured by the Russians and escaped a prisoners' transit camp to return to Warsaw. According to Jerzy Zubrzycki 'He wrote his story at my request in June 1952 and I have supplemented it with some additional observations arising from our conversations. It is significant that the original story presented here, without any alterations, is in English.'

I began to plan my escape from German-occupied Poland to join the Polish Armed Forces in England. In the summer of 1940 I set out on foot across the Carpathians to Hungary, thence to Yugoslavia and on a small Greek ship to Egypt. In December 1940 I arrived in Great Britain. I knew little English at that time.

I was sent to a Polish training unit in Scotland but after some 6 months spent on training I decided to apply for leave to supplement my University education, seeing no purpose in wasting my time in the 'armed idleness' of a camp life. For one year I studied at Liverpool University's School of Architecture and having completed my Degree Course I went to London to work at the Polish Ministry of Reconstruction. My task at the Planning Staff of the

Ministry was to assist in drawing up plans for the reconstruction of Polish industrial centres. Thus – I thought – my chance had arrived when I could contribute something to the realization of my youthful ideals of 'better homes for workers.' While I was at the Ministry I established several contacts with British architects and town planners. I also published an article in the 'Times Review of Industry' on the 'Housing of Light Industry' and then two more articles in specialized journals. Two English engineering firms made tempting offers to employ me but I turned them down as I was fully convinced at that time that there would be no impediments to my returning to Poland at the end of the war.

In the summer of l943 I was recalled to my unit and subsequently sent to the Polish anti-aircraft Regiment in Dover. There I flung myself into military routine with great enthusiasm. In the Autumn of 1943 I was promoted to the rank of Captain and in the Spring of 1944, just before the V-1 'Season' began, I was made a Battery Commander. For this promotion I was much envied by older professional officers who were not specialized enough to be given command of a heavy AA Battery with its intricate Radar system and other scientific devices at the vital sector of British Coastal Defences.

During my stay in the vicinity of Dover I first met my wife. She was then a welfare worker with the W.V.S. and used to drive a mobile canteen. Strangely enough, our first conversations centred on political and social problems. She was an active member of the Fabian Society and aroused my interest in British Socialism.

From June 1944 onwards my battery played a crucial part in fighting the 'doodlebugs.' Several times I was commended for my excellent results much to the displeasure of my Regular Army colleagues.

In the Spring of 1945 a Senior English Officer inspecting my Regiment found that in my Battery no disciplinary measures had been taken for the preceding 6 months. He did not seem to view this fact with satisfaction although I argued that the excellent morale in my Battery was due to the fact that I had tried to maintain discipline, not in accordance with the feudal dogma of military regulations and traditions, but in accordance with the principles of team co-operation enforced in industry. The angry Colonel took my remark much to heart, especially when I added that I was not a Regular Army Officer and now that the hostilities had almost ended I would be glad to leave the Forces altogether.

Shortly after this unpleasant interview I was released and having decided meanwhile that my return to Russian-dominated Poland was pointless I signed a contract with one of the firms that had offered to employ me in 1943. I also became an Associate Member of the Town Planning Institute (A.M.T.P.I.). I have been with this firm ever since advancing quickly from the position of a Junior Architect to that of an Acting Head of the Planning Staff with some l5 architects and draughtsmen working under me.

In the Summer of 1945 my Fiancee resigned her membership of the Fabian Society in protest against the treatment of Polish problems at successive Big Four conferences which were endorsed by the British Labour Party. We were not married till the Autumn of 1946 and only after I had been given a substantial rise in my salary. We have bought a bungalow in Sussex where we spend our weekends. We have one child – a girl – Maria Patricia.

I don't think I am assimilated, I have only adapted myself wholly to British ways of life. I consider myself to be a Citizen of the world, not a given country. Any person I come across is judged by me not according to his national label but according to his moral and intellectual qualities. I have only one life to live – and because I live in Britain I have to adapt myself to British Ways of Life. After all – I eat their bread. Once I earn my living in this country – why should I stick to my pre-war national loyalties.

J. Zubrzycki, *Polish Immigrants in Britain: a Study of Adjustment* (The Hague: Nijhoff, 1956) 206–7.

85) Eric Ferron, a Jamaican soldier, travels to Britain, 1944 [I.]

Born in 1925 in Jamaica, Eric Ferron arrived in Britain as a member of the armed forces in 1944. He left the RAF in 1947, trained as a psychiatric nurse and eventually became a professional social worker. His autobiography is an intimate account of life in postwar Britain: the stress on the difficulties of everyday life within an often racist society. Man, You've Mixed *was written over a number of years and published in 1995. Ferron writes 'I put this book together because I hope that young people who feel there is no hope may read it and that it will convey to them a strength that will enable them to withstand their difficulties . . . I hope the book will also be read by adults who will see how pain can be put to constructive uses'.*

Early one morning in 1944, after nearly two months in the RAF camp in Jamaica, we were awakened and taken by lorries and trucks to Kingston Harbour where a big ship, the SS *Cuba*, was waiting. We were not told we were going to England, but then we always knew we would go.

All through my boyhood I was constantly hoping the time would come. We all did. We had heard about Queen Victoria, about Rodney and Nelson, all the great English sailors and soldiers. Buckingham Palace. Windsor Castle. We had seen pictures of these great buildings and of places in all the great countries of Europe.

I had joined up because I had wanted to get away, do something new, something different. I did not tell my parents I had applied until after I had been accepted. They objected, of course, but by then it was too late. I wanted to get into the war, but most of all, I wanted to see England. I had no intention of staying away for any length of time; it would be more of a visit to do my service and then come back. I boarded the ship in great excitement. It was a childhood dream fulfilled. I was on my way to England.

It was to take 28 days. As we sailed away from the island everything seemed possible, from finding German submarines to seeing King George. We were excited. We did not know what we were getting into. Some English boys back in camp in Jamaica had told me I would like it when I got there, but, once we sailed, I found I was soon missing camp life and the routine.

My time there had been one of hard work and concentration. I had wanted to learn and do my best. The group of boys who joined up with me were all eager to prove themselves. Now on the ship, we were all like overgrown schoolboys. A rumour went round that a German submarine had been sighted. We flew into a panic. But the scare passed and we sailed on to New York.

Here we stopped for a day and people lined the wharfs to cheer us. They were kind. We felt accepted. We felt proud. They called us 'British' boys. We left New York in a convoy of 30 ships. There were nearly 3,000 men on our ship. As we sailed into the Atlantic we wrote letters home. I thought of my mother and sisters and the island. I always told my mother whatever I did. I had always been close to her and this parting made me realise my dependence even more. I kept her up-to-date with life on board ship, how the boys played cards and cheated each other, how different the boys from the other islands were.

In mid-Atlantic, one of the English sailors told us it was the graveyard of English shipping and this was the first time a convoy had passed the point without a ship being sunk. The destroyers and escort ships fired their guns in salute. Only a few hours after that, our convoy was attacked. You could see the fire out to sea. We heard over the radio that one of the ships had been attacked and sunk. That frightened us. We lay in our hammocks waiting for a torpedo to come through the side. It was the first time we had seen war, except on the films.

It was October and getting colder. A storm lasted a whole day and a night. A lot of us couldn't eat. The food wasn't what we had been used to. I had never had potato before, not this kind of potato. I had never had a meal without spices. No curry. But we said to ourselves: 'We are men. It is only for a while.' We didn't know then that for some of us it would be years and years.

The second attack was at night. Most of us were asleep. We didn't see much of it, but we heard two ships had been sunk. The next night we were told to be sure not to show any lights on deck. One of the boys wanted us to be attacked again. He wanted to see these Germans for himself. He wanted to get a photograph of a German ship to send to his sister.

The journey seemed endless. It was as if we were going round the world. One minute they said we were going north to Canada, then it would be that we were stopping again in America, and then that we were going to Europe.

We thought that maybe the plans were being changed to out do the Germans. But we did not know; no-one told us.

We were happy enough, although there was always a tinge of sadness. We had left home for the first time and for the first time I was with boys rougher than myself. They too were Jamaicans, but they were from other parts of the island. Sometimes there were scuffles. The Jamaicans would fight each other over little things; they also fought the Barbadians, the Trinidadians and the Guianese. Indeed the Jamaicans were everywhere – always the proudest group, always feeling themselves to be the most capable, the strongest and the most intelligent. It is something about the Jamaican, he always feels himself better than the others. He is from the big island, they are from the little ones. The boys from Barbados were timid and gentle, the Trinidad boys were more defiant but generally more friendly to the Jamaicans, the Guianese were somewhere in between. However, it was all new to me. I learned a lot about the West Indies on that journey.

We sailed on and we talked to each other. Foster, a friend I'd joined up with, and Robbie and Martin, who I'd got to know in camp, were together, just the four of us.

On the twenty-seventh day, they announced that we would see England the next day. We stayed up nearly all night. All we could see were shadows, dark clouds, but no England. The air was colder, there was not so much wind and the sea was calm.

In the morning we woke up to see the land – land for the first time in so many days. I remember coming up on deck, seeing the coast and running down to tell the boys. Within minutes there were hundreds and hundreds of us looking ashore, but fog was coming up and we soon lost sight of it. It wasn't until night that we really came face to face with England – or, as we soon discovered, Scotland. We arrived in Glasgow harbour and the ship anchored a few miles out. We waited hours for the order to land, but were told to sleep on board that night. The following morning we woke up early and found ourselves tied up in dock. 'This is really it', I thought.

The country was white. I couldn't understand how a country could be so white. Every tree and every house was covered in snow. We put it in our cups and started to eat it, but the sailors told us not to because it was dirty.

It was mid-afternoon before the gangway was opened and we began to land. There were crowds of people to greet us. They waved and cheered and gave us boxes of chocolates, biscuits and cigarettes. They were kind, they were nice people. I felt happy. It was a great country after all, but it was cold! We came off the ship in our thousands and poured into the waiting trains. All along the way through Scotland, people stood and waved to us. Everything was so new and wonderful and we were so proud to be there.

E. Ferron, *'Man, You've Mixed': A Jamaican Comes to Britain* (London: Whiting and Birch, 1995) 1–4.

86) 'N', a Ukrainian, travels to Bedford, 1948 [I.]

John Brown's detailed study of immigrants in the Bedford area c.1970 presents an investigation of eight national groups and their place within the community together with a discussion of related social issues. The author describes his purpose as 'to understand the condition of life and the problems of each of the main immigrant groups', and he tries to achieve this by a discussion of national backgrounds and cultures, of their interaction with British culture, and of personal experience. 'At times this is reported', Brown writes, 'at times directly quoted, usually with concealed identity. Often the device of "representative voices" is used'. As a result of this technique few biographical details are available, though Brown clearly carried out extensive interviews. The only details available on 'N' (pseud.), for example, are that he was taken from his smallholding in the Ukraine in 1941 to work as a slave labourer in Germany between 1942–5. He subsequently lived through the dangerous, anarchic conditions of the early postwar years before moving to the Bedford area in 1948 under the British-sponsored Displaced Persons scheme.

> Americans collect many people in camps. First of all, many sent home, mostly east Ukrainians, because Russian subjects. That was terrible. People not want to go. Many suicide. Throw themselves from high buildings or from transport. People desperate. Then Americans stop mass deportations. Let people choose. Start screening. Let forty, fifty people at a time in big room. Raise right hand, swear to tell the truth. Then fill in form. Nationality. Subject. . . . What is this? Ukrainian? Not possible. Just Pole or Russian. 'No, no,' I say, 'I am Ukrainian.' Then big trouble. American MPs come in, and everyone shouting. . . .
>
> Well, in 1947, they ask DPs in English zone if they want to go England; 1948, same in American zone. All young people want to go England. So at last begin three-month journey, Munich to Cambridge. All mixed up together, no one know which which. Russians put down 'Ukrainian' so not to go back. Some Ukrainians put down as Poles. I have 'Pole' on my card, so I cross it out and write 'Ukrainian'. When we come to England, Polish interpreter say : 'He is not Ukrainian. He is Pole.' I say, 'How can you put for horse, cow?'
>
> We told we have choice of three jobs. Agriculture, coalmine, brickyard. But at Cambridge, they say, 'All up to thirty-five go to coalmine.' Many say no, not want to go. Stay there six weeks, and very good food. Very good. After, they stamp card for farm work. . . . Later, after contract finish, come to Bedford for brickyard. Kempston Hardwick hostel.

J. Brown, *The Un-Melting Pot* (London: Macmillan – now Palgrave Macmillan, 1970) 60.

87) Donall Mac Amhlaigh travels to Northampton, 1951 [I.]

Born near Galway, Ireland, in 1926, Donall Mac Amhlaigh left school at the age of 15, did mill, farm and hotel work, and eventually joined the First

Battalion of the Irish Army, spending three years in his beloved Galway with an Irish-speaking unit. In 1951 he left the Army and moved to England to work with his fellow countrymen in the Health Service, building, light engineering and service industries. An Irish Navvy *covers the years 1951–7. Written originally in Irish* Dialann Deoria (The Diary of an Exile) *was a successful and important documentary account notable for a strong sense both of the language Mac Amhlaigh was writing in and of the uses to which an exile can put language. The English translation was published in 1964. The author died in 1989.*

I stood on John Bull's territory for the first time in my life on Tuesday morning when I got off the Irish Mail at Rugby. I don't count Holyhead for that's really Welsh and there was as much Welsh spoken there as there was Irish on a fair day in Derrynea. I lost my friends in the customs hall and I never saw them again. And what a to-do there was about our bags! You'd think that we were carrying priceless jewels instead of the few old rags we had. There was one man who shoved on to the counter an old battered case that was tied with a bit of rope to keep it shut.

'What have you got here?' said the customs officer.

'Yerra, nothing at all,' said my lad with a grin.

'Open it up, all the same,' said your man.

'Sure, it's hardly worth my while,' said the lad.

'Look here, you're only wasting both our time. I can't let you through until you open up that bag.'

'Fair enough,' said my lad and drew out of his pocket a bloody big knife with which he cut the rope around the case. The lid jumped up just like a Jack-in-the-Box and out leapt an old pair of Wellington boots that had been twisted up inside it. Devil the thing else was in the case – not even a change of socks. A melancholy wintry little smile crossed the face of the customs officer as he motioned to your man to get along with himself.

I slept most of the way from there to Rugby and, when I left the train, I had a two-hour delay before I caught the train to Northampton. My heart sank altogether then as I stood and looked around at the dirty ugly station. Everything looked so foreign to me there. Round about six o'clock hundreds started pouring into the station, pallid pasty faces with identical lunch boxes slung from their shoulders. They were all getting the train to work and their likes were getting off the train at the same time coming to work in Rugby, I suppose. God save us, I murmured to myself as I thought that nobody in Ireland would be even thinking of getting out of their beds for another couple of hours yet!

D. Mac Amhlaigh, *An Irish Navvy: the Diary of an Exile* (London: Routledge, 1964) 5–6.

88) Jamaicans travelling to Britain, 1956–60 [I.]

Harry Goulbourne's article is an early attempt to establish a framework for the study of black labour history in Britain. Within this structure the author provides illustrative interview excerpts which, he states, were based on discussions – tape-recorded in 1975 – with workers in the south London districts of Brixton, Camberwell, Peckham and East Dulwich. All but one of his informants was Jamaican. They all had rural upbringings, and had settled in London in the 1950s and 1960s.

> **How much was the fare [from Jamaica] in those days, can you remember?**
> (Wife): Oh, I paid £85.13.0
> (Husband): My own was £85, that's right.
>
> **Did you have to save-up to do this? Did you have to borrow? Was the money hard to come by?**
> (Wife): Well, at that time my husband was here, so it was quite different you know.
> (Husband): Not really because I used to do lorry business, you know; and after finding that things wasn't working all right, I just set out, you know.
>
> **To the same question another worker from Jamaica responded thus:**
> It was easy for me really, because we wasn't that badly off. I was a mason-builder, and we could find the money easily.
>
> **The same worker went on:**
> Well, I had a brother at the time over here, and a sister, and they want me to come – 1956. I refused – they even sent me the fare; 1956 my sister sent me the fare and I didn't come. 1958, sent me the fare again, I didn't come until 1960. Well, most of my friends was leaving – coming to England – all friends and cousins . . . so I was coming from work one Friday and I saw them going to the Travel Service place – I went in with them . . . Well, I booked my passage at the same time because I did have money with me.

H. Goulbourne, 'Oral history and black labour in Britain: an overview', *Oral History*, 8 (1980) 25–6.

89) Goram Singh Khera travels from the Punjab to England, 1960s [I.]

Saheli Winter's account of the Asian community in Gravesend, Kent – from which Goram Singh Khera's comments are taken – was the result of a local oral history project carried out in the early 1990s.

> I was only a few years old when my uncle Kartar Singh Randhawa left India and come to England. It was a big talk of the village. I grew up knowing that

out there somewhere is England. When I started school I had this dream that when I grow up I shall go to England. That dream came true when, along with my three uncles, I started for England, very excited and enthusiastic. Coming to England was really something great. I was not frightened at all because of the company of my uncles. We landed here and the first thing we did was get jobs and start making money. We used to earn £4 per week working on a building site.

S. Winters, *Nobody Sleeps on the Rooftops Now* (Gravesend: AIM, 1994) 3.

90) Prafulla Mohanti explores Surbiton, 1960s [I.]

Prafulla Mohanti arrived in Britain in 1960 after having qualified as an architect in Bombay. He worked as an architect in London, went to study town planning at the Leeds College of Art, and later returned to London where the Greater London Council employed him. Writer, artist, and sometime yoga teacher, Mohanti draws a detailed, thoughtful portrait of British society between the early 1960s and the early 1980s – an era of economic, industrial and racial turbulence.

I sat by the window watching the lingering twilight. I was not prepared for it and found it difficult to go to bed. It gave me a totally different sense of time. When Tom and his mother said goodnight I wondered how it could be night when there was still daylight outside. In India the sun sets around six in the evening all the year round and there is a clear division between day and night.

I was used to sleeping on hard beds made of wood with a thin cotton mattress and in the village I often slept on a straw mat on the mud floor. But the bed Tom had supplied for me was too soft and I felt uncomfortable. So I sat cross-legged on the bed and meditated. My mind and body gradually relaxed and I was able to sleep.

The next morning the birds sang and woke me up. I looked through the window and saw the sun shining again. The grass in the garden looked like a green carpet. I saw the squirrels jumping from branch to branch. Around eleven I went out on my own to do some shopping. The streets were quiet with very little traffic. I seemed to be the only person from India. Many prams were parked outside the shops. I had never seen such big fat babies with round, pink cheeks before. When I returned to the flat and told Tom 'I saw some beautiful fat babies in trolleys', he replied, 'They're National Health babies.'

I did not know what he meant but when he took me to his doctor to register he explained the National Health Service to me. Everyone, young and old, received free medical care. I thought of the sick and the starving people in India. Many of my childhood friends had died and I am lucky to have survived. My aunt had told me that when I was a baby I had a terrible cough.

One day I stopped breathing and my mother put me in the courtyard so that I could get some fresh air. Everybody thought I was dead but after a while I started breathing again. A few days earlier a woman from another settlement had come to see my mother. She did not have a child of her own and held me in her arms. My aunt thought she had cast her envious eyes on me and that was the cause of my illness. Mothers put black spots on their children's foreheads to protect them from 'nazr' eyes, 'the envious look'. That day my mother had forgotten to put the mark on me . . .

Tom's mother told me how happy she was to have her son back in England. She never visited him in India because she did not think she could endure the heat or face the beggars. She liked her cottage in the country, its garden, the apple trees, and the roses. To her Surbiton was a lifeless suburb and she came there only to see her son.

I thought Surbiton was a good example of suburbia. I had read about London suburbs during my course in architecture. These were the places where people lived and travelled to London every day to work. There were a few blocks of flats, but most people lived in detached or semi-detached houses with front and back gardens. In the mornings I saw men with brief cases hurrying to the station to catch their trains. They returned between five and seven. In the afternoons the streets were deserted and I wandered around admiring the flowers in the carefully laid out gardens. Near the station there was a small shopping street with a cinema hall and several pubs. The shops were always well-kept with an attractive display of goods. I liked Waltons. The fruit was clean and polished, graded to size, and kept neatly in boxes. I was surprised to see pineapples, bananas, and oranges as I knew they grew only in tropical countries. The flowers in the florists were so beautiful that I examined them to find out if they were real. I smelt them but they did not have any scent. The shop assistant had been watching me. 'Can I help you?' she asked. I had gone into the shop to admire the flowers but had not wanted to buy any. I was embarrassed and asked her to select a small bunch of flowers with a nice smell. I gave them to Tom's mother. She smelt them and said, 'What lovely freesias.'

The prices in the shops were clearly marked and I noticed there was no bargaining. It made shopping easy but dull. Shopping was an exciting expedition in India. We selected the fruits and vegetables, watched them being weighed, and bargained about the prices. But in Surbiton the shopkeeper was annoyed when I picked up a pear to see if it was ripe. I looked out for bazaars and open-air markets, but there were none. Newspapers were left unattended on the pavement, with a box containing coins. I saw a man stop, take a paper, and put some money in the box. In an Indian city everything would have disappeared in seconds.

The local shops and the milkman delivered groceries and milk in proper milk bottles. The laundryman brought the clothes. They put them outside the door and every week collected the money which was left in envelopes.

The door was rarely locked. I thought English people were very honest and wrote to my parents about it.

Tom laughed when I asked him if the milk was pure. 'It is not only pure, but you can get as much as you like', he replied. In India, milk was in short supply and was rarely pure except from a few dairy farms. But their milk was not enough to meet the huge demand in the cities. Water was added to the milk and sold at different prices according to the degree of dilution. In my village the milkman was requested to bring pure milk for the babies. Sometimes to assure the customers that the milk was pure, he brought the cow to the door and milked her in front of them.

P. Mohanti, *Through Brown Eyes* (Oxford: Oxford University Press, 1985) 27–9.

91) Bodrul Alom on migration from East Pakistan, 1967 [I.]

Born in East Pakistan (present day Bangladesh) in 1955, Bodrul Alom followed his father to England in 1967. He describes here the mass migrations from his homeland from the mid-1950s to the 1970s. Alom's comments were recorded as a part of Jonathan Green's interview project with immigrants describing their experiences and perceptions of Britain in the years after 1945.

People from east Pakistan, now it's called Bangladesh, started arriving in this country in the mid-1950s. Some of them had worked on the big ships and they began realizing that immigrant labour forces were very much needed in this country. So they began coming to this country to fill that need. Prior to that there had been Bangladeshis involved with World War II, fighting as colonial troops. So, through coming here as merchant seamen or fighting for the British in the war and learning something about Britain, people decided to start coming to settle here. Initially most of them worked as sailors, then as labourers, then gradually they moved into the clothing trade. Some people did work in factories, in light industry. After that, in the '60s and early '70s, some people decided, since there was still work available, to bring over their relatives and associates and members of their family. They came in on work vouchers. From them the news spread, mainly by word of mouth, and people began applying to their appropriate High Commissions to come and settle in this country.

J. Green, *Them: Voices from the Immigrant Community in Contemporary Britain* (London: Secker and Warburg, 1990) 30.

92) Mary Lennon on migration from Ireland, 1982 [M.]

Mary Lennon arrived in London from Ireland in 1973. Her comments were a contribution to a conference called 'Black and Immigrant Women Speak Out and Claim Our Rights', held in London in 1982.

> I came to live in England in 1973, and I came then mainly because the work opportunities were better here than they were in Ireland. At the time I had about four aunts on both sides of my family who had emigrated. Along our road every family had aunts and uncles who had emigrated. Because emigration was a way of life and had been for a century and a half, it was just something we took for granted. But I gradually realised through living here that there was nothing about immigration that should be taken for granted. That basically it wasn't a fact of life that Irish women had to emigrate in the numbers that they did. That the reason why they did was because Ireland had always been treated as an appendage of Britain. It was treated as an appendage in the sense that our land was taken from us; that our industries were prevented from developing if they should compete with British industry; that it was a predominantly rural country because it was important that Britain had a country nearby that could supply it with food when it started to industrialise. There was nothing accidental about it. There was nothing natural about it. It was a systematically developed policy whereby Ireland's fate and rights were always subordinated to the fate of Britain.

S. James (ed.) *Sisters and Strangers: Women, Race and Immigration* (Bristol: Falling Wall Press, 1982) 72.

Settlement and Work 2

93) Lithuanians and Poles in the Lanarkshire coalfields, 1907 [I.]

Evidence from a government report on Scottish immigrant labourers

> . . . I have watched for years the conduct of those men; they are far more amenable to discipline than our own men. It is the universal testimony of the managers that these men are much more amenable to discipline, and that they will do what they are told. If they know that they are obliged to do a thing they will do it, and they are a striking contrast to a good many of our own workmen in that respect. I have only so far come across one case of a trifling accident, apparently, where one of those foreign workmen was the cause of another man meeting with an injury.

First Report of the Royal Commission on Mines, Cd 3548, Q5022 (1907).

94) Neil Sinclair's family history in Tiger Bay, pre-World War One [I.]

Born in Butetown, Cardiff ('Tiger Bay') c.1940, N. M. C. Sinclair's affectionate, intimate account of the district's history and his own upbringing there gives a unique insight into this long-established multi-racial community. 'Wherein', the author states, 'emerged an Afro-Celtic culture amidst its intra-cultural and multi-ethnic heritage'.

> It was through her acquaintance with Maggie that Agnes learned all about life in Tiger Bay. Meanwhile in the Bay, as a result of her stern upbringing, Maggie became known as 'Straight Jane And No Nonsense'. Nonetheless she became wife to Joseph Friday, a huge black man known as 'Pop Friday' who originally came from Guyana, South America. In those days it was British Guiana. They eventually settled down at 5 Somerset Street in Grangetown with dreams of living happily ever after. After all World War 1 had yet to begin.
>
> Having followed 'Straight Jane And No Nonsense' down to Tiger Bay, Agnes soon met up with one of Pop Friday's sea-going friends, 'Iron Ford'. This

handsome young man clearly swept Agnes off her feet for they too were soon to be married. Iron Ford, of course, was not his real name. He was James Augustus Headley. Like my grandfather, Danny Sinclair, known in Tiger Bay as 'Gravy Eye', Iron Ford came from Barbados. Bridgetown to be exact. But not just a touch of the Ashanti was he. Carib blood was in his veins too. His ambition, like Gravy Eye's, was to escape sugar plantation life and head for Queen Victoria's land. But as a lad he was disembarked from his ship in Cuba. There he worked as a trolley car driver. One fateful day he had the misfortune to run over a man in a Havana street and thought he had killed him. In panic he boarded ship as soon as was possible, signing on as 'Joe Ford'. His job was cabin boy. Then destiny brought him to Wales, where his first view of life in Britain was in Tiger Bay.

Said to be mean-tempered and stern, characteristics that well earned him the name Iron Ford, he still softened enough at the sight of Agnes whom he married and who subsequently gave birth to Beatrice, my mother, while living in lodgings in Peel Street. And of that street old Mrs Pervoe was midwife to my mother's birth.

As no land work was available to black men in those times, Pop Friday and Iron Ford had to make many seagoing ventures to make ends meet. Eventually, Iron Ford was able to get lodgings for his family in Grangetown at 27 Somerset Street near Pop and 'Nana Friday' as Straight Jane And No Nonsense had by then become known.

N. M. C. Sinclair, *The Tiger Bay Story* (Treforest: Zenith, 1993) 29–32.

95) Anant Ram settles in Coventry, World War Two [I.]

See note on extract No.82.

How did you come to Coventry?

With peddling business over, the factory work also finishing soon, I was not happy in London. Also there was some trouble in London. On one occasion, I was caught and charged for black-marketeering. I was fined. Our friends advised me and others to move on. I knew some other people including Gurdas and his uncle from a village, Basava. I thought I would seek their help. They were living in Coventry, I got their address, this was 38 Spring Road. At that time, several other Punjabis were also living there. Among these were, Gurbathan Singh, Ratan Singh from Uppal village and Gurdas. There was also another Punjabi from Nawan Pind living with them. Thus, I had someone to go to in Coventry. So, I came to Coventry in 1942. Our Coventry friends accommodated all of us who came down from London. They gave us lodgings. Another group of Punjabis had rented another house, this was in the same road, number 50. Here I also learned a bit later, these Punjabis had formed an organisation, the Indian Workers Association. On this street, there were four houses in all rented by Punjabis. It was the usual practice among

Punjabis, not to charge rent from new arrivals until they had some paid work. Rent was seven shillings per week. This included a common kitchen and everyone shared the housework.

What sort of work did you manage to get in Coventry?
My friends in Coventry advised me on how to find work and how to make enquiries in a factory. Ratan Singh asked one of his friends, Kartar Singh, to help me in finding some work. A number of us found some contract work at Moreton Marsh, where an aerodrome was under construction. I was in-charge of cooking for thirty-five or forty people. After this had finished, we again looked for work. I was offered a job involving night shift, the work involved handling a machine in a medium sized factory. This was the Second World War time. Coventry was bombed only a few days earlier. I think the factory was making some components for the war, but I am not sure. The factory operated piece-work. There were men and women working alongside each other. A fellow Punjabi from Jandiala village also worked in the same factory. I got along well with him.

What was pay like and how much money did you manage to save?
I was able to earn around seven pounds every week, although it varied as we were paid piece rates, so I tried hard. After paying seven shillings for the room, another pound would buy plenty of food and drinks. All the rest was saved and sent home. Letters from home started arriving later during the war years, some were censored. We had to write short letters. We took care to send money in smaller quantity as there was a fear of its loss through the post.

D. Singh Tatla, 'This is our home now: reminiscences of a Punjabi migrant in Coventry', *Oral History*, 21 (1993) 71.

96) A Polish ex-soldier becomes a laboratory cleaner, 1950 [I.]

Born in 1919, this un-named former geography teacher was demobilized from the Polish forces and exiled in Britain after World War Two. After two years work in a vegetable nursery near London he found employment at the British Museum Natural History section.

My work is rather heavy and dirty for it involves the cleaning of natural history laboratories. Wages are low, but enough to live on for a single person and a teetotaller like myself. What I like about this job is that it makes it possible for me to see various geological and zoological exhibits which can be studied at close quarters. Moreover, I have an easy access to all the London museums and so I can study my subjects (geography and geology) much better than several professional scientists. Every evening I attend lectures in the Geography Department of King's College and occasionally special courses of lectures given in the Imperial College or the Royal Institute of Science. Last Autumn I attended a course of 12 lectures on 'The Pleistocene Glaciation in Great

Britain and its effects.' On Sundays I take part in geographical excursions organized by the Geological Museum and King's College. I spent most of my demobilization gratuity on a collection of 1,500 slides covering the course of general geography in a grammar school. I hope they will one day be used by a Polish school or university when my country is liberated. I have very few Polish or British friends but I am happy in my present work because its nature enables me to preserve an intimate contact with the subject I taught in Poland.

J. Zubrzycki, *Polish Immigrants in Britain: a Study of Adjustment* (The Hague: Nijhoff, 1956) 173.

97) Eric Ferron looks for accommodation in Surrey, *c.*1950 [I.]

See note on extract No.85.

When I had just started work in a hospital in Surrey, I applied by telephone for a room advertised in the local paper, a front room on the first floor at two pounds ten shillings a week, which was as much as I could afford at the time. The lady asked me to come round and see it that evening after I had finished duty. I went round and knocked on the door. She opened it, looked a little taken aback and said: 'Oh! Was it you on the phone?'

'Yes', I said.

'You're sure it was you? You sounded so different on the phone. I didn't know it would be you.'

'Who did you expect it would be?'

She flustered. 'Well, I don't know really. I thought it would be a white man I suppose. It sounded like it on the phone.'

I didn't respond but asked to see the room. Just a minute; and she shut the door. She could at least have left it open I thought. I also had a feeling I wasn't going to get the room. She was back in a few minutes.

'I'm so very sorry but my husband phoned just this minute and told me he has offered the room to a friend at work.' She was sorry I had wasted my time coming all this way but she hoped I would understand.

I said: 'If you'd known I was black would you have asked me to come?'

'Well, to tell you the honest truth, no, I wouldn't.'

'Why not?'

'It's very difficult round here. I personally have nothing against coloured people but people round here are a funny lot. I believe there's black and white in all of us but people round here don't see it like that. I couldn't risk it.'

'What is there to risk?'

'It's not because of what they think. But you must understand how difficult it would be for me. No one would speak to me. I'd go into a shop and no one would speak.'

'Is it really as bad as that now?'

'Yes', she said, and she seemed to be apologising. 'But surely you can stand up to what people say. You're your own boss in your own house.'

'And you're a very good talker', she said, 'What is your language? Where do you come from? You speak English very well.'

I told her. 'I see. I thought you must have learned to speak English when you came here. I'm so very sorry about all this.'

She seemed a good woman and she was beginning to listen.

I decided to risk it.

'Since I've been talking to you I've got the impression you are a kindly honest woman, yet you began by hiding something.'

'I'm not hiding anything.'

'You know your husband didn't telephone. You knew when you opened the door that no one else had taken the room. You knew you'd decided you wouldn't let it to a black man. Why couldn't you be honest with me?'

She thought for a minute, then she said: 'Would you like a cup of tea?' I said I would and she invited me inside.

'It seems so awful really. Of course, my husband didn't telephone. I feel terrible about it. I've read about people rejecting coloured people and I never thought I'd do the same thing. But it's the neighbours. And my husband is very strict about who he has in the house.'

I said nothing.

'What about in Jamaica? Do you get on with the white people there?'

'Yes I do. There's no difference. But we don't seem to let rooms in Jamaica. Everyone has their own house.'

'What about in the towns?'

'Perhaps. I don't know. I've always lived in the country.'

We talked on. I felt that there was a woman for the first time trying to be honest about her colour prejudice. She was talking to a black man face-to-face and finding out that he was a human being who felt deeply about being rejected but who could take it, and discuss it. She didn't know what to do.

'You might like to see the room now you are here.'

It was just as she had described it over the telephone, a big room, well furnished and warm. 'I provide meals because there's only one kitchen.' We went back downstairs. She told me about her husband and her little boy who had just done well in his exams at school. And the time passed pleasantly. 'I could talk to my husband when he comes home. He might let you have the room.'

But I didn't want the room now. I had felt insulted but I was pleased. I'd done my job. She would remember meeting a black man, finding he could talk English and wasn't a monster.

E. Ferron, *'Man, You've Mixed': A Jamaican Comes to Britain* (London: Whiting and Birch, 1995) 58–60.

98) An Asian man arrives in Bradford, 1950s [I.]

The speaker was born in 1938. His recollections are recorded in Destination Bradford, *one of a series of publications by the Bradford Heritage Recording Unit. The book and the exhibition on which it was based use large format photographs alongside brief quotations with minimal bibliographical details on the speakers.*

> I still remember the day when after about three months of getting my first job in this country I was treated like a slave by one of the supervisors. For the sake of my dignity and self-respect I had to leave that job. I also remember that on the night following this incident I wept for about two hours, regretting my decision to come to this country. I simply wanted to go back home. All the images of Britain which I had acquired through my education and acquaintance with a few British people in Pakistan were shattered.

Destination Bradford: A Century of Immigration (Bradford: Heritage Recording Unit, 1987) 32.

99) Donall Mac Amhlaigh begins work as a navvy, 1950s [I.]

See note on extract No.87.

> It was as much as I could do to drag my body out of the bed next morning. I managed to get up; however, and off I went down to Regent Square to meet the man from Cornamona as I had arranged the previous day. Curran is his name but he's known as Mike Ned. We moved off down to Town Centre where we got on the wagon of the contractor that's doing this work in Towcester and away we went. We hadn't got the job at this stage but we went out 'on spec' and, thank God, we got the job: A lot of others came out looking for work also but some of them were sent away. I was lucky that I got a job so readily, especially as I didn't particularly look like a navvy at all – or not much.
>
> We were sent off to the store to get tools – picks and spades and crowbars, and then we made our way down to where they were breaking the ground. The engineer had marked out a big square where Mike Ned and myself were set to work, excavating to a depth of four feet. Mike Ned has been on this work since he left school and it was worth while to see him using the pick and digging at the hard ground. I thought I was as good as him and I started off like the hammers of hell belting at the ground with the pick but for all that I did I might as well have stayed at home.
>
> Mike Ned, however, showed me how to go about it properly – not to lift the pick too high and to hit in the same place always and not to be hitting haphazardly with it. I worked better after that and I tried hard because I didn't want to have any of the lads saying: 'What kind of a man is that that can't work like a proper navvy?' We worked away and when the first break came

at ten o'clock I had blisters on my hands and my back felt as if somebody had been laying about it with a stick.

We got our tea out of a big bucket and every minute of the ten-minute rest was like heaven. When the whistle blew to call us back to work, it was as if a judge was sentencing me to death; it couldn't be avoided, however, and back into the hole went my companions and myself. I kept on doing my best and shovelling but, no matter what I did, I wasn't as good as the next man. When we had a certain amount done, Mike Ned told me to change around with him; he started working on my portion and he wasn't long tearing the stuff out. Just about then the ganger came round and he said:

'Good lads, ye're doing all right. Now would ye come up behind the mixer for a while?'

My heart sank at this for I had heard so much about the same malignant mixer that I had no wish at all to go next nor near it – until I was more experienced in the work at all events. We went along anyway and what I was told to do was to shovel the sand into the hopper. Four men are supposed to work on a mixer of this kind – one driver who also throws in the bags of cement, one man who shovels in the sand and two others who shovel in the gravel – and indeed it's necessary to have the lot of them when you have a dumper or two taking the concrete away from the mixer as fast as it comes. Eight shovelfuls of sand to twice that amount of gravel and one bag of cement are the proportions laid down.

The job I had was no trouble and I could see that Mike Ned and the man with him were working much harder than I was. Shovelling sand is different from shovelling gravel; the man on the gravel puts in twice the effort. When I had worked a while at the sand, the man who was carrying the bags of cement came over and said:

'You're new to the game so I'll give you a break. Take over the bags, you, and I'll do the hard graft.'

I thanked him and did what he said but it wasn't long before I found out that the rogue had tricked me for heaving the bags was slavery compared with what I had been doing. One hundredweight was in each bag and, while the weight itself was nothing to me, for I had often carried as much, it was the devil and all to be doing it again and again without a break while the dust from the cement would choke the devil himself.

'The devil's luck to you,' said Mike Ned. 'Why didn't you stay as you were and not be such an eejit ?'

He's a great worker, Mike Ned, though he's hardly there at all, as you might say. He's never idle for a minute and as soon as the hopper is filled, he starts piling the gravel up in a heap. Any time he got the chance, he came over and heaved a bag of cement for me. I don't know at all how I'd have got through the day but for his help. I was ready to fall by the time the dinner break came and only half the day was gone by then. We wolfed the sandwiches of bread that we had with us and drank a drop of tea. I'd have given my two eyes for a pint of milk at that minute if it could have been got.

I don't know how I got through the rest of the day. I'd be exhausted and as weak as a cat and then I'd gather enough strength to keep going for another while. Be that as it may, when six o'clock came and it was time for us to go along on the wagon that would bring us homewards, I was as happy as if I was being driven in the King's own car.

I spent the night at home.

D. Mac Amhlaigh, *An Irish Navvy: the Diary of an Exile* (London: Routledge, 1964) 29–30.

100) Tang, a Chinese cook, works in southern England, 1961 [I.]

Born c.1928 in Mong Tsen Wai, New Territories, Tang (pseud.) arrived in London in 1961, and like many of the individuals in Ng's anthropological study became a restaurant worker in Britain. Tang's story is presented as an illustration of the background many Chinese immigrants came from, and of the importance of village and kinship in bringing workers to Britain. Ng states that he carried out his interviews between June 1963 and April 1964, that his interviews with restaurant workers from the New Territories were carried out mostly in the Cantonese dialect, and that he made contact by visits to the Chinese only associations, clubs and gambling houses in London

Tang, a Cantonese, came to London in May 1961. He was born and brought up in Mong Tseng Wai, the principal village on the Mong Tseng peninsula in the north-western part of the New Territories; the 500 inhabitants of this village are all Cantonese and mainly surnamed Tang. He is a bachelor, 33 years old, and comes from a family of five younger brothers and one married sister; the brothers, like him, are unmarried because they cannot afford to marry. Both his parents are still alive; in spite of their advanced age, they still personally manage a small plot of the family farm.

Tang got his first job as a cook in a Chinese restaurant in London through one of his *t'ung heung hing-tai* (fellow-villagers); the latter had since returned to the village. His parents being poor did not have sufficient money to pay for his boat fare and other necessities such as warm clothing in a cold country, so they borrowed HK$ 1,000 from two *t'ung heung shuk pak* (i.e. village uncles). Tang had to sign a contract for it, agreeing to repay the loan plus 3% interest at the end of one year; he considered the rate of interest high. However, within four months he was able to pay the debt completely; when asked how he could do so in such a remarkably short period of time, he said, 'Because I have determination [*k'ut sam*] to pay back as soon as possible.' Tang, it should be added, is a teetotaller, non-smoker, and non-gambler. In addition to having repaid his parents the sum of money which they lent him when he left for England, he is now able to remit about £100 annually to them. He also made arrangements to have his younger brother aged 30 brought over here.

According to Tang, loans from fellow-villagers could sometimes be obtained without interest; but when the rate of interest was stipulated, the borrower had to pay within the specified period, normally one or two years, sometimes even three years. Should he fail to repay the loan at the time agreed to, the interest rate might be doubled. It is almost impossible for the debtor not to honour the obligation of repaying the loan, because 'people are aware who owes whom; and if he refuses to pay, friends will "laugh" [*siu*] at him. How much a person earns in England is known to the village from which he comes, for when a worker writes home, he will invariably mention how much so-and-so earns and this news will soon spread to the entire village.' Tang added that in his village almost every one knew one another.

Since Tang came to England he has worked in several places. His first job as a cook was in a Chinese restaurant in East Ham; as mentioned earlier, it was obtained through the recommendation of one of his *t'ung heung hing-tai.* As an inexperienced cook, he was paid £8. 10s. a week. After three months there he left the restaurant. He told the writer that one day several 'teddy boys' had a five-dish meal at the restaurant; when the time came for paying the bill, they insisted that they had eaten only four dishes and refused to pay for the fifth. Thereupon a heated argument took place between the customers and the waiters, and eventually led to an exchange of blows. Tang, on hearing the squabble, rushed out from the kitchen and joined in the fight. After the incident, he, being new in England, felt 'somewhat uneasy in his heart' and so he left the job.

Again through the introduction of a village clansman, he was given a job in a Chinese restaurant in the Soho area; since he had had some experience in the kitchen, he was made a second-grade cook with a weekly wage of £10. After a year he became a *shuk shau*, i.e. an experienced hand, and was confident enough to give up his job to a fellow-villager who had some difficulty finding one because he was new in this country.

Tang, again through the help of a *t'ung heung hing-tai*, secured a more highly paid job in a restaurant in Kensington; he was paid £11. 10s., weekly but now for the first time he had to find his own accommodation; this had been provided in the first two jobs. Because of the long distance between his lodging and the restaurant Tang left the job after nine weeks there and got another in Watford, with a still higher wage: £12 a week. When a fellow villager needed extra hands to assist him in his new restaurant in Kent, Tang was offered a job at £12. 10s. a week; he accepted it because 'we are from the same village and we should help one another'. So he left the restaurant in Watford, again after nine weeks there, and joined his clansman's restaurant in Kent. Unfortunately, Tang and his clansman employer did not get on well and within three weeks they had a misunderstanding and Tang gave up the job. At the time of interview, Tang was still unemployed. But he had recently turned down a job paying £13 a week because the kitchen in which he would have to work was very dirty. He was still very confident that he would get a job soon since his *t'ung heung hing-tai* were on the look-out for any vacancy for him.

Tang was staying at a lodging-house whose owner also owned two Chinese restaurants in London. There were ten rooms in the house; the room occupied by Tang was barely furnished and uncarpeted. The number of occupants in a room could be increased by setting up more beds in it. Tang paid £1 a week for his bed.

Tang, though he had been here for nearly two years, still could not speak English; had he been able to, he would have preferred to work as a waiter. 'Those who cannot speak English have to work as cooks or dish-washers', remarked Tang. To him, waiters were more *sz man* or 'refined'. He complained that restaurant workers had to work long hours and that employers were able to conceal this fact from the 'blind government'.

K. C. Ng, *The Chinese in London* (Oxford: Oxford University Press, 1968) 38–41.

101) Prafulla Mohanti finds work as an architect, 1960s [I.]

See note on extract No.90.

To gain experience in architecture it was necessary for me to get a job, my first in England. I wrote to an architect in London. I knew his name because one of his books was prescribed for my course in Bombay. My teachers had told me he was famous. I drafted a letter and showed it to Tom. He smiled and without saying anything he changed it completely. 'My respected Sir' became 'Dear Sir' and my opening sentence, 'I most humbly beg to submit', was crossed out. 'Yours faithfully' replaced 'I have the honour to remain, Sir, your most obedient servant'. He ended the letter with 'Looking forward to hearing from you'. After a few days I received a reply calling me for an interview. The letter was addressed to 'P. Mohanti Esq.' I asked Tom what 'Esq.' meant. It was a polite substitute for 'Sir' or 'Mr' he said.

The architect's office was situated in a small Georgian terrace near Tottenham Court Road tube station. My A–Z map helped me to locate it. Tom had emphasized that I should be punctual and I got there in time for my interview at eleven.

I reported to the receptionist, who asked me to wait. After a while a man came up to me and introduced himself as the architect's partner. He helped me to carry my drawings upstairs to his room. I thought how considerate he was as this would never happen in India where the employers feel superior and use their employees like servants.

The partner was in his mid-forties, dressed in a conservative style. His room was old-fashioned with antique furniture. I was taken aback, first by the building and then by the decor, as the firm was famous for designing modern buildings.

I showed him my drawings. He examined them with great interest and said, 'I like your drawings. We like Indian architects; they're good and conscientious. But you haven't got any experience in this country.'

'If all the architects I go to say they can't offer me a job because I have no experience in this country, how do you think I'll gain experience?'

He smiled. From the expression on his face I knew he was not expecting that reply from me.

'All right. I'll give you the job.'

He showed me round the office and explained the type of work they were doing. It ranged from small housing projects to large scale office development. He introduced me to Tony, the architect I was going to work with.

His secretary brought us coffee. While drinking it he said, 'We have employed Indian architects before, but never black architects. We don't want to offend our South African clients'. Later on, when I moved around London, I saw notices in estate agents' windows: 'No blacks, no Irish, no children, no dogs'.

I was amazed that educated professional people could have such views and express them openly. The architect was honoured for his contribution to religious architecture. There were very few Indians in London. They were usually scholars, students, or the sons of the rich. When I saw an Indian in the street I felt happy. We stopped and talked to each other. The students and scholars lived in hostels around Fitzroy Square. A few Indian restaurants and grocery shops had opened to cater for their needs. The Government of India managed a hostel for Indian students, mostly doctors. They worked hard to get their qualifications as soon as possible in order to return to India. Some were married and had left their families behind.

I started my job a week later. I was worried I might not be able to recognize the architect who interviewed me. English faces looked similar to me then and I had difficulty in distinguishing one from another. But as soon as I saw him I knew it was him. That gave me confidence.

The office hours were from 9 to 5.30. I got up early in the morning and travelled by train and underground. They were always full and I had to stand all the way. The journey took nearly one hour and when I arrived wearing all my new clothes I felt so exhausted that I had to sit down quietly for half an hour to recover . . .

Tony was an associate architect in charge of several projects. Apart from me there were three young assistants in his section. They all found difficulty in pronouncing my name correctly and Tony suggested I should be called 'Paul'. I did not like the idea and they asked me if there was a shorter version for 'Prafulla'. I said there was none but my parents called me 'Kuna'. They found that easy but I felt strange at first as 'Kuna' means 'the little one'.

Tony was friendly and kept us all amused. To my dismay my first job was to design a lavatory. Plumbing was not my favourite subject but I was being paid for my work and I could not refuse. I referred to books and magazines on sanitation, designed the lavatory, and produced a set of working drawings. I was relieved when they were not only accepted by Tony but also by the partner – an expert on plumbing, Tony told me later. I was immediately given another lavatory to design. I thought I would be spending the rest of my life designing lavatories.

I visited several architects' offices nearby to find out what they were doing but was disappointed by what I saw. I met a couple of young Indian architects doing work similar to mine. Like my office, instead of designing they were simply assembling, providing space to accommodate prefabricated fittings. The manufacturers were telephoned and their representatives came round to show us their literature. They also brought samples. Materials were selected to suit the design and the price. Most of the work was done on the telephone. I often wondered what would happen if the telephone system broke down.

P. Mohanti, *Through Brown Eyes* (Oxford: Oxford University Press, 1985) 34–6.

102) Satya and her family set up home, *c.*1970 [I.]

Sociologist Ursula Sharma describes Satya, Rampal and their children as a 'representative' immigrant family, by which she means not educated or middle class. Like the majority of their peers the family are from a rural background (Punjab), have a young family and manual jobs – Satya works in a factory; Rampal as an electrician for the Ministry of Works – and a home in the west London suburbs. Sharma's study tells in turn the stories of Satya and Rampal based on tape recorded interviews over a number of sessions, presumably made around 1970, and with minimal adjustment to their accounts.

We ourselves have always supported ourselves through our own efforts, and now we are gradually getting all the things we need. We started looking for a house as soon as we had enough money for the deposit, about two years ago. We went to an estate agent, but we did not like the houses he showed us at first at all. One house belonged to some Pakistanis, but it had no fence between the front garden and the road. Leave your door just a few inches ajar and anybody's dogs and cats could get inside from the street. I told my husband, 'I don't like this house. Let us look for one with a better garden, where our children can play safely.' Then we saw some better houses, but they were all too expensive. After all, we were not sure that we would be able to get a mortgage easily, for many say that coloured people are not given mortgages readily, or at least can only get them at high rates of interest. When we saw this house I told the agent that it suited us well but it was too expensive. I asked whether the price could be reduced a little. 'Look these people are not babies, that they can be fooled into dropping £700,' he said, 'but we can certainly try. Please yourself.' So we went to see the owners ourselves. Only the owner's wife was at home, and we had to bargain with her in broken English because we did not know very much English at that time. We eventually managed to make ourselves understood and she agreed to lower the price somewhat. We accomplished this without any help from others, so cannot other people do the same?

We have decorated the two downstairs rooms in our house now that the better weather has come; the front room has beautiful shiny paper and gold coloured curtains to match, and the back room has flowered paper and a new carpet. We did all the work ourselves at the weekends. And my husband laid new lino in the kitchen and fixed strip lighting there. What I should really like now is a proper bathroom; our bathroom is downstairs and has not got a decent wash basin. I have heard that you can get a grant for your bathroom, but you would have to pay the money back, wouldn't you? And we can't afford that on top of the mortgage just now. A few weeks ago my husband bought this refrigerator second hand for a few pounds, along with some other good second hand furniture from a friend of his. And I have ordered a pair of gold earrings from an Indian goldsmith – the latest design from India. They cost about twenty pounds, gold being cheaper here than it is in India.

Except for the house itself, of course, everything we have bought we have paid for in cash. I dare say some people's houses have nicer carpets than ours and they run big smart cars, but you'll often find that they have hardly a penny left to themselves each month by the time they have paid all the hire purchase instalments they owe for these fine things. I don't believe in running up debts – I have seen the trouble it leads to – and if we have the good things we want it is because we are as careful with our pennies over here as we used to be when we were in India.

U. Sharma, *Rampal and His Family* (London: Collins, 1971) 204–5.

103) Junine Hinsman on laundry work, 1978 [I.]

Born c.1960, to Jamaican parents who settled in Britain, Junine Hinsman reluctantly left school at the age of 16 against the wishes of her parents, who had hoped she would become a music teacher. Because of the poor economic situation in Britain in the mid-1970s, which left the Hinsman family close to poverty, Junine could only find work in a laundry. T. J. Cottle's collection of 'life studies', as he refers to them, of which Junine's account is one example, resulted from two years of intensive interviewing (without a tape recorder) in the mid-1970s. An American living and working in London, the author talked to a large number of West Indian families with the intention of producing 'portraits of people, not an analysis of their lives'.

It ain't like school, you know, working for some small-time laundry. I mean, there's nothing you have to learn. Old Buzzy, after the first ten minutes, she says to me, hey, Junine, is this all there is? I mean, is this what you been doing all these months? I said, what the hell you think I've been doing, making airplanes? What could anybody do in a laundry that no 3-year-old couldn't do just as good? All she could do was shake her head, you know, like she couldn't believe it. But you told me you liked it here, she told me. You said you liked it. I told her, I told you I liked it here 'cause without this I ain't got a thing in the world, baby, not a thing in the world. I am in the laundry business, I told her. I am in cleaning, I ain't in show business, or in the happiness business. I'm in laundry. From school-leaving to laundry. So she said, well, can't they find something more interesting for us to do? So I told her, hey, you want to go ask Mr. Charles, he'll tell you he'll look into it, and baby, your old parents not only ain't going to see the outside of their nice little sixth-floor home, they're going to die up there from starvation and you won't be able to find another job to get the money you'd need to pay some man to go up there and carry them downstairs. You keep your mouth shut and keep folding up those sheets. So you know what she says to me? She says, Junine, you're a part of the system. You're working for the man like a slave. Baby, I told her, you go right ahead and call me anything you like. You want to call me a slave, then that's what I am. Working for the man, sure I'm working for the man. That's exactly what I'm going to keep on doing too, 'til someone comes along and tells me he's got a better deal for me. If slavery pays me for forty hours a week and an hour off for lunch, then slavery's my business. I'm only taking what they're pushing. The man says hop on one foot, hop on one foot, long as he says, until I die if I have to. They don't give you no choices in this game.

T. J. Cottle, *Black Testimony: The Voices of Britain's West Indians* (London: Wildwood House, 1978) 88.

Childhood and Home Life 2

104) Social distinctions among Jewish neighbours in Manchester, 1920s [I.]

Bill Williams records the following details of the speaker's biography. 'Born in 1916, Hightown. Father came to Manchester from Russia with his parents in the 1870s. Clerical Workers.' Williams' article uses oral evidence to outline the shortcomings of existing historical accounts of Jewish life in late 19th and early 20th century Manchester, in this case the myth of communal solidarity.

> The Levines were . . . she was an English woman, born here. He was foreign. But she was more foreigner if you understand what I mean. And they were, I don't know, they were, the family were more foreign, they were different from us, you know what I mean . . . a different outlook, they were a religious family, very religious family, but they were brought up more in a foreign way than we were. They have a different outlook on life, you know what I mean. Well, for instance, or, we were never allowed to take food outside. And if we wanted bread and butter, or bread and jam 'inside'. When you've eaten it, then you can go out to play. You don't eat and play. They would sit on the garden wall there eating nuts, it didn't matter if the shells were on the floor, you know, this kind of thing. Rougher, rougher in . . . a rougher way, I should say, a more foreign way. They weren't rough. I wouldn't say they were rough. They were . . . can't explain . . . they were – ah different – more – the more working class outlook, if you understand what I mean.

B. Williams, 'The Jewish immigrant in Manchester: the contribution of oral history', *Oral History*, 7 (1979) 48–9.

105) Anglo-Chinese families in the East End of London, 1935 [I.]

A relatively hostile journalistic account of East London's immigrant communities notable for an almost complete lack of personal contact with the local population.

We went out into the street again. I remarked on the number of white women standing about. They were wives of Chinese, my friend said. He assured me that there was only one Chinese woman in all the colony. The Chinese made very good husbands, kind and industrious; and if anything goes wrong with the marriage it is generally the English wife who is to blame. They are not usually Poplar women, however, who marry them, but girls from less fastidious Hoxton: Poplarites have a healthy prejudice against mixed marriages. The little Anglo-Chinese children are common features in the streets hereabouts, easily distinguishable by their slant-lidded black eyes and straight black hair. The English children admit them readily to their companionship, and except in appearance, there is no difference between them. The little half-castes speak the same Cockney language and play the same games and appear to be universally popular youngsters.

There is a Sunday School where the regular attendants include about forty of these children, generally considerably more intelligent than the pure English child of the locality. But the critical age for Eurasians is about sixteen – often they then throw back to the lower type.

H. Thorogood, *East of Aldgate* (London: George Allen and Unwin, 1935) 146.

106) Refugee children leaving for England, *c.*1938 [I.]

As the title We Came as Children: A Collective Autobiography *implies, this is an account by one particular cluster of immigrants: Europeans displaced around the time of World War Two who came to settle in Britain. While this approach effectively obliterates individual life stories (with the exception of some longer testimonies) it does allow a glimpse of the variety of immigrant experiences among a relatively cohesive group.*

¶ From my father's diary: . . . a continuous rush and chase from one agency to another; each week new decrees with their requisite documents, etc.; a chaos in which nobody knows what is happening and which, when all is settled, turns out to have been futile.

¶ It was only on the way to the station that our parents informed us that they would have to stay behind 'to clear up a few things'. My brother and I were to travel to England alone. He was seven and I was eight years old.

¶ The prospect of going to England appealed to me above all as an adventure. That we had no relatives or any connections in that country did not deter me. In any case the separation from my parents would be only temporary, since I would be spending at the most two or three years there, just a waiting period until our turn came when we could be re-united in the U.S.A., our ultimate goal. I was sixteen years old.

¶ I left home with several hundred other children in December 1938. My mother insisted on kissing me over and over again, and I got impatient with her demonstrativeness, not realising of course that this was to be out final

parting. I have often wondered since what she must have felt as a result of my impatience. I was eleven years old.
¶ Leaving home – I find I have only vague recollections of seeing my parents at the station, but I seem to remember more vividly the pleasures of the great adventure ahead – going across the sea to England. Somehow I appear to have missed any feeling of wrench, or more probably my parents – who were very sensible – managed not to show any sign of sorrow at the parting. It was all matter of fact, and see you shortly either in London or in Palestine. Rather the kind of farewell that sensible parents give a boy scout off to his first camp. I was thirteen years old.
¶ I remember crying bitterly and saying: 'Please, Mummy, please don't send me away.' I was eleven years old at the time.
¶ My father wrote numerous letters to people abroad in the hope that they could help him to leave, but all in vain. Guarantors, visas, quotas, money – these legal obstacles could not be overcome by him.
¶ I think it is difficult to separate the effects of being a refugee in a strange country from those of being separated from my parents. I was only five years old when I arrived.

K. Gershon, *We Came as Children: A Collective Autobiography* (London: Victor Gollancz, 1966) 19–20.

107) Inge, an Austrian refugee, describes life in England, *c.*1939 [I.]

Born c.1927 in Vienna, Inge was forced to leave her parents and come to Britain as a child refugee. This account is part of a private diary written in German. See also note on extract No.106 and Introduction to Part II.

I am twelve years old and have come with my sister to live in the house of Mr. and Mrs. Roberts. We have a governess, and English Miss (like in a book). Mr. and Mrs. Roberts are very upset because she told them that I am lazy and don't learn English as well as I could. If I knew English life would be easy!

Yesterday evening in bed I remembered how I had prayed to God to send me to England. Well – He granted my wish. And now I lie in bed and pray that I may soon be allowed to return to my parents, to Vienna without Hitler. Vienna is my home. I shall always remain a Viennese at heart.

When my parents found fault with me, which happened quite often, I took it to heart and thought: it's for the whole of my life. But when people in a strange country (and strangers) find fault, I immediately think the worst – that they want to bully me, don't like me, etc. When they say to us: 'Take your coats, it's cold,' I feel that this isn't said out of love for me but so that they don't lay themselves open to criticism, because they are responsible.

Mrs Roberts said: 'We give you a home, and you must keep it nice,' and I thought: and if you don't keep it nice you won't give us a home?

When I laugh I suddenly think: What have I got to laugh about? How frantically I envy other children who are able to be together with their parents. To be in a foreign country is a punishment to me! When I am dead they will have to put on my grave that here lies a child who died of homesickness.

Today Mr. Roberts told me that he would send me to an institution if I wouldn't speak English. It is only recently that I have come to love my mother-tongue above everything else. I have never had this feeling about it before. Here, everybody speaks English, from babies to grandfathers. It hurts me to hear it. And when I hear or read German somewhere, it makes my heart beat faster . . .

Where is my good temper, where is my sense of humour, my ability to enjoy life? Everything is gone. I don't care about anything – except being together again with my family. Then nothing would matter. God should have protected me from the days I am living through now.

My friend is here with her parents, and she is homesick too – for Vienna. She is homesick once and I am doubly homesick.

I have had a terrible scare, because – I can hardly write it down – because if I start going to school perhaps I shall have to continue until I am old enough to leave. I thought that I had come for a year. Now Mr. Roberts says that we would take the exam to enter school perhaps only next summer, because I still know so little English. Next summer one year will be up! They must think three to five years. Or perhaps even longer. But after the first year they will no longer have a strong healthy child.

Yesterday we were talking about Germany. Mr. Roberts asked Lieselotte: 'Didn't you have anything to eat any more?' Lieselotte: 'Oh, it wasn't as bad as that. Only, no butter, no meat, no fruit and no milk. But enough to live on.' 'Then why did you come to England?' (This might have been interpreted as a reproach, but he said it unsuspectingly and of course he meant all Jews.) 'But we couldn't live there – haven't you heard about 10th November? We couldn't go into a park, a theatre, or use a tram. In the street, anybody could do what they liked to us, the men were imprisoned, we were thrown out of our homes.' 'Oh, I see.' He found it impossible to understand, but looked very sad and seemed to be taking it to heart. He said: 'I expected to find you very nervous, my wife and I were surprised that you weren't.' (I must say he is at times a little tactless.) But soon we were talking about something else. I know, only someone who has been through it can understand, and to be honest, I wouldn't be able to understand it either.

Today I saw a letter from Mutti to Mr. Roberts lying open in the table and I read it. And in it it said something like this: I am glad that you like Lieselotte so much, and I hope the same will be the case with Inge, who is a happy, jolly child (was it once).

A relative has been visiting. She gave us sixpence and Lieselotte asked if she could accept it. Mrs. Roberts said: 'Of course, you are her adopted nieces.' That means in other words that we are her adopted CHILDREN. That is very nice of them but please, Mr. and Mrs. Roberts, don't say it, it hurts me almost as much as if you were to say 'we hate these children'. We are not your children, no, no, never!

K. Gershon, *We Came as Children: A Collective Autobiography* (London: Victor Gollancz, 1966) 57–9.

108) Weronika R., a Polish refugee, sets up home in Yorkshire, 1949 [I.]

Born c.1927 in Poland, Weronika R. was deported as a slave labourer by Germany in 1943. After liberation she went to a Displaced Persons camp. In 1948 she arrived in Britain and became a mill worker.

Weronika was a girl of 16 when in 1943 her parents and herself were deported as slave labour to Germany. The train which conveyed her to Germany was bombed by the allied planes in the vicinity of Leipzig. Both her parents were killed. She was sent to the province of Hanover where she worked on a German farm. After the Liberation she went to live in a D.P. camp. In 1948 she arrived in England engaged to work in a cotton mill in Rochdale. There she discovered that she was pregnant but was unable to establish the identity of the father of the child. The child was born in February 1949. Weronika attempted to get rid of her child by starving it and then by selling it to a Lancashire couple for £100. When this was reported to the Police she was arrested and the child taken into the custody of a Catholic religious order. Weronika was sentenced to six months' imprisonment. While she was serving her term in Durham she was looked after by a Polish Welfare Officer who in the meantime arranged for her to live in a Polish housing estate in Yorkshire. When she came there her identity and her past were only known to the Polish R.C. priest. Weronika found employment in the local industry and established close friendship with a number of Polish women living on the estate. She seems to be quite happy and hopes to marry a Polish labourer in the near future.

J. Zubrzycki, *Polish Immigrants in Britain: a Study of Adjustment* (The Hague: Nijhoff, 1956) 185–6.

109) Anant Ram's family life in Coventry, 1950s

See note on extract No.82.

When did your family come to join you?
My wife came in 1958. My son had joined me earlier in 1952. I bought my first house in 1961. This was the most happy period of my life. My daughters were married away in my absence. My father had looked after family matters in my absence. When my father died I could not go. I regret that very much now. My wife passed away here in 1987.

Have you kept in touch with folks at home?
I went back to my village in Punjab only once, in 1970. It was a rather hurriedly planned visit as I had to go to sort out a simmering dispute with another family. I stayed there for three months. I do miss many things from home. Nowadays there is not much contact with my village though some relatives still write to me. However, given the conditions in the Punjab now, it is better here.

What are your views of England and life over here? Would you regret dying here?
Well, we had no idea of foreign lands, we were in reality just illiterate villagers. We had only heard of other places, foreign countries. We just knew that the English rule over us, nothing more. We came to know the world after living here. This is a country of good life and I am quite contented with my life. Our family is into the third generation, my grandchildren are now well settled here. I do not think I could have done better. No, I think I would not regret dying here. Many of our Punjabi people now die here. It is the same for all of us. I am part of our community. This is our home now, isn't it?

D. Singh Tatla, 'This is our home now: reminiscences of a Punjabi migrant in Coventry', *Oral History*, 21 (1993) 73.

110) Paul George encounters London for the first time, 1960s [I.]

Born in Grenada, West Indies, c.1950, Paul George was 16 when he wrote this account.

When we landed at Heathrow we were shown where to go. We had a little money. I remember eating a box of smarties. Finder, Kathleen and Pauline was busy looking round and saying – 'Are we in England, when do we reach?' Some people came, they were looking at us, they was speaking funny. Then a lady came and ask our names, hugged and kissed us. It was our Mummy.

We were led away, we was looking round – could this be England? No hills, all flat land. We went into a car, looking around at the scenery. Mummy and daddy talking, none of us talking back, just said yes or no. This place looked so strange. We had been travelling a long time. We stopped in front of a house. It had a wall in front. We got out, someone opened the door, we got in. It was strange inside and nice. It had a carpet and other things. We went into a room, it was big with chairs and a television. We saw our eldest sister, Avis, who had come up before us. It was a Sunday, Tarzan was on the television. I watched it fascinated, having never seen one before.

They gave us rice and peas and stewed chicken to eat and pineapple juice with ice. We watched television, there was so many things. I went out the front, the door was locked after me. I was looking round, the sun was shining.

> I wanted to get back but which was the house? I could not tell the difference. I was lost but someone opened a door of the house I was standing in front of and called my name, I ran inside. They took us upstairs, when I was coming down I fell down and felt funny.
>
> They gave me some money; they said it was three pence, I thought it was three cents. I went out and asked in a shop for three cents of sweets. The man must have understood because he gave me some sweets.

P. George, *Memories* (London: Commonplace Workshop, 1976) 15.

111) A Punjabi boy's race education, Bradford, 1960s [I.]

Robert Perks gives the following comments on his subject's autobiography. 'The interviewee was brought up in Manningham [Bradford] and was one of the first Asian children to enter Bradford's educational system, he was able to highlight the changes in policy and attitudes as more migrants arrived and as younger Asians began to respond to the emergence of overt racism and discrimination.' Perks' interviewee was a Sikh man, born in 1954 in Punjab, India, who wished to remain anomymous.

> . . . As a child, a young child, I never realised I was an Asian kid, the only Asian kid in the school or one of very few, and . . . the earliest memory I have of realising that I was different was actually when more people had come across and there were more families and things settling in, and that's probably when I was about twelve. And there was some discussion started by the teacher, or the teacher was pointing to somebody, and she was trying to convince the pupils, or try to tell them that all human beings are the same, and they shouldn't have these prejudices and if you think they smell, Japanese people think we smell because we smell of meat because we eat meat. And its . . . and I became conscious then actually, you know, I felt embarrassed, and I felt very conscious that somehow I was different. You know . . .
>
> **Not until then?**
> No, not until then.
>
> **So was it a change in attitude amongst the people around you, or in yourself?**
> First of all I think it was a change in attitude in people around me er . . . not to me, I mean I don't . . . not to me at that stage, or not to me ever actually, because one of the things I remember, and other Asian youngsters will say this, is that the other used to comment at all 'Oh I didn't mean you', after making a sort of . . . 'you're all right', you know, 'you're one of us.' So it wasn't to me . . . but it was, it was reaction towards others that started coming out, because . . . now there were others. And unfortunately there's a connection between me and those others which I couldn't escape even

though they themselves tried to say 'Oh it doesn't affect you because you're one of us.'

R. Perks, '"You're different: you're one of us": the making of a British Asian', *Oral History*, 15 (1987) 67.

112) An Italian teenage girl's view of parental authority, Bedford, 1970 [I.]

See note on extract No.86.

Well, you know, you go to work and someone says 'I went out with my boy-friend last night.' Went to a dance or went out somewhere. When they ask: 'What did you do?' I have to say I stayed in, helped my mum, watched the telly, did the washing-up. Italian parents, they are more particular than the British. If you are late home from work, 'What were you doing?' When you want to go out, 'Where are you going?' They expect you to do what they say. Sometimes it's difficult. You want to go out somewhere and your mum says you will have to ask your dad. Women have no say. Dad's the authority. Well, perhaps he comes back tired from the brickworks. Just wants to sit down and watch telly. Perhaps he can't be bothered to talk about it. He just says, 'I am your father. You will do this or that. No argument. Finish.' Maybe, now and then, they will let you go to the Italian youth club. That is all right, more or less, although they have their doubts about that. Anywhere else is not all right.

It is not always all right with me. You see your English friends from school or from work doing all those things you can't do. Well, I don't like to argue with my parents. I wouldn't want to do anything to hurt them. I know how bad they would feel if I did. But when it comes to marriage, that will be something different. Who I marry will be my own business. I don't know if I will fall in love with an Italian or an English boy. But whoever it is, it'll be me who will have to live with him for the rest of my life, not them. So it will have to be my choice then.

J. Brown, *The Un-Melting Pot* (London: Macmillan – now Palgrave Macmillan, 1970) 91.

113) A Punjabi boy in school, Bradford, 1960s–70s [I.]

See note on extract No.111.

. . . when I left Green Lane and went to Frizinghall, although in Green Lane I was in the top five, at Frizinghall I was put in the second stream, not the top stream, and I had to do well in the Christmas exams and got in the top stream. In Frizinghall, at the final exams, I came second through out the whole school, because I was (inaudible) . . . common, and second in the top stream, and when I went to Belle Vue I was put in the third stream. And even my deputy headmistress made a fuss about that, but they didn't move me to the top stream where I felt I naturally belonged. And then, I mean, I put down an option for a language because I came top in French. You see my interest in languages was already developing, and . . . I got left with a choice of er . . . handicraft, which I was useless at, woodwork, which I hated, and music right, which I . . . (laughs) . . . again, you know, I wasn't interested in the slightest. And, and not German which I wanted to do as my other option. And eventually I had to go just stand in the German queue and just join the class to get in, and as I say I went on to do 'A' Level. And again at the Christmas exams I had to prove myself again, to get into the top stream, which I did. But I mean I couldn't understand that at all. Personally I think, you know I'm on a different level. I mean obviously I've had things shouted at me, not by people I know, but other people you know . . . 'Wog' or, or whatever, and things which hurt and things which I'd turn round and be ready to fight people . . . at that stage of my life anyway. And I'm sure, I mean I can't clearly remember, but I'm sure I must have got into one or two situations because of that. I remember once in the dinner queue, em . . . I was just sat down eating as the queue was going by, and it, it's a remark . . . it's something and nothing, but I can remember the other person saying you know, he was stood up because he was in the queue and I was eating, he said 'Well chop-chop', in a very funny accent, and I took that as a racist remark, and I stood up immediately and I think I threw a glass of water over him or something, but I can remember that kind of thing happening. And I was ready, you know, ready to fight it out at any time.

R. Perks, '"You're different: you're one of us": the making of a British Asian', *Oral History*, 15 (1987) 70–1.

114) Satya on elderly relatives in immigrant families, 1970s [I.]

See note on extract No.102.

Once we had settled in here the next decision which we had to make was whether to invite my husband's father over to join us. Before we had left India we had told him that we would always send him money anyway, and so we did. We never wanted him to feel resentful or say 'They went away and deserted me.' We did not fear that he would not be properly looked after; in India some neighbour will always tend a sick person or bring water to an invalid who finds himself alone, and anyway my brother-in-law had agreed that the old man should live with him. But we did not want anyone to feel bitter about the matter or to say after we had gone, 'That is all very fine for you – running off to England to earn money while we are left to care for your old man.' Even though we sent plenty of money people might have gossiped and we did not want them to say, 'They left the poor old fellow to starve.'

People notice things and we did not want to feel any cause for shame in front of them. But I soon came to realise from what I saw of the condition of elderly Indians brought to this country that we would certainly have been doing wrong to bring my father-in-law over here. I have seen it happen over and over again and it is people's own fault; the old people get their son's letter from England telling them of his prosperity and their hearts begin to blacken. 'They are having a fine time over there,' they think 'they are not sparing a thought for us left behind in India.' (Fine time indeed – they don't know how hard you have to work over here to earn your money.) Or they feel discontented that their sons do not write to them more often – as though anyone over here had time to sit down and write to India every day. So the son brings his old mother or father here, and at first they are delighted. 'Now we shall be with our son at last,' they think as they step into the plane. 'Everything will be all right; every day they will give us meat to eat, even wine if we want it. We shall pass our old age in ease and luxury.' And suppose an old man arrives on a Saturday everything is all right for the first day; and on Sunday he likes England very much also. But when the son has to run to his work and the daughter-in-law to her factory! They know that the old man may not know how to use the gas stove or the geyser and the other appliances which we use over here, and they know that it may be dangerous for him; if he were to turn on the gas and forget to light it he might be dead before anyone arrived home and found out. So they leave some food already prepared or pack something in a Thermos flask. And when the poor old fellow has to eat stale food at mid-day he begins to think, 'I was all right where I was in India. At least over there I got food fresh and hot from the stove. Did I come so many miles just to eat stale bread?' And when the young people come in from school or work they are tired out. 'Make us a cup of tea,' says the old man as soon as his daughter-in-law appears, or, 'What about some nice hot vegetables now?' But she is so tired and stiff from standing and running around all day that she can't jump up that very minute to fulfil his demands. So the old man gets angry and peevish – because in India the young people wait on their elders and respect their every wish. 'She didn't even ask if I felt hungry,' he says to himself. 'All very well calling me "father-in-law" and then not even making me a cup of tea when I need it!'

The old people get bored and lonely over here, too. It is hard enough for us to learn a new language and adjust to new ways, but they are past the age when they can adapt easily. If they want company while the others are out all day, or if they want to know something, whom can they go and ask? An old person here is as helpless as a child and must rely on someone else coming to tell him. He cannot understand the people around him, nor can they understand him. I can get a baby-minder for my baby, but where could I leave my poor old father-in-law?

U. Sharma, *Rampal and His Family* (London: Collins, 1971) 197–9.

115) Jamie Pinkerton on the family responsibilities of a son, 1978 [I.]

Born c.1965 in Britain to Jamaican parents who settled in London, Jamie Pinkerton (pseud.) was 13 years old at the time of this interview. See also note on extract No.103.

You can see with your own eyes how things stand with me and my family. We got three boys, all of us in school, but me thinking I'm about to leave. No purpose in it for me. Maybe my brothers will think different, but for me there's no future there. My grandmother has been sick long as I can remember. I think maybe she gets the right help and the right medicine, but how can I be sure? I don't make visits to hospitals to see how they're treating everybody. If I had to guess, I would say my school and her hospital are just about the same. They're both all right. They could be worse, but you know from just looking at us that we aren't getting the best deal this city is offering to people. My mother, well, she'll keep taking care of us, and taking care of my grandmother. Probably when my grandmother dies, my mother will go hunting around for some other old lady to take care of, just so she has something worthwhile to do. My mother's unemployed too, you know, like my father was when he was here. She hasn't got a job that pays. So what's she going to do? She shops, she stands in the queue at the post office collecting all the payments she gets each week, and then what else can she do? If she didn't have my grandmother to worry over, she'd be looking around for work. This way she has a little satisfaction in her life, if you can call that satisfaction. My brothers, like I say, go to school, and as long as they stay out of trouble we don't have to worry about them. See how I say 'we', like I was becoming the father in my family instead of one of the sons. Well, maybe a little of that is happening; maybe a lot of it. Somebody has to be the man there, and with my father still away I guess it has to be me. My mother doesn't turn me into a father, but my brothers do. I got to tell them all the time, 'Hey, don't look at me, man, I don't earn the money around here.' I don't think Henry understands where the money comes from at all. It's sort of sad for him because he can't even remember his father, my father. It's like he really never had a father. We got pictures of him, and the letters he sends. My mother and me, we'll go shopping and buy something for him and tell him it came from my father, but it doesn't help him. He can't remember him. How could he?

T. J. Cottle, *Black Testimony: The Voices of Britain's West Indians* (London: Wildwood House, 1978) 25–6.

116) Warren Oster on the psychological effect of poor housing, 1978 [I.]

Born c.1920 in Jamaica, Warren Oster (pseud.) arrived in London with his family c.1960. According to T. J. Cottle, Warren had lost count of the number of flats the family has rented over the years. See also note on extract No.103.

> It pulls me so far down, my home. I come back from work, you know how this can be true, and I reach the corner, the turning even into the street where I can see the building, that's all, just see it, and it's like I've just remembered something that I was supposed to get, but it's too late now to get it. So I must go home, every night of my life with this feeling that something important hasn't been taken care of. Does this make sense to you? It's like some men receive their sad news in the post. My sad news is the house. I think of it, and it is my sad news; I see it, I wake up in it, I go to sleep in it, and this is my sad news. I haven't done so poorly in my life that I should have it this way, you know. Not at all, not at all. I tell myself, Warren, you did the best you could, you could even say you did better than all right, too. I talk this way to myself, as you know. But then I see it, between other buildings, down the road, it's waiting for me. It's waiting for me like it wants to tell me something, give me a message, and the message is: Warren Oster, you are a liar. You tell lies, only to yourself, but this still makes you an evil liar. I am an evil liar. I tell myself, I do all right, I've done good for years, years running into more decades now than I want to count, but my home tells me, you couldn't have done all that well and end up coming home every night to this kind of place. This isn't a coming home to a successful sort of place. Not by any stretch of the imagination, my imagination or anybody else's.

T. J. Cottle, *Black Testimony: The Voices of Britain's West Indians* (London: Wildwood House, 1978) 130.

117) Doreen Grainger on past and present, 1978 [I.]

Born c.1965 to Jamaican parents who settled in Britain, Doreen Grainger (pseud.) was aged 11 and living with her parents in Clapham at the time of this interview. See also note on extract No.103.

> See, that's what's important about history; that you can sort of be alive when you weren't really alive. That's why teachers should tell you about the people who were alive then, and not just the things that happened. Because then you can pretend that you were alive too, when they were alive, or you'll pretend that you will be alive when you know you won't be alive any more. You can pretend that what's going to happen when you're not here is what happened to people a long time ago when you weren't here either. That way, learning about history is like making believe you could live three different

> lives instead of just one life: the life you have, the life people had before you were born, and the life people are going to have after you die. So you can know about things and pretend about things too. Maybe things have always been the same; I don't think so, but maybe for some people they are. But people don't look like they did millions of years ago, so how could other things be the same?
>
> I was just thinking, maybe what I want to know about history is whether everything will be for my family like it is now. I mean, it's fun to know about other people, but I want to know whether it will always be like this for me and my family. And then how will it be when I get older, and then very old? Nobody can see the future, but they can see what history was like, only not the kings. The kings don't tell me anything about me, or anybody I know. They only tell what it's like for the important people, rich people, like in government. Maybe that's why we study them, because the rich people in government like the kings, they tell the rest of us how we have to be, so maybe that's why we have to read about them, although my teacher doesn't say this. One thing that isn't fair is just reading about the rich people who lived long, long ago. They, for sure, don't tell me anything about me or people like us. Except there's always rich people, so maybe I'll have to get rich so somebody will write a history book about me. But that's for sure never going to happen. All you have to do is figure out a little what happened to your own family long, long ago, and you know *that's* never going to happen. I guess history makes me sad sometimes.

T. J. Cottle, *Black Testimony: The Voices of Britain's West Indians* (London: Wildwood House, 1978) 156–7.

118) Nazrah on the reputation of a daughter in an Asian family, 1989 [I.]

Born c.1975 Nazrah (pseud.) is a Muslim born in Britain. At the time of her interview she was looking forward to moving back to Pakistan with her family. Audrey Osler's Speaking Out *is based on group discussions with three sets of fourth year students (aged 14–15) in Birmingham secondary schools over a period of six months. The author's purpose was to ensure 'that people had a chance to hear what black girls and young women had to say about life, and about their own lives in particular'.*

> At home we're different, but when we go out we're expected to behave in a certain way. It's the same between Britain and Pakistan. Here we can do things which our parents wouldn't expect us to do if we were in Pakistan. In Pakistan we'll be expected to act in a more ladylike and disciplined way. When we are at home here we can relax and be ourselves. But when we go out people can look at us and tell other people about our behaviour. News passes fast. At home we can be wild ones, hitting whichever of our brothers and

sisters go past, and telling each other to shut up! When we go to someone's house we don't do that. It's got a lot to do with reputation.

Sometimes, if I've had an argument with my parents, I feel like shouting out: 'All you care about is the reputation!' because arguments are always about something which has happened in front of somebody. With Asian families reputation is the first thing because if you've got a bad reputation nobody wants to know you. You've got to keep that reputation going. It's very important for girls because when the time comes for them to get married if they've been seen to behave well then that will be an extra boost if they want to get married to a particular person.

Izzat means 'reputation', 'honour', the same thing. In Asian families it's the thing. The woman takes more responsibility for izzat than the man. If you get followed by boys, for example, most Asian parents are likely to blame it on the girls not the boys. They might swear at the boys but you get looks of disapproval from your parents. My dad will shout at the boys but my mum will look at us, give us dirty looks saying, 'You've called them upon us.'

A. Osler, *Speaking Out: Black Girls in Britain* (London: Virago Upstarts, 1989) 98.

Community 2

119) A Greek Orthodox church service, London, 1903 [I.]

In his journalistic account of 'Some Foreign Places of Worship in London' F. M. Holmes includes a description of religious ceremonial practice among London's Greek Orthodox believers.

From the flashing sunlight of a bright spring day we turn into the crowded Church of St Sophia, Moscow Road, Bayswater. The large congregation has risen to its feet. Priests, generously arrayed, advance from the richly painted altar-screen towards an open space under the dome. One, the Archimandrite, bears a lighted candle in his hand, while a sonorous voice proclaims in modern Greek, a sentence which may be thus interpreted:

All come and take the light that never sets, and embrace Christ, Who has risen from the dead.

The second priest, and the lay-reader after him, light their candles at that of the Archimandrite, repeating the sonorous proclamation, and then persons from the congregation move forward, not in a hurried, disorderly rush, but quietly, one or two at a time, and light the tapers which they hold in their hands, at the larger candles borne by the priests. These individuals among the congregation in their turn allow their neighbours to do likewise, and thus the light is passed round the church to nearly everyone in the large and beautiful building. It is the service of the Resurrection, celebrated on Easter Sunday, in the Greek Church. The lighting of the candles is symbolic, and is said to represent the new light which came into the world with Christ – the new teaching of the Gospel.

The service proceeds. The choir sings superbly. The sonorous voice sounds frequently.

The crowded congregation – or by far the greater number – remains standing throughout, though the service lasts for nearly two hours. The dark southern faces appear very attentive, and the worshippers make the sign of the cross at frequent intervals. Some who might be Greek sailors, though dressed in their best, are here; others evidently are prosperous merchants. It is a festival service, the church is light and bright and ornate, the gleam of hundreds of candles shines on rich marbles, and during the morning the priest proclaims:

If any be pious and a lover of God, let him enjoy this beautiful and bright festal gathering. At the close, when the last notes of the choir have died away and the sonorous voices are heard no more, the priests make their way through the throng to tables by the main entrances; and there they distribute gaily coloured genuine Easter eggs to the crowds of worshippers according to ancient custom and as a sign of rejoicing.

G. R. Sims (ed.), *Living London*, vol. 3, (London: E. Arnold, 1903) 229–30.

120) 'The First War of Tiger Bay', 1919 [I.]

See notes on extract No.94.

Killing and burning appeared in the streets of Cardiff and were soon to arrive at Somerset Street in Grangetown.

At that time Beatrice Headley was ten and had just celebrated a party with all the neighbouring children who unlike her were white. They had all gone home after thoroughly enjoying themselves, having consumed jelly and blancmange and the like. Then, quite suddenly, chaos! A neighbour excitedly appeared at the front door shouting, 'They're on their way! Get him out or they'll kill him!' Agnes ran with James to the back door encouraging him to flee over the back wall to safety else he should die or be beaten senseless if the rioters found him in the house. As James fled Agnes took Beatrice by the hand and rushed upstairs to the landing. Beatrice knew nothing of the 'whys and wherefores' of all this commotion and was more confused than terrified as she hid away among the folds of the skirt of her mother's long, dark, floor-length dress. Sombre clothes were customary in those days. They did not know what happened at Pop and Nana Fridays across the street but out of the many voices roaring in the street one was heard to say, 'Not here! Next door!'

Light from a flashlight could be seen through the glass window of the front door as Beatrice and her mother peered down from the landing. Suddenly, a few thuds and the door was broken through. While men ran into the downstairs rooms, Beatrice in her fear implored her mother to hide themselves under the bed, the safest place in the world in the mind of child. But it wasn't them that the rioters wanted. Iron Ford, who had already escaped, was their prey.

Disappointed at not finding him they began to ransack and destroy the home. Agnes was attacked and struck to the floor while rioters poured paraffin over the living room table about to set fire to the house. 'Better not!' a voice blurted out, 'It's not their house!' With that they left.

Holding on to each other in fear was the only consolation for mother and daughter as they awaited the arrival of a constable. The police arrived the following day and for all her troubles Agnes was blamed for marrying a black man! Beatrice was now keenly aware that she was 'coloured' and needed to know what this was all about. Her mother however was too stunned to console her, being unable to get over the loss of her cozy little home. It was not long before a visit was paid by the landlord who demanded that they leave or he would evict them. He wasn't having his property nearly burnt down on account of any black man. So into the streets they went . . .

In Tiger Bay things were different. The 'Bayites' were armed to the teeth. Chinese restaurateurs provided 'plenty pepper' to the housewives, pepper which was hurled into the faces of the horses on which the white rioters rode down into Bute Street. As the horses reared up and the white men fell, Tiger Bay men, women, boys and girls of every race and nationality you can think of pounced upon them and gave them the hiding they never forgot. Legend still proclaims Tiger Bay as a dangerous place to go!

No, there were no easy or defenceless victims to be had here. Tiger Bay was a fortress. In the days to follow, police manned the two bridges that were the northern entrances to Tiger Bay – the one at the top end of Bute Street and the one at the top of Canal Parade. Both bridges spanned the West Junction Canal. As the white rioters approached the bridges on horseback they were told by the police that if they 'went down there' they entered at their own risk because 'They are ready for you down in the Bay'. There were a few West African, West Indian, Arab and Somali families living in Herbert Street and the surrounding areas, just outside the protective enclave of Tiger Bay proper. They however did not fare so well.

Tiger Bay was the safest haven in Britain for men of colour. The people of Tiger Bay fought well for this tiny piece of land, for their community's right to be. Our Celtic mothers fought in this battle too and preserved a harmonious multi-racial way of life which forms one of the most endearing aspects of community life in the history of South Wales. In honour of that early valiant struggle this battle should rightfully be referred to as the 'First War of Tiger Bay' to commemorate the community's keen spirit of togetherness. The legend of the knife-carrying inhabitants of Tiger Bay may have its root here in the need for self defence against a violent and hostile host nation.

N. M. C. Sinclair, *The Tiger Bay Story* (Treforest: Zenith, 1993) 32–5.

121) Joe Clough, a Jamaican in Bedford, 1919–68 [I.]

Joe Clough was born on Jamaica in 1886. He arrived in England in 1906, working first as a personal servant and later as a bus drives. In the Great War he was an ambulance driver in France. Afterwards he worked as a taxi driver in Bedford until 1949, then ran his own taxi business until he retired in 1968, aged 82. See also note on extract No.86.

The only immigrant of note [before the Great War] is a man of colour. His name is Joe Clough. He has a unique place in the town's history, and it would be just to call him the doyen of Bedford's immigrants.

Born in Jamaica in 1886, he came to England in 1906 as personal servant to a rich Jamaican doctor and planter. When his master returned home, Joe became a London bus driver on the No.11 route between Liverpool Street and Wormwood Scrubbs. In 1911, he married his English wife, Margaret, two years older than himself, whose father kept a Pub in the City. As an ambulance driver in France throughout the First World War, he was proud that everywhere he was liked and accepted, 'No trouble, no trouble at all nowhere. Nobody mentioned my colour. I was like a king there. They even made me captain of the cricket team.'

Demobbed in 1919, he settled soon after in Bedford, working as a bus driver until after the Second World War, and then running his own taxi business from 1949 until his retirement in November 1968. He was then 82. A flood of retirement cards and good wishes marked Bedford's affection for Joe. 'People have been so kind,' says his wife; 'I think he's the luckiest coloured man living.'

He can recall only three incidents that have marred some fifty years of life in Bedford. The first was at a corporals' dance in Kempston Barracks just after the First World War. A captain demanded drunkenly 'Who gave that damned nigger an invitation? Get him out of here.' Joe perforce withdrew. Later, he received a regimental apology. Some time after, he was temporarily laid off from his job through false reports that other drivers objected to his colour. He was quickly reinstated and everywhere won respect as an excellent and steady driver.

The most dramatic incident took place in the Second World War. Walking back from the garage one night, passing near the river, he was noticed by three American servicemen.

'Hey, see what I see? Let's get the black bastard!'

'Nobody talk to me like that. Don't think I'm a blinking mug.'

'Come on, let's pitch the bastard into the river.'

'You are not in America, you know. You're in Bedford and don't forget it.'

At this point appeared a British Army corporal, who knew Joe.

'Don't you dare touch him, he's one of us.'

'We squared up to them,' said Joe, 'and all the Americans turned away liked whipped dogs.'

Unknown to Joe, his wife 'raised Cain and Abel' with the American authorities. An American officer visited their home to apologise.

As driver, character, and private person, Joe has total acceptance in Bedford. No doubt the fact he was unique helped make it so. No doubt the pattern could never be repeated. But this is not the whole explanation. One should also reckon what he has given to Bedford. Skill and integrity in his profession: a constant and kindly involvement in community life, giving

> readily, demanding nothing: and with these things, a pattern of family life to disarm the harshest critic. What he and his wife have made between them is not a small thing. They live deservedly in peace and in the town's esteem.
>
> Now things change, Joe recognises: relationships deteriorate, attitudes to colour harden, the situation everywhere becomes 'a bit niggly'. On the one hand, he regrets those immigrants whose bad behaviour taints the reputation of their fellows: on the other, the instances of local people refusing jobs to properly qualified coloured men. The time of danger, he says, will be when the new generation of immigrants are educated and come to compete with local people for the skilled jobs. 'That's when the trouble going to start.'

J. Brown, *The Un-Melting Pot* (London: Macmillan – now Palgrave Macmillan, 1970) 23–5.

122) The Welsh Chapels in Liverpool, 1890–1930 [M.]

Merfyn Jones identifies the speaker here as Mr C. T. J., born 1906, Liverpool. The author states his intention was to examine the internal workings of the immigrant community, since apart from one remarkable published source, 'information of this kind is virtually non-existent'.

> The people who went to Princes' Road (chapel) and paraded the Princes' Boulevard on a Sunday morning, you know there were streams of them . . . these people paraded the Boulevard, went to the very end of the Boulevard whether you passed where you lived or not . . . because you were someone of some consequence, you know, and dressed for the occasion, I mean . . . fantastic really . . . they really did fancy themselves . . . There were a lot in cotton, insurance, banking and so on. They weren't all bank managers you know, clerks and that sort of thing, awful lot of them. The second generation people had had the advantage of decent schooling. It was the ambition of Welsh parents to try and get them into the Collegiate or the Institute, particularly the boys, that's who they used to bother about most, and once they were there, they found it fairly easy, through Welsh connections, to get into the banks, particularly the Midland, and into the insurance offices, the Royal in particular.

M. Jones, 'Welsh immigrants in the cities of North-West England, 1880–1930: some oral testimony', *Oral History*, II (1981) 34.

123) Irish Catholics in the Gorbals, Glasgow, 1920s–30s [M.]

Father Canning's recollections were originally recorded c.1980 for the BBC Radio Scotland documentary series Odyssey.

> Religion was virtually the only security they had, 'cause they hadn't much of the world's goods and they found comfort and strength in their religion. Also they found security in that they could go for example to the local priest and he was there to assist them in many ways, very often doing things that we now take for granted – like writing letters, getting houses, jobs and so on. Also fighting their battles for social equality. So the priest played a very important role in their life and also the Church afforded them an opportunity for meeting their fellow countrymen, or fellow county men, or even fellow townsmen and this itself was a source of help to them, because they were able to rely on each other.

B. Kay, 'From the Gorbals to Gweedore', in B. Kay (ed.) *The Complete Odyssey: Voices from Scotland's Recent Past* (Edinburgh: Polygon, 1996) 6.

124) Donall Mac Amhlaigh celebrates St Patrick's Day, 1950s [M.]

See note on extract No.87.

> *Feast of St. Patrick of the Gael.* A box of shamrock arrived from home this morning. I was free for the first part of the day and I went out to Mass. I couldn't believe that there were so many people from Ireland in the city. Every fourth person that I met had the shamrock up and the church was full to overflowing. After Mass, they hung around outside the church just as they do at home and I have to say that I never saw such fine strong men and such lovely girls for a long time. I was pleased and proud to see them like that for those up where I work are pretty poor types.
>
> I wandered off down the city by myself and dropped into a pub where the Irish gathered. To tell you the truth I wouldn't have been able to go in for a drink but for the fact that Bert, my room-mate, gave me a pound that morning. He asked me if I was going out for a few drinks in honour of the Saint. I said I wasn't. He then tried to find out the reason for this as he found it incredible that an Irishman wouldn't have a drink on St. Patrick's Day. He sensed soon enough what the trouble was and he said nothing more but pressed a paper pound into my hand. There was one generous Englishman for you although as a race they're not noted for liberality.
>
> The Admiral Rodney was the name of the pub I dropped into and it was full to the doorways with fine Irish boys, all of them knocking back their pints. I made my way in and got a drink for myself, keeping an eye out the whole time in case I'd see a man from Connemara. There weren't any there, however; it seemed that most of the men were from the County Mayo. These lads had none of the foreign airs that the women up at the hospital had and, but for their being dressed so well, you'd have thought that you were back in a pub in the West of Ireland on a fair-day.

They have the habit here – the Irish as well as everybody else – of moving from pub to pub instead of staying in the one place as we do at home. When the fun was at its highest in the Rodney, the boys started moving off. At first, I thought they were going off home for their dinner but when I asked one of the men he said no, they were going down to the Bull. The crowd down there would come up to the Rodney and so on. I thought to myself that I had better get down to the Bull to see what was going on there that was different from here so I followed the crowd out.

The lads here are very friendly and, unless you were careful, you'd be in the company in no time and they'd be buying drinks for you. I wasn't in any position to be joining company like that for I had only the pound Bert had given me and I wanted to keep something out of it for later in the evening.

One of the men down at the Bull had an accordion and was knocking great music out of it. There was hardly a jig or a horn-pipe that he didn't play and I could feel the heart rising inside me. I'd have given anything to have been able to stay until closing time but I had to go on duty at one o'clock and I was late for the dinner already.

D. Mac Amhlaigh, *An Irish Navvy: the Diary of an Exile* (London: Routledge, 1964) 10–11.

125) A musical evening in Tiger Bay, 1950s [I.]

See note on extract No.94.

When the Annex closed at midnight and there was nowhere else to go you could always find a welcome at Mrs Grahams on the corner of Sophia Street and Canal Parade. In that little front room Tiger Bay stomped the night away. There you could hear Ritchie Valens sing 'La Bamba' or Sam Cooke sing 'You Send Me' and you could listen to all the Rhythm & Blues groups you never heard on the BBC. And if the electric went and there was not a 'shilling' between us there was always Mrs Graham's pots and pans and Mingo could play a mean quatro (four string guitar).

Another venue that closed at midnight, expelling its Bacchanalian night revellers into the streets of Tiger Bay in search of more fun, was the Cardiff International Athletic Club – known to everyone as the 'CIACS' (pronounced 'Kayaks'). All opposing rugby teams, including the Fijians and Moaries, were entertained there after the game – no matter who won or lost. At that time the club was located at the top of Bute Street near Custom House Street right next to the Bute Street railway bridge.

A staircase of several flights led you to the top floor where you would discover a dance floor that appeared to be bouncing away as the stomping Kayak revellers were enjoying a Saturday night revel. The Taylor Brothers, who could do a good Mills Brothers interpretation of 'Up A Lazy River', were a regular feature – to the joy of all the members, who couldn't resist singing along. And of course the team had to sing the by then traditional round of 'The River Boat Song'.

Once out in the street 'the Boys' made there way to Old Loudoun Square and many a night in my back bedroom I wished I was old enough to go out and join them. You could hear them strumming guitars, singing risque calypsos like Lord Kitchener's 'Kitch Come Go To Bed' or doing their imitation of the Platters to songs like Paul Anka's 'Diana', The Diamonds' 'Little Darling' and Roy Hamilton's 'Unchained Melody'. In those days there was definitely high life in Loudoun Square. But sooner or later the night would go quiet again.

The hottest teenage night spot in Tiger Bay, the 'Sixpenny Hop', was located, would you believe in the Old Vestry (This building, which is still standing, once stood at the corners of North Church Street and West Church Street.) Scores of local youth queued up outside for the doors to open to hear Bobby Freeman sing 'Do You Wanna Dance' or Danny and the Juniors' 'At the Hop'. Thanks to Father Bradley and Father Lewis (both of St. Mary's Church) and to Rita Ali (now in Denver, Colorado) and Sandra Cockle (now in Truro, Cornwall) and me, Tiger Bay kids had the best value for a 'Tannner'.

I remember when Joe Erskine ('Joey') won his big fight. Crowds were around his door in Old Angeline Street opposite the Bute Pub in Nelson Street. There among the crowd was Clara Graham ('Mingo' to us) with guitar in hand, Hannah Graham and Pepsi (Peter Findlayson that is). The crowd were all singing the calypso 'Hold Him Joe!'

N. M. C. Sinclair, *The Tiger Bay Story* (Treforest: Zenith, 1993) 72–3.

126) Polish political refugees, 1951 [I.]

A view from The Newer Statesman and Nation *(8 December 1951) on the limit of Polish postwar assimilation.*

The observer, doing his best to be objective, cannot escape the conclusion that politics to these people means no more and no less than the fight for the 'liberation' of their countries. In their political literature, page after page, is the assumption that war is certain; 'In the future war . . .'; 'When the next war breaks out . . .'; 'The next war will be carried on with all the forces available until the total annihilation of one of the adversaries.' It was curiously disturbing to read this in a Lancashire terraced house during the opening weeks of the Sixth Assembly of the United Nations. These are people, it seems, who indeed have a vested interest in a Third World War. And it is ominous that many of them have now been over here long enough to consider taking out naturalisation papers, but hardly any of them have done so. Ask them, and they all give the same reply: 'We are grateful to you, of course, but this is not our home. Some day we will really go home.' The tragedy is that this attitude is really so human and understandable; they have families and friends to the East of the Iron Curtain. It may be that, if the forces of peace should prove greater than those of war, these unfortunate people will slowly forget their past, and look instead towards the future of their children, born in Lancashire. But ultimate 'assimilation' will probably have to wait for another generation.

J. Zubrzycki, *Polish Immigrants in Britain: a Study of Adjustment* (The Hague: Nijhoff, 1956) 167.

127) Summing up the Notting Hill riots, 1959 [I.]

Urban Sociologist Ruth Glass here provides a detailed summary, with a numbers of passages from contemporary eyewitness and commentary sources, of the Notting Hill disturbances of 1958.

On September l5th, Mr. Justice Salmon gave judgment in the trial of the nine 'nigger-hunting' youths. It was an exceptionally severe sentence, and it has, therefore, become a very controversial one. It was meant to have a deterrent effect, and it probably had that effect, at least for a time. For after September l7th, it could be said that the temperature in and around North Kensington had become normal again. Standards of normalcy had, however, changed. Since the 'riots' sporadic aggression against coloured people in those marginal parts of West London has become routine, though it does not follow a regular curve. It has been an uneasy truce. Mr. Justice Salmon told the nine offenders:

'It was you men who started the whole of this violence in Notting Hill. You are a minute and insignificant section of the population who have brought shame upon the district in which you lived, and have filled the whole nation with horror, indignation, and disgust.'

The Judge expressed a view current at the time. The upsurge of aggression in West London was so disturbing that everyone wanted to be reassured. 'Why had it happened?' 'Who was guilty?' 'Is it over now?' It is perhaps not surprising that the answers were circumscribed; they tended to simplify rather than to clarify the search for causes and culprits.

Thus there was widespread agreement that it was a 'minute' group of young hooligans or 'teddy boys' who were responsible for the troubles in Nottingham, and even more for those in Notting Hill. Some sections of the Press were blamed. It was said that their sensational treatment of the news had had a snowball effect: it had excited young 'ruffians'; and it had also attracted the 'morbidly curious' sightseers, whose presence had made it so difficult to restore order. There was talk of the influence of fascist agitators, who were, however, regarded as another 'insignificant' lunatic fringe by many commentators. And there was even some straightforward 'witch-hunting': a well-known American columnist explained (in the *New York Herald Tribune*) that the disturbances in Nottingham and London were the result of a

Communist conspiracy – indeed, of the same conspiracy that had accentuated racial friction in Little Rock, and fomented riots in the Southern states of his own country. This was the one theory that – as the *Manchester Guardian* said – 'had not occurred even to the most Right-minded commentators in Fleet Street'. Nevertheless, as the point had been made, some people thought it appropriate to add it to their repertoire.

Another parallel set of explanations was sought not only in the problem of white trouble makers, but also – or even more – in the 'Colour Problem'. There were those whose instinctive first reaction to the disturbances was to argue, explicitly or implicitly, that there would be no racial friction if there were no coloured minority in this country; or that the quantity of friction is determined by the number of coloured migrants. Hence it was their contribution to the discussion to ask for immigration control. There were others who adopted a more sophisticated approach: they probed the characteristics and habits of coloured newcomers. This was done with diverse intentions – positively and negatively, on the basis of more or less scanty information. But however the probing was done, there was still far more dissection of the coloured minority group than of British society.

Thus although there were other lines of thought as well, the predominant accounts of the causes of disorder tended to be evasive and tautological. Stripped of the verbiage, they said not much more than that it is the coloured people who represent a colour problem; or that a small irresponsible section of the population had acted irresponsibly. This was a typical summary: 'Those involved in the recent outbreaks invariably appear to have been ill-educated, unskilled and irresponsible. Few white participants have been other than teen-age hooligans. Most of the coloured people have been West Indian labourers, frequently from Jamaica.' It was a deceptively simple sum of disorder, and while many of the items were correctly noted, something went wrong in the addition.

It is true that there were many young people involved in the disturbances – in London even more than in Nottingham; but not everyone who took part, actively or passively, was young. And the young live in an adult society. The 'youthful thugs' were roaming around in an environment in which their actions were not discouraged; indeed, it seems that they were definitely encouraged by some of their elders and betters. They rarely met white opposition. While there were many people who preserved their sense of decency in the turmoil of Notting Dale – some white housewives did the shopping for their coloured neighbours who dared not go outside – active defiance of 'nigger-hunting' was rare. There were not many who had the determination of the greengrocer's wife who stood outside her door facing a violent crowd.

The 'teddy boys' had the sanction of their own back street society; more important still, they were operating in terms of their own social code – in deliberate opposition to the region of remote official authority beyond their back streets. 'Nigger-baiting' was their new form of social protest, a particularly convenient form because it was, apparently, tacitly accepted by some sections of both worlds; indeed it combined the worst of both worlds – the worst of their inside and of the outside world.

Was that not made clear by the sightseers who came to watch aggression? And were the many hundreds who stood by as mere spectators any less to blame than the few young 'hooligans' who acted in the performance? It is unlikely that the actors would have continued without the spectators.

It is probable, too, that the more sensational accounts in some sections of the Press intensified the pathological excitement. But they did not create it; it was there to be intensified. And in general, the press played a positive role – not only by acknowledging the importance of the events, but also by the critical editorial comments on them.

Objective difficulties accentuated the tension between coloured and white at that time. There was a minor recession – and thus increased competition for unskilled jobs – in Nottingham. Both there and in London, the housing problems in the zones of transition were acute. And the latter, in turn, contribute to the awareness of social and cultural differences between 'natives' and newcomers. But such problems exist at other times and in other places without causing an explosion. Indeed some of them exist more strikingly in the districts of fairly dense coloured settlement than in the actual foci of disorder in London.

Moreover, the widespread assumption that Notting Hill is a 'coloured quarter', and that it was the ghetto-style mode of living of the new minority which largely explains the disturbances, is not confirmed. There are as yet no coloured ghettoes in London; there are only a few streets with clusters of coloured people, and these streets were not the main scenes of violence.

Why then did the 'riots' break out in the Shepherd's Bush-Notting Dale-Paddington belt? Why there and not elsewhere? The actual concrete frictions between white and coloured were not most intense in these places. It is the friction between white and white which is symbolised in these districts and for which outlets have to be found. All the current unrests are rolled into one in these streets. They are a panorama of the schisms in British society which cause disturbance, singular and plural. And once the turmoil starts, it is bound to spread because it is not self-contained. The 'trouble makers of Notting Hill' acted out tendencies which were latent in all social strata. They were shouting what others were whispering.

That was the lesson of the 1958 disturbances. They revealed that there are in mid-twentieth century Britain not 'two nations' but several, which are estranged from one another. And both the disorders and the comments on them also showed more clearly than any previous events the all-pervasive British ambivalence towards colour. Most important, they proved that in so ambiguous a situation, aggressive fringe groups, though 'minute', are not 'insignificant'.

R. Glass, *Newcomers: The West Indians in London* (London: Centre for Urban Studies/George Allen & Unwin, 1960) 142–6.

128) A Methodist minister on West Indian church services, London, 1959 [I.]

These comments were made by a Congregational minister who worked in Willesden and who helped many immigrant settlers in the London district. Ruth Glass recorded his account for her study of West Indians in 1950s London.

'. . . because I still felt that many of our West Indians were not being spiritually satisfied with our services . . . I began to hold a week-night "Evangelical Service" in the hall, particularly for West Indians. These services I ran myself each Wednesday night and always invited one of the worshippers to lead the "Testimony Time" and another to speak. We had some wonderful and inspiring services and I learned many choruses as well as a whole new technique in worship.'

'Gradually we built up within the meeting a small orchestra, as one by one our Jamaicans either purchased an instrument of their own, or brought along friends who played an instrument. Our guitars, tambourines and trumpet could be heard all down the street, and I have often wondered what passers-by imagine to be happening inside our Tin Tabernacle! The rhythm at times would be particularly hot, and has been described by one of the young people in my church, who himself enjoys a bit of "Rock'n Roll", as being the type that "sends you". Our normal pattern of worship would follow a regular line, although the time allowed for each item in the liturgy would vary according to the number of worshippers and the way in which the Spirit moved. We generally started with a hymn from Redemption Songs, which is the hymn book we normally used. This would be followed by a period of free prayer, in which all the worshippers would kneel and say their own prayers aloud until one by one they fell into silent meditation. The prayer time would then culminate in a petition offered by the leader, and finally the repetition of the Lord's Prayer. After this we would have another hymn and then Testimony. Between each testimony, or possibly two or three testimonies, we would have choruses led by the chorus leader and each one being quickly picked up by the various instruments comprising our orchestra.'

R. Glass, *Newcomers: The West Indians in London* (London: Centre for Urban Studies/George Allen & Unwin, 1960) 203–4.

129) A Sikh marriage ceremony in Bedford, 1960s [I.]

See note on extract No.86.

The girl's father came to England for a holiday. He was also looking for a suitable boy for his daughter. By chance he met one of our friends, who told him that we were religious people, and well-known in the Sikh community. This friend brought him to our house for a social visit. He did not let us know at that time what he came for. But talking to us, he came to know about our family, how we think and what we do. After a period of time, the friend told us that he was interested in discussing a marriage arrangement. Then, of course, we began making inquiries about his family. We knew already that it was a very nice, very religious family, and that he was a leader of his community. Each year he takes a pilgrimage of people to Mount Everest, which for us is a holy place. He is a very saintly person. And we think, if the parents are religious people, then surely the children will be the same. So we began to negotiate. First we had to see that the surnames of the father and mother differed from ours, for we must not mix the same bloods together. Then he invited us to come to India to see the girl, or for our relatives in India to do so on our behalf. We knew enough of the family to think this was not necessary, but we arranged to exchange photographs.

Of course, we consult with the boy. We do not wish to be dictators. If he had had objections, we should not have proceeded. Now we are much more flexible than we used to be. Of course, it is not just a matter of the photographs. The important thing is that boy and family have the feeling of accord in the mind with the other family. We believe that marriages are made in heaven, and that in making this union, we are enacting the pattern of God's will.

The son takes up the story:

'The day we received the photographs, I was in Coventry all day. When I got back, and came into the room, my parents had taken my photograph off the mantelpiece and stood hers in its place. I did not know where to turn. My mind went blank. I could not speak because I was shy. My mother said "Do you like this photo" "Yes," I said. "But are you sure? Do you really like it?" "Yes," I said, "it's a very nice photograph." They would have seen from my face if I did not like it.

'Both she and I, as Sikhs, are seekers for God. Like moths, we seek His light and to merge with that light. And it is through the world that we come to our Creator. Through human relationships that we achieve salvation. For us, marriage is another, necessary stage of understanding in the search for perfection.

'At the engagement ceremony, they asked me to come and sit in the centre between the men and women before the Guru Granth Sahib, the holy book. And when I was seated there, her uncle, as the oldest and nearest member of her family in the absence of her parents, came and sat next to me on my left-hand side. First, he touched my head, which is the Sikh sign of love and affection. Then all asked for a towel to be brought, the symbol of the bond. This was placed round my neck and draped in front of me into a fold or bag. Then her uncle placed a dried date (shhorara) in my mouth, which I had to eat. This means the contract is made. He placed a ring on my finger and in the bag pieces of coconut and gifts of money. The coconut means a blessing, and the pieces will be kept for the wedding day next year. Then my mother was required to make her gifts of coconut and money, I and after this, family and friends all put in their gifts. Our next door neighbour, Mrs Readman, an English lady, she also put a garland of flowers about my neck. As the towel grows heavier, this symbolises the burden of worldly things. At the wedding ceremony itself, I shall share this burden with my wife. We will carry it together. This burden, which the love of God will make as nothing to us.'

J. Brown, *The Un-Melting Pot* (London: Macmillan – now Palgrave Macmillan, 1970) 121–2.

130) Pakistani isolation in Bradford, 1970s [I.]

This commentary is taken from Verity Saifullah Khan's essay on Mirapuri villagers in Bradford.

Mirpuris in Bradford generally have minimal contact with the indigenous population. Men employed in the textile industry, for example, work long hours on all-Pakistani night shifts. The little time for relaxation is invariably spent with friends and biradari (kin) in Bradford or other towns. Most Mirpuri women do not go out to work, partly because it is considered to be un-Islamic and partly because there are no close family members with whom they can leave their young children. Women living in a neighbourhood with a high percentage of Pakistanis visit nearby friends or relatives and shop in Pakistani shops. Contact with the local population is limited to visits to the supermarket, post office, clinics, and other relatively impersonal and official settings.

J. L. Watson (ed.) *Between Two Cultures: Migrants and Minorities in Britain* (Oxford: B. Blackwell, 1977) 76.

131) Anita on Birmingham community relations, 1989 [I.]

Anita (pseud.) was born in Edgebaston, Birmingham c.1975. Her parents are Hindus from Gujarat, India. See also note on extract No.118.

In this newspaper report about what caused it [the Handsworth riots of 1985] there was some rubbish about noisy parties. I don't think it was any of that. I think it was police harassment, and there's racism and, well, unemployment. The police have some good ideas but they just go about them in the wrong way. I guess the police – I can't really judge them because individually some of them are right horrible people and some police I guess must be all right. I can't speak.

Between Black and Asian people, between some it's a problem how they get on. Like, if an Afro-Caribbean person went into an Asian person's shop

> some Asian shopkeepers keep a special eye on them. Yet if an Indian person went in they'd be all right. It depends on the individual really because there's not many problems between them. The newspapers do seem to exaggerate a lot of stuff and particularly if a paper is biased they'll put whatever they write just to back their own sort of opinion.

A. Osler, *Speaking Out: Black Girls in Britain* (London: Virago Upstarts, 1989) 46–7.

Another Culture 2

132) Welsh language and cultural identity in Liverpool, *c.*1900 [M.]

According to Merfyn Jones, Mr A. W. H. was born in Manchester in 1925. See note on extract No.122.

> The thing was, I think I was rather like someone, you know, whose got a wooden leg – you can't imagine life any differently . . . I don't think it's good for one's character, for one's maturing, I think it puts it off many, many, years because you learn to be one thing here and another thing there. If somebody said to me, 'Make your mind up. What are you?' and it had to be one or the other I'd say Welsh every time . . . Because I wouldn't have kept my language and things . . . I always remember my grandfather saying 'Eu Gwlad a Gollant, Eu Hiaith a Gadwant' (Their country they will lose, their language they will preserve) and to me, that is me. But, I think if we had it all over again, I think immigrants should . . . become absorbed – they've no right to play with the kids' lives. They should . . . come in this country and become this country. I think, I know, it was a very big strain, I think it interfered . . . with my educational progress, because to me school was my social centre, it wasn't just school . . . Different people reacted in different ways, my brother, he withdrew into himself.

M. Jones, 'Welsh immigrants in the cities of North-West England, 1880–1930: some oral testimony', *Oral History*, 9 (1981) 39–40.

133) An anti-Jewish riot in Leeds, 1917 [I.]

Comments from an eye-witness police report on events in June 1917.

> With regard to the disturbances which occurred on Sunday evening, the 3rd inst., these commenced about 7:30 p.m. in the Jewish quarters, viz, The Leylands, when a large number of women and boys commenced to break the windows in the shops occupied by the Jews . . .

On Monday, the 4th instant, expecting that the disturbances would be renewed, I made arrangements for a large number of regular Police, augmented by a large number of the voluntary force of the Special Constabulary, to be located in various parts of the city. The disturbances were repeated about 7 p.m. and a large number of arrests were made, chiefly of boys, youths and females, and with the exception of one case – that of a woman charged with inflicting grievous bodily harm upon one of my Detective Inspectors – they were all dealt with by the Stipendiary Magistrate, Mr Horace Marshall, the following day.

I continued to keep up the reserve Police, prepared to deal with any further disorder, but I am pleased to inform you that no further outbreaks have taken place.

PRO/HO 45 10810/311932.

134) The tourist trade in London's Chinatown, *c.*1935 [I.]

See note on extract No.105.

What a joke these professional 'underworlds' are! Limehouse (to give it its popular name, though it is really in Poplar) may have been a very wicked place once, but it is tame enough to-day. As an 'underworld' it is a fraud. Publicity has killed all the pretension to that title. When smiling ladies and gentlemen swarm out of motor-coaches by the score and run all over the place trying to buy opium as souvenirs, what can poor Vice do but seek a more congenial secrecy? It would be much more appropriate now if charabancs 'to London's Underworld' were to start from Limehouse instead of from the West End for Limehouse perhaps we could clean up the West End then.

However the Limehouse 'underworld' legend brings innocent profit to the Causeway and its purlieus. Its Chinese signs and shop names give it a certain picturesqueness and make the eyes of tourists to bulge. You can buy curios, interesting things there – uncommon little china bowls and dishes in the ancient Chinese rice patterns (the grains of rice make flecks of transparency where the piece is held upon the light; joss-sticks; ginger in pleasing Chinese jars; China tea – anything, in fact but 'snow'. The Chinese lodging houses have not the sinister appearance of those in Pennyfields. One or two Chinese restauarants cater impartially for Western and Oriental taste. In one, we ate excellent chop suey, and drank China tea from delicate little handless cups, while a loudspeaker did its best to defeat any romantic imaginations I might have harboured by giving us the latest sporting results and the political news from Westminster. The proprietor was a benevolent old Chinese with a face full of humorous wrinkles, and I suppose that the man with the smart dark suit and correct Western manners who served us, speaking perfect English was his son.

In another Limehouse restaurant, I had to be content with a cup of cocoa and slice of cake, served by an obvious London woman, the Chinese proprietor's wife.

H. Thorogood, *East of Aldgate* (London: George Allen and Unwin, 1935) 149–50.

135) A Ukrainian learns English customs, 1948 [I.]

See note on extract No.86.

Afterwards, they told us we go to England. There were stories of fog and rain. And when I came to England, I had three words only, 'water', 'knife' and 'eat'. At first we spent one year and a half in a POW camp at Mildenhall in Suffolk, working on agricultural land. We had eighteen shillings a week, nine shillings in real money, nine shillings in camp money. In 1948, we were discharged with £30 for clothes and for what else we wanted. Then we were classed as 'Displaced Persons'.

We did not speak English, so we had to keep together. We went first to a sugar beet factory at Bury St Edmunds, then to Sudbury and Snettisham. Everywhere we lived in camps. I had a little book of English, and when it happened I had 'flu, two weeks in such a way, I learned all the little book by heart. In Snettisham we also had English lessons from interpreters. I learned very much from the pictures. The Picturedrome – that was my best teacher. You listen. You watch people move. You make connections, what they say and what they do. You begin to learn.

Then you go for a walk. You pass someone, and you say, in English for the first time, 'Good afternoon'. In my country, if you go by anybody, you have to greet them. In England, they turn away. Don't answer. That hits you. You feel very bad. You think they don't like you. Then you think more. Perhaps it is because they think you were in German army. Then you understand that in England they do not make such greetings. You learn to be careful, what to do, what not to do. In Italy, back in POW camp, they used to say 'Do not speak to English woman unless she smiles at you. Otherwise, trouble.'

Then we were told the camps would be ended. We were given three choices of work. Coalmine, brickyard, sewage farm. I chose brickyard. In 1950, I came to Kempston Hardwick hostel.

J. Brown, *The Un-Melting Pot* (London: Macmillan – now Palgrave Macmillan, 1970) 61.

136) A Polish woman describes domestic service, 1949 [I.]

Maria was born in Wole, a village in central Poland, in 1927. In 1943 she was deported to Germany as a slave labourer. After liberation she lived in the Displaced Persons camp in Allenbach, and in 1947 volunteered to become a refugee labourer in England under the Ministry of Labour 'Westward Ho' Scheme. A year after she wrote the letter reproduced below she attempted suicide and a local magistrate ordered her immediate deportation to Germany. Zubrzycki notes that he never met Maria, but based his account on private letters, official records and interview notes in the possession of a Polish Welfare Officer.

> [Maria] arrived in England in November 1948 and after a comparatively short stay of just under three weeks in a transit camp she went to work as a domestic servant for a British family near Market Drayston. Maria described her work in a letter to the Federation of Polish Women in Great Britain.
>
> 2nd January 1949.
>
> Respected Ladies!
>
> When I landed in England a leaflet was given to me by a Polish gentleman who acted as interpreter for English officials. In the leaflet it says that I am to write to you if any harm is done to me. Well, I don't know whether my present tortures are really as bad as the treatment I received from the Germans, but they seem very bad and so I appeal to you, Madam, to speak to the Ministry of Labour and ask if I can be released and transferred to a lighter job. I shall willingly assist in a tailor's shop as I can sew and mend clothes. I am employed as a maid in this house and I have to do all the chores for 14 hours a day. There are two adults and three children. The children tease me very painfully and call me different names which I do not understand but I know that they are not nice. The wife of my employer wants me to serve her breakfast in bed every morning and she never gets up before 11 o'clock. And believe me, Madam, these people live like pagans, they never seem to pray and when I dress the children in the morning they do not know how to make the sign of the Cross. Last week we had the Feast of Nativity but the woman did not let me go to Mass in the nearest Catholic Church. She often says that if I want to go to Mass I can only go on Wednesday afternoons.
>
> Dear Lady, please do something about it and take me away from this place. I want to work among my compatriots.
>
> The letter quoted above was followed by another one week later and finally the Federation of Polish Women asked the local office of the Ministry of Labour whether Maria could be transferred to one of the Polish hostels. The Ministry did not agree and pointed out that Maria had come to Britain to serve a three year's contract on conditions laid down by the Ministry. All that the Ministry agreed to do was to release Maria from her present job and transfer her to a cotton mill in Oldham.

J. Zubrzycki, *Polish Immigrants in Britain: a Study of Adjustment* (The Hague: Nijhoff, 1956) 212.

137) Eric Ferron reflects on an Anglo-Jamaican marriage, 1950s [I.]

See note on extract No.85.

Not long after returning from my first sad visit home to Jamaica, I went to see an old RAF friend up in Liverpool. He had asked me to go up and meet his new English wife. We all went to visit the wife's mother while I was there. It was the first time my friend had met his mother-in-law, she had refused to come to the wedding. He told me she had invited him to meet her about a month ago but he hadn't the nerve. I'm sure he asked me to visit them just then so that I could support him.

The mother was a cold serious woman who seemed to me to have had a hurtful life herself. Her first words to her daughter were: 'I wondered whether you were coming or not.' The girl explained we had had to wait for a bus. 'More excuses', said the mother. She didn't greet my friend and took no notice of me whatsoever. When we got inside the house she said: 'Which one of you is the husband?' The girl introduced my friend. 'Are you both from the same country?' My friend was still too nervous to speak so I told her we both came from Jamaica. 'It's funny how you look so different.'

'In what way?' I said.

'You're much darker than him', she said.

'You get dark and not so dark where we come from.'

'Very funny.'

'But mum he's got white blood in him', the girl said, he told me his grandparents had some mixture and he is a throwback.

'So what are you?' the mother turned angrily to my friend,

'Are you half-caste or a quarter?'

He attempted to speak but she went on, 'And what happens when you get her pregnant? What colour will your children be?'

Again the girl replied for him. 'Our children will be nearly white Mum because if he's only a quarter and my baby's half that means he'll be nearly white.'

I sat on and listened astounded to these two, mother and daughter, discussing in this curious way how much black and white the baby would have. It was so cold. They spoke with no feeling or interest about the child who would be born into the family. I didn't know what to say and I didn't want to interfere but I could sense how my friend was feeling. The mother changed the subject and asked about his job. He managed to tell her he was a mechanic.

'And when do you go back to Jamaica?'

He said he didn't know yet.

'Are you going with him? she turned back to the girl.

'I don't know. We haven't discussed it.'

'Don't you talk about these things?'

'Give us a chance, Mum. We've only been married a few months.'

'Do you think you'll like living in his country away from us?'

'I won't know till I get there, will I?'

It was cold, right through. I wanted to leave. It wasn't my problem. But my friend implored me to stay. It was late when we returned to their house and the girl was in tears. She told us her mother was like that with everybody first time. 'But I think she'll like you', she said to her husband. Then she went to bed and we sat down again and talked.

'Man, this is a funny country, 'he said. 'People up round here say they like coloured folks but they don't really. You marry one and suddenly they don't like you any more. I married her because I love her. I've got a good job and I've got this house and I can provide for her. My folks all want to meet her. They're so delighted. This is the first time I've seen her mother and you saw what happened. This is a strange country. They don't seem to think about their children's happiness. Can't they forget their own silly pride for the sake of their own children?'

There wasn't much I could say. 'These are the things you will find, but the most important thing is that you love her. You should be able to fight for her and stand up for her. She'll need you.'

I left next day and returned to London and thought of the sad scene I had witnessed. In one evening, in one hour, in just a word or two, happiness could be destroyed. This girl and her boy had tried so hard. All they needed was for someone close to them to say: 'I wish you well.' But they were denied even that.

Perhaps it was then much harder for the girl. Women depended so much on the personal relationships in their family circle, a man had other possibilities, his job and his public life where he could seek prestige.

E. Ferron, *'Man, You've Mixed': A Jamaican Comes to Britain* (London: Whiting and Birch, 1995) 80–6.

138) Speaking Irish in England, 1950s [I.]

See note on extract No.87.

I started to try to teach Nick some Irish. Though he'd like to know it, however, the devil hasn't enough patience to learn anything. We made up a plan to pull the wool over the eyes of the foreigners so as to pretend that we always spoke Irish among ourselves. Nick knew a good deal of songs from school and what we arranged to do whenever anybody would be listening to us, was that I would say conversationally a line of poetry: 'What will we do without timber?' Nick would then answer with the next line: 'The last of the forest is down'; I would follow with the next line and so on. We planned to laugh now and again and to appear to be angry from time to time. We got a chance to do it this afternoon when there were some Poles and Ukrainians standing around the back door enjoying the first bit of sun I've seen since I came here. Nick and I came to the door pretending that we were delighted to see the sun shining at last. I looked up at the sun and then as if I was commenting on the weather, I remarked: 'What will we do without timber?'

'Oh! be gor, the last of the forest is down,' said the lad.

I stretched myself lazily and said:

'Kilcash and its house are forgotten.'

'And its bell will be heard no more,' said Nick. I let on that I was feeling a bit down and I made a face.

'And what the divil about that place where the oul' wan lived?' I said.

Nick gave me a kick on the ankle.

'Stick to your lines,' he said venomously. I had put him off his stroke with my improvisation and he couldn't think of what came after the idea in that line. I rescued him then, however, with:

'The duck or the goose won't be heard there.'

'Or the eagle above the bay,' he replied.

The foreigners were all ears by now and I could see that they were amazed at all this Irish. They started looking at us with a new respect, even that Ukrainian Pizzarenko whom Nick was always annoying and challenging. We were well away, I'm telling you, but for Nick's sister arriving at that very moment and hearing what we were at.

'Well, there's a good man,' she said to me, 'teaching Nicky Irish and when he was at home he'd learn nothing.'

All the foreigners burst out laughing and Nick almost jumped up a mile in the air in a fit of rage. He threw a malevolent glance at Pizzarenko and started leaping around with his two fists up and shouting: 'All right, Pizzy, put them up. Come on and fight like a man. I'll teach you to laugh at the Irish.'

But your man Pizzy sloped off to his own room breaking his heart laughing.

Nick is in a blinding rage ever since and it's not safe to talk to him, never mind anything else.

D. Mac Amhlaigh, *An Irish Navvy: the Diary of an Exile* (London: Routledge, 1964) 14–5.

139) A Jamaican view of British politics and religion, 1956–60 [I.]

See note on extract No.88.

Did you feel that British politics had anything to do with you?
I did admire MacMillan and . . . when he was Prime Minister, The 'wind of change' and all those things. I remember all that in the fifties.

Did you vote at all?
Only recently . . . 1970.

Why didn't you vote before that? Didn't you think it was important?
I wasn't so interested at the time . . . General Election 1959 – that was the one I was very interested in MacMillan – never had it so good when the winds of change . . . that was the one I remember very much.

And with respect to trade unions, he had the following to say:

Did the unions here strike you as being fairly different from the unions in Jamaica?

Oh, yes. Well at that time the feeling was negative, it was no good. Just take your money and that was that – you never got anything out of it. Certainly the whiteman got something out of it.

But the unions were never officially hostile to black labour? Would officials of the unions make public statements against black workers?

No. They say it privately but not publicly.

As regards religion he went on:

Let me ask you about your religion . . . when you first arrived presumably you didn't find any of the churches of your denomination?

No, I used to go to Baptist Church. It was something similar to Church of God. I didn't try Anglican. I knew of them from back home.

Why?

I didn't believe in them! I didn't believe they were true.

H. Goulbourne, 'Oral history and black labour in Britain: an overview', *Oral History*, 8 (1980) 30.

140) Prafulla Mohanti celebrates Christmas in London, 1960s [I.]

See note on extract No.90.

I looked forward to my first Christmas in England with great anticipation. Around November the atmosphere changed and the shops started displaying special Christmas goods and decorations. The main shopping streets were illuminated at night.

Tom and his mother brought out their address books and prepared lists of friends and relatives. 'Christmas is the time to remember friends and relatives and send them cards', they told me. They bought their cards but I drew mine. I thought it was more personal and my list was short.

In India there is a religious festival practically every month. My village school closed for several days at Christmas. We called it 'Xmas holiday' but did not know what it meant. For the autumn festival of Dassera my father came on a long holiday with presents for me. There was a great sense of participation in the village and my mother prepared many kinds of cakes which we ate and distributed among our friends.

I was disappointed when I was told that my office would close for only two days, but I noticed my colleagues taking time off to do their Christmas shopping. A secretary told me she had been buying her presents since the previous Christmas and had even kept some which were given to her. I noticed that the closeness of the relationship was measured by the price of the presents. There seemed little religious significance, but the shopkeepers were happy.

Christmas also meant party time. I did not like parties in England. Guests stood in little groups clutching their wine glasses, gossiping with their friends, and ignoring the others. But the office Christmas party seemed different. We all joined in, there was plenty to drink, and everybody was friendly. I was also invited to other office parties. In the week before Christmas there were two or three every night. It was a time to be nice to everybody, but after Christmas the smiling faces became gloomy again.

I liked the habit of giving presents; it was very Indian. I bought several small packets of the best Darjeeling tea available in London to give to my friends. I gave a packet to a colleague in the office. She was very pleased and said it would go with the Christmas cake. After Christmas she came up to me and said, 'Prafulla, we enjoyed your tea very much, but it blocked up my sink.' I had forgotten to warn her that the tea had large leaves. On Christmas Day I woke up in the morning to find a stocking on my bed, full of little presents. Tom's mother said Father Christmas must have left them.

We had spent many hours the previous day decorating the flat. In one corner of the living room we placed the Christmas tree with all its ornaments – light bulbs, stars, and an angel. Attractively wrapped parcels were piled round its base. We hung Christmas cards on strings and put them round the room. Tom's relatives started arriving at eleven, one by one, carrying presents in their arms. The flat vibrated with greetings: 'Happy Christmas'; 'Happy New Year'.

The table was laid with the best china and the family silver. Tom was very particular about the drinks and had bought champagne, sherry, wine, whisky, gin, brandy, port, and liqueurs. We started with champagne for the Christmas toast. Although I drank very little alcohol I was persuaded to take a sip.

Tom's relatives looked at me with curiosity. 'You are the Indian friend we have been hearing so much about.' I smiled but felt like an exhibit. Tom had explained to me that he had invited his five cousins because they lived on their own.

Tom's mother had spent the whole of Christmas Eve preparing the meal. I knew the menu but was shocked by the sight. I was not expecting to see a huge roasted bird filled with stuffing. Tom was the carver. When he sharpened the knife, started cutting large slices of turkey, and scooped out the stuffing with a spoon, I wanted to get up and run away. In India we never serve whole animals or birds; they are cut into small pieces and hidden by the curry sauce. But I forced myself to stay at the table and gradually settled down to enjoy the food. Roast potatoes and sprouts were served with the turkey, care being taken to give everyone equal portions of white and dark meat.

The Christmas pudding arrived. The lights were put out and the curtains drawn. Tom poured brandy over the pudding and lit it. Everyone applauded as blue flames flickered. What a waste of good brandy, I thought. It was used as medicine in my village. We slowly ate our way through the vast quantities of food as though we had never eaten before, pausing briefly to hear the Queen's speech. Tom's mother produced a box of crackers. We pulled them, put on the paper hats, and read out the mottoes. Then the ceremony of the presents began. Everybody behaved like little children, opening parcels and reading the messages. Tom read out a letter from his aunt in Australia sending greetings to the family.

I was touched by the present from Tom's mother. It was a pullover and a pair of gloves she had knitted herself. I had seen her knitting but had not realized she was doing it for me. 'It's not the present but the thought that counts', Tom's mother said.

In the early evening we went out for a walk. The streets were deserted, the houses had their curtains drawn but I could see lights filtering through. In some windows decorated Christmas trees were clearly visible. For one day the family had come together and the outside world was forgotten. When we returned to the flat we found tea and Christmas cake on the table, prepared by Tom's mother. I had presented her with a tin of Indian tea, which she served with great pride. But I heard some of the relatives complaining it was not strong enough for them. I knew tea drinking was a ritual in England but very few seemed to bother about the quality. Their taste was affected by drinking too much 'English tea' and they were unable to appreciate the taste of pure Indian tea.

P. Mohanti, *Through Brown Eyes* (Oxford: Oxford University Press, 1985) 44–6.

141) An Irish Catholic view of Protestants, 1960s [M.]

See note on extract No.98.

It was totally different to what I'd expected. No ogres around corners you know. I'd been told as a child you could tell a Protestant because they'd have a big Satan's mark on their forehead, you see, and I was a soldier of Christ, it was my job to shoot them. But I never found anybody with a mark on their heads. So I mean thing's just didn't turn out to be what I'd expected.

Destination Bradford: A Century of Immigration (Bradford: Heritage Recording Unit, 1987) 28.

142) Sikh, Muslim and British community relations, 1960s [I.]

See note on extract No.111.

I mean I used to come home fighting all the kids with black eyes and everything quite regular, and then get a beating from my dad as well for being in a fight. You know, I mean, I remember quite often after school you know, being involved in scraps, and the . . . interesting, and one of the interesting ones I'm telling you about, a prize one was . . . You see having been there so long and already speaking English and being academic, I used to be in a higher class than most of the other Asians. And when they first – I never noticed it before but when they started coming in they'd be learning English or something and they'd be in a lower class. And my friends were already there, I mean like Derek I used to go to school with and somebody else used to come from round our area, and most of them in a sense used to be white or there used to be some Asians, so . . . I think they went to different schools. Most of them used to be white. And the Asian kids, there were a few problems here. One was that I wasn't a Muslim, I was a Sikh, and they were far more aware of that than I was because they'd just come from Pakistan. Me being brought up here, I mean I didn't have a clue about what the problem was between Sikhs and Muslims or anything. It didn't you know, it just didn't . . . I wasn't aware of the . . . but they were, and er . . . so, you know, and partly because I'd got white friends, you know they began to have some antipathy towards me sometimes; and one day one of these lads was picking on . . . (and some of these lads were quite . . . much older than we were actually because I think they'd just been stuck into that school for want of somewhere else to put them, but they weren't the right age. But they had to learn English or something so they were there. So you know they were a lot bigger than some of us there). One day one of these lads was picking on Derek who as I say was one of my best friends, and er . . . I went into defend him I said 'Hey', you know, and this person was a bit scared of me. I think I must have hit him or something and he backed off. But he had a friend called Johnny and his family's been here quite a long time as well. Now, so what . . . it was basically a fight between us two, and he was being egged on by these other people, and we went and fought it out, and I still . . . and we're best friends still to this day actually, me and this Johnny after that incident. But he was telling me that, you know, they were all pushing . . . part of the egging on was that I was a Sikh who hung round with English kids, and you know 'You should fight him as a Muslim'. And they wanted him to do it again, but he told them to, to get lost actually, eventually. So you know I was aware of those things happening, but I wasn't really part and parcel of that group of people.

And then on the other hand did British people look at you as a different sort of Asian?

In one sense they did because I mean most of these lads, you know, spoke very little English and I did, and I spoke probably with a, with a natural ease you know, virtually having been born in this country. And that's partly the thing you know, 'You're different, you're all right', syndrome. But in respect of that, in respect of the fact that I was aware, becoming aware that there was something wrong with, you know, they didn't consider me part of them, it still didn't help me when comments were made about other Asian people, because I still wasn't totally aware of what the things were, and what the difficulties were. And, you know . . . at Belle Vue yes, there was a lot more Asian people there, and there was Asian boys there and there was something called the 'Immigrant Hut', where Asian boys went to learn English. And there were white boys coming from all kinds of ways and there were obviously a lot more comments which I became more and more aware of. And even there I had to have one or two fights to establish my credibility before . . . after that I wasn't really bothered by anybody . . . and again things which had begun to develop at Frizinghall, which were end of term fights between Asian boys and white boys, and boys coming from other schools. And I can remember vividly at Belle Vue one time when the Asian boys had to band together and march down the road as a phalanx column, I mean it was a phalanx virtually, to ensure their own safety. And I can also remember now, we're into the early 'seventies, and in 'sixty-eight I can remember things about skinheads coming to Bradford in 'seventy-one and, and beating up Asians and black people. And I can remember, you know, things about repatriation, and I can remember leaflets going round school which were from something called the, was it 'The Yorkshire Campaign against Immigrants'? Things like, which said things like 'If you sit against, sit next to an Asian in a class you are bound to catch smallpox', and things like this. So yes, I was becoming more and more aware of myself, what I was, and, and these things that were happening, and I was . . .

R. Perks, "'You're different: you're one of us": the making of a British Asian', *Oral History*, 15 (1987) 70.

143) Jaroslav Madylus on double cultural identity, 1970 [I.]

See note on extract No.86.

Years ago, I felt more English than Ukrainian. When I went to school, all my friends were English. Then, when I was about twelve or thirteen, I started to turn back towards my parents. I began to find, in many ways, that to be Ukrainian, there was much more interest, more meaning, like. Now I'm proud to say I am Ukrainian. Anyway, if I said I'm British, my name would give me away. It's more honest just to say 'I'm Ukrainian'. And I've found out, over the years, that with the British, if you say, 'I'm Jaroslav Madylus' straight out, then they accept you. But if you're, well, apologetic, or you try to hide that you're Ukrainian, or you cover it up, then they're not so keen on being friends.

When I first went to grammar school, you know, they'd laugh at me. Some used to call me 'wog'. I suppose they didn't know a better word. Just joking it was with most of them. In the end, I told them: 'Look, my parents came here because they're political refugees. Because they've lost their own country. My mum and dad couldn't go back now, or if they did, maybe they'd never come back. Perhaps it would be the same for me, unless I had a proper British passport.'

Now I know what I am, that I'm Ukrainian, I no longer have to worry. I feel at ease. This girl I went out with last night, I said my name, and she burst out laughing. She said, 'You any relation to Engelbert Humperdinck?' We got on great. I think you gain so much from having, like, two ways of life. Here, in this house, this room, it's all Ukraine – (cushions and chair covers beautifully embroidered by his mother; pictures of saints, of cossacks and of Ukrainian leaders murdered by the NKVD; a carving of the Virgin Mary and a Ukrainian doll in national dress) outside, it's all England. It gives you a chance to compare, to choose what you think best. You know, I wish it was possible to have lots of parents of all different countries. British, Ukrainian, Italian, West Indian, the lot. Then you would know every way of life. You could choose the best of each.

J. Brown, *The Un-Melting Pot* (London: Macmillan – now Palgrave Macmillan, 1970) 63–4.

144) Rampal's views on 'colour', 1970s [I.]

See note on extract No.102.

I am the kind of man who must reflect upon what he sees and hears and I often wonder in my heart why English people do not think well of coloured people. It really is a matter of colour, because they do not feel the same way towards white foreigners. Those who have the right coloured skins never get stopped at the airport, they just show their passports and go straight through. No one asks whether they are of good or bad character. White foreigners who come here to work have nothing to fear; their skin is the right colour and so there is no danger for them. Suppose I had come not from India but from France or Holland or Germany. Then no one would tell me to clear off. I would still be a foreigner, wouldn't I? But no one would abuse me. My children are being brought up here, but they will think of themselves as Indian and will live as Indians because so long as their colour is not white, English people will not regard them as British. A coloured man is easily picked out just because he is coloured. His skin tells you who he is when you are still far from him. If only the government could pass some law to change the colour of people's skin or the scientists would invent some drug to make either all the coloured people white or all white people coloured, then perhaps all would be well. But our colour is different and it cannot be changed.

U. Sharma, *Rampal and His Family* (London: Collins, 1971) 96.

145) Christopher Hope on foreign Britain, 1990 [I.]

Born in South Africa in 1944, Christopher Hope moved in London in 1974. After working as a teacher he became a full-time writer. See note on extract No.91.

> Given my prior impressions of England I decided that Plato was quite right to kick poets and writers out of his republic – they tell the most dreadful lies. My very sharp images of that settled, civilized, 'other place' had only a minute tinge of truth in them. Britain was a deeply foreign country, populated by the most unruly natives. A very strange and turbulent place. The only thing one had in common with the natives here was the English language. That was the only connection. The British made it quite clear that we were foreign. It was more complicated for them because unlike other people from elsewhere, we were also white. So we seemed like them, but the moment you opened your mouth, and the way you reacted to what you found around you, distinguished you immediately. Particularly in places outside London. Eerie it is. The echoing emptiness of the countryside. I found it remote, strange, still and deeply foreign. Your exoticism was a wonderful thing to behold in the eyes of your neighbours. But it wasn't their recognition of our foreignness that struck me, rather it was the other way round: to me their foreignness was so profound and disturbing and was made all the worse by the fact that I spoke the language. I had felt that I was at least a little bit English, and I discovered painfully, over a period, that I wasn't.

J. Green, *Them: Voices from the Immigrant Community in Contemporary Britain* (London: Secker and Warburg, 1990) 101–2.

146) Mrs Stanowska on self and memory, 1995 [I.]

Mrs Stanowska was born in Poland c.1929. In 1940 the Russians deported her to Siberia. From there she went to Persia and after another move from Tehran to Africa lived for five years with her mother and two sisters. Her father, who had fought with the Polish Army, was stationed in Scotland and his family arrived there in 1948. Mrs Stanowska met her husband, also a Pole, in Britain in the early 1950s. They moved together to set up home in a Midlands textile town. Bogusia Temple states that the interviews for her article took place in 1991.

> I often think about the person I might have been. I wanted to be a teacher. Everything seemed to be in its place. My parents had a farm which would go to my brother and I would be a teacher. We would look after each other. He died in a labour camp. I went to Siberia . . . I saw things a young girl shouldn't have to see. I think about those days all the time. As I grow older I think about them more. I remember peoples' faces and what I did and saw as if it was yesterday. It's more important than yesterday. I think about it and talk about it with others who were there. Is that young girl me? Is she me? People don't understand that for us it was not a long time ago and it still

> makes us cry. We mourn for ourselves and for those who loved us and were part of ourselves. (Author's translation)

B. Temple, 'Telling tales: accounts and selves in the journeys of British Poles', *Oral History*, 23 (1995) 61.

Searching for a Place 2

147) Maurice Levinson on 'racial cleavage' in the Jewish East End, London, *c.*1930 [I.]

Maurice Levinson was born in 1911. His autobiography includes an affectionate, disturbing account of an East London childhood.

I left the men trooping into the public-house and made my way home. The evening was cold, and the lighted stalls in Middlesex Street gave a pleasing warmth to my diffident mood. I crossed Aldgate into Whitechapel Road. The pavements were congested with the usual crowds. The young men in their Sunday suits were parading up and down, with inviting glances at the girls as they passed. Beggars and hawkers passed by with trays suspended from their necks. Fat women with young babies, and pretty girls with their men escorts. The Rivioli picture house threw out a luxurious glow as I passed. Underneath me I felt the distant rumble of a passing train. The very air was tense and humid. And then I met Stokey. He came towards me with a shy sort of unobtrusiveness. His head looked more massive than ever. His eyes were large – far too large even for the immensity of his face. His large rounded lips exposed a layer of reddened gums and a line of uneven teeth. The small cloth cap he wore made his ears look grotesque – as though fate had given them to him because they would fit nobody else.

'Oh, it's you!' he said, stopping awkwardly in my path. An uncomfortable silence followed. We stood and gazed at each other. He looked ill, and a wave of pity surged through me. Nobody like Max could ever live without pain. The pain about him was having to move amongst his fellow-beings. And the sad part about it was that Max was far from being a fool. Nobody could say he was stupid. So few people terminated their lives by opening an artery in their wrists. Hanging, drowning and jumping from skyscrapers seem more obvious ways of dying.

Max was deeply conscious of the racial cleavage amongst the people with whom he lived. It bewildered him to think that an accidental origin of birth should cause him so much unhappiness. He suffered great misery from this complex. He felt that the implications of entering this world were too great for him. He always maintained that the best and worst that could happen to a Jew was to have been born a Jew. I never found cause to argue with him over this point, as it held all the logic of an illogical remark. Max also maintained that the idea of being born was not his. Here again I couldn't argue. Max was much too sensible about things. He saw things in a clear unblinded light. He saw truth, and it made him sad.

We turned into New Road. At the junction of Commercial Road we crossed into Hessel Street. Hessel Street always affected me with a sort of mystical sadness. It is long and narrow, with stalls on either side. The vendors were all Jewish. They stood by their barrows and yelled themselves hoarse. They swore, pleaded, and implored. They yelled at each other and passed remarks and felt anger and showed pleasure. It was a small island of Orientalism in a sea of Christendom. Sometimes I watched a lonely Gentile wander self-consciously between the heavily-laden stalls. I used to wonder what thoughts entered his mind. I wondered if he felt as some of the younger Jews feel today. Maybe he felt guilty of having been born. Maybe he hated the Jews, and didn't know that the effort to stamp out a religion succeeds in fostering its growth.

M. Levinson, *The Trouble with Yesterday* (Bath: Cedric Chivers, 1946) 64–6.

148) European refugees describe their 'naturalization', 1940s–50s [I.]

See note on extract No.106.

¶ Originally we had come into the country on a temporary basis and throughout the war no official announcement was ever made that we would eventually be allowed to stay. My brother joined the United States Army and after ninety days he became an American citizen. My cousin, who happened to have a Polish passport, could join a fighting force. But because I had a German passport I was not even given a rifle until 1941. Frenchmen who joined the Free French in England were promised that they could if they wanted to take British nationality after the war. No such promise was made to us and 'German' servicemen who were discharged became again enemy aliens under police supervision, though they might be drawing a British Army Pension. Right till the end of the war there was no security, you might say, of tenure.

¶ Naturalisation – the first step to establishing roots.

¶ I was naturalised under a special scheme introduced after the war for young people like me who had gone into foster homes and whose parents were dead, as we could not be legally adopted until we were British subjects.

¶ I married an Englishman when I was eighteen and from then on I ceased to be a refugee. I became a British subject on my marriage and no longer had to conform to restrictions imposed on aliens. My life then took the path of many other young wives during wartime.

¶ I stopped feeling a foreigner when I joined the Army – even the pioneers because you wore a uniform, what unit you were in doesn't matter. Once you get naturalised you're as good as the next man. You pay your taxes, you can vote, you can sit on a jury, you can do anything you like.

¶ In 1947 I asked the Czech Embassy to revalidate my expired passport. The official's mistrust, his probing questions – searching for what? – made the interview end disastrously with me tearing the old passport in half and throwing it at him. It was then I sought naturalisation. The Home Office official was an ex-rugger blue, and we discussed a recent international at great length. It was only afterwards that I realised how informative the interview must have been – more subtle, and much more effective, than the other one.

¶ Naturalisation was something I had forgotten about until the early 1950s, when not being legally British was a hindrance in business. Until then I had virtually overlooked the fact that that I was still technically 'German'. Thus I embarked upon this legalisation of something that I had already established in fact with those around me.

¶ My wartime residence in the U.K. was not taken into consideration when I applied for permission to file my application for naturalisation. This I could only do on the fifth anniversary of my last entry into the U.K. The certificate of naturalisation was granted in 1957, but first I had to renounce my Czech citizenship. By that time, I was the father of two daughters. British-born and educated, our daughters knew only one country, and to them Czechoslovakia is, to quote the words of a British Prime Minister, 'a small far away country', and those who lived there were 'people of whom we know nothing'. This is out home, this is where we belong.

¶ I am naturalised British and consider this state an understatement of my actual position, which is that I am no different in any essential respect except accident of birth from any other British citizen.

¶ I have never become naturalised. I was still under eighteen when my father was naturalised and we were told that I would have to apply again myself later. I am married to an Englishman, that does not automatically make me English – that was stopped after the war, when so many German girls married British soldiers. During the war, I wanted to join the Wrens, I wanted to join them so badly and I couldn't have done even if I had been naturalised then – you still had to have British-born parents. So I don't see that it matters. To my sister, being naturalised mattered terribly. She wanted to be British, and that was that. But I think it was a mere formality. I feel so strongly English that it would make no difference to me. I am married to an Englishman and my three children are English born. So that satisfies me.

¶ I was naturalised in 1947, but must admit that my change of nationality had meant little to me, a mere technical formality. I do not 'feel' either English or German; indeed my experiences have made me acquire a deter-

minedly international outlook, and I am suspicious of most forms of so-called patriotism.
¶ Naturally we shall always remain 'naturalised' citizens, the fact of not having been born here will always made us somewhat 'different'.
¶ My father, sister and myself were naturalised after the war, but I nevertheless continued to feel that I really was a refugee. From time to time people would ask where I came from, or when I was returning 'home', and then the awfulness of the situation would be brought home to me once more. Some refugees no doubt come to terms with it, but I never could, and to this day I resent having my provenance enquired into, I suppose because it reminds me that I am different from other people, or at any rate in the minority. I did not meet with any unpleasantness on this account, either during the war or after, but if anything did go wrong – if I didn't get a job, or promotion I wanted, I frequently believed, rightly or wrongly, that this was due to my being a foreigner.
¶ I did not become naturalised until my marriage until 1951. This is after all a mere formality, I am no different now to the 'bloody foreigner' I was before – I still have my accent, I am only British and never English, and even my passport gives the game away by stating my place of birth.
¶ I feel at home in England and I feel I have been accepted for what I am. True enough I am still different from the ordinary run of people, despite having become a British subject, and the man in the street still becomes aware of it when we have closer contact.
¶ I have now been married for fifteen years and have two children, and we are comfortably off. But in all these years of British Citizenship we find that whereas we certainly don't feel like refugees any more, we don't seem to be fully integrated either. It takes more than one generation to do that.

K. Gershon, *We Came as Children: A Collective Autobiography* (London: Victor Gollancz, 1966) 126–9.

149) Eric Ferron visits London, and an English home, 1940s [I.]

See note on extract No.85.

We were posted together to an army camp in Buckinghamshire to go on a course in the Royal Army Medical Corps. Ben said it was near London and he would like to take me there. I was thrilled as I wanted to see London. I felt so good. Ben said we could stay with his family. We had ten days leave to come the following month. I wrote my mother that I was invited to an English home and Ben was taking me to London. My mother wrote back delighted and asked me to send a photograph. Ben gave me one and I sent it to her. . . .

Ben and I hitch-hiked to London. I wanted to see everything – all in one day. Ben said it would take months it was so big and there was a lot of waiting to do. It was odd that when we arrived Ben didn't take me straight to his home. We went to a YMCA hostel. I thought maybe his family were away on holiday, but I wondered. That evening we went to the pictures and afterwards I asked Ben.

'I think we are better off spending a few days by ourselves first. I want to surprise them. We'll see as much as we can and then we'll go home. You know how parents are. They won't let you out of their sight, so we'll have some fun first.'

I accepted this. It seemed reasonable. We went to the dog track, to Wembley to see the Harlem Globe Trotters, to Buckingham Palace, to Windsor and to Tower Bridge. I saw so much, it was wonderful. It seemed endless. There was so much to write home – letters and letters to my family. Then on the Saturday evening Ben said: 'There's a pub I used to go to near my house. We'll go there, have a drink and then go home.'

The lady behind the bar was kind, although she did call me 'Sambo'. She offered me a drink on the house, which I thought was nice. 'You're always welcome here' she said. This I did think strange. I had supposed that everyone was welcome in a pub. We had our drinks. Ben was gloomy. I tried telling him stories about the boys, but they did not seem to register. Then he said suddenly: 'You see that man over there in the cap? That's my father.'

'Your father? Well, aren't you going to talk to him?'

'When I've finished my drink.'

He did finish his drink and then went over to his father. I watched them both talking and looking over at me. Then they came over.

'Dad, this is Eric, the friend I told you about. This is the man you refused to have home. Look at him, shake his hand. Go on shake his hand. He doesn't bite!'

His father's head dropped. I felt bad, as if I could go through the floor. My whole world crumbled. The women behind the bar tried to cheer me.

'Never mind, we like you. Some people are so stupid about black men. Take no notice, you can come here any time you want.'

All this was just background noise to me, all I could think was: Why doesn't his father want to see me? What have I done? In a curious way I felt guilty, as if I was in the wrong. Then I heard Ben's father's voice: 'Pleased to meet you. I don't hate you, why should I? I don't know you. Never seen you before. Take no notice of my son. He's had too much to drink.'

'No I haven't' Ben said, 'you wrote and told me not to bring him. I've got the letter in my pocket. You know damn well! I wrote and told you about him. How do you think I felt when you wrote and told me not to bring him? I didn't know how to tell him. I never told him. But I thought we shouldn't go back without letting him know the truth.'

Everyone in the pub was now listening. The woman came from behind the bar and put her arm around me. 'This country has got some funny people in it. But we aren't all like it. You mustn't let it upset you. There's good and bad everywhere.'

She was trying to help, but I just stood there shocked, suddenly disillusioned, somehow guilty. I didn't know what to say, where to look. I didn't know why I felt so anxious. Ben's father went back to his friends, but before he went he said to Ben: 'You can bring your friend round to meet your mother tomorrow. See you at home.'

Ben and I left the pub and took the bus back to the YMCA.

Along the way we didn't talk. We went up to our room and he sat down on the bed and wept . . .

Next morning Ben said we could go home to his family.

'Why should I', I said.

'Don't be a bloody fool. Come and show them you're better than they are.'

I wondered if I was even good enough. But we went. His mother and sister were there: his sister very cheerful, his mother quiet and older than I had expected. She greeted me.

'Come in and sit down. Let me take your coat. I heard all about last night. Ben you were naughty to talk to your father like that in front of people.'

To me: 'We don't hate anyone. You mustn't get it wrong. People round here are just not used to coloured people and they would talk if they saw a coloured man come into our house. So we thought rather than embarrass you we'd tell Ben not to bring you. Anyway, that's all past and you're here. Now, what will you have to eat?'

It turned out to be very pleasant. We stayed about three days. We were out most of the time, Ben's sister came with us. His father was friendly but all along I had a suspicion that he was just putting up with me. They were polite and cheerful but I did not feel close. I was aware of the distance and could feel the rejection.

E. Ferron, *'Man, You've Mixed': A Jamaican Comes to Britain* (London: Whiting and Birch, 1995) 9–13.

150) Sikh religious practice in Gravesend, 1950s onwards [I.]

See note on extract No.89.

By 1954 Cloran Singh from Jandialy came to Gravesend and he brought our Holy Book in 1955 and set up a room in the house for it. We used to go there for weekends to say our prayers. By 1957 we gathered enough funds and brought a house in Edwin Street for setting up a Sikh Temple for the community. The community grew bigger and bigger and soon we needed a proper place to meet the needs. So, in 1968, we bought a church building in Clarence Place which is now our Temple, known as Guru Nanak Darbar. It seemed too big at that time, but is not enough now to cater for the community needs. So the community here bought another two buildings, military barracks in Trinity Road and one building in the Grove to meet the religious, social and educational needs.

As the community started settling, we started thinking of meeting their other needs. For religious functions we now had the Temple, for our own intellectual gratification we formed parties. Some joined the labour party, others Indian Workers' Associations. So we started to celebrate our religious festival, Viasakhi, as well as our National Day on August 15th, the Independence Day. We used to invite prominent members of the host community and Lord and Mary Murray were our guests on these occasions. We entertained sportsmen and other leading figures from India. The Chairman of the Hockey Team, who brought the Indian team to attend the Olympics in Helsinki, enjoyed our hospitality.

Things changed now. Since the attack of the Golden Temple at Amritsar we turned back to our religion. We started growing our hair and beards and temple-going became more than a weekend routine. Now I go to work during the day, to the temple in my spare time and mind my own business and family. No time for politics or national heroes.

S. Winters, *Nobody Sleeps on the Rooftops Now* (Gravesend: AIM, 1994) 6–7.

151) Simi Bedford on rediscovering Africa, 1959 [I.]

Simi Bedford was born in Lagos, Nigeria, in 1941. After attending an English boarding school she went on to university and a career mainly in television. See note on extract No.91.

In 1959 I rediscovered Africa. I had to wait a year before going to university and my parents had bought a house in Wembley Park and a load of my Nigerian cousins were in England by now, studying, and I began to met them all. We formed this whole circuit and my life then went from being totally English to being totally African. I was back in the fold. They were all like me, refugees from this English education system. Every Saturday, at different town halls, there would be a Nigerian dance. Fela Kuti would play Nigerian High Life music – which didn't interest the West Indians, so it was all West Africans. We spent a lot of time going to parties at the High Commissions. There were four, one for each area of the country. I went around with this group, mainly black or Asian. Suddenly you could give up trying to look like Sandra Dee or whoever. There was the Ronettes. Changed our lives. Suddenly black girls were seen as beautiful. You went from being this hideously ugly Frank Bruno figure to being Ronnie Spector. It was quite extraordinary. By the time I went to university in 1960 black was where it was at. All that soul music. Then here were all these fine art students at Durham University who were into Benin bronzes and African masks and tall thin women and suddenly here were these people saying, 'You are a great beauty.' I thought, 'This is all right then.'

J. Green, *Them* (London: Secker and Warburg, 1990) 245.

152) Eric Ferron becomes a social worker in London, *c.*1960 [I.]

See note on extract No.85.

In my work as a social worker, as well as in my private life, it is not unusual for people to talk to me about black people quite bluntly and without any embarrassment to them or pain for me. Often I find people so full of colour prejudice and so in need to talk it out that paradoxically they do not seem to see that I am black too. To them I am just another friend of the family. I remember my contact with one family whose young daughter got into all kinds of trouble with men. Her mother was particularly upset and bitter one day when I went round to see them.

'My daughter is pregnant by a coloured man! A coloured man, Mr Ferron!' I was not all that surprised. She went on: 'There's plenty of fellows in the street, white and black, and I know the white ones aren't much cop in this area but that would have been better than with a black man.' Her face grimaced in disgust as she said it. I listened to her outpouring and when she paused for a moment I told her I shared her disappointment that the girl was pregnant but now it had happened she would need her mother's help.

She must see that she wouldn't have to face it alone.

'But what about the people in the street?' the mother said

'How do you think they will react when they know? She's not married. That's bad enough but having a black baby is worse.'

'The neighbours will talk anyway', I said, 'That's something we all have to live with. But the important thing now is that she mustn't feel rejected.'

'Well she can't stay here! There's no room for a baby. And when her father hears of it he'll throw her out.'

I murmured something about hoping they would see their responsibilities a bit more constructively instead of just responding to their own immediate disgust, and I offered to talk with her father as I knew him well. A few days later they invited me over again. All three of them were there and the father had already been told.

'I don't want a little black bastard in my house! You can take it and go and live with him whoever he is.'

The girl was embarrassed. 'But Dad, Mr Ferron is a black man too. How do you think he feels when you say things like that?'

'Mr Ferron is Mr Ferron as far as I'm concerned.'

And it was true. I was Mr Ferron, who worked with the family; they had a problem and had asked me to share it with them. It just so happened that the problem was their daughter having a black baby. I went into some detail with her father about how important it was for him to concern himself with the girl's future and not to reject her but to give her a chance to prove herself. They talked about abortion but they decided there would not be enough grounds. Tempers cooled a little as we talked and the discussion turned into a sober exercise between the parents and myself. I said I would talk to the young man if they thought it would help and the girl said she would arrange it for the following Monday.

I met him and he turned out to be the kind of fellow I hoped would never leave the West Indies, arrogant, indifferent and casual, the kind who creates trouble and gives all black immigrants a bad name. 'Why should I talk to you? What are you anyway? Some kind of protector of the young?'

I said I was a friend of the family and told him to sit down and listen. If he wanted to prove he was a man, now was the time.

What was he going to do about it?

He said nothing, then: 'How do you know the kid's mine?'

I said I didn't know, only he and the girl knew that, but we had been told the child was his and I wanted to know what he was going to do to help. Could he help pay for its upkeep, for instance. He agreed he would. He even put it in writing.

When I saw the family again they were surprised and relieved he had agreed to pay something. It would help because they were a poor family, but they also needed help to accept the fact that their daughter was pregnant and unmarried and that they would have a black grandchild. Gradually, the mother managed to hold down her fear of the neighbours and the pregnancy took its course and the girl gave birth to a fine healthy boy. The parents visited her every day in hospital and took her and the baby back home when the time came. Also her father began to take to the baby. 'My grandson', he would say, 'You may be a little black bastard but you're my first grandson.'

His elder daughter was married but had no children. As he began to move towards the new baby she became jealous and wanted to share in. The young mother resented her interference. We were facing a new problem. I could only help by trying to get them all to discuss it instead of quarrelling and then avoiding each other. The girl had to see her sister's gesture as helpful and accepting, that she was not rejecting her but wanted to share with her. Soon the girl got herself a job and the grandmother gave up her own job to look after the baby. Help came for the girl, late but in time.

E. Ferron, *'Man, You've Mixed': A Jamaican Comes to Britain* (London: Whiting and Birch, 1995) 87–9.

153) Rampal on the insecurities of immigrant life in London, *c.*1970 [I.]

See note on extract No.102.

> It is just because we are guests in this country that I often feel afraid and insecure about staying here. English people will tolerate coloured people here only as long as they need them. Those who are necessary to them have their demands met quickly enough. If I were a doctor or a scientist I would be in a position to ask for things and my requests would probably be met, but people like myself come here as labourers and if we lose our value they will soon tell us to go. They will tell Indian scientists and doctors to go as soon as they no longer need them. The things which you cannot do without are dear to your heart and you will not abuse them readily, but what you do not need you have little regard for. We are vulnerable here because we are insecure and this is humiliating for us, a matter of shame. If the government decides to turn us out, no amount of marching up and down with flags and petitions will do us any good. If the foreman abuses us and fires us, no amount of protest will get us back our jobs. An Englishman can answer back because he knows the language, he can stand up for himself. He does not depend on the good will of others and can easily get another job in any case.

U. Sharma, *Rampal and His Family* (London: Collins, 1971) 99.

154) Alcoholism and despair among Latvians in Bedford, 1970 [I.]

See note on extract No.86.

> The Latvians are the saddest of all. Despairing drinkers. They'll drink for days on end. All heavy drinking. And come Sunday morning early, seven o'clock, they will be knocking me up for more. No matter what . . . but never any violence. Never trouble. And no matter how drunk they are, they wouldn't dream to swear in front of me. Those Latvians are gentlemen to the death. Some of them, I think, died really in the war. They saw too much. And they know they cannot go back. They have accepted that they will die here. In that state, some people turn to religion, some turn to drink. . . . Those Latvians are the most lost of all. I have one, he is deaf and dumb. He doesn't want a hearing aid, he doesn't want to know anything any more. He just cut himself off. And now he has drunk himself out. He is waiting to die.

J. Brown, *The Un-Melting Pot* (London: Macmillan – now Palgrave Macmillan, 1970) 52.

155) Asian political activism, 1970s [I.]

See note on extract No.111.

> . . . I mean in terms of when I started taking note of politics to do with race, em . . . during the . . . I mean when was the Ugandan crisis? early seventies, then there was the Malawi Asian one, and the way the press had dealt with that had begun to put an impact on me, and also interested me in

> immigration control and immigration laws, and how they were affecting things. So that was already coming into my consciousness, and it's one of the things that we discussed when we met. We . . . we all agreed on the need to form something in 'seventy-six, and I don't think we did particularly anything about it at that stage apart from continue to just talk about it. And, er . . . there was already something in Bradford called . . . No, what happened was that we started talking about the need for something independent in Bradford, not necessarily a black organisation then, but something to fight the National Front influence in Bradford because they were selling papers and all kinds of things. And we talked about some kind of ad hoc committee to start with, and then I'd to go away, I think. This might have been when I was still at university. I'd to go away to France or something to work as part of my course, and when I came back something had been formed called the 'Ad Hoc Committee against Racism and Fascism'. This had been our idea, started in the Library cafe. So that was already going and, and I'm just wondering how we moved on from that. (Long pause) . . . I'm not sure when or how we particularly moved on from that, but what I do know is that in 'seventy-six in Southall there'd been an incident where an Asian youth had been murdered, Gurdit Chagger. And that had a big impact on us and we decided that we'd have to do something now and that we'd have to . . . you know, not hang on the coat tails of, you know, the white left any more and organise our own community. And, er . . . through organising the meeting, er . . . did we organise the meeting? No. Ah, somebody organised the meeting, I've got it now. There's a guy called, a young lad called . . . oh, Surinder, and he was a Labour Party member of, or supporter of Militant, or his father was any way, he called a meeting in a pub on Leeds Road, to sort out some kind of youth organisation, which we went along to, and we decided to call another meeting. Anyway this other meeting which happened in the Albion, a group of about eight or ten of us went along, and there was Surinder . . . But what happened was the IWA.

R. Perks, '"You're different: you're one of us": the making of a British Asian', *Oral History*, 15 (1987) 72.

156) Elaine on black identity, 1989 [I.]

Elaine (pseud.) was born in Britain c.1975. Her mother is English, her father Jamaican, and the family live in Erdington. She has a strong interest in history and politics, especially in Northern Ireland. See also note on extract No.118.

> I hang around with a lot of white people and they seem to me to have a problem about this. Marcia's quite clear about it: she sees me as Black. The first person who said 'Afro-Caribbean' to me, I didn't know what she was talking about! I just said to her, 'I'm Black!' A lot of my white friends say, 'No you're not Black, I see you as white.' I really feel like screaming, saying: 'I'm not white, I'm Black!'

Sometimes they are calling everybody names around me, using words like 'nigger' and I look at them and they say, 'Oh, God, I didn't mean anything.' Sometimes it really causes some bad arguments around me and sometimes I just say, 'Forget it!' When people say 'Paki' I really start arguing, I really start getting involved. My mum told me I must learn not to react like that, but I can't stand it when someone says, 'I didn't mean to be racist, but . . .'

A. Osler, *Speaking Out: Black Girls in Britain* (London: Virago Upstarts, 1989) 83.

157) Muhammad Ali on integration and Asian identity, 1990 [I.]

Muhammad Ali was born in Kashmir in 1942. He arrived in Bradford to be with his father in 1969. See also note on extract No.145.

It's very difficult to say whether people want to integrate into the mainstream society or not. People who have tried to integrate have had such bitter experiences. When I was at school there were a few Asian kids who considered themselves as English, as white. What they said was that they considered English to be their mother tongue – although it wasn't – and they didn't really want to mix with other Asian or Muslim boys. They wanted to adopt the English culture completely and they did their best to do so. We called them 'natives' and we generally teased them. We all left school and went our own ways. Ten years later I met some of them and they had become completely different. At least two had grown beards, become very religious and were completely involved in the Asian community. I asked them why. They said that they had tried their best to mix with the white community, but they had given up. The English would never accept them, when it came to the crunch they would always be isolated. When it really came down to being accepted as part of English society, it was impossible, and they found a lot more security in their community. This must stem from colour. It's not just the English attitude to foreigners. Apart from colour there was nothing about these boys that made different from the English. That was the only difference. They had accents, they ate English food, drank in the pub, made the same jokes. Everything was the same except the colour of their skin, so logically, by a process of elimination that had to be the cause of their rejection. They might throw away their Asian identity, but still they were excluded.

J. Green, *Them: Voices from the Immigrant Community in Contemporary Britain* (London: Secker and Warburg, 1990) 251.

158) Yasmin Alibhai on Asian-British identity, 1990 [I.]

Yasmin Alibhai was born in Kampala, Uganda, in 1949. She arrived in England as a post-graduate student in 1972 and stayed on after Idi Amin excluded the Asian Ugandans. See also note on extract No.145.

My identity is very much that of a British Asian, which is not the same as being an Indian born in India. I don't see culture as a static notion. I see it as a volatile, ever-changing, re-processing dynamic, and it has to be if it's going to survive. What is important to me is that certain values that are gained through being Asian in origin, are extremely valuable in this very cold world. So I don't care who my son marries, or if he prays or whatever, but what is important is the lessons that my mother taught us: how you think about yourself, that you don't think that the world owes you personal happiness which is the central philosophy of life in the West. The question of individual fulfilment at the cost of anything: personal happiness becomes a kind of apple to which everybody is entitled. Our lives are not like that. At least fifty per cent of our happiness is defined by the family or the community. From the time you are a child you learn to sacrifice a part of your life. I admire those values. I don't want to lose them, because if you've got that belief it isn't that difficult to look after the old, it isn't that difficult to occasionally make decisions which hurt you but which hurt others less. I don't find this in Britain or in the West generally. The spinal fluid of the West remains based on this central principle every individual has the right to go for personal happiness and personal fulfilment, and that's the most important thing. It's completely different in the East: you learn that you are important but not the most important thing in the world. The circle immediately around you, and all the circles beyond that are equally important if not more so.

J. Green, *Them* (London: Secker and Warburg, 1990) 242.

159) Cindy Blake on culture and personal history, 1990 [I.]

Cindy Blake was born in Boston, Massachusetts in 1952. She came to England in 1978 to marry her fiancé, and worked as a journalist before becoming a novelist. See also note on extract No.145.

I absolutely do think there is an immigrant experience which makes no difference whether you're upper-class American or born in some wretched village in Pakistan. Because what you're talking about is, among other things, having no history. So that you can't say to the person you're with, remember something we did together five years ago, or look at that building, that's where I used to live. You can't refer back and you're very cut off: I think that nobody takes in properly what a major upheaval it is to move countries, and that you don't yourself until it's too late . . . You don't realize what culture actually means. What it means to be able to refer to having seen Mr Ed on television, having the same jokes, having the same references. When you can't share those you feel somehow missing. I think that that's why it's very difficult to be an immigrant. So you haven't lived through the same experiences and even when they're supposed to be similar – the 60s for instance – they can actually be so different. All those points of references have moved

> and you're left without a grid to chart anything. And you're supposed to start from the beginning, but at any age after 0 it's very hard to start from the beginning and build up another grid, especially if it's a grid that you're not particularly fond of.

J. Green, *Them: Voices from the Immigrant Community in Contemporary Britain* (London: Secker and Warburg, 1990) 248.

Part III
Migrant Place Stories from the 18th to the 20th Centuries

Introduction to Part III: Migrant Place Stories from the 18th to the 20th Centuries

Peter Leese

Part III of *The British Migrant Experience* presents first-hand accounts recording the development of migrant communities within the major cities, county towns and rural districts of mainland Britain. These are not histories of particular communities in particular cities, because first-hand migrant accounts do not give this kind of detail. Rather, Part III provides a series of cross-sectional studies which slice through time so as to allow insight into the lives of certain groups of migrants in parts of Wales, Scotland and England, and, by implication, into the lives of wider regional communities. The extant sources are patchy – capturing in words a sense of place, be it a neighbourhood, a city or a region, is an elusive task because it depends on static description rather than dynamic events; nevertheless, the collected stories highlight the local character of the British nations and regions.[1]

The migrant communities that develop in each region all have their own local history: they are inflected by the geography, work patterns, wealth or poverty of the districts in which they dwell. In some instances migrant groups established themselves in a particular location over many decades, while in others their presence was either dispersed or their numbers were so small that a particular minority was hardly visible.[2] Some communities could be well organized and supportive, others riven with rivalries and divisions, still others could merely 'boast' of isolated gestures of communal assistance. The accounts in Part III make it also clear that poorer migrants, particularly those from overseas who travelled from the eighteenth to the early twentieth century, had a bounded awareness of where they were or how their present location might differ from some other part of the country. They knew the name of their destination, were taken or moved directly there when they arrived in the country, and remained within a small group of native-speaking fellow-countrymen in lodgings, workshops and places of worship. The psychological impact of local and regional adjustment is difficult to pin down; the wider processes of cultural adjustment are easier to embrace. What might be said with certainty is that it did influence migrants' everyday experience, as they tried to cope with local accents, or with regional religious and work practices.[3]

To illustrate some of these local character stories and to address related issues raised by Part III, this introduction analyses the accounts dealing with the South. Moreover, in the case study section it discusses additional material, which concentrates in part on that most archetypal of British immigrant localities, the East End of London. To begin with, the concept of place should be defined in relation to three centuries of migrant experience.

Any description of 'place' has clearly to refer to more than a particular region, town or neighbourhood. Significantly, it must relate to distinctive forms of human interaction with locality: to the connections and disjunctions of rural and urban landscape; to the constantly shifting ephemera of local climate and personality as well as to the immovable landmark. In the eighteenth and nineteenth centuries especially, when servants might be restricted to a small but largely rural or proto-industrial landscape, or when tramping labourers and artisans moved between fields, workshops or kitchens, a sense of place meant association not with distinguishing landmarks, but with open landscapes, particular work practices and accents.[4] Some of the accounts reproduced here are thus intended to register specific instances of movement over a few miles, or sometimes over much longer distances, as servants and agricultural labourers moved around the country (183–6; 188). Place may also be taken to mean the creation of a self-sustaining and self-contained ethnic enclave, and there are thus a number of references to Irish and Jewish community at different times and throughout the country (193, 194). A fluctuating sense of territorial ownership is also detectable in some accounts: when social investigators feel themselves in 'alien' districts of the city (197); when migrants create neutral zones, such as markets, where they could usually act in public without fear of harassment or reprisal.[5] The reception of migrants into local community varied geographically. In some of the smaller towns of Scotland or Wales, for instance, acceptance was a matter of tolerating, or not, religious difference, un-unionized labour practices, or parochial attitudes (234, 236, 237). In the twentieth century Jewish, Polish and Irish communities settled well into the landscape, which meant that they could uphold their own traditions and values with partial communal acceptance (247–50).

Overview of Part III

The South charts a much larger region than the great metropolitan magnet of London; the extracts point to Bristol (Avon), Exeter (Devon) and Gravesend (Kent) as well as the Irish, 'Asiatic' and migrant labour presence in the western districts of the south. Inevitably, however, it is London that has always drawn the majority of migrants and immigrants both from home and abroad as well as many talented social writers eager to investigate the

London scenery. There are few accounts that could better those presented here by Henry Mayhew (on a Moroccan street trader; 167) or J. T. Smith (on Joseph Johnson; 169), though J. Salter (168) on 'Asiatics' of the West Country comes close. Besant and Thorogood (170, 172–3) contribute to the early twentieth-century discussion on race politics; A. S. Darby (171) gives a delightful child's-eye view of his engagement with the Italian community in Luton; and Guran Singh Khera (174) describes the early settlement of the Punjabi community in Gravesend. Returning to London, Ruth Glass and Mike Phillips (175, 176) provide two portraits of the black community (see also case study below).

The Midlands and East Anglia is an amalgamation of two regions that encompasses recent heavy industrial development such as car manufacturing, the older tradition of crafts and trades in Birmingham, and the smaller rural communities of Norfolk or Bedfordshire. Consequently it is an area with diverse migrant communities: a Jewish settlement in Birmingham (177) as well as European newcomers from the mid-eighteenth century (178); servants as well as labourers and craftsmen criss-crossing the district through the eighteenth and nineteenth century in search of employment (171, 185–8); displaced European refugees reluctantly settling after World War Two and the Hungarian Uprising of 1956 (189). In more recent years the post-colonial settlements have led to the establishment of large immigrant communities in Birmingham and Bedford for instance (191), and to ethnic tension revealed most notably in the 1958 'riots' in Nottingham and the 1985 disturbances in Handsworth, Birmingham (190).

North West England together with several Midlands cities including Birmingham and Coventry, has been the preferred home for many migrants because accomodation and cost of living are generally lower than in the South. Of the accounts presented here members of the Shaw family (192), travelling in the late eighteenth and early nineteenth century, were most obviously driven by economic necessity, but migrants from Ireland and Wales, from Italy and India (194, 204, 201, 206), among others, settled in the North West for similar reasons. The Jewish communities in the region, especially Leeds and Manchester (193, 198–200, 202, 203), attracted most attention – naturally so, because Jewish working practices and communities were the object of both sympathetic curiosity and malign discontent from the 1880s to the Great War. In recent years oral historians have recovered many less obvious aspects of Jewish life during this period.

North East England has a long history of Irish settlement in Cumbria, Northumbria and Durham, dating in some cases back to the seventeenth century, and peaking at around five per cent of the total population. However, the selection here concentrates on two groups: Jews in the eighteenth and nineteenth century Sunderland (207–10), and Arab seamen in South Shields (214–30) in the interwar period. The Sunderland Jewish community established itself in the eighteenth century, but it was through connections with Lithuania that the Krottingen Jews began to arrive after the 1860s. A fascinating insight into Arab–English community relations, notions of patriotism, racial purity and mixed-race relationships is offered by the long run of letters reproduced from the *Shields Daily Gazette*.

Scotland has its own unique mix of migrant groups, who tended to gravitate towards Glasgow, and especially its slum district, the Gorbals. Two of the accounts here also register the presence of internal migrants: William Cameron's (232) witty recollections of his early 'cadging' career in 1815, and N. Morris's (240) journey of initiation from Stornoway to Glasgow in 1889. The Irish presence is well-established throughout the nineteenth century (234, 236, 237, 245). Other less well-known groups include 'Asiatics' (238); Poles and Lithuanians (confused at times), although present in Scotland both earlier and later, were recruited in large numbers in the late nineteenth century to work in the steel factories and mines of Lanarkshire (235, 241). Irish and Indian accounts represent the increase in these two migrant groups in twentieth century Scotland (245, 246). Finally, the story of recent Polish immigrantion to Scotland is told (249).

Wales, for reasons of geography, has always had a strong Irish presence both in the cities and in the countryside – there is a kind of border zone where the two nationalities have mixed and co-existed (258, 261). At certain times too, for example during the 1882 Tredgar riots, and for both religious and political reasons, the Irish were the object of violent demonstrations (255). This section also notes the English, Jewish and Spanish presence in Wales (254, 251, 259, 260). Aristcratic Englishwoman Hester Thrale comments acerbically on the Welsh countryside as a provincial backwater (*c*.1795; 252–3). There are two notable childhood memoirs here: W. H. Davies recollections of the Italian presence in Bedlinog (*c*.1914; 257) and Neil Sinclair's reminiscences on Tiger Bay (1940s; 262, 263).

Case study 3: local identity as negotiation

Markéta Luskačova became a migrant in 1975 when she moved from Prague to a quarter of the English capital that has been the entry point for new arrivals for over three hundred years: the East End of London. Ten years earlier as a sociology student in Slovakia Luskačova had made an anthropological photographic study of village pilgrims; now, as a newly arrived immigrant, she turned back to photography as a nuanced, subjective language that could help understand her own situation and describe it to others. In 1991 a collection of her work was put on display at the Whitechapel Gallery, and in the catalogue for the exhibition a British friend C. Killip commented on the connection between Luskačova's awkwardly spoken English, her beautifully spoken Czech, and her use of photograph. '[Her] lack of skill in speaking English has had a paradoxical effect', he writes, 'as it seems to heighten her ability to see Englishness, as any eloquence for her in this country is through her photography.'[6] As they depict the people and streets of the East End markets, Luskačova's photographs simultaneously testify to the power of language, in this case a visual language, to root the newly arrived into their adopted home, to shape a sense of place, personal and communal identity. The London writer Iain Sinclair thus describes this imaginative process in Luskačova's work: 'By her listings of particulars she makes an overloud somewhere into an estranged and marvellous nowhere. She detaches the fertile chaos of Cheshire Street from the rest of London. Her animal traders under the railway arches are fictionalized through documentation. The album of images becomes a self-portrait.'[7]

In this process of fictionalization and self-portraiture, we are able to observe how migrants' expressions of self within their adopted community allow them to bridge cultures and re-invent selves. Furthermore, whether or not these fictions and self-portraits are well articulated or incoherent, oral history or published memoir, they also give an insight into the development and sustenance of three mutually inclusive forms of identity. First, personal identity: as Iain Sinclair notes, by observing, recording and interacting with a local population the immigrant provides an oblique self-portrait. The only image of Luskačova in her album, for instance, is glimpsed in a mirror that stands casually in front of a shop, but her sense of locality and of self, of a particular place seen through fresh, unaccustomed eyes, marks her whole collection of photographs. Second, local, communal identity: by examining Luskačova's work we are able to observe a rich, vital community that has a long history of immigrant arrival and settlement without reference to its past or past conventions of representation. The photographer interprets for us a localized, particular form of London Englishness. Third, national identity: as Killip notes, Luskačova's failure as an English speaker is also her success as an eloquent witness to Englishness. Since the East End has an exaggerated, clichéd place in the collective image of English national identity, Luskačova's work provides a rare opportunity for self-reflection.

There is a limit to the usefulness of migrant testimony however. Iain Sinclair traces it in his remark that Luskačova's photographs make 'an overloud somewhere into an estranged and marvellous nowhere'. By definition, migrants lack a past: their birthplace becomes a faded snapshot in their own mind, and a hazily imagined postcard to their new neighbours. Hence the advantage of seeing without a set of local cultural conventions might equally be a disadvantage, because the best it can produce is an estranged, marvellous nowhere. In analysing migrant narratives that relate to local, regional community, it is difficult, therefore, to build any kind of objective, comprehensive picture. The pieces of the jigsaw just won't fit together to make an un-jumbled, definitive image of the host community, the immigrant community, or the interaction between the two. Instead, in memoirs, autobiographies and reminiscences, migrants give oral equivalents of *Photographs of Spitalfields*: portraits of self, community and nation reflected in mirrors, composed in fragmentary observations, particularized in life-experiences.

If sources of host and migrant testimony are too few and too fragmented to give a full picture of immigrant arrival and settlement, let alone the psychological or social processes of identity adjustment, they can nevertheless provide an historical model for the process of identity formation. Southern England is an interesting case study: because of its seaports, especially Bristol, which drew slaves, migrant and immigrant labour, as well as religious and political refugees; and because of London, which attracted every kind of international and internal migrant. The extant sources for southern England come in the eighteenth century from court record or newspaper advertisement for escaped slave; in the nineteenth to the early twentieth century from religiously and politically motivated reportage or travelogue; in the last fifty years from autobiography or else oral history. In observer accounts of migration, the narrative of exclusion marks out local identity: defined according to place of birth, cultural and historical knowledge, religious faith, skin colour, useful work skills, and ability to contribute to the local community. In migrant accounts, the narrative of inclusion marks out local identity: defined according to employment, language skills, minimized or maximized cultural differences and religious devotion. In both cases, a polarized account seems to defy the workaday reality of cooperation and antagonism between stranger and local. As if each collection of details is an idealized bargaining position for the negotiation of identities, a position which is imagined and shaped through the dialogue and discussion of everyday experience, but which can be articulated in its most idealized form as a monologue. Native and migrant accounts of local community need to be seen as mirror images then: they reflect, distort and interact with each other; they depend on one another for their sense of self-definition. As Mike Phillips, the modern day journalist and long-time observer of black London has put it, migrants and hosts come to share a locality, and by doing so they also share 'an identity which is difficult and which has to be constantly negotiated' (176).

Accounts of migrant communities in southern England during the eighteenth century show only one side of this bargaining however, that of the host. John Latimer's chronicle of Bristol, published in 1893, uses evidence of this kind, especially from court proceedings and newspapers columns, to strikingly convey the depth of loyalty and inclusive sense of community felt by the city's population: their suspicion of outsiders, their unwillingness to accept settlers unless on carefully qualified conditions. Latimer notes that around 1700, for instance, place of birth was strictly checked and defined to ensure that only qualified traders and craftsmen did business within the city boundary; those who were born in neighbouring districts or out-parishes were 'foreigners' (160). Outside traders paid fines when caught engaging in what to the local population was 'illicit' business activities within the Bristol city boundary (fines increased from £5 to £20 in 1703); spies were encouraged to produce information that would lead to the prosecution, conviction and exclusion of out-parish strangers. Any youth from beyond the city boundary who wanted to acquire a trade through apprenticeship had to pay a fee or be hounded out of town. There were, however, notable exceptions to these rules – when a craftsman with new skills could be added to the town: for instance, when William Bonney set up his print shop in 1695, or when a watchmaker was allowed to set up business in 1700 by making a present of a watch and dial and promising their upkeep for life.

The reluctance to accept out-parishioners or other native migrants may be accounted for by the speculative involvement of many local merchants in the lucrative sale and purchase of black slaves. As Roger North, Baron of Guildford noted in 1742 'A poor Shopkeeper, that sells Candles, will have a Bale of Stockings, or a Piece of Stuff for *Nevis*, or *Virginia* &c. and, rather than fail, they Trade in Men'.[8] Such slaves, indeed, appear to have been a more acceptable sight in the streets of early eighteenth century Bristol than native 'foreigners', though they lived and died in servitude, were seen only when parading in the streets as a mark of their owner's status, and were viewed as novelty and commodity. Latimer's native account is remarkable, then, for its broadly inclusive definition of both British and overseas 'foreigners'. It shows how their acceptance was conditionally linked to usefulness and status: the presence of French Huguenots is noted with approval in 1726, for instance, when the Corporation of Bristol granted a plot of land for a chapel to be built; yet in August 1740 the court of quarter sessions fixed a rate of 6s. 6d., including food, for the ship masters who were charged with returning Irish paupers who had landed in the city to their native land (161).

Nineteenth century narratives of local migrant community in southern England are more common, recorded both by migrants themselves and their host community observers. Generally, however, the available sources document only one side of this dialogue between foreigner and local, that of the inquisitive or intrusive observer who comes to relate his tale to the wider community, and in these accounts the foreigner is often irreducibly 'alien', even when he is resident of long standing and at least partly absorbed into the locality. J. Salter's *The Asiatic in England: Sketches of Sixteen Years' Work Among Orientals* (1873), for instance, is an account of the author's missionary work in the southern parts of England, including London, Bristol and Bath (168). Salter's report describes travelling to these 'alien' enclaves to share the Christian faith with Jews, Muslims and Hindus. His safe passage through these foreign, enclosed societies, as he sees them, is evidence of 'Divine care in such work'. The author's regard for 'Asiatics', moreover, both affectionate and condescending, is typical of middle class observer in the later Victorian era who went to working class and immigrant districts like East London and elsewhere to document, photograph and report in the belief that he was 'scientifically' recording a culture as strange and incomprehensible as any missionary might find on the 'Dark Continent'.[9]

Henry Mayhew's *London Labour and the London Poor* (1851) is an early exception to this spirit of enquiry in providing verbatim testimony from nineteenth century migrants to the capital, for instance, from a Moroccan rhubarb seller. This man's narrative – a story of business success in London, setting up shop in Exeter, and then return to London for want of acceptance or profits – shows, significantly, how migrants sometimes failed to connect with any local community, finding both their own and their host culture inert and unresponsive. 'We take and trust, and lose all our money,' says the trader (167). 'T'oders never kept a sop before, and not one of us was English scholar; we was forced to keep a man, and datway we lose all our money.'[10] The rhubarb seller's account therefore, as a result of his disconnection with his host community, has only a sketchy sense of local identity, place settlement, or the rewards of settlement. This failure to connect with the host community, expressed in hazed details, collapsed time spans and unremembered place names, is also a mirror image response to the abject certainties of the religious or scientific observer; a monologue that reflects the hard bargaining of negotiated local identities.

Accounts of the late nineteenth and early twentieth century show a growing yet impersonal curiosity towards immigrant communities. Social investigators and journalists who venture into migrant districts saw them as closed, foreign societies, and described them with antipathy and resentment: they were places to buy exotic mementoes, observe curious scenes, or avoid altogether if judged unsafe. As W. Besant wrote in his account of East London's Chinatown in 1903, 'it is considered quite safe to visit the place, at all events in the daytime' (170). Similarly in the 1930s another journalist, George Thorogood, entered the same district with 'a vague feeling of fear' and regarded Whitechapel Road as 'abandoned to the alien invader' because of the strong Jewish presence in the district (172, 173). Here the sometimes questionable spirit of Victorian scientific investigation is further tainted by frightening stories of alien invasion, Great War atrocity propaganda and interwar anti-Semitism. After World War Two, however, the rise of autobiographical writing, oral history and multiculturalism reveal more clearly than ever that migrants and immigrants own a sense of local identity, which closely matches a sense of cultural, social affinity.[11]

In *Man, You've Mixed* (1995), for instance, Eric Ferron, a Jamaican who came to Britain in the 1940s, defines himself against southern Englishness, rejecting London and, instead, finding kinship with northern Englanders and Scots. 'I always found an immediate kindness in the North,' he writes (205). 'I've never had this feeling in the South, certainly not in London. People seem indifferent. You had to have a lot of nerve to approach them because you felt they might rebuff you.' Ferron's autobiography also sets up a series of contrasts: cold and warmth, politeness and informality, indifference and friendship, south and north, which help the author define his own values and sense of self. In doing so, he implies that 'foreigners', whether from overseas or just beyond the city limits, do not engage in an entirely random settlement process determined only by material necessity and chance. They also make active locality choices based on temperamental preference that reduce cultural difference and make identity negotiation consensual as well as confrontational. While Ferron writes that the indifference of Londoners has not changed during his half-century residence in the capital, Mike Phillips, a West Indian from the generation that came after Ferron, argues that the identity of London has itself changed as a result of the presence of outsiders. 'I belong to London because London is partly what I have made it', Philips states (176). 'When I look at London now it's not an alien city any more . . .'

If we accept the idea of the changing development of self-identity and interiority through the centuries, the development which roughly coincides with the rise of industrial and post-industrial modernity, then regional distinctions provide a particularized measure of how interiority and self-identity are experienced in time and place. The lack of knowledge to compare and contrast language, landscape or tradition, as they once were and as they now are, means that by definition the makers of migrant narratives cannot give an objective history of regional development. However, what migrant narratives can provide, when taken together with native accounts, is a record of local identity negotiation; of incremental, time-bound, bargaining for social and cultural adjustment that constantly remakes the locality and its inhabitant. The outcome is a gradual clearing vision which eventually allows both migrant and host to recognize accent, observe and respect custom, accept imported and indigenous landmarks. In this light Markéta Luskačova's photographs of East London's streets and markets are part of a long tradition whereby hosts and hosted engage, interpret and accommodate each other. The hard-won result, if won at all, is a sense of belonging that comes from reworking both locality and self.

Notes

1. For a general introduction see also: R. Lawton, and C. Pooley, *Britain 1740–1950: An Historical Geography* (London: Edward Arnold, 1992); V. Yans-McLaughlin, 'Metaphors of self in history: subjectivity, oral narratives and immigration studies', in Yans-McLaughlin, V. (ed.) *Immigration Reconsidered: History, Sociology and Politics* (Oxford: Oxford University Press, 1990) 254–90.
2. While London is exceptional for the number and variety of its migrant populations, this is as true in the Capital as elsewhere. See, for example, N. Merriman

(ed.) *The Peopling of London: Fifteen Thousand Years of Settlement from Overseas* (London: Museum of London, 1994). Among the numerous more specialized studies see, for instance: C. Withers and A. Watson, 'Stepwise migration and Highland migration to Glasgow, 1852–1898', *Journal of Historical Geography*, 17 (1991) 35–55; or D. Russell and G. Walker, *Trafford Park 1896–1939* (Manchester: Manchester Studies/Manchester Polytechnic, 1979).

3. For examples of regional studies see J. Brown, *The Un-Melting Pot* (London: Macmillan – now Palgrave Macmillan, 1970); K. E. Collins, *Second City Jewry* (Glasgow: *the Jews of Glasgow in the Age of Expansion, 1790–1919* Scottish Jewish Archive, 1990); C. Hughes, *Lime, Lemon & Sarsaparilla: the Italian Community in South Wales, 1881–1945* (Bridgend: Seven, 1991).
4. See for example E. J. Hobsbawm, 'The tramping artisan', *Economic History Review*, 3 (1951) 299–320.
5. See for example the photographs by L. Maholy-Nagy, in M. Benedetta, *The Street Markets of London* (London: John Miles, 1936).
6. M. Luskačova, *Photographs of Spitalfields* (London: Whitechapel Art Gallery, 1991) 26.
7. R. Lichtenstein and I. Sinclair, *Rodinsky's Room* (London: Granta, 2000) 7.
8. P. Fryer, *Staying Power: The History of Black People in Britain* (London: Pluto, 1984) 38.
9. J. Salter, *The Asiatic in England: Sketches of Sixteen Years' Work Among Orientals* (London: Seeley, Jackson and Halliday, 1873), 230, 238–9; S. Dentith, *Society and Cultural Forms in Nineteenth-century England* (London: Macmillan – now Palgrave Macmillan, 1998) 103–27.
10. H. Mayhew, *London Labour and the London Poor* (London: George Woodfall, 1851) 454.
11. C. Steedman, 'State-sponsored autobiography', in Conekin, B., Mort, F. and Waters, C. (eds) *Moments of Modernity: Reconstructing Britain 1945–1964* (London: Rivers Oram, 1999) 41–54.

The South

160) The movement of 'foreigners' in and out of Bristol, *c.*1700 [M.]

John Latimer details the local history of eighteenth century Bristol and surrounding areas from contemporary sources. See also Introduction to Part III.

On one point, however, all ranks and parties seem to have been thoroughly in unison – namely, in the exclusion from the trade and industry of the city of those not born within its boundaries. Every one coming from outside these limits – even from Clifton or Redland, or the out-parishes of St. James or St. Philip – was stigamatised as a 'foreigner,' and often treated as an enemy deserving extermination. In 1696 the Corporation passed a by-law, prohibiting every person not a freeman from exercising a trade or opening a shop within the city, 'whether with or without latesses or glass windows; butchers, cobblers, or hoxters alone excepted.' The penalty upon an interloper was £5 a day. In 1703 the fine was raised to £20 on each conviction. The authorities, it is true, acted capriciously in the matter, sometimes shutting their eyes to incursions from outside, and sometimes encouraging informers to prosecute, and convicting all and sundry. Minutes exist of several foreigners' shops being 'shut down' and the goods therein seized to defray the penalties; while the dealings of 'one foreigner with another' in the city were presented by one grand jury as a great grievance to legitimate traders. In 1695 William Bonny, a printer, was permitted to set up business, the Chamber believing that a printing house 'might be useful'; but he was forbidden to sell books. In 1700 a watchmaker was allowed to open a shop on presenting a 'curious watch and dyall to be set up in the Tolzey,' and undertaking 'to keep the same in repair during his life.' In the same year the Council empowered the mayor, 'there being a confederacy among the cooks now in the city,' to confer the freedom on any 'able cooks' that might come down from London; the freedom being also granted to an interloping brushmaker, because there was no other in Bristol. The applications of other strangers were rejected, or such heavy fines were imposed for admission to the burgess roll as to be practically prohibitive. Many other restraints on business, mostly imposed by the

> incorporated trades in the city, affected the citizens themselves, and must have operated grievously. Before commencing business on his own account, a man was required to serve seven years' apprenticeship in Bristol to a member of his trading company. No shopkeeper not being a tailor was allowed to make or sell linen or woollen stockings. A skinner was forbidden to buy skins used by the trades of whitetawers and glovers. No glover was to make points, and no pointmaker was to make gloves, no carpenter was to meddle with the work of a joiner, and *vice versa*. Neither joiners nor carpenters were to furnish customers with hooks, bolts, hinges etc., or to make any use of any tools, save those made by the Smiths' Company. No one except a member of the Cutlers' Company was permitted to sell a knife. Articles produced by suburban joiners and carpenters, including rough boards and planks, were forbidden to enter the city. A similar law interdicted the admission of casks and washing pails. No butcher was to cook meat for sale. No victualler was allowed to buy country bread, or even to bake in his own house. Tilers were forbidden to lend a ladder to a carpenter or mason. No baker or barber was to open two shops. Interloping artisans from other neighbouring districts, and enterprising country youths seeking to raise themselves by exchanging a rural for a town life, but unable to pay an apprentice fee, were hounded out of the city as soon as they were discovered, and people harbouring such 'inmates' were prosecuted. The law which prevented a trader or an artisan from changing his occupation for a more eligible one was common to the whole kingdom, but was not the less onerous. Under an Act of Elizabeth such a change could not be made without passing through a second apprenticeship of seven years, and the members of the trading companies were always on the alert to maintain this preposterous restriction on individual energy.

J. Latimer, *The Annals of Bristol in the Eighteenth Century* (n.p: Butler and Tanner, 1893) 20–2.

161) Slaves in Bristol, early 18th *c.* [I.]

See note on extract No.160.

> It will be seen from the above extracts that the commanders of slaving vessels were allowed to transport a few slaves in each cargo for their personal profit. It was doubtless through this custom that so many Negro slaves were brought to England, and lived and died here in servitude. The post of captain in a slaving ship was a lucrative one, and those who gained it were prone to make a display of their good fortune. Their gaudily-laced coats and cocked hats are often mentioned by contemporary writers. As their wills bear witness, they were accustomed to flaunt large silver, and sometimes gold, buttons on their apparel, and their shoes were decorated with buckles of the precious metals. But the most distinguished mark of a captain in the streets was the black slave

who obsequiously attended him, and who was often sold to a wealthy family when the owner again embarked for Africa. Sometimes, as has been already shown, a black servant was bequeathed to a friend by will. Female negros reached this country in the same manner, and were purchased for domestic service. The House of Commons Journals for March 16th, 1702, in reporting evidence given before a committee, described a witness as a slave to a Jew merchant in Holborn. 'She had lived with him,' she deposed, '14 years as a slave.' The newspapers of the first seventy years of the century contain scores of advertisements concerning the sale or elopement of blacks held in slavery. A few examples may be interesting. In the *London Gazette* of January 17th, 1713, Captain Foye, of Bristol, offers £5 for the capture of 'a Negro called Scipio, aged about 24,' who had escaped. In the same journal for July 5th 1715, Mr Pyne, the Bristol postmaster, undertakes to pay two guineas and expenses for the recovery of Captain Courtney's Negro, aged about 20, 'having three or four marks on each temple and the same on each cheek' – which were presumably testimonies of the affection of his master. (Captain Courtney, it will be remembered, was one of the commanders of the fortunate *Duchess* privateer.) Nothing, perhaps, better indicates the distance which separates us from the reign of George I. than the fact that the postmaster of Bristol was the agent employed to recapture a slave living in Bristol, and that this fact was published in the official organ of the Government. In *Farley's Bristol Newspaper* for August 31st, 1728, Captain John Gwynthen offers for sale 'a Negro man about 20 years old, well limb'd, fit to serve a gentleman or to be instructed in a trade.' In the *Journal* of November 15th, 1746, Captain Eaton announces the evasion of his Negro Mingo, whom he had owned for eight years, for whose recovery he promised a guinea. 'All persons are thereby forbid entertaining the said Black at their peril.' Josiah Rose, of Redcliff Street, advertised the elopement of his Negro boy, aged 13, in the London *General Advertiser* of April 8th, 1748. In the *Bristol Journal* of June 23rd, 1750, appears: – 'To be sold, a Negro Boy of about 12 years of age. . . . Inquire of the printers.' The *Bristol Intelligencer* of January 12th, 1754, offers for sale, to 'any gentleman or lady who wants a Negro Boy,' a lad of 14 years, recently landed. The *Bristol Journal* of March 12th, 1757, publishes the elopement of a young Negro called Starling, who 'blows the French horn very well.' His owner, a publican in Prince's Street, offers a guinea for his capture. A week later it is announced that the Negro of Captain Bouchier of Kensham, has escaped; while on the 22nd September the evasion is published of the Negro servant of Captain Ezekiel Nash, who offers to reward the person giving him up, and threatens to presecute any one secreting him. On the 15th April, 1758, the same paper offers £5 for the recapture of a 'Malotta Boy,' absconded from one McNeal, of St. Philip's Plain, who also menaces legal proceedings against a detainer of his property; and on the 14th April 1759, Captain Holbrook advertises a 'handsome reward' for the recovery of his 'Negro man named Thomas.' *Felix Farley's Journal* of August 2nd, 1760, contains a pithy adver-

> tisement: – 'To be sold, a Negro Boy about ten years old. He has had small pox.' A Liverpool paper of 1766 has an announcement of the sale by auction in that town, on the 12th September, of 'Eleven Negro Slaves.' In the *Bristol Journal* of June 20th, 1767, we have: – 'To be sold, a Black Boy, about 15 years of age; capable of waiting at table;' and the same paper of January 9th, 1768, offers for sale 'a healthy Negro Slave named Prince, 17 years of age; extremely well grown.' Some of the fugitive slaves are described as wearing silver collars round their neck, engraved with the owner's name.

J. Latimer, *The Annals of Bristol in the Eighteenth Century* (n.p: Butler and Tanner, 1893) 146–8.

162) Gabriel Treves and the Jewish settlement in Exeter, early 18th c. [I.]

C. Roth's mid-20th century account describes the history of local Jewish communities across the country.

> The earliest settler here [Exeter] in modern times seems to have been an Italian snuff-merchant, Gabriel Treves, who arrived some time before 1735. He was followed over from Italy by his nephew Joseph Offolenghi, who became converted to Christianity. The uncle did not treat the apostate with as much kindliness as the latter optimistically expected, and the consequence was a spate of polemical publications. It does not appear from these that there was any sort of organised Jewish life in Exeter at this time. Nevertheless, in an address given in 1853, on the occasion of the rededication of the Synagogue, it was stated that the congregation had been founded in 1728; that an inscription dating to this period could still be deciphered in the burial-ground; and that a place of worship had been dedicated about 1734.

C. Roth, *The Rise of Provincial Jewry* (London: Jewish Monthly, 1950) 59.

163) George Watson's move from Yorkshire to London, 1736 [M.]

George Watson was born near Hull in Yorkshire c.1671. He worked in his home county, London and Kent as a servant, and later became involved in smuggling on the Isle of Shippey (the present-day Isle of Sheppey – on the Thames estuary at the mouth of the River Medway). Watson's testimony was noted down during his trial for involvement in smuggling activities in 1736.

> 1. George Watfon, Fifty-five Years of Age, of honest Parents, five Miles from *Hull* in Yorkfire, and not Education at School, and not much knowledge of religious Matters, neither was put to any Trade; but when of Age, he ferv'd Gentlemen in the Country; and having paft his Time fome Years nigh to the Place of his Nativity, he came to *London* as a Gentleman's Servant, and from thence he went down to *Kent* in the same Station, where he liv'd for fome

Time, and did labouring Work in the Country, till at laft he fettled, and commenced Farmer in the *Ifle of Shippey*, where he Married a Wife, and had fome Children, his eldeft Daughter, now in *Shippey* with her Friends, and in Service; and his Son about fourteen Years of Age, in Service of a Gentleman upon *Finchley-Common*; thefe two were of the firft Marriage; his Wife of the Isle of *Shippey*, about fix or feven Years ago, when he thought fit to give over his Farm, (upon Advice of thofe who he took to be his Friends, though in effect they now appear to have been the Reverfe) and to convert all his Stock to Money, which he was to employ in the Smuggling-Trade, they having perfuaded him, that there was much more Money to be got that way, and that he could not fail enriching himfelf foon: This Advice he follow'd to his deftruction; after he took this Refolution, he never was eafy in his Mind, but was perpetually in Trouble, and expos'd to the Danger of his Life; he and all his Companions having been fort of abandon'd, defperate Men, refolv'd to hazard their Lives upon every Occasion, when any Soldiers, or Cuftom-houfe Officers, endeavoured to difturb them in running uncuftom'd Goods.

George, after throwing up his Farm in *Shippey*, apply'd himfelf wholly to Smuggling, in which however he had been concern'd almost fince he was a Boy, particularly all the Time he liv'd in the Ifle of *Shippey*, which was Twenty-feven Years, at the End of which Time he brought his Family near this Town, and took a Houfe in *Finchley* . . .

Proceedings at Sessions of Peace. City of London and County of Middlesex, 2, 1735–1740, 63–4.

164) John Pinnock travels from the West Country to London, 1750s–60s [M.]

Born c.*1732 in East Stoke, Wiltshire, John Pinnock worked as a servant in Froom (Somerset, present day Frome), Romsey and Winchester (Hampshire) and Aldgate (London). His account was taken down during an official settlement examination in 1771. See also Introduction to Part I.*

Who on his oath saith that he is thirty nine years of age and that he has a wife named Jane + that he was born Earl Stoke in the County of Wilts and that he served his father John Pinnock as a servant while he attained the age of Twenty one years, at the expiration of which time, he has worked at Froom in Summersetshire, at Romsey in the County of Hants, and after that at Winchester in the said county at neither of which places did he hire a house or pay any Tax whatsoever, and that from Winchester he settled in London and hired a house of Thomas Hewlett of the Parish of Aldgate at the date of six pounds a year and that he lived in the said house eight years and that serving the said . . . he never paid any taxes whatever but what taxes he paid was by master Thomas Hewlett and further the examinant saith not [.]

Settlement Examinations (Settlement Papers, Overseers of the Poor), Parish of Bedford St Paul (1771) Bedfordshire and Luton Archives, Bedford, P 1/13/4.

165) Seasonal labour in London, 18th c. [M.]

See note on extract No.21.

> Besides the unending flow and ebb to and from London, there were thus two main tides of seasonal immigration. That of the Irish travelling on foot, often in family parties, from Liverpool, Chester and Bristol, and finding shelter chiefly in St. Giles and Marylebone. These arrived before the hay harvest began and filled the streets of London with beggars. Secondly, that of the lascars, who were deposited in the eastern riverside districts from the East India Company's ships to live for some months in more or less enforced idleness, some of them drifting to the common lodging-houses of St. Giles. There was another seasonal migration to London, that of the women who came on foot chiefly from Shropshire and North Wales to work in the market-gardens round London and returned in the autumn. They were employed in picking fruit, gathering peas (hence the old name of codder), weeding, haymaking and especially in carrying loads of fruit to Covent Garden. Their earnings at the end of the century were only five or seven shillings a week as compared with ten or twelve paid to men for the same work. But they slept in barns and outhouses and lived chiefly on garden produce allowed them by their employers, so that they returned to their homes with a little fund for the winter. They would carry a heavy load of fruit from Ealing or Brentford to Covent Garden, about nine miles, and would sometimes make the double journey twice a day. Londoners admired their gay, healthy appearance and neat clothes. There was a corresponding exodus from London of men and women who spent the winter in the workhouse and went out in the summer for tramping or harvesting, but it is difficult to see how these could compete with the Irish and the sturdy country people who worked so hard for such small pay.
>
> This constant flow to London tended to make it always overcrowded. The outlets for an ever-redundant population (in spite of a general shortage of many kinds of labour) were the army and the navy (enlistment under the pressure of starvation being reinforced by the press-gang and the crimp as well as the penal system); indentured emigration to the colonies, and removal under the poor law and the Vagrant Act. Press-gangs directed their energies not only against seamen, but against those whom their officers chose to consider idle fellows, the attempt on Tom Jones being a case in point; 'neither law nor conscience forbid this project,' said Lady Bellaston, 'for the fellow, I promise you, however well drest, is but a vagabond, and as proper as any fellow in the streets to be pressed into the service.' Magistrates encouraged the application of this principle. In 1776, for instance, the Lord

> Mayor refused to back the press warrants for the impressment of men in the City but ordered the City Marshals to go in force to search the public-houses and take into custody all 'loose and disorderly men' and bring them before him. Those who, like Goldsmith's private centinel, could not give a satisfactory account of themselves, were sent by the Lord Mayor on board the tender for service in the Navy. 'By this judicious step,' says a contemporary annalist, 'many idle persons were obtained, and the more industrious escaped being illegally forced from their friends and families'. The magistrates of Westminster took similar steps, great numbers, it is said, were obtained in this way . . .

M. D. George, *London Life in the XVIIIth Century* (London: Kegan Paul, Trench, Trubner, 1925) 140–2.

166) The establishment of a Bristol Synagogue, 1786 [I.]

See note on extract No.160.

> The Weavers' Company in 1786 had become so diminished in numbers that they ceased to maintain a hall. The building was transferred to the Jews, who decorated it in what Mr Barrett terms 'a neat expensive manner,' and opened it on the 15th September as a synagogue.

J. Latimer, *The Annals of Bristol in the Eighteenth Century* (n.p: Butler and Tanner, 1893) 470.

167) A Moroccan trader in Exeter, 1851 [I.]

See note on extract No.27.

> After I been selling my rhubarb for two years, when I fust come here, I save about a hundred and fifty pounds, and den you see I agree wid tree oder of my countrymen to take a sop (shop) in Exeter. De oder tree was rhubarb-sellers, like myself, and have save good bit of money as well. One have seven hundred pound; but he have brought tree or four hundred pound wid him to dis countree. Anoder of de tree have about two hundred, and de oder about one hundred; dey have all save deir money out of de rhubarb. We keep our sop, you see, about five year, and den we fall to pieces altogeder. We take and trust, and lose all our money. T'oders never keep a sop before, and not one of us was English scholar; we was forced to keep a man, and dat way we lose all our money, so we was force to part, and everyone go look for hisself. Den we all go selling rhubarb again about the country, and in London; and I never able to hold up my head since. When I come back to de rhubarb times is getting bad, and I not able to save no more money. All I am worth in de world is all I got in my box, and dat altogether is not more dan ten shillings. Last week I havn't a pound of meat in de house, and I am

> obliged to pawn my waistcoat and handkerchief to get me some stock. It easy to put dem in, but very hard to get dem out.

H. Mayhew, *London Labour and the London Poor*, vol. 1 (London: George Woodfall, 1851) 454.

168) 'Asiatics' in the West Country, 1873 [I.]

See note on extract No.52.

> Some of the towns in the west, – Bath, Bristol, Cardiff and Salisbury, were visited for the first time. I arrived at Bath in the after-part of the day, and soon found that Avon Street must be the chief place of my search; but wending my way down there, I found that long, narrow street is a state of commotion. A fight had taken place; a man had been stabbed, and was taken to the hospital. Among such excitement of Irish and English, including men, women and boys, I thought it better to defer my visit until the morning. I speak of this to illustrate some of the spots I have repeatedly visited in various parts of England, yet without any insult. Those who are acquainted with such spots as Pitsey and Gloucester-lane, Bristol; and Ann-street and London Apprentice-street, Birmingham; Pockthorp, Norwich; and Ann-street, Cardiff, cannot but be sensible of the Divine care in such work. And yet in these localities of want and vice there are Asiatics living who never hear of the truth but by such a visit. In Bristol I met with three who resided in the Home, and spoke of its advantages. In Cardiff were two others who had resided in the Home.

J. Salter, *The Asiatic in England: Sketches of Sixteen Years' Work Among Orientals* (London: Seeley, Jackson and Halliday, 1873) 238–9.

169) Joseph Johnson, street entertainer, 1883 [M.]

See note on extract No.29.

> The succeeding plate displays the effigy of Joseph Johnson, a black, who in consequence of his having been employed in the merchant service only, is not entitled to the provision of Greenwich. His wounds rendering him incapable of doing further duty on the ocean, and having no claim to relief in any parish, he is obliged to gain a living on shore; and in order to elude the vigilance of the parochial beadles, he first started on Tower Hill, where he amused the idlers by singing George Alexander Stevenson's 'Storm.' By degrees he ventured into the public streets, and at length became what is called a 'Regular Chaunter.' But novelty, the grand secret of all exhibitions, from the Magic Lantern to the Panorama, induced Black Joe to build a model of the ship Nelson, to which, when placed on his cap, he can, by a bow of thanks, or a supplicating indication to the drawing-room widow, give the

appearance of sea-motion. Johnson is as frequently to be seen in the rural village as in great cities; and when he takes a journey, the kind hearted waggoner will often enable him in a few hours to visit the marketplaces of Staines, Romford or St Albans, where he never fails to gain the farmer's penny, either by singing 'The British Seaman's Praise,' or Green's more popular song of 'The Wooden Walls of Old England.'

J. T. Smith, *Mendicant Wanderers through the Streets of London* (Edinburgh: W. P. Nimmo, 1883) 19.

170) London's Chinatown, *c.*1900 [I.]

See note on extract No.69.

Nearly opposite this house is a small street which contains the Chinese colony. Compared with the Chinese colony of New York, part of which I once visited, one sweltering night in July, that of London is a small thing and of no importance. Yet it is curious. There are not, I believe, more than a hundred Chinese or thereabouts, in all; they occupy a few houses in the street; there are one or two small shops kept by Chinamen; it is considered quite safe to visit the place, at all events in the daytime; I was myself taken there by one who was personally known to the shopkeepers. There was not much that was attractive and interesting offered for sale, except Chinese playing cards, which are curious; conversation in Pidgin-English is difficult at first, but one quickly acquires enough of the patois. There is a boarding-house for Chinese in the street; the ground floor we found furnished with a tiny joss-house, in one corner, and a large table which occupied nearly the whole of the room; the stable was covered with Chinamen sitting and sprawling; they were wholly absorbed in a little gamble with dominoes and small Chinese coins; their absorption in the changes of the game was complete.

W. Besant, *East London* (London: Chatto and Windus, 1903) 204.

171) Italian street traders in Luton, *c.*1910 [I.]

Born in 1905, A. S. Darby's reminiscences of his childhood in Luton were published in 1974, two years after the author's death.

The Italian community were self-supporting, versatile and hard-working, becoming organ grinders, ice-cream vendors, hot-pea merchants and roast chestnut purveyors, according to season. An elite few were fine craftsmen, specialising in mosaics and the shaping of composition of hat boxes. They were a volatile people, excitable and gay, lending a deal of colour to the town. The older generation never really mastered the English language, and when 'Wetweather' called us 'Bloody fukky monkies' she was unaware of any obscenities.

'Wetweather' was an old Italian woman who stumped the streets with a barrel organ, never forsaking her Italian dress. She had jet-black hair, enhanced by gold earrings, and wore a traditional fringed head-shawl patterned in chocolate and green. A wide belt round her middle held in place a shirt and underskirts of various shades, so back or front she always looked pregnant. The long skirt almost hid buttoned boots of shiny black leather but when she rested her foot on the wheel of the barrel organ, the boots allowed just a peep of her red stockings. Eyes like liquorice peered from a hooked nose of great length, her wide mouth compensating for the affliction. Skin the colour of Christmas pudding completed the portrait, reconcilable with an aged 'Mona Lisa'. We believed the legend that she made it rain, hence her name 'Wetweather' – thought she was a witch, and rarely pestered her. When we did, it was to chant from afar 'Wetweather-wetweather, go away, make it rain another day!'

The ice-cream man, with his gaily painted ice-cream barrow dispersed dollops of 'Hokey' from metal tubs surrounded with ice, delving with a wooden spatula, emerging with the concoction and scraping it on a bone-hard cornet and wafer. The Hokey was gritty with particles of ice added to give bulk, and the 'cream' could never have originated from a cow's udder. Nevertheless, we licked away at it. The portion was generous, it was cold and sweet, only knocked us back a ha'penny, so who cared.

The hurdy-gurdy man most appreciated was he with the monkey. The little animal, decked out in velvet coat and tasselled cap, was wide eyed and sorrowful, tethered to a long chain. It was taught to go round with the hat. Armed with orange peel and apple cores, we quickly filled it, the monkey with squeaks of delight retreating to the end of the chain and wolfing down the freely given fruit. The organ man, gesticulating with rage all the time tried to pitch the titbits off the animal, the monkey making lout ticking noises. With one hand apparently glued to the handles, the monkey man continued to grind the classics with the 'show must go on' complex whilst we chuckled and jigged to the music. Finally he gave up, grabbed the monkey and shuffled away, lugging the cumbersome music maker with him.

The roast-chestnut man who took up his station in the alley at the rear of a pub was very popular, the proceeds of a returned empty bottle ensuring hours of warm glow, basking in the heat from his fire. Even when it rained we kept dry under the corrugated sheet, spread over the stalls . . .

A. S. Darby, *A View from the Alley* (Luton: Luton Museum and Art Gallery, 1974) 31.

172) The Jewish East End of London, 1935 [I.]

See note on extract No.105.

I started one Sunday night from Whitechapel Road, a good beginning and a good night for such a ramble, especially if one would realise how completely this part of London is held by aliens. The northern side of Whitechapel Road has the most magnificent pavement in London; so wide, flanked by such a noble breadth of road that it seems made for gaiety. If this were Paris it would be crowded with pavement cafes and the Parisians, seated over coffee and cigars, would be as the sands of the sea. But London has abandoned it to the alien invader. An English name over a shop is a rarity. It is thronged, but not with our people. The lads and lasses who promenade it have the lustrous eyes and raven hair of the Ghetto; the faces of the older ones bear the indelible stamp of Eastern Europe. You see more beards in ten minutes than you would in ten days in all West London.

Yiddish was the general language among these older ones. It fell constantly on my ears and eyes from Aldgate to Mile End. I preferred it to the loud Cockney English of the young Ikeys and Rebeccas.

'Can you read zat?', a father asked his son pausing at a Yiddish poster. The boy wore a public school cap. The cut of his good clothes and his general bearing were very English-schoolboy. I remarked his averse expression as he shook his head, his look of dumb unhappiness as he listened to his father's eager translation. He was not finding the melting-pot a pleasant place.

Across the road a smart Jewish wedding party could plainly be seen in the upper room of a restaurant, enjoying the publicity of the long, uncurtained window. The bride, still bridally arrayed, sat in the middle. Glasses were raised, and a young man rose as if to respond to a toast.

I turned of Whitechapel Road, attracted by one of the narrow side streets that cut through the Commercial Road. It was called Plumber's Row. The total unexpected change of scene delighted me. The little wooden-sheltered houses, the square basement areas guarded by iron railings like miniature bear-pits, and there irregular frontages, lit by street lights and the gentler lights gleaming from upper and lower windows, made it like a lane in some country town — until I noticed that, behind most of those lighted windows tailor' workmen sat in their shirt sleeves cutting and stitching and machining, with bent head and curved backs. The infernal diligence of Jewry!

H. Thorogood, *East of Aldgate* (London: George Allen and Unwin, 1935) 132–4.

173) The Chinese East End of London, 1935 [I.]

See note on extract No.105.

On another of my night perambulations I came upon a dingy, narrow cutting that slanted off West India Dock Road in the direction of Poplar High Street, with the name 'Pennyfields' inscribed at the entrance. Promptly I turned aside and entered it; for Pennyfields means Chinatown. This was, by all accounts, the bad place. I would have to look at it.

And to tell the truth, on that first occasion I was glad when I was through Pennyfields. It was the only streets in the miles of East London that I traversed by day and night that inspired me with any real fear.

Not that anyone showed signs of molesting me. Quite a number of men were in it, many of them Chinese, with a few Lascars and negros and a good sprinkling of whites; and several white girls were to be seen, too. They took very little notice of me. Yet there was a heavy sense of menace about that street, a furtive look, a treacherous air, that made me uneasy. The occasional street lamps shed little light into its profound gloom. There were practically no shops among the low and squalid houses to shed reassuring gleams on the narrow pavement. Every other house seemed to be a Chinese lodging-house. Before the opened doorways the yellow-faced, slant-eyed Orientals stood in little groups, mostly silent, smoking cigarettes. The passage behind them, empty and faintly lit receded into the mysterious depths of the lodging-house, and for all its empty look it gave an impression of concealing danger as if at any moment a signal might fill it with a turmoil of scurrying men. Any one of whose doorways presenting that interior glimpse with its air of false emptiness, put on the stage would have created the right sense of melodrama about to begin.

But it was not the Chinese out of doors who gave me a vague feeling of fear. They seemed harmless enough. It was the curious demeanour of the white loafers with whom the Chinese made no association.

H. Thorogood, *East of Aldgate* (London: George Allen and Unwin, 1935) 141–2.

174) Guram Singh Khera in Gravesend, 1954 [I.]

See note on extract No.89.

My uncle's friend Bhagat Agla used to live in Gravesend. He was the only foreigner in this town and used to work at an refinery on the Isle of Grain. They needed some work force so he came to London and brought us down here. All four of us cramped in the same house he used to live in and we went to work at the same place he used to work. We were young and single, knew nobody here, so worked all the hours we could lay our hands on. The money was good, almost double what we used to earn in London. We spent very little because we didn't have time to spend it. Our uncle bought us a house in Peppercroft Street. Then within six to seven months, we managed to save enough to buy a large four storey house in Pier Road (1954) and all of us moved there. The weather was a lot colder then. There were no bathrooms in the house, we used to go to public bath once week, had our hair cut to save washing it and to mingle with the community. Everybody became clean shaven.

S. Winters, *Nobody Sleeps on the Rooftops Now* (Gravesend: AIM, 1994) 3–4.

175) Race riots in Notting Hill, London, 1958 [I.]

A report in the Manchester Guardian, *2 September 1958. The article is included in Ruth Glass's discussion of 'attitudes' in her study of West Indians in 1950s London.*

This was one incident that occurred on September 1st:

It comes as a shock to hear the ugly phrase 'lynch him!' on English lips in an English city. But it must be reported that these words were used not once but a dozen times yesterday afternoon. . . . The object of this venom, a young West African student, was running for his life down Bramley Road, followed by a gang of young toughs who had set upon him, kicked him and twisted his leg before he could escape. Dashing into a greengrocer's shop he persuaded the owner's wife to bolt the door and hid himself in a back room until the police came and rescued him. By that time a crowd of two hundred white people had gathered on the pavements and in the roadway, and it took the combined efforts of police on horseback, in radio squad cars, and twenty constables on foot to disperse them.

The incident took place not fifty yards from the scenes of the worst fighting in the so-called 'race riots' at the week-end . . .

Long before trouble actually broke out in Bramley Road yesterday afternoon there had been an unhealthy mood in the streets of Notting Hill. It was not a normal Monday, for there was hardly a black-skinned person to be seen in the shops or on the pavements . . . At the street corners, knots of young men could be seen gathering and occasionally being dispersed by constables on foot patrol.

Into this ugly situation stepped an outsider who had no inkling of what was in store for him. Mr. Seymour Manning is a 26-year-old African student who is at present living in Derby. He had come down for the day to see friends in Notting Hill, and though he did not know it he was under close observation from hostile eyes from the moment he stepped out of the Latimer Road Underground Station.

In the four hours that I had been in this area he was only the third coloured person that I had seen venture out of doors. I watched him disappear up Bramley Road. A few minutes later there was an outburst of screams and jeering and I saw Mr. Manning sprinting back towards the Underground, his tie and blazer streaming out behind him. As his three pursuers closed in, he turned in desperation and flung himself into the doorway of a greengrocer's shop, turned, and slammed it shut. A moment later the shopkeeper's wife . . . appeared in the doorway, locked the door behind her, and turned to face the trio of toughs. She had two friends with her – a housewife of her own age and a boy in his teens.

She kept them at bay until the police arrived a few minutes later. Soon after the first two constables came to her rescue, a radio car arrived, and after that came full reinforcements. It was during the interim period, before it was clear

> that the police were on their way in force, that people on the opposite pavement called out for a lynching. I went up to one of the young men, who looked to be about 25, and asked him what he had against the African in the shop. 'Just tell your readers that Little Rock learned us a lesson,' was the reply.
>
> Another youth, who had also been calling for a lynching, turned to me and said: 'Tell them we've got a bad enough housing shortage around here without them moving in. Keep Britain White.'

R. Glass, *Newcomers: The West Indians in London* (London: Centre for Urban Studies/George Allen & Unwin, 1960) 138.

176) Mike Phillips on black London identity, 1990

Born in Georgetown, Guyana, 1941, Mike Phillips settled in England after following his father there in 1956, since then has become a well-known journalist, academic and novelist. He is the co-author of Windrush: The Irresistible Rise of Multi-Racial Britain *(London: HarperCollins, 1998). See also note on extract No.145.*

> The crucial thing to me is the sense in which the black community is a bastard offspring of England. What interests me now is the sense in which blacks and whites in England, and especially in London, are coming to share a difficult identity, an identity which is difficult and which has to be constantly negotiated. Neither side is quite aware of what they are doing, even while they are engaged in the process. Most black people have more relationships with white people than they do with black people. When you go to work you're not working only with black people; you might even be the only black person there. So this theme interests me: the sense in which we are negotiating our identity in this country, what the country is, what the nations is, what we all are, without being conscious of it. The other thing is about London, the way in which I belong to London because London is partly what I have made it. Maybe a tiny part, but still a part that me and my brothers and sisters and friends have made it. When I look at London now it's not an alien city any more, it's a city that we've partly reconstructed. When white people say derogatory things about London, the inner city problems and so on, what they're really talking about is the black community. And what I say is, 'Bugger their luck' – because we ain't going nowhere.

J. Green, *Them* (London: Secker and Warburg, 1990) 249.

The Midlands and East Anglia

177) The Jewish settlement in Birmingham, early 18th c. [I.]

See note on extract No.162.

> The Birmingham community must be one of the oldest in England, but it is impossible here to go into great detail regarding its origin. According to the late Arthur Franklin, a member of the family, Moses Aaron, was born in Birmingham in 1718 of Hungarian Jewish parentage. Though this may not be absolutely correct, one may at the least assure that the family was resident there at an early date. The earliest cemetery is said to go back to 1730, but of this too there is no documentary evidence. These dates are however approximately confirmed by the statement on the *Jewish Chronicle* account of 1842 that 'our nation has had a congregation here for upwards of 120 years,' – ie since about 1720.

C. Roth, *The Rise of Provincial Jewry* (London: Jewish Monthly, 1950) 32.

178) Recruitment of skilled workmen from Europe to Birmingham, 1750s [M.]

A late 19th century account of the movement of continental craftsmen to the Midlands.

> At that time the Boultons lived, and had their workshop, on Snow Hill, which was yet a very rural neighbourhood, only sparsely built upon, and in close proximity to the open country. They were known as 'toy-makers,' a term sufficiently understood in Birmingham as signifying a maker of buckles, buttons, and trinkets and ornaments of steel, which were at that time very fashionable, and gave rise to the famous phrase applied to Birmingham by Edmund Burke, 'the Toyshop of Europe.' [in 1756 they built a Soho Factory 2 miles outside Birmingham] One of the chief aims of the firm was to obtain skilled workmen, in order to establish a school of designers who should give to the production of the Soho Factory an artistic style and finish not attainable else-

> where. One of the secrets of Boulton's great success was that he 'would buy any man's brains,' and never grudge the price. By this means skilled workmen were attracted to Soho from all the chief cities of Europe, and, in consequence, the productions of the firm became more varied.

R. K. Dent, *The Making of Birmingham. A History of the Rise and Growth of the Midland Metropolis* (Birmingham: J. L. Allday, 1894) 142–3.

179) John Smith, a servant, moves from the Midlands to London, and back, 1770s [M.]

Born c.1754 in Halston, Northamptonshire, John Smith worked for seven years as a servant in London, and then in Leamington, Warwickshire. His account was taken down during an official settlement examination in 1776.

> 22 yrs. b. parish Halstone Northamptonshire 'where his parents Resided under a certificate of Crateon [Creaton] in the said County of Northampton hre staid there some time afterward he saith he went to west haddon in the said County from thence he went to St Swithin's Lane London . . .* to live with Thomas Sylvin Esq with him this Examinant saith he Lived for 7 years and a half but made no agreement with his said master nor never** was hired he hath since Lived with the revn Mr Wheeler at Leamington in the County of Warwick was hired for a twelvemonth but did not stay his full time with him neither received his full wages.' [30 October 1776]
>
> * in the Parish of St Swithins
>
> ** His wife named Jane and Daughter Jane aged two years

Settlement Examinations (Settlement Papers, Overseers of the Poor), Parish of St Swithins (1776) Warwickshire Record Office, Bedworth, DR 225/327/14–87.

180) The Birmingham synagogue, *c.*1780 [I.]

William Hutton (1723–1815), Quaker and successful bookseller in Birmingham, was also the author of a history of the city.

> We have alfo among us a remnant of Ifrael. A people who when mafters of their own country were fcarcely ever known to travel, and who are now feldom employed in any thing elfe. But, though they are ever moving they are ever at home: Who once lived the favourites of heaven, and fed upon the cream of the earth; but now are little regarded by either: whofe foceity is entirely confined to themfelves, except in the commercial line.
>
> In the Synagogue, fituated in the Froggery, they ftill preferve the faint refemblance of the ancient worfhip. Their whole apparatus being no more than the drooping enfigns of poverty. The place is rather fmall, but tolerably

filled; where there appears lefs decorum than in the chriftian churches. The proverbial expreffion 'as rich as a jew,' is not altogether verified in Birmingham, but perhaps, time is transfering it to the Quakers.

It is rather fingular, that the honefty of a jew, is feldom pleaded but by the jew himself.

W. Hutton, *An History of Birmingham to the End of the Year 1780* (Birmingham: Pearson and Rollason, 1781) 122.

181) Sarah Whatton, a servant, working in the Coventry area, 1770s [M.]

Born c.1759 in Woolston, Sarah Watton worked as a servant in the west Midlands. Her account was taken down during an official settlement examination in 1779.

b. Parish of Woolston, aged c.24 'at a proper age she went to service & lived a year with Wm Collier of Stoke in the County of City of Coventry: that she then was hired by Wm. Cooke of the Parish of St Nicholas in the Borough of Warwick with whom she fulfilled three years services successively under so many different Hirings: that at Kenilworth Statutes in ye year of 1777 she was hired for a year by Joseh White of ye Parish of Bedworth in ye said County Baker served ye full time & received her stipulated wages, & has since then done no act whereby to gain a settlement she not having been hired to Wm Chaptin of Brinklow till 3 weeks after Michaelmas 1779.'

Settlement Examinations (Settlement Papers, Overseers of the Poor), Warwickshire Record Office, Bedworth (1779) DR 225/327/88–132.

182) The Jewish community in Nottingham and Birmingham, late 18th and early 19th c. [I.]

See note on extract No.162.

My earliest record of a Jew in Nottingham in modern times back to 1763–4, when Moses ben Jacob Ballin, of Nottingham, was admitted a member of the Great Synagogue in London; while a Sephardi artist, named Abraham Osorini, was resident there in 1788. There is evidence as early as 1805, for in that year Joseph Crool, one of the first Anglo-Jewish preachers and writers (who may have been its minister and factotum) published there a discursive work entitled *The Importance and Necessity of a more general knowledge of the Hebrew Language.*

In the course of the next few years, the Jewish population grew. The founder of the community, according to local report, was a certain David Solomon(s), a Russian Jew who settled in Nottingham in the eighteen-twenties. In 1822 his name figures in a application made for a piece of ground to be used as a Jewish cemetery . . .

A little later in the nineteenth century there was a small influx of German Jews, as to the other industrial cities of the Midlands, who did a good deal for local prosperity but drifted away from the Jewish community entirely: a typical instance was Lewis Heymann (1803–1866), from Hamburg, of the firm of Heymann & Alexander, who founded the Nottingham lace curtain industry in the middle of the century and was Mayor of Birmingham in 1857.

C. Roth, *The Rise of Provincial Jewry* (London: Jewish Monthly, 1950) 87–9.

183) John Clare travels from his native Helpston to Wisbech, 1808 [M.]

See note on extract No.7.

I started for Wisbech with a timid sort of pleasure and when I got to Glinton turnpike I turned back to look on the old church as if I was going into another country Wisbech was a foreign land to me for I had never been above eight miles from home in my life I could not fancy England much larger than the part I knew.

J. W. and A. Tibble (eds) *The Prose of John Clare* (London: Routledge and Kegan Paul, 1951) 20

184) John Clare walks to Newark-on-Trent in search of work, 1813 [M.]

See note on extract No.7.

I felt quite lost when I was here though it was a very little town but I had never been from home before scarcely further than out of sight of the steeples I became so ignorant in this far land that I could not tell which quarter the wind blew from and I even was foolish enough to think the sun's course was altered and that it rose in the west and set in the east I often puzzled at it to set myself right but I still thought so.

J. W. and A. Tibble (eds) *The Prose of John Clare* (London: Routledge and Kegan Paul, 1951) 28.

185) Rebecca Prutten, a servant, moves from Amptill to Hertford, 1823 [M.]

Rebecca Prutten worked as a servant in Bedfordshire and Hertfordshire in the second and third decades of the 19th century. Her account was taken down during an official settlement examination in 1823.

The examination of Rebecca Prutten Single Woman respecting her settlement taken on oath 20th May 1823. The examination saith that the short time before Michaelmas 1816 to the best of her recollection as to the year, she let herself for the year to Thomas Pomfrey of the Parish of Amptill in the county of Bedford Gentleman at the wages of fifty shilling that she went to her masters' service on Michaelmas day + served Mr Pomfrey in the parish of Amptill till the Michaelmas day following when she again let herself for a year to Mr Pomfrey at the wages of Three pounds and served him also that year in the parish of Amptill – And the examination further saith that she has not since live in any service for a year and that she is non resident in and chargable to the parish of Hitchin in the County of Hertford and that she is ill and unable to be removed.

Settlement Examinations (Settlement Papers, Overseers of the Poor), Parish of Amptill (1823) Bedfordshire County Record Office, Bedford, P 30/13/4.

186) A 'tramping' agricultural labourer, 1840s [M.]

See note on extract No.9.

We went on to Oxford, where I started to work for about two months, and stopped all that winter in Moreton-in-the-Marsh. There was no work to be got; but we had made enough in the harvest to keep us through the winter. In the spring time, when our money was gone, we came on to Warwick, where we bid a few days, while our two or three shillings lasted us. On the Saturday morning we found we'd got nothing left, and no victuals for the next day.

Says I, 'Whatever shall us do, old gal?'

'I'm sure I don't know, Bill; I thought "Brommy" would have been to see us, or Abram Baxter,' she says. 'I made sure they'd have seed us and given us a shilling or two. I'll bet a guinea,' she says, if that "Brommy" don't come now, I'll never give him nothing no more.' . . .

When we left Warwick on the Tuesday morning, we went to Birmingham and stopped till harvest time came round again. We went to Coventry on purpose to show my missis 'Peeping Tom' (it is an old image stuck up in the corner of the street), and then we came back to Birmingham. From thence we travelled to Wolverhampton, Stourbridge, Worcester, and Malvern, walking from thirty to thirty-three miles a day. We have done thirty-six sometimes.

At Ross we bid a twelvemonth; and from there my wife and I set off on a tramp of more than four hundred miles, stopping every night, and walking all day. It took us a month and three days. We never did a bit of work all the time. It was a bad harvesting, and we had saved money enough to keep us till we came to my mother's in Essex, where we stayed with the old lady three days. After that we went to Stratford for one twelvemonth, and saved money to carry us into Kent and keep us through a good bit of the harvest, by which we made ten pounds, and came to Chatham. There my wife was taken ill with the fever, and I had to wait upon her day and night. She was ill very nigh a twelvemonth period altogether; and I had to nurse her as best I could, and clean the house, and cook, and make her gruel and everything, for we could not afford to pay a woman to help us. We did not get to work again till next harvest, when we had to sleep in a barn, and we both of us got the ague together; and I could not do much work then. When we got a little better, a man took pity upon me, and put me watchman over two houses. I was there about three weeks, and then he got me another little job, and we got a few shillings together and took our things out of pawn. From that I went to work up at Rochester Bridge; and, when winter came on, I got in a tunnel at Ford Ret, for about three months. It was rather chokey kind of work, all done by candle-light, and the smoke makes the air thick and misty. Once, when I was in Dorsetshire, I was in a tunnel that fell in at both ends. There was only one man and me and some horses buried in it, and he drove a hole through the ground (he was about eight hours doing it), and then he and me got out, and left the horses in for three days and nights. We had to lower corn and water to them through a hole till we could dig them out again; but we were none of us hurt. When I went away I left my wife at Chatham, and used to send her five shillings a week; and she saved money out of that! I was away nine weeks, working at different places, and went down to see mother. From Essex I walked to see my sister, who was in service in London, forty miles in a day, and she paid my fair to return home to Chatham; and a man came after me to go work in Chatham Dockyard, for Mr R—. I staid there two years and a half, and then Mr R— sent me up to London, where I have lived ever since, working in different places under different masters.

Ever since then things have seemed to go the right road with me.

J. Burnett, *Useful Toil* (Harmondsworth: Penguin, 1974) 62–3.

187) Irish labourers in the Black Country, 1856 [M.]

See note on extract No.26.

There is undoubtedly a great decrease in the Irish population of the district. In Wolverhampton the Irish-born, who were 3,491 in 1851, were but 1,687 in 1881. After thirty years the survivors out of a given number of people would not be very much greater than this, but the new comers ought to count for a considerable number. The diminution in some of the other towns of the district has been considerably greater than in Wolverhampton, particularly in Bilston and Darlaston, not simply in the Irish-born, among whom you but seldom now hear their native tongue, but also in their descendants.

Perhaps the most graphic description we have of the 'Black Country' is from the pen of A. M. Sullivan, who visited the district in 1856. This was but a few years after the rush of our people into England to escape from the Famine. Most of those, therefore, he found at this time were Irish-born.

Speaking of them in parts of Darlaston, Oldbury, and Wednesbury, he says – 'The Gaelic tongue is now more often heard than the language in which Thor and Woden were praised and glorified.' At this time they had become numerous in the district, and their employment was of the most rude, laborious, and unhealthy kind. In fact, he says – 'It is lives that are bought and sold in the furnaces and forges of South Staffordshire.' He describes the district around Wednesbury, with its 'mounds of fire and sheets of flame, with a forest of stacks belching out smoke.' Here there was at the time a population of 15,000, of whom he estimated that probably one-fourth were Irish. In describing the part of the town inhabited by the Irish, he says – 'In very many of the houses not one of the women could speak English, and I doubt that in a single house the Irish was not the prevalent language.' It will be remembered how Father Sherlock was sent to minister to the Irish of Bilston, one of these Black Country towns, because he could hear their confessions in their native tongue.

Mr Sullivan describes the terrible ordeal our people passed through in these early days of their appearance in South Staffordshire, and how the English miners 'rose up against them and tried to expel them by fire and sword.' 'Many were,' he says, 'killed, many were murdered in the works at night of whom no word was ever heard or trace ever found.' His informant said – 'If we went into a public-house to drink, and that an Englishman came in, we were struck dumb; if he asked for our pipe and didn't get it, he'd pull it out of our mouth. We dare say nothing, for there was neither law nor justice for an Irishman: Many changed their names. We got reckless, too, and used to drink and fight and riot, and would have gone wild and savage outright if it wasn't the mercy of God sent us a priest.'

Visiting West Bromwich and Oldbury, he says he found the Irish employed at laborious tasks that required great physical strength more than skill, such as charging and cleaning out the blast furnaces, and removing the slag. 'Having,' he continued, 'seen the Irish in their homes, I was anxious to see them at their work. Threading my way through smouldering heaps of ironstone, undergoing the process of roasting, and coal being converted into coke, I reached a gateway, in which were lying in all directions piles of pig iron, and masses of metal of every shape and size. A constant roar, as of a hurricane through the shrouds of a frigate, only louder by a hundred times, filled the air to the utter absorption at times of the hundred other noises that assailed the tympanum. On entering the precincts, my profane curiosity changed into awe and wonder. I found myself about to witness a marvellous event – one of King Vulcan's revels! That great, ponderous vat, eighty feet high, belted and ribbed with iron bands as closely as the network of a balloon – that mighty cauldron was about to be tapped; iron was about to run like wine! See how the imps of the iron god prepare for the flow of the liquid fire; through smoke and dust and darkness they flit about naked, their limbs and muscles strong as the metal girders that brace and bind the roof above them. All seems to be ordered by gesture; no voices may be heard here save those raised in the grand chorus which ever and anon swells into thunder on the ear, now sinking, now rising, now allowing the ringing sound of the cold metal, or the heavy blow of the weighty sledges to be for a moment distinguished amidst the thorough bass of the awful roar that stunned the visitor on entering. This proceeds from the powerful steam-bellows – the caged Boreas – that blows the furnace. At every gust the very ground seems to quake and tremble. It takes a little time to acquire confidence and composure in such a scene as this. And now a bustle is observed in the group standing near the surface: a canal has been cut leading to a pit dug in the ground. One of the firemen strikes, with his iron pole, at the base of the furnace wall, a few strokes, and a glare bursts on the faces of the group, and a fiery fluid rushes through the canal, and deposits in the pit. This, however, is not the stream – this is not the libation that is to flow for the Fire King. In a little while the deposit cools, and we discover that it is only the scum or dross – called "slag," that is being drawn off from the metal in the furnace. When it has flowed for ten or twelve minutes a movement is perceptible among the firemen, indicating that something of importance is about to take place. One or two of them run along by the canal that leads to the 'furrows,' throw themselves on their knees, pat with their hands and smoothen the sides, or dust out the bottom of it most carefully, which done, they take their stand at its head, close to the huge vat, and now – now – shower the blows of their weapons at its base; again and again, when a shout of horror and dismay bursts from your lips, as you see a fountain of liquid fire dash out almost in their faces; as it sweeps along the canal it fills the whole space, to a distance of twenty yards, with a scorching glow, white, sparkling, and dazzling, quite painful to the sight, and yet these wondrous beings, calm and undismayed, walk by it, play with it, all but handle it and feel it. One can scarcely credit that it is metal he sees there flowing in a stream with ripples and waves, and even spray rising on its surface; a glance at the spot to which it is flowing and we perceive that the furrows are nearly all filled with the molten iron thus cast into "pigs," the canal which fed them being technically called the "sow." When the metal has all run out the opening through which it flowed is once more securely blocked up with fireproof material, and the furnace again charged. I ascended to the platform from whence this operation is performed, and watched half a dozen brave Connaughtmen at the task. The furnace is a circular tower about eighty feet high and thirty feet diameter at the base; tapering to about fifteen or twenty feet at the top; within some ten feet or so of which are large openings through which the charge is shot. The "charge" consists of fixed proportions of coal, coke, limestone, and ironstone: the latter having already been subjected to the process of "roasting." The mass is fired and – in a hot blast furnace – burns twelve hours before tapping, by which time the molten metal has settled at the bottom. In cold blast furnaces twice the time is needed; in the former the air which is blown into it passed through red-hot pipes and entered the furnace at a heat sufficient to melt lead by one puff of its fiery breath.

'Rain was pouring heavily as I held converse with these men on the platform, yet they wore but little clothing, and from this little, saturated and dripping, the heat of the furnaces was driving a dense cloud of steam. In the snows and sleets of December, mid biting frosts and drenching rains, they are in this way exposed to the sudden and extreme changes of temperature – they are at the same moment being drenched and scorched, broiled and frozen; the strongest constitution sinks under subjection to this fearful trial, and the average duration of life, consequently, here is appallingly brief. Accidents, too, are numerous and of constant occurrence.' . . .

Since Mr Sullivan visited the Black Country, and so lovingly traced the footsteps of his poor fellow-countrymen, there has been a great change in the industries he studied so closely.

At Oldbury, one of the places he visited, there has been even more tragic waste of Irish flesh and blood than anything he saw. Those employed at the copper works there or elsewhere may commence the work fine, stalwart, young men, full of life, of powerful bone, and with sinews like iron – but they only last a few years. They have good wages, but no wages could repay their suffering. After a time their teeth become destroyed, they have bleeding at the nose, and other symptoms of arsenical poisoning. In comparatively a few years they become prematurely aged and mere wrecks of humanity. When unable to do the work required they are not discharged, but set at jobs in the yard and kept in employment while they live, which is not very long. It is circumstances like this and those described by Mr Sullivan that, no doubt, account for what one sees with sorrowful eyes in some places in this country – the Irish apparently melting away like a snow wreath.

J. Denvir, *The Irish in Britain from the Earliest Times to the Fall and Death of Parnell* (London: Kegan Paul, Trench, Trubner, 1892) 417–21.

188) Henry Broadhurst, stonemason, travels to find work in East Anglia and the South, 1850s–60s [M.]

Henry Broadhurst was born at Littlemore, near Oxford, in 1840. The son of a stonemason, he joined his father and brothers in the trade aged 13. In 1872 he became the Stonemason's Society delegate to the TUC; in 1873 Secretary to the Labour Representative League; in 1875 Parliamentary Secretary to the TUC. In 1885 he became a Member of Parliament and was Under-Secretary of State at the Home Office in Gladstone's government. The following extract from The Story of his life from a Stonemason's Bench to a Treasury Bench. Told by Himself *(1901) describes his early years 'on the tramp'.*

As I have said, the church at Wheatley was nearing completion, and the discharge of the hands in the mason's yard began. My turn soon came, and I found myself – a hobbledehoy – out of employment. All my endeavours to get work in Oxford and the surrounding district failed. Business was slack and masons were a drug in the market. So, as it happened in Robinson Crusoe's case, 'my head began to be filled with rambling thoughts'. I quickly made a decision to seek my fortune further afield, and from that moment I never again permanently resided under my parent's roof. I started on my venture into this raw life on Monday morning with high hopes and cheerful countenance. The night before my foot had kicked something in the pathway, and a patient search in the blackness of a pitch-dark night had been rewarded by the discovery of a rough purse full of coppers. I took this treasure for a happy omen; and, indeed, before the end of the week I had found employment in the town of Buckingham. My life there, and subsequently at Banbury in Bedfordshire, where I stayed nearly a year, passed uneventfully in the exercise of my trade.

About this time I paid my first visit to the Metropolis, where I found employment for a short time in the firm of George Myers and Son. Like all country-bred lads, I was astounded by the life and movement of London. The teeming masses of humanity rushing in all directions, bent, as it appeared to me, on getting clear of their neighbours, yet never succeeding in shaking off their pursuers, the roar of the streets, and the glare of the lamps at night-time, inspired in me a curious mingling of fascination and distaste. The same conditions were reproduced in the workshop. Above, below, and around me machines throbbed and whirled ceaselessly. The homely surroundings and social interests of the country life had no existence here; life seemed a new thing, almost unearthly. I began to long for the sunlight on the quiet fields, the green hedgerows, and the music of the woods. Even the Houses of Parliament, with the great Clock Tower, my chief delight, could not compensate for the absence of the joys of rural life. A few month's stay in modern Babylon was quite sufficient for me, and, gasping like a fish out of water, I set my face towards the open country.

After a week's wandering I found employment at a country house near Pangbourne, in Berkshire, a most delightful spot. The beauty of these new surroundings, and their contrast to the close air and grim streets of London, inspired me with a strong desire to make a long stay here. Unfortunately, the work I was engaged upon was soon completed, and in a short time I found myself back in London. My return route lay through Reading and Windsor, and as I possessed a little money I made the journey by easy stages. In those days railway fares were much higher, and most working men, even though they had the means, regarded travelling by rail as an expensive luxury, only to be indulged in by the lazy and foolish.

On my arrival in London I found that a firm of builders, Lucas Brothers, were in want of masons in Lowestoft, and that they were paying the passage by sea to Great Yarmouth of employees engaged in London. Here was a chance offer which suited me. I had never seen the sea, much less sailed upon its heaving breast. Accordingly, I found myself aboard a crazy tub of a steamer pounding heavily down the Thames. Besides ordinary passengers, I found a number of other masons bound on the same errand as myself. In such company the day and night passed rapidly and jovially, and so liberally did I contribute my quota of the entertainment that when the steamer reached Great Yarmouth I had not a half-penny to bless myself with. My companions were in no better case, so we were forced to tramp to Lowestoft, though this proved less a hardship than we expected, as the distance turned out to be only ten miles.

After a stay of a few months I left the coast and found my way to Norwich, little suspecting that my wanderings were to cease for the next six years.

J. Burnett, *Useful Toil* (Harmondsworth: Penguin, 1974) 314–16.

189) Irish and Hungarians in Daventry and Northampton, mid-1950s [I.]

See note on extract No.87.

Daventry is not much of a place; most of the people go to Northampton twelve miles away to do their shopping and, indeed, there weren't many to be seen around today.

A couple of letters awaited me when I got home, one from Father Eric and another from Patrick Dollart. Both of them had been addressing me in Irish and Eileen told me that the postman had enquired if she had a Hungarian staying in the house. I'm telling you that if I'm staying here for a while, he'll recognise Irish when he sees it.

For the matter of that, there have been a good few Hungarians around here since the Rising and natives, since they got to know them properly, don't care for them at all that much. Just before Christmas, the people in one of the villages nearby made a house available for a Hungarian family that had escaped. The villagers filled the house with furniture and laid on a store of food and coal for the family also. You'd imagine that the poor exiles that had suffered so much would be thankful for all this; but no, it was quite otherwise. They stayed in the house for one night only and then went into Northampton to inform the authorities there that they wanted a house in the city since they weren't used to country life.

I was in digs myself with some of them in Northampton and, from what I saw of them, I didn't think they were very willing to put up with much in the way of privation. They were all dressed nicely and, although we had the best of food in that house, they were never satisfied. From beginning to end they were complaining and grousing. I'm not saying that they haven't as much right as anyone else to kick up a row but you'd think that, after suffering so much hardship and deprivation in their own country, they would be prepared to put up with a few little difficulties here and there. At the same time, we have to pray to God that none of us have ever to suffer the amount of cruelty and persecution that they had to put up with from the Russians.

I walked into Daventry and said a couple of prayers in the church there. It's only a little chapel for there aren't many Catholics hereabouts. There were a few people gathered together at the corner and I thought of home and how the boys would gather at a similar corner commenting on anyone that passed by. But this crowd are not at all like the groups that collect at the corners in Ireland. They have no conversation other than what can be said in short sharp sentences. To listen to them, you'd be convinced that they knew no word of two syllables or more. They perpetually chew gum like cows chewing the cud and I doubt of they ever have any thought that wouldn't equally occur to a cow.

D. Mac Amhlaigh, *An Irish Navvy: the Diary of an Exile* (London: Routledge, 1964) 140–2.

190) Race riots in Nottingham, 1958 [I.]

Urban sociologist Ruth Glass here provides a detailed summary of the Nottingham disturbances of 1958. This extract, which quotes extensively from contemporary sources, comes from her study of West Indian London in the 1950s.

On Saturday, August 23rd 1958, a fight between a coloured and a white man started just at closing time, around 10 p.m., outside a public house in The Chase, a decaying Nottingham district, where a considerable number of coloured people are concentrated. The exact cause of the fight is obscure; various versions have been told, publicly and privately. But it is clear that the fighting spread within a few minutes. Several white men were stabbed by coloured men. Their attacks – and the immediate rush of rumours of their attacks – caused counter-attacks and threats against the coloured, in general. '. . . dozens of men and women were injured by knives, razors, palings and bottles.' A hostile shouting crowd of about 1,500 people gathered. At first, no more than two or three policemen were standing by; and apparently it took some time for police reinforcements to arrive. The fire brigade was called in. 'It was an ugly riotous crowd and fires could have been started,' said the Assistant Chief Constable of Nottingham later to the Press. 'Several coloured men were removed by the police for their own safety. A number of them had cuts and bruises.' Eight white people – including a policeman – were taken to hospital. It took 90 minutes to restore order: by midnight, the crowds were dispersed.

But that was neither the end of the matter, nor had the events of that night been a case of spontaneous combustion. Those who knew the district and the situation had been aware of growing tension for some time before. Coloured people had been molested, humiliated and beaten up by white men ('. . . vaguely known as "teddy boys", though their age range seems to run from over 20 to at least over 30.'). There had been frequent assaults of that kind, particularly during the fortnight preceding the riotous Saturday; and there had been widespread rumours that further warfare was imminent. The police thought that the initial fights of coloured against white on the Saturday night had been a reprisal for the previous attacks on coloured people.

> '. . . the Assistant Chief Constable (of Nottingham) confirmed that there had been assaults. He said that two white men were on remand charged with robbery with violence against a coloured man. The attacks made by "teddy boys" in the past fourteen days were responsible for Saturday night's outbursts. The coloured community, he said, apart from a few isolated cases, was "very well behaved".'

On Monday, August 26th, The Times reported 'All Quiet Again in Nottingham', but many of the other national newspapers were less optimistic – and less restrained. Some of them had picked up the 'teddy boys' story in a distorted form. Real boys – perhaps teddies, but certainly adventure-hunting or aggressive youths – from near and far took the cue and invaded the district. It was not quiet in The Chase; there was mounting tension. Everyone was waiting for the next Saturday night.

The rendezvous was kept on the following Saturday evening, August 30th. In St. Anne's Well Road, the scene of the previous week's disturbances, there was a large mixed crowd – 'teddy boys'; sightseers in cars and on foot; reporters; some local white people, but hardly any coloured ones: they had been advised to stay indoors and were anxious to do so. And there were police patrols who kept the crowds moving. It was reported that there was a 'milling mob' which grew to about 4,000 people during the evening. A car with three West Indians in it passed through and was stopped.

> 'Cries of "let's lynch them", and "Let's get at them", went up as the crowd, many of them teddy boys who had poured from public houses, tried to smash their way into the car. Beating on the windows, they tried to overturn it. . . . Finally police forced a path through them and told the coloured men in the car to "go like hell". They did.'

Later on, there was more trouble; it started, so it was said, when a cameraman lit a magnesium flare to 'film a scuffle between a small party of youths'. The crowds, which had begun to disperse, rushed back, thinking there was a fire. There was great agitation and shouting – for example, as was said subsequently in the Magistrate's Court, 'Find some niggers'. 'By this time all coloured people appeared to have left the streets . . . an ugly white versus white clash developed as police vans came into the area.' Some of the fighting was directed against the police, but no policeman was injured. More than fifty people were taken to police headquarters, and 24 boys and men (whose ages ranged from 16 to 45) were charged under the Public Order Act.

Next day the Chief Constable held a Press conference and said:

> 'This was not a racial riot. The coloured people behaved in an exemplary way by keeping out of the way. Indeed, they were an example to some of our rougher elements. The people primarily concerned were irresponsible teddy boys and persons who had had a lot to drink.'

On the following Saturday evening, September 6th, there was again a crowd in the district, though a much smaller one than previously. Again there were 'nigger-baiting' incidents. A siege of some coloured people's houses developed into a missile battle between the tenants who threw milk bottles from the upper floors and the crowd below who bombarded the houses with bricks and bottles and broke windows. In a dark side street coloured men were chased; five were assaulted. But the police vans arrived quickly, and the fighting was stopped.

There was no further news of anti-colour mass hysteria in Nottingham. But there was a footnote. A bus company in an adjacent town advertised coach tours to see 'the terror spots of Nottingham'.

R. Glass, *Newcomers: The West Indians in London* (London: Centre for Urban Studes/George Allen & Unwin, 1960) 130–3.

191) Nazrah on Asian life in Birmingham, 1989 [I.]

See note on extract No.118.

I think Birmingham from the outside view, and from my view, is really dead and really trashy. You look around and there's rubbish everywhere, and I think it's segregated as well. Because if you look at Stirchley and Kings Norton and more up that way, Asians and Blacks get less and less. And if you go up to Selly Oak it's mostly Asians and Blacks everywhere up to Handsworth. And Solihull, again, gets all whites.

People think that the area you live in reflects the class that you are. When we say to someone that we live in Small Heath they say: 'That's a really bad area; don't you want to get out?' Yes, we do want to get out, but we love that area because it is our home. We can't go out because there's loads of gangs there, but still, we've sort of grown to like it more and more. I don't think my dad has or my mum, but us kids have. We've grown to like it and we've made some really good friends without our parents really coming into it. Because most of the people we know it's through our parents. But in Small Heath whichever shop we go into we make friends with them.

A. Osler, *Speaking Out: Black Girls in Britain* (London: Virago Upstarts, 1989) 39–40.

North West England

192) The movements of the Shaw family, late 18th century [M.]

See note on extract No.3.

> Mary Shaw my fathers sister, & daughter of Benjn & Hannah Shaw, was the youngest Child, Born in grasdale about 1759 or 60 – She lived with her parents all the time they lived, She was employ in the house & in knitting & spinning &c She married when she was about 30 years old one John Davis, son of Jacob & Nanny Davis of their town a waller (as they called them) or builder & flager & Slater plasterer &c by him she had 2 Sons, the first Jacob & 2 d Benjamin, the first died in this town Preston about the year 1804 – the other went for a Soldier and never returned – after her parents died they went to Kendal to live, with an intent of getting a better living, this might be about 1796, then they shifted to this town, (Preston) about the year 1801 and lived several years, John following mason work and her Brother Edward who always lived with them sometimes turned a laith wheel, Sometimes Strook [wielded a hammer] for the Smiths, & Sometimes tended a Steam Engin &c while they were in Preston their Son Jacob died about 14 years ago, and Benjn went to be a Soldier, & never came back – after this they went back to their own countery and are living yet for anything that I know.

A. G. Dent, *The Family Records of Benjamin Shaw Mechanic of Dent, Dolphinholme and Preston, 1772–1841* (n.p: Record Society of Lancashire and Cheshire, 1991) 16.

193) The Jewish community in Leeds, early 19th c. [I.]

See note on extract No.162.

> The traditional date for the foundation of the Leeds community is 1840. Jews were, however, resident here before that date. Lazarus Levi 'a Jew well known in Leeds' died in 1799, in his 105th year; and, if he settled there in the prime of his life, he should have arrived no later than 1750. He was father, perhaps,

of Moses Levi, who was recorded in the press to have been baptised in 1772 on his marriage to a certain Mrs Gordon. He had been in business in Briggate as a silversmith since at the latest 1758 . . .

From these data it would appear probable that some sort of organised Jewish life developed in Leeds in the course of the eighteen-twenties. Up to 1846, services were held in a room in Bridge Street, and thereafter in Back Rockingham Street, where there was accommodation for 70 persons; while a plot of land in Geldard Road was granted on May 12th, 1840 by the Earl of Cardigan for use as cemetery, at a nominal price of £2. It was not, however, for another generation that this community, now the third in size in the entire country, began to play a part of any importance in Anglo-Jewish life.

C. Roth, *The Rise of Provincial Jewry* (London: Jewish Monthly, 1950) 81–2.

194) The Irish community in Manchester, 1844 [M.]

*Leon Faucher, French by birth, journalist by profession, like his near contemporaries Friedrich von Raumer (*England in 1835, *1836), and J. G. Kohl (*Ireland, Scotland and England, *1844), was a continental observer and commentator in the Industrial Revolution. He is also the author of* Etudes sur L'Angleterre *(Paris: 1845).*

In the midst of this immense population you easily distinguish the Irish portion, which amounts to 35,000 or 40,000 in number.* The English stroll in small groups, or wander about solitary, unless they have some subject of great moment to discuss, such as a rise of wages or a reduction of the hours of labour. The Irish are perpetually in a state of agitation. Often they assemble by hundreds at the corner of Oldham and Ancoats streets. One of their number reads in a loud voice the Irish news, the addresses of O'Connell, or the circulars of the Repeal Association; and afterwards, the whole is commented upon without end and with great clamour, by the closely pressed crowd. They are so strictly organised, that in the twinkling of an eye, one or two thousand can be collected at any given spot.

For several years the Irish labourers formed the most abject portion of the population, their dwellings were the most dirty and unhealthy and their children the most neglected. It was in the cellars occupied by them that the illicit distillation of ardent spirits was carried on. Misery of every description, fever, roguery, debauchery, and theft, were rife among them; their neighbourhood was the chosen retreat of vagabonds and criminals; scarcely a day passed without some disturbance or without some serious crime.

* The population of Lancashire is 1,667,000, of which there are 21,000 Scots, and 105,000 Irish.

Happily, however these features of the Irish portion of the population have undergone a remarkable change. The labours of Father Matthew, assisted by the Catholic clergy were the commencement of this work of reformation amongst them. They drink less, and consequently there are fewer disturbances. On Sunday, July 22nd, 1843, 20,000 of them publicly took the pledge of abstinence from spirituous liquors, and the following day the apprehensions for drunkenness and crime were reduced one half. The publicans complained loudly. Gin palaces which used to have fifty customers at a time, could now count but fifteen or twenty. But what is most remarkable, is the care taken by the priests in the education of the children. In this town where the little ones run about in the streets barefoot and in rags whilst their parents are in the gin shops, and where the police take annually more than five thousand children, which have been lost, or abandoned by their parents, the Catholic chapels are kept open during the evenings and form a species of asylums, where the young boys and girls pass their time in singing hymns and listening to the instruction of their pastors.

I have seen upon a Sunday, from five to six thousand of these children in procession, under the banner of St Patrick, and in partial neatness (*demi-propreté,*) and decency of this juvenile assemblage, is the greatest as well as the most unexpected progress which I am able to record.

M. L. Faucher, *Manchester in 1844; its Present Condition and Future Prospects* (Manchester: A. Heywood, 1844) 28–31.

195) Mixed relationships in Liverpool, 1849 [I.]

Herman Melville (1819–91) signed on as a merchant seaman for a round trip to Liverpool in June 1939, aged 20. Ten years later he published Redburn *(1849) based in his Liverpool trip.*

. . . three or four times I encountered our black steward dressed very handsomely, and walking arm in arm with a good looking English woman. . . . Owing to the friendly reception extended to them and the unwarranted immunities they enjoyed, the black cooks and stewards of American ships are much attracted to the place.

T. Lane, *Liverpool: Gateway to Empire* (London: Lawrence and Wishart, 1987) 117.

196) Sanitary conditions in Liverpool, 1871 [M.]

From an official report describing the living conditions and potential health hazards among the Irish community in Liverpool.

It is not possible to alter this without surrendering the commercial supremacy of Liverpool, but some precautionary measures may be taken. Arrangements for the proper and healthy accommodation of emigrants, both Continental and Irish, so as to separate them completely from the permanent population, by locating them only in a certain district, would afford the best chance of stomping out or limiting the spread of an epidemic disease brought with them; and although it might be impossible to do this in the case of Irish, or other labourers, who enter Liverpool in search of work, still, even here precautions might be taken, whenever it is known that epidemic diseases are prevailing in the localities whence they come.

. . . But the local causes which aid the spread of these diseases (and which are all important as being removable) exist also in Liverpool to an unusual extent.

E. A. Parkes MD FRS and J. Burdon Sanderson MD FRS, *Report on the Sanitary Condition of Liverpool* (London: Parliamentary Papers, 1871) 51.

197) 'Monkey Abraham' and other 'Orientals' in Manchester and Salford, 1873 [I.]

See note on extract No.52.

This was the Missionary's first visit to Manchester, and being a stranger in that town, he engaged the services of this 'native Christian' to conduct him to the various Orientals in it. In the course of that dirty day the human sewers of Manchester and Salford were overhauled, the warrens of twenty were entered, and the imperishable bread of heaven sent before the starving wanderers. The visit was repeated the next day with pleasing success. He went down one dirty little avenue in Salford, that seemed very much like squeezing into the neck of a glass bottle, which was dignified by the 'right of way,' was passed; but here Jan Abdoolah kept a lodging-house, and five Asiatics were with him. Among these a candle was lighted for the Lord, with an effect that will not be easily forgotten. A Javanese and five natives of India constituted the audience; one of the latter had been brought up in a Missionary school in Indian, and had been taught the truth, and perhaps valued it, but the cares of his shifted life had choked it, or it was found to have no root and was therefore scorched up . . .

Another man is noteworthy, because he was famed in Manchester; a tall old man, whose body had wasted in the western sun, leaving little more than skin and bone. Like the patriarch's son, he wore a coat of many colours, which was contrasted with evident design; a large ring hung round his neck, made of silver, and a number of smaller ones of the same metal, hanging one in the other, depending from each ear, and he rejoiced in a name as singular as his appearance: 'Monkey Abraham.' It was a name not chosen but earned, and any one who saw the ape-like attitude he assumed, with his ridiculous ornaments, would never doubt how well he merited the appellation. But as we miss a singular flower plucked from our garden, so suddenly Abraham was missed from Manchester; and the Missionary saw no more of him till he turned up again in the Whitechapel Road in the East of London, with coats, rings, and paraphernalia entire; but he had obtained a board with a printed paper on it, which was suspended from his neck, telling the piteous tale of his master's death, and his destitution in consequence. The Missionary spoke to him, expecting to be identified; but Manchester was a long way off, and probably both the Missionary and his teachings were quickly banished from his mind, and he sought to defend the statement on the board by giving name and place, and other invented particulars. 'Why Abraham! don't you know me?' 'Oh, Padre, is it you? I don't know you. Pardon what I said.' His deceit was commented on and condemned. But he conceived the falsehood to be necessitated and justified by his want of means.

J. Salter, *The Asiatic in England: Sketches of Sixteen Years' Work Among Orientals* (London: Seeley, Jackson and Halliday, 1873) 224–6.

198) Manchester Jews, 1880s [I.]

See note on extract No.54.

The Jews in Manchester, numerous as they are now, were very few in numbers a hundred years ago; and, even within the recollection of a gentleman now living, the number of tradesmen of their nation in the town might almost have been counted upon the fingers. They were so few that it was only about the year seventeen hundred and eighty the first synagogue was founded by Mr Nathan. This, we believe, was an upper room in Garden Street, recently pulled down. The Rev. Moses Margoliouth, a converted Jew, tells us in his history of the Jews in England that the Halliwell Street synagogue was founded in eighteen hundred and six, but was for some time without a regular minister, and that Mr Isaacs of Liverpool came over once a fortnight to preach a sermon. He tells a curious story of a split from Halliwell Street by some of the members, which scoffers may pronounce characteristic. It is to the effect that the pretext was afforded by some dissatisfaction concerning a charge made for the special prayer for the repose of the soul of a departed relative. The ordinary price for each soul was two-and-sixpence; but some members thought several souls might be included for that money, and, as the wardens protested and refused, they decided to leave Halliwell Street and return to Long Millgate.

One of the rooms used in the earlier part of this century was situated over a joiner's shop in Ainsworth Court, Long Millgate; and belonged, it is said, to a relative of Harrison Ainsworth. A notable preacher who officiated in Halliwell Street was Dr Schiller, formerly a rabbi in Hungary, who during the struggle for independence joined the army and became a major, but eventually had to flee; he came here, was elected rabbi, and regularly preached in the above-named synagogue. Concerning the number now in Manchester, we cannot obtain any exact information, various estimates being given, the highest of which is ten thousand; but this is formed upon no very reliable data, and is not improbably an underestimate. Some notion may be formed of the important item they form in our local population from the fact that they have five principle synagogues – of which the Old Hebrew Congregation is the parent one – and not less than about fourteen minor ones, or 'Hebras', which are principally used as meeting houses for prayer, and are largely if not chiefly patronised by immigrants.

These people are foreigners from various countries, who knowing little of any language but their own, naturally gravitate each towards those of his own nation, and get ministers who can lead their devotions in their own languages. One of the principal synagogues is that of the Portuguese, so called, comprising the Jews from Portugal, Spain, Italy, Morocco, Algiers and the Orients. Another is that of German and Polish Israelites, – some of the most orthodox of all; and there are also 'British Jews,' a congregation posing to some extent as reformers of the church, who are regarded as being not without a suspicion of heterodoxy. One recent development of their misguided zeal is the establishment of an organ . . .

W. Tomalinson, *Bye-Ways of Manchester Life* (Manchester: Butterworth and Nodal, 1887) 31–3.

199) Jewish sweaters' living conditions in Manchester, 1888 [I.]

A report by the Special Sanitary Commission on 'Sweating among Tailors of Liverpool and Manchester' that was conceived to reflect contemporary concerns about the new immigrants and published in the respected medical journal The Lancet.

Manchester, as an abode for sweaters, posseses some notable advantages over London. The town is comparatively new; the streets are therefore wider and there is more air and more light. Further, it so happens that the greater number of Jew sweaters have settled in the district of Strangeways, where they have found houses in some instances built for an altogether different and higher class of tenants. Somehow the higher class tenants did not think fit to live in this quarters, and this, so far as public health is concerned, is a fortunate circumstance, for thus many of the Manchester sweaters are located in a better class of houses than those generally occupied by the sweaters of, for instance, London and Liverpool.

The Lancet, 21 April 1888.

200) Jewish women market traders in Lancashire, 1880s–90s [I.]

See note on extract No.55.

The strong, independent woman of the shtetl did not disappear completely, however. A minority of Jewish women continued to carve out careers for themselves in the market trade: Benny W. explains how his brother, a former machiner, was introduced to the market trade through his mother-in-law:

> She was a market man and she taught him the markets . . . He'd never been on the markets and he didn't know how to speak to a customer, or where to buy or what to do.
>
> Rose M.'s mother came to England from 'a small place in Kovno Geberne, Lithuania' in the 1880's. She soon after met her husband who, partly at her instigation, set up a tailoring workshop in Manchester. Although the workshop did reasonably well and although they had ten children, Rose's mother earned an independent livelihood, not in the family workshop, but out on the markets over 'the length and breadth of Lancashire'. Rose recalls,
>
> 'My mother had never been in the workshop . . . she was always on the markets. From the time that I recalled my mother, she'd always been going on the markets . . . She always told us, "Don't depend upon your husband's wage. Go out and earn your own." '

She was a most remarkable saleswoman. In the end, she finished up in the bigger markets, like Blackburn and Oldham. The market trade gave Rose's mother an independent income which she did not divulge: 'I couldn't tell you what my mother made, because she spent here and she gave there. She was very, very charitable and nobody ever knew . . .'

The market trade had three important advantages for women. Firstly, its flexibility: although Rose's mother might go on the markets every day of the week, she was not tied to fixed hours and daily attendance, as in factory work, but could suit her own convenience. Further, it required little initial capital outlay or specialised training. In Rose's words:

> You can get right on, in those days. You can go on a market. The stalls weren't full. You could say to the superintendent, 'Have you a stall?' He asks you what you sell. You say . . . 'Right, sell'. So it was as easy as that. And you didn't need a lot of money to start with. And that's why they went on the markets.

R. Burman, 'The Jewish woman as breadwinner: the changing value of women's work in a Manchester immigrant community', *Oral History*, 10 (1982) 32–3.

201) The Italian community in Liverpool and Manchester, 1901 [I.]

A survey carried out by the Italian Consul General in 1901 of the expanding Italian community in two major northern cities.

> Our compatriots living in Liverpool are about 300 in number, the majority of them are organ-grinders, street ice-cream vendors; statuette makers from

Tuscany, and other various workers . . . This small colony, spread in the numerous districts of this large city . . . , has little cohesion and few individual relations among its members.

In Manchester there are probably some 1,250 Italians; many organ-grinders, ice-cream and statuette makers and vendors; and, to a lesser extent, labourers, small shopkeepers, commercial clerks, waiters; etc.

L. Sponza, *Italian Immigrants in Nineteenth-Century Britain: Realities and Images* (Bath: Leicester University Press, 1988) 16.

202) The choice of occupation among Manchester Jews, 1896 [I.]

Bill Williams records the following details of the speaker's biography. 'Born 1878, Vilna, Lithuana. Father a synagogue official. Arrived in Manchester alone in 1891 and took lodgings in Fernie Street, Red Bank. Capmaker.' See also note on extract No.104.

The existence of certain trades in the Jewish area is, of course, a reflection of the economic pattern of Jewish life in Eastern Europe: skilled workers brought their trades with them. The question is why they were followed by the unskilled majority (and often by a second generation), particularly when the trades in question were notoriously unstable and exploitative. The answer may well lie in the narrow concentration of immigrant residence: in Manchester, in two closely-connected slum districts, Strangeways and Red Bank. Once drawn into these districts by ties of kin, country or friendship, the availability of cheap and congenial lodgings or the accessibility of essential communal facilities, immigrants were drawn naturally towards certain trades by the social network in which they lived. The point was put sharply by a Russian [*sic*] immigrant who arrived in Manchester in 1896 at the age of 13:

Why did you choose capmaking?
Well, I had no other trade. Somebody recommend me . . . They took me to the factory and they showed me how to learn to do the capmaking.

Who took you?
A friend. No relation at all. No relation.

How did you meet this friend?
I don't know how I met him. In the street, talking. Standing in the corner. He said, 'Sonny boy, what are you looking for?' Zocht, 'I'm looking for work,' 'What sort of work?' Zocht, 'I have no trade at all.' Said, 'Come with me.' He took me to the workshop and showed me how to do it with an iron, with everything.

B. Williams, 'The Jewish immigrant in Manchester: the contribution of oral history', *Oral History*, 7 (1979) 47.

203) Sabbath work among Manchester Jews, 1906 [I.]

Extracts from three interviews are cited here. Bill Williams records the following details of the speaker's biographies: (1) Born 1908, Stockport. Father an immigrant of 1906. Credit draper. (2) Born 1895, Vitebsk, White Russia. Father a tea-traveller. Arrived in Manchester, 1910. Wholesale draper. (3) Born 1917, Cheetham. Grandfather a Rumanian immigrant. Clothes dealer and market-stall holder. See also note on extract No.104.

A similar situation is revealed in the case of shopkeeping and the itinerant trades. For the credit draper – a traveller selling domestic textiles and clothing on the basis of small weekly payments – Saturday was the most important day of the week, an essential collecting day if the weeks wages of his customers were not to be drunk away in the pubs. The daughter of an Austrian immigrant described the work of her father, who became a credit draper in 1906 and built up a profitable 'round' in the Stockport area:

But they [the Jewish credit drapers] used to work on the Saturday?
Yes, yes. But we didn't do things . . . We were told what dad had to do for the business. That was our living and our bread and butter, it couldn't be helped. But we weren't allowed to do anything . . . We had a fire goy (gentile) who came in to do the fires and mother didn't do any cooking on the Sabbath and we didn't ride on the Sabbath or do anything like that.

Even the local Rabbi turned a blind eye: 'It was Mr Dove who lived next door. Oh, he was a wonderful man. On Saturday, even on a nice day he wouldn't go out in the afternoon after he'd been to shool (synagogue) in the morning . . . He wouldn't go out in case he embarassed his congregation if they met him and they were on business.'

For marketmen, amongst whom were many Jewish immigrants, Saturday was the critical day of the week. An immigrant from Vitebsk who toured the Lancashire textile towns with a drapery stall shortly before the First World War told me: 'We explained it to ourselves this way. We thought, "It's a necessity." That's how it was. You couldn't make a living if you didn't work on a Saturday in England.' Shopkeepers too opened for at least part of the Sabbath, even in the solid immigrant districts of North Manchester:

What about religion in the home, in the shop?
Very strict. She [his mother] was very strict.

Kosher?
Strictly kosher . . . She was strictly kosher. When Friday night came along, everything was laid out, white table-cloth on the table, brass candlesticks lit, the wine and the challah (twisted sweet bread) was put on the table, kiddush (blessing) was made, which is the Friday night prayer and . . . we knew it was Shabbos. On the Shabbos morning, naturally she opened the shop. She'd make us go to school . . . She was that orthodox that she wouldn't even tear

> paper on Saturday even though she had to serve. Any brown paper that she had to wrap up, she had it cut in squares ready so that she didn't have to cut it or tear it on the Shabbos. Although she had to work, she didn't want to make more sins than she absolutely had to do. Pieces of string. We had balls of string. Well she cut them in different lengths beforehand so that she could tie the parcels up without making an initial sin as it was considered.

B. Williams, 'The Jewish immigrant in Manchester: the contribution of oral history', *Oral History*, 7 (1979) 46.

204) The Welsh Chapel network in Manchester, 1890–1930 [M.]

Merfyn Jones identifies the speaker in the first quotation as Mr C. T. J., born 1906, Liverpool. The second and third quotations are from Mr A. W. H., born 1925, Manchester. See also note on extract No.122.

> 'It was like this – in all these chapels the deacons and the people who ran these chapels were almost all wealthy. In the chapel I went to, Great Mersey Street, Tom Phillips, he's gone long ago . . . he was an Estate Agent, and he had come here as a young boy, and he had arrived quite poor, but he had worked himself up. He . . . had his own place, his own company, . . . and he knew of other builders and he could help if, say if a boy came from Wales, if he went to the chapel, if he started attending the chapel, there would be someone in that chapel who could help him to get on . . . to get him work. I'll give you an example, there was an organist in Great Mersey Street chapel . . . and he had got a job on the railway, on the Cheshire Lines and he became Traffic Manager, and he had a lot of authority, well there were three or four young fellows who had jobs with the Cheshire Lines, and they didn't have to start at the bottom, he was able to give them jobs higher up the ladder. And they all got on, just because Edwards gave them a start . . . And that was the influence of the chapel, and the influence of these men who came from Wales and bettered themselves – they helped. If you wanted a job on the docks well there were plenty of men working on the docks: "come with me Monday morning. You'll get a job."'
>
> The chapels operated as unofficial Labour Exchanges for the Welsh community bringing together, as they did, employers and labour. But, even more significantly, the chapels offered a familiar framework which kept the Welsh migrants in touch with other Welsh men and women (they also, of course, offered a highly efficient dating system) and gave shape and coherence to their lives:
>
> 'There was that system, say that Mary Jones came up from Trallwng or somewhere, her chapel would send up a letter. Now the evening service would be . . . hymn, reading, prayer – very long prayer informing higher authority of

everything that happened – "Thou knowest Lord that this week we have seen Mrs. Jones" you know, whatever, and then a hymn and then a collection while the organ played (I was the organist so I knew to turn it up) and then the sermon, then a hymn and then the seiat. And that is when they'd stand up. Now this was the thing, you see it wasn't just church, it was the nostalgia centre for everybody because the minister would then stand up and he would give out the news: "I'm sorry to say that Mrs. Williams of 24 Lloyd Street is no better . . . , They went into every detail. "We are sorry not to be seeing Mr. Morris for two whole weeks, but we are sure that the spirit is willing." '

Following the local news came the crucial process of accepting the newcomers:

'And then they would come reading the letters. He'd ask Mr. Morgan, the Secretary, to stand up now and "I'm glad to say that I've received a letter this week from whatsitsname chapel in Pwllheli." And it would read like one of Paul's letters: "To our brothers and sisters who are worshipping in the chapel at Upper Brook Street, Manchester. Greetings!" And this would go on to say that "we are commending to you our sister or our brother who has been a faithful member and worker at the this and that and the other". And then you were on the books. If you went away and took your letter with you you were still a subscribing member sort of thing. And this kept you, wherever you went, in this thing. You were watched over weren't you, and your parents back in Wales knew you were on the narrow path because your letter had been read. "And will the dear brother stand up?" And we all had a good look, or better still at a dear sister, and that was that. So there was this network, and there was this network of care . . .'

M. Jones, 'Welsh immigrants in the cities of North-West England, 1880–1930: some oral testimony', *Oral History*, 9 (1981) 37.

205) Eric Ferron in Manchester and Glasgow, 1947 [I.]

See note on extract No.85.

Manchester was my kind of town. I was seeing it for the last time before going south. Nothing good had happened to me in London so far. But Manchester felt like home. It was like Jamaica to me, the only place I felt really happy. The people were friendly and cheerful to me, and they seemed used to coloured people. I liked the North and Manchester was the centre. Colour did not seem to be such an issue here. The only discussion about it had been with some students when I was on a course in Manchester. I remember some of us being invited by an Englishwoman to her house where we met two politically minded men. They were talking about the problems of race and colour and she suddenly turned to us and said: 'You're no different from the rest of us. No different at all. You're just as good and just as bad. Unless you believe this and accept it you'll go round thinking you are different and you'll be treated different.' When we left she said: 'Remember what I said. You'll need it to keep going. It's the only way to live in this country.'

I remembered her words. They served their purpose many times.

There were other towns in the North where the people made me feel good. Once in Blackburn I wanted to see a friend and couldn't find his house. I was walking down this long street and it was raining hard. It had been raining all day. A woman from a house across the street called out: 'What do you think you're doing, walking in this rain without a coat? Come inside at once and dry your clothes! You'll catch your death of cold!' And she ran across and pulled me inside. She didn't ask any questions. I started to apologise. I couldn't protest. I said I was just looking for an address. 'Doesn't matter about that now! Go up and take off those wet things and put these on'. She put some dry clothes and a big warm dressing gown in my hands and I went upstairs and took off my uniform, heavy and soaking wet, dried myself and put on the dry clothes. I came downstairs. There was a huge coal fire burning in the living room. She hung my clothes in front of the fire and she talked to me. I explained again I had come looking for this address and couldn't find the house. She was able to tell me the people I had been looking for had moved about a year ago but they were still only two streets away. I told her I hadn't heard from them for over a year but I had been passing through and thought I would look them up. She said: 'Don't worry. My husband will take you round there when he comes home.'

She made me tea and fussed over my uniform to get it dry without crumples. 'You men! Just like overgrown babies. No sense. Never have a proper coat on. Walking in all that rain.' To her I was just another man stupid enough to walk in the rain without a coat. She seemed to enjoy mothering me and I certainly needed it. Her husband came home. He accepted the strange sight of a cold wet black man sitting in his chair wearing his dressing gown as if it happened all the time. I was there over two hours talking with them and drinking hot sweet tea. Then he took me round to the house I had been looking for.

I had always found this immediate kindness in the North. What troubles I had were little pinpricks, usually from children who didn't know and wanted to find out. Further north still, in Glasgow, I never felt different from anyone else. No one seemed to go out of their way to embarrass me. I felt accepted as just another customer in the cafes, the pubs, the dancehalls. I found people wanted to talk to me, to tell me about Scotland and the injustice they had suffered from the English. Yet they seemed happier than the people I met in the South. They talked to you. If you asked the way they were quick to answer and to help. I'd never had this feeling in the South, certainly not in London. People seemed indifferent. You had to have a lot of nerve to approach them because you felt they might rebuff you. You asked the way. 'I don't know. I'm a stranger here too.' The police were always helpful and so were the taxi-drivers, but you never got far if you depended on people in the street. Maybe all the people you asked were strangers. It's a big town, but sometimes you doubted that so many people could be strangers. They sat in the tube train and read their papers and if they brushed you and stepped on your toe they were polite and said: 'So sorry'. But you had the feeling that if you were to collapse they wouldn't even notice, they would step over you and pass on their way. Maybe I was wrong about this. But I had had no reason to think otherwise during my time there so far. As I reflect now after all these years I wonder whether London really can be so indifferent as it appeared to me then, because it was in London that I was eventually to settle. Back in 1947, on my last Saturday in Manchester, it was the last thing I expected to do.

E. Ferron, *'Man, You've Mixed': A Jamaican Comes to Britain* (London: Whiting and Birch, 1995) 38–40.

206) Prafulla Mohanti in Leeds, 1960s [I.]

See note on extract No.90.

I went to see the accommodation officer, who had a well-furnished spacious room to herself. She was in her fifties, neatly dressed in a green floral-patterned frock and a green hat. She wore heavy make-up and her lips were red. I produced a letter she had written to me referring to emergency accommodation. 'But we don't have emergency accommodation' she replied. I realized there was no point in arguing and requested her to find me a room.

She searched through her files, telephoned somebody, and arranged a room for me. She wrote the name and address on a piece of paper. It was already four in the afternoon, my lecture started at six, and I decided to go the next day.

I had great difficulty in finding the place. It was in the suburbs and there was no direct bus. I had to ask several people how to get there. The house was situated in a well-kept terrace with a front garden. I climbed up the steps and rang the doorbell. A young woman opened the door and looked surprised to see me. `The accommodation officer has sent me. You have a room for me.'

'Oh no, no', she replied. 'The room is gone.'

Before I could say anything she closed the door in my face. I felt like an Untouchable. I remembered how the Harijans in my village were not allowed to enter the houses of the high caste Hindus. Even the doors of the temples were closed to them. In Bombay I was told that before Independence there were exclusive clubs for the British displaying notices, 'Dogs and Indians not allowed'. Even after Independence the Breach Candy swimming pool in Bombay excluded Indians, claiming it was a private club. When an Indian was able to swim the English Channel he was invited to use the pool. That created a precedent and gave the swimming club an excuse to allow Indians to join as members.

I returned to the college by bus, disappointed. The woman conductor gave me my ticket, smiled, and said, 'Thank you, luv.' My three days at the YMCA were at an end and I had to leave. It was the weekend and the Education offices were closed. After great difficulty I found a small hotel to stay in for a few days. On Monday I went to see the accommodation officer again. This time she was all in blue, with a blue hat.

'Why didn't you tell her I was from India? She shut the door in my face.'

'You are imagining things.'

'I am staying in a hotel. It's expensive and I can't afford it. You must find me a room.'

'You can't say "I must find you".' She seemed to find fault with everything I said. I left.

I wandered around Leeds. Wherever I looked I could see only grey-grey buildings, grey churches, and grey skies. A thick layer of dirt had collected over the Victorian Town Hall and nobody had bothered to clean it. But when I went to the school and saw friendly faces I felt optimistic. I decided I must somehow overcome the difficulties and complete the course.

That night I kept wondering why the accommodation officer had not been helpful. What did I do to offend her? There was nobody like Tom to advise me. I was translating my Oriya expressions into English. Saying 'please', 'thank you', 'excuse me', and 'sorry' had not yet become a habit. Sometimes I thought I might have said the wrong thing but did not know how to put it right. My Indian friends faced similar difficulties and were so afraid of being misunderstood that they avoided meeting English people.

The hotel was comfortable but too expensive for me. After a few days I moved to a bed-and-breakfast place nearer the college. It was run by an elderly couple. He was an invalid and had lost one of his legs in the war. He had an artificial leg but was very active. He even drove a car. They were kind and wanted me to stay with them permanently but I could not afford it. I started looking for a place on my own. Every day I bought the local newspaper and searched through the advertisements for suitable accommodation. When I telephoned and said I was from India I was usually asked about the colour of my skin. I always got the same reply, 'The room is gone.'

One day I saw an advertisement for a room near the school. I telephoned and a woman's voice answered. I explained to her that I was a student from India and looking for a room.

'I have asked somebody to come at ten. Could you come at nine-thirty?' she said.

When I arrived the landlady was waiting for me. She was small, thin, and her skin was as dark as mine. While showing me the room she told me she was a Jew from Rumania. She lived with her husband in a suburb of Leeds and had a number of houses which they let.

The room was on the ground floor of an old Victorian terrace house. There was a fireplace with a gas fire, a large window overlooking the road, and a partitioned area with a sink and a small gas stove. Lighting was free but there was a meter for gas. The bath and toilet were on the first floor. The room was large and the rent was a little expensive. As I was trying to make up my mind the doorbell rang.

'Do you want the room?' she asked. 'Otherwise I'll let these people have it.'

Immediately I said, 'Yes, I want the room.'

I moved in the same day. The owner of the boarding house helped me with my luggage.

I felt relieved to have found a room of my own in Leeds. But I became aware of four walls and a ceiling. I felt alone and lonely in a box, suspended in a space where I thought people were hostile to strangers. I missed my village and my parents and their love. For the first time I realized what love really meant. I received so much of it in my village that I had taken it for granted. The expression of love is natural in India.

P. Mohanti, *Through Brown Eyes* (Oxford: Oxford University Press, 1985) 67–9.

North East England

207) Daniel Nicholson moves from Carlisle to Bedford, 1770 [M.]

Born c.1742 in Barnsley, Yorkshire, Daniel Nicholson was an apprentice calico printer in Carlisle from the age of 10 to 13. He later travelled to Great Driffield in Yorkshire and eventually on to Bedford, where he married in 1770. His account was taken down during an official settlement examination of the same year.

> The examinant saith that he is ab. 28 years of age and was born at Barnsley in the county of York and that he was put out an apprentice at about the age of 10 years to William Cookson a Callicoe Printer at Carlisle in the County of Cumberland to serve for the term of three years wch term he served as an apprentice to the sd Wm Cookson at Carlisle aforesaid and soon afterwards by this examinant let himself as a hired servant for one whole year to John Gray of Great Driffield in the County of York Callico printer for the sum of fifteen pounds and received of the said John Gray his whole years Wages and afterwards worked with the sd. John Gray by the week for the space of abt six Months And further saith that he hath not gained any other subsequent Settlement since he left the sd John Grays service at Great Driffield aforesaid. This examinant further saith that on the Second Day of December One thousand seven hundred and seventy he was marriyed at the Parish Church of St. Paul in the town of Bedford aforesaid to one Mary Hull who resided in the parish of St. Paul aforesaid and is now living and resident with this examinant at his Quarters in the Parish of St. Paul aforesaid. And further this examinant saith not.

Settlement Examinations (Settlement Papers, Overseers of the Poor), Parish of Bedford St Paul (1770) Bedfordshire and Luton Archives, Bedford, P 1/13/4.

208) The establishment of the Jewish community in Sunderland, 18th c. [I.]

From a detailed local history of Sunderland Jewry published in 1956. Here the author traces the earliest records of settlement in the region.

Practically all available authorities on the subject agree that Abraham Samuel was the first Jew to settle in Sunderland. Shortly after his arrival he was joined by his brother Hart (or Mark) Samuel. Very soon after that there came a family by the name of Davis, and two single men, Barnard Cohen and Lambert Levy. These two 'married into the families of Abraham Samuel and Mr. Davis.' [*Jewish Chronicle*, 11 January 1861.]

Abraham Samuel, Jeweller and Silversmith, 'was the outstanding Jew in town'. He died in 1794. His place of business 'was at the corner of Burleigh Street and High Street East'. One daughter married Israel Isaacs of London in 1792. Another married Barnett Cowen in 1795. His son Philip married Miss Ornaberg of London in 1796, and his other son Lazarus married Ann Davis of Sunderland, 'introducing us thus to a second family'.

The fact that Sunderland was chosen as the place for marriage by an Edinburgh dentist and a London widow, confirms that Sunderland was already well-established as in important community in 1791.

A. Levy, *History of the Sunderland Jewish Community* (London: Macdonald, 1956) 34.

209) Polish Jews in Sunderland, 18th c. [I.]

See note on extract No.208.

The suggestion has been made that the newcomers who brought about the 'split' of 1781 were probably Chassidim. That they hailed from Poland there appears no doubt, since they named their Congregation 'Polish'. It is therefore important to examine the political and economic conditions prevailing in that country in the second half of the eighteenth century which forced them to emigrate.

Expulsions, as mentioned by Dr. Roth, were indeed mild affairs compared to the atrocities that were being committed in Poland in that period (1760–1780) . . .

The Jews who managed to flee probably made for the nearest seaport, viz., Danzig. From this busy port there were frequent sailings to England, perhaps more so to the Tyne and Wear on account of the coal trade. It is therefore not unreasonable to assume that many of them came to Sunderland; hence the 'Polish' Congregation of 1781.

A. Levy, *History of the Sunderland Jewish Community* (London: Macdonald, 1956) 35–6.

210) The establishment of the Krottingen community in Sunderland, 1860s [I.]

See note on extract No.208.

> [T]hey emigrated [from Krottingen, Lithuania, *c.*1870–80] for two reasons. Firstly, because economic conditions were bad, but chiefly in the case of men of twenty-one or under, because they did not desire to be enslaved to the Czar's army for twenty-one years, which was then the period of service. Lithuania was then, as now, under the yoke of Russia.
>
> Quite as many, if not more, Krottingers emigrated to the United States and Canada, but not all could afford the fare, whereas a ship from Memel or Danzig brought them to the Tyne and Wear for a matter of shillings, especially if the passenger was willing to 'give a hand' on board ship.
>
> Barnett Bernstein is a case in point. The son of a struggling carpenter, he was forcibly taken into the Czar's army as a lad, and after some years of service he was allowed to visit his parents in Krottingen, and from there he escaped to England. He was the first Krottinger to settle in Sunderland, about 1859.
>
> Mr Bernstein was soon followed by relations, close and distant; many of these eventually became prominent members of the community and active in the work of the Hebrew Congregation. To mention but two who were still well-remembered, Simon Olswang and Israel Jacobs.

A. Levy, *History of the Sunderland Jewish Community* (London: Macdonald, 1956) 93–4.

211) The Irish community in Newcastle, 1872 [M.]

An account describing the polarized but substantial Irish community in North East England. See note on extract No.51.

> In the neighbourhood of Newcastle they [the Irish] are chiefly employed as labourers in the docks on public works, and in mines, or in iron foundries – that is, in all works requiring the greatest strength, energy and endurance – and in every instance they are found to be abreast or ahead of their competitors. In Newcastle, from a combination of causes, there are classes and varieties of labour to be obtained which are met with in few other places. It is the chief centre of the coal and iron trade of the North – a commercial part ranking among the highest in scale of tonnage, and one of, if not the chief centre, of the English shipbuilding trade. In the multifarious employments belonging to each and all of these, Irish labourers, skilled and unskilled, are to be found; and in every instance – taking into consideration the short time they have been settlers in this locality and the difficulties which they have to surmount – a fair proportion of their number have won for themselves foremost positions in the ranks of their fellow-workmen.
>
> The population of Newcastle, according to the Census of 1871, is 130,000. Of them there are over 30,000 of Irish birth or Irish descent in the first generation, or about one in four of the total population – that is a proportion nearly equal to that prevailing in Manchester. But with this exceptionally large proportion of Irish to English in the town, there political influence, which

ought to be great, is extremely limited. I have it on the written authority of leading Irishmen in the town who have the longest and best acquaintance with its political condition, and the best opportunity of arriving at a judgement of the political power possessed by the Irish element, that 'there is no other town in England of the same Irish population where the Irish have less political weight than in Newcastle . . .'

The social state of the 30,000 Irish in Newcastle will best be gauged by a reference to the employments in which they are engaged and the positions which they otherwise hold. In this respect they fairly contrast with their kindred in most other towns – indeed with all except Manchester and Liverpool. There are among 400 business men of various grades and conditions, and over 4,000 skilled artisans, that is about 5,000 – or nearly one in six – who have worked upwards from the severest drudgery to a condition of comparative prosperity. There is still in the rank and file of labour, or dependent on it, 25,000. Of these there is a considerable number, particularly females, whose employment in factories and shops constitutes a species of skilled labour, but not of such a character as to raise those so engaged above the level of the ordinary labourer. In a community so constituted, and situated in the midst of a people where many are wealthy – the great bulk of the people in easy circumstances, and even those living by labour – in virtue of their being in previous possession – holding most of the best places – the social standing of the majority cannot lend much weight to their position. But if social position were to be meted by their highest standard of virtue and spiritual superiority, the contrast would be wholly in favour of the Irish. Dr Todd's test of an angel from Heaven coming down to seek the best and purest, irrespective of social distinction, would certainly find himself at home in more Irish than English houses in Newcastle.

H. Heinrick, *A Survey of the Irish in England* (1872), ed. A. O'Day (London: Hambledon, 1990) 117–8.

212) The expansion of the Krottingen community in Sunderland, 1890s [I.]

See note on extract No.208.

On the second day of Pentecost, 1889, the town of Krottingen was gutted by fire. Practically the whole of the Jewish population, numbering some two thousand, lost not only their dwellings but their entire possessions. Not more than 5 per cent were covered by insurance, and most of these were under-insured.

The fire emanated from a row of thatched-roof cottages situated in the lower section of the town known as the 'Devatkes', and inhabited by Catholic Sisters of Mercy. Being 'Yom Tov' [Holy-day], the Jewish community was having an afternoon siesta, and by the time they awoke the greater part of

> the town was engulfed in flames. The cause of the fire was an unswept chimney set ablaze by an overheated cooking-oven.
>
> Already at that time a large number of Sunderland's Jewish community were natives of Krottingen. When the news of the tragedy reached Sunderland prompt action was taken. A fund-raising committee was formed, and the Rev. A. A. Green, then minister of the Sunderland Congregation, was sent to Krottingen, and there, with the assistance of the local Rabbinate, he distributed the funds.
>
> Though the sum raised at Sunderland was comparatively large, yet, when Mr Green returned and reported on the appalling conditions prevailing, a public appeal was decided upon . . .
>
> It took several years for the town of Krottingen to be re-habited, when it functioned again as of old. Meanwhile, many Krottingers emigrated, the majority to Sunderland, for the reasons that, firstly, they had relatives there; secondly, the fare was comparatively cheap.

A. Levy, *History of the Sunderland Jewish Community* (London: Macdonald, 1956) 94–5, 98.

213) The Italian community in Newcastle, 1890s [I.]

From a survey of the expanding Italian community in North East England.

> Similar information, although with fewer attempted figures, was given in the reports [by the Italian Consul General] for the northern counties, in 1893:
>
> > The Italians [in Newcastle] of good social station may be counted on the fingers of one hand . . . ; they form the aristocracy of the colony, and next to them, but across a huge social gap, we find the humblest class of Italians: the itinerant musicians who, in some periods of the year, become ice-cream street vendors. Street musicians may be 30 to 40 in Newcastle; 10 between North and South Shields; 5 in Sunderland.
>
> In 1902, the consular authorities estimated the Italians in and around Newcastle to number about 500, although to this figure the zealous official added the children
>
> > who are more than 300, few of whom appear in the civil registers of this Consulate, despite my efforts to promote such registration, in particular the children who attend the Italian School, which I have established [in Newcastle] in November 1901. In the rest of this Consular District there may be 250 of our fellow-countrymen: about 100 in Middlesborough and Stockton; another 100 or so between Sunderland, Hartlepool and Darlington; about 50 between Redcar and Scarborough. All of them are mainly [sic] engaged in the trade of selling ice-cream, statuette making (from the province of Lucca) and itinerant organ-grinders.

L. Sponza, *Italian Immigrants in Nineteenth-Century Britain: Realities and Images* (Bath: University of Leicester Press, 1998) 17.

214) A letter against Arab seamen in South Shields, 1920s–30s (1) (*Shields Daily Gazette*) [I.]

The following sequence of letters [Nos.214–29] gives a vivid insight into the professional and personal rivalries within the South Shields shipping community from the end of the Great War to the slump of the early 1930s. The letters are roughly uniform in style and language and rarely signed other than with a pseudonym; it seems plausible to argue the style and content of these stories was adjusted for publication.

Letters [Nos.214–22] voice the common accusations made against the community of Arab sailors across the country. Nationally the population reached several thousand during the Great War, mostly concentrated in the Bristol Channel ports, Cardiff and on Tyneside. Welcomed as a pool of reserve labour during wartime, and accepted nominally as British by dint of the occupation of Aden, after the war, work and professional rivalries as well as straightforward racial hatred (Letter [No.218] for example) led to constant challenges to Arab employment rights as well as both physical and verbal attacks. (During the South Shields Arab 'riots' of 1919 and 1930, for example.)

While walking through the Mill Dam this morning my attention was attracted to an unusual crowd round the Shipping Office entrance. Being curious, I walked across to find out what the commotion was about. I was soon to be made wise. A British ship signing on, and to my disgust engaging Arabs whilst hundreds of white men were walking the stones outside, many of whom, I daresay, had never tasted breakfast that morning. How such a state of things is allowed puzzles me. Our noble Prime Minister during the war boasted about making the country a fit place for heroes to live in. I and many others, I daresay, think a man is a hero who can live in it.

During the time these men were being engaged I heard expressions of disgust on all sides, and thoroughly agreed with them. Why are these men, or the greater part of them, not sent back to the country they belong to? People may say, 'They did their bit during the war'. Granted, but so did our own men but when anything happened such as the ship being mined or torpedoed, they were the first to rush for boats or rafts. I hold no brief for anyone, but when you see a state of things such I had the 'pleasure' of witnessing this morning, you begin to think seriously and wonder whether, after all, the country you belong to was worth fighting for.

Signed ONE WHO ALSO DID HIS BIT

R. I. Lawless, *From Ta'izz to Tyneside* (Exeter: University of Exeter Press, 1995) 88.

215) A letter against Arab seamen in South Shields, 1920s–30s (2) (*Shields Daily Gazette*) [I.]

Is it not time the Labour Bureau, the Board of Trade and the men's unions were tackling the question of aliens getting employment on British ships in preference to British sailors and firemen who are quite willing and eager to fill such posts, but instead are shouldered aside and cast on the dole? Is this the reward they receive for services rendered, to be replaced by crowds of Arabs etc? Who is to blame for such a state of things?

Surely the shipowners cannot truly say there is no preference shown towards the coloured section who during the war had to be forced to do their duty at the revolver's point, as the seafaring fraternity are well aware.

It was only on Monday of this week, I was passing the New Quay where there was a dispute about Arabs vs white men which resulted in the business of signing on being held up for two or three hours. Another ship paid off the same day with the same class of men, a Cornish company this time. Whatever are the captains and officers thinking of to prefer such men instead of their own nationals? Let us raise the cry, 'British men for British ships'.

Signed A WHITE MAN

R. I. Lawless, *From Ta'izz to Tyneside* (Exeter: University of Exeter Press, 1995) 88–9.

216) A letter against Arab seamen in South Shields, 1920s–30s (3) (*Shields Daily Gazette*) [I.]

The time is a long way overdue for our Union officials to tackle the job of having Britishers in British ships. If you remember when some Arabs were before the police court at South Shields, the solicitor who appeared for them told our officials that as these men paid their contributions the same as a white man, they had the same right to have work in our ships. Now, what had our officials to say to that? Nothing; they did not answer; they simply had not a leg to stand on because the solicitor was right.

I have my union card in front of me now, and on the front of it in big type is printed 'The National Sailors' and Firemen's Union of Great Britain and Ireland'. Now, were these Arabs born in Great Britain or Ireland? I say no; a few of them are British subjects, and very few at that. The majority are Turkish Arabs that walk into Aden, and then reckon they were born there. Now was it the intention of the white men who paid the first contributions and joined the Sailors' and Firemen's Union to allow Arabs to take the bread out of our white children's mouths? I say no, emphatically no.

Therefore it is the fault of the present-day officials of the union that is the cause of all this trouble of keeping the white man on the unemployed list while taking contributions from the Arabs. I say chuck them out and make it a white man's union, the same as it was when it was started.

Signed A MILL DAM WHITE MAN

R. I. Lawless, *From Ta'izz to Tyneside* (Exeter: University of Exeter Press, 1995) 89.

217) A letter against Arab seamen in South Shields, 1920s–30s (4) (*Shields Daily Gazette*) [I.]

I am a seaman myself and I find it most degrading after I have signed on a British ship to find that our sleeping berth is only separated from the Arabs by a narrow alleyway and all other accommodation had to be shared with the Arabs. The only reason I can see for it, is that Arabs will accept food at less than the rations which regulations of the Board of Trade allows every seaman and also to work overtime without demanding money in return, which a British seaman would justly claim and stand out for.

I agree that British seamen that are a credit to the world should refuse to sail with Arabs, but I cannot see that the responsibility lies with us as much as it does with our union, whom we pay to look after our interests. I only ask, sir, that your readers will imagine that they were being replaced at their different trades by Arabs, then they will know how every British seaman standing on the Mill Dam feels, if they broach the subject to him.

Signed A.B.

R. I. Lawless, *From Ta'izz to Tyneside* (Exeter: University of Exeter Press, 1995) 90.

218) A letter against Arab seamen in South Shields, 1920s–30s (5) (*Shields Daily Gazette*) [I.]

To say that an Arab is the equal of a Britisher – I don't know whether to laugh or get mad when I think of it. Why not ten per cent of them are British subjects even although they claim to be. As for their bravery during the war the less said about that the better; from my own experiences, and those of my friends, half the Arabs lost during the war died of fright before the sea got them.

The Union was built up by white sailors and firemen and a going concern long before Arabs came here to deprive white men of work, and gain for South Shields the name of Cardiff the second. I am sure it would not go bankrupt now if all the Arabs were out of it. My advice to these gentlemen as they are too thick-skinned to see they are not wanted, is to get while the going is good. Furthermore, I don't merely dislike Arabs, I hate them.

Signed 'BURGOO'

R. I. Lawless, *From Ta'izz to Tyneside* (Exeter: University of Exeter Press, 1995) 90.

219) A letter against Arab seamen in South Shields, 1920s–30s (6) (*Shields Daily Gazette*) [I.]

Would you spare me a little space regarding the unemployment among seagoing firemen of South Shields? Surely something can be done, seeing two thirds of the ships that are signing on here at present are taking Arabs, while so many of our own townsmen are walking about practically starving. Where are the Labour Exchange officials, whose duties, I understand, include that of trying to find work for the unemployed? Can they not help to put a stop to this? And what about the Union and Federation Officials, can they do something to discourage the signing on of these men who are taking the bread out of the mouths of our own men?

I think it is about time we got on to the same footing as our North Shields friends, who prefer to give their own a chance.

Signed SUFFERER

R. I. Lawless, *From Ta'izz to Tyneside* (Exeter: University of Exeter Press, 1995) 90–1.

220) A letter against Arab seamen in South Shields, 1920s–30s (7) (*Shields Daily Gazette*) [I.]

We live in a country that sincerely believes in fiction invented by priests and as a result have been blinded to greater things that pertain to our own general welfare. Darwin and others have taught us that the human race and apes have descended from a common stock so there can be no harm in the admission that the Arab is a distant relation. Theology is of very little use to the seamen standing day after day looking for employment, afraid to go home for an hour lest some ship should sign on in his absence, only to find out that white men were not wanted as Arabs were engaged. Mr Bergman blames the shipowner and looks for the remedy there, mindful of the fact that they have exploited every race from Norway to China. We have the remedy in our own hands and must use it by making it a test at every election, municipal and national, until the law of the land is no foreigner shall be engaged while a Briton is available.

Signed FREEDOM

R. I. Lawless, *From Ta'izz to Tyneside* (Exeter: University of Exeter Press, 1995) 91.

221) A letter against Arab seamen in South Shields, 1920s–30s (8) (*Shields Daily Gazette*) [I.]

We are told the Arabs served the country well. Yes and were well paid for it. It wasn't for love of the country; it was the big money. See how many would serve the country for the tanner a day as our lads had to do. What a rush? But it would be to their own country. Yet still they come, can get work while the white man is left out, simply because he was away fighting for the glorious sum of 6d and hasn't got a book; he hasn't a chance now. Yet the Arab must have the run of the town because he served the country well. I wish we had a few more men like Councillors Smith and Watson who dare speak their mind and stick to what they say, to limit them and give our own men the chance they were promised and have waited for since the war. All they ask is work, yet 33,000 alien firemen are in British ships, while we have six to seven hundred unemployed seamen.

Now where is the justice there? Certainly there isn't any for the Britisher. It almost makes one feel ashamed to think they belong to this land fit for heroes to live in.

Signed 'MAXWELLITE'

R. I. Lawless, *From Ta'izz to Tyneside* (Exeter: University of Exeter Press, 1995) 91–2.

222) A letter for Arab seamen in South Shields, 1920s–30s (1) (*Shields Daily Gazette*) [I.]

Letters [Nos.222–9] support both the work record and the personal character of the Arabs in South Shields. These letters point out the hypocrisy of accepting migrant labour in wartime and rejecting it afterwards; of blaming Arab men for 'stealing' white women while reportedly South Shields men treated women with less courtesy and consideration. See also note on extract No.214.

Re the coloured seamen of home ports is there not one Englishman who knows a good word to say of the Arabs? One cannot but think of the altered opinion of these so-called coloured seamen since 1914–18. Is their war service so soon forgotten? It must be admitted that there are hundreds in this country who have no right to be called British, but whose is the fault that they have many of them obtained registration certificates? On the other hand there are hundreds settled in this country since they finished their war service and are living peaceably and are good citizens. What is more they were born in Aden and as such pay homage to the English flag. Yet they are stated to be aliens, and have as their nationality 'Seamen'. If one knows what nationality this is, well, they are ultra-clever. Apart from all this, what is the N.S. and F.'s Union going to say about and do with the hundreds of pounds paid by these men in contributions? Many are forced to pay the whole of their debts which they have incurred during unemployment before they can sign on. Is there no Englishman who will brave the prejudice of his fellow countrymen by saying a good word for those who are of a different religion, and look to a Christian country to treat them in a Christian manner.

Signed G.Y. of P.C.

R. I. Lawless, *From Ta'izz to Tyneside* (Exeter: University of Exeter Press, 1995) 95–6.

223) A letter for Arab seamen in South Shields, 1920s–30s (2) (*Shields Daily Gazette*) [I.]

We live in a country that professes to be Christian, but which pays little heed to that teaching, that 'one is your father, even God, and all ye are brethren'. Colour should not make the above void, not parrot phrases such as 'once an Arab always an Arab', a saying which is generally meant to suggest a lot more than is said. Instead we should remember that character is not something confined to white skins, nor depravity to brown skins, for they are both to be found under both black and white skins, and our colleges and universities are proving that many a noble soul inhabits a dusky skin. As regards our own seamen being unemployed because of them, let us put the responsibility on the proper shoulders, namely those who employ them because of their cheapness for that is where the trouble lies. That is why they will still be coming here in increasing numbers even though they should have difficulty in finding lodging room, and it is to our shipowners at the other end that we must look for the remedy.

Signed C. BERGMAN, 2 Challoner Terrace East, South Shields

R. I. Lawless, *From Ta'izz to Tyneside* (Exeter: University of Exeter Press, 1995) 96.

224) A letter for Arab seamen in South Shields, 1920s–30s (3) (*Shields Daily Gazette*) [I.]

How many white men get ships and after cashing advance notes lose their ship through drink? Many a poor widow who cashes the note is robbed of the money. I can safely speak of one respectable widow that she has been robbed of practically £100 or more by white men cashing advance notes and forged notes and leaving ships. You won't find an Arab do such a mean, dirty trick. Some white men do want work, and some are too lazy to work, even when work has been found for them. They are quite content to sponge their drinks as long as they have the dole or the Guardians to keep them and their families.

Signed JUSTICE

R. I. Lawless, *From Ta'izz to Tyneside* (Exeter: University of Exeter Press, 1995) 93–4.

225) A letter for Arab seamen in South Shields, 1920s–30s (4) (*Shields Daily Gazette*) [I.]

Give any Arab a chance to go down the mines or any other work he is put to and I will guarantee however hard it is he will not shirk his job. Half the Englishmen on the dole are there through their own fault, being too lazy to look for work. When they receive the dole what do they do with it? Nothing but gamble and waste money on horses and drink. As to all the talk about Britishers not wanting to be employed in the same vessels as Arabs, well I am disgusted with our so-called Britishers. If Arabs are not needed in England send them, their wives and children to Aden. I for one would gladly go and I know then what would happen; the bread you are taking from them will be taken from England in various ways.

I wonder if Fairplay One and Two know where all their foodstuffs come from? What is there in England to boast about; only coal and vegetables. They are forgetting it is the coloured man's country they depend on. What would England do if Arabs were to do the same to them as England is doing to the Arabs.

Signed ARAB'S WIFE

R. I. Lawless, *From Ta'izz to Tyneside* (Exeter: University of Exeter Press, 1995) 97.

226) A letter for Arab seamen in South Shields, 1920s–30s (5) (*Shields Daily Gazette*) [I.]

. . . much has been said for and against these unwanted, but honest coloured British citizens, and very human children of God. Man was made in God's own image by God himself. This Jewish God had no special idea of colours. In fact nowhere in the Bible is it mentioned what colour the first man was. This religious and racial prejudice is (to anyone who has studied history and theology) the outcome of an old Christian dogma of self aggrandisement and barbaric egoism. If the Arabs are useful, keep them, but if no longer useful exterminate them, repatriate them. They have colour; they are heathens and unclean. In short an 'eyesore' in the town to our sanctimonious Christians. And if they do get £9 per month instead of a handful of dates? What did our Christian, capitalistic shipowners get by means of their service? Mohammed, an Arab camel driver, delivered his people from the cruel tyranny of the Christians in AD 570. We are different now, we have changed all that, we are more charitable, more civilised, intellectually superior. Yes, Sir, we have learnt

> the art of hypocrisy to a fine art. I have translated this from my husband's written views – an Arab.
>
> Signed MRS SAID RODMAN, Frederick Street, South Shields.

R. I. Lawless, *From Ta'izz to Tyneside* (Exeter: University of Exeter Press, 1995) 97–8.

227) A letter on British–Arab marriages in South Shields (1) (*Shields Daily Gazette*) [I.]

In this discussion on mixed marriages (Letters [Nos.227–9]) it was the white wives of Arab sailors who claimed that their husbands treated them better than their white peers and, moreover, that they had the right to choose freely whom they should marry.

> I would like 'Arab's wife' first to understand that no mixed breed child is or ever will be as good as the child born of white parents. As regards dirty white children, well, if an Arab child was never washed it would never be known, as black is a good standing colour. As to Arabs never being in prison for neglect, as many of these Arabs' wives have never been married they cannot prosecute any Arab they co-habit with. They have no claim on them. It is only luck, in many cases I know, that has saved the Arab from prison. A white man can be found and identified but it takes you all your time to identify the Arabs. How many Arabs have escaped prison for lashing their so-called wives with whips and sticks? Only on one occasion was the law lucky enough to get the Arab. There is no escape for a white man for such conduct . . . 'Arab's Wife' says build an Arab school. I wonder if she thinks the education authorities are mad. I say send the Arab children over to Aden and then they will be united and educated among their own.
>
> 'A Holborn Resident'

R. I. Lawless, *From Ta'izz to Tyneside* (Exeter: University of Exeter Press, 1995) 183.

228) A letter on British–Arab marriages in South Shields (2) (*Shields Daily Gazette*) [I.]

> With all due respect to the Arab community, I maintain that no self-respecting white girl is going to marry an Arab for love alone. Then what is it that draws them? Not the Arab's beauty surely! No, it is the dress that these men can offer, the pleasures they can indulge in. When these are the bait, with a little kindness thrown in the type of man does not matter.
>
> Furthermore, the Arabs can always be relied upon to pick the prettiest girls: the ugly ducklings being left for the white man, with the exception of the girls who have their self respect. Also an Arab can get a job where a white

man has not a look in; they refuse to sell themselves cheaply. 'An Arab's Wife' says the Arab children are as good as the white children. True, but are the mothers that bear them as good as their white sisters?

There are dirty people wherever you may go but these are a class unto themselves. There are poor white people who are scrupulously clean, both with themselves and their children, many of them having to go to bed in the suit they were born in, until their clothes are washed. But they are clean? Again, 'An Arab's Wife' says that all Arab shildren are both clean and well-clothed. Does she refer just to her own children or does she go about blind-folded?

In conclusion, let me say that so long as there are girls with no self respect, so long there will be these detestable mixed marriages. If a white woman is good enough for a white man, why is not an Arab woman good enough for an Arab.

'Adsum'

R. I. Lawless, *From Ta'izz to Tyneside* (Exeter: University of Exeter Press, 1995) 183–4.

229) A letter on British–Arab marriages in South Shields (3) (*Shields Daily Gazette*) [I.]

I am a white woman, having a family of six (four sons and two daughters) and I say that there are just as good Arabs as bad.

I have often noticed when in a car if any white woman or girl were standing they would get up and offer them their seat: that shows respect to us white people. On the other hand there are dozens of white men who would sooner see one drop than give up a seat in a crowded car.

As for the coloured men being inferior, well, it may be only in stature, but they are kind and gentle to their wives and children and that is more than a great deal of the so-called white men can say.

Even if the coloured gentlemen of Holborn had to resort to sell oranges they would do it willingly to support the white wife they chose to share their lives and their kiddies; they look after their own and take care of what they have. Again I say that is more than a lot of our so-called white men do. If white girls find happiness and kindness and comfort in their Arab husbands, I think that is all that is required.

'White Woman of Six'

R. I. Lawless, *From Ta'izz to Tyneside* (Exeter: University of Exeter Press, 1995) 185–6.

230) Eric Ferron in Cumberland, 1940s [I.]

See note on extract No.85.

Up in Cumberland the camp was near a small town by the sea. There were only a few Jamaicans there. One hot afternoon four of us were lazing around on the beach when two children came by, a boy about eleven and a girl a few years younger. They stared at us very hard but didn't say anything. We were gazing out to sea, happy to feel the sun on our faces. They came back and stared again, but still didn't say anything. The little girl was obviously longing to speak, but the boy took her hand and pulled her away. Then they passed by again; this time they stopped and she said: 'Hello'.

'Hello' I said.

'You see!' She turned to the boy: 'He does speak English.'

'Yes' I said.

'And you wear clothes.'

'Yes.'

'And you wear shoes.'

My friends got impatient: 'Why do you answer all these questions?'

'Well if she thought we didn't wear clothes and didn't speak English now she's finding out it was wrong and she's learning something. I don't see why we shouldn't help her.'

'Our teacher told us that black men live in trees and they don't wear shoes and they don't wear clothes and they don't have houses.'

'You can tell your teacher now that you met some black men who do wear shoes and clothes.'

My friends were furious now. Why should we educate these stupid kids just because their teacher was ignorant? The children ran away and we started a big argument. Don't people here know that black men wear clothes and speak English? Surely they know about their own Empire? It's theirs, isn't it? Don't they know the difference between the dominions and the colonies? Don't they know how we got here? Are the teachers really so ignorant or do they tell the children lies? We were angry with the teachers but I couldn't be angry with the children.

The first words a little niece of an English friend said to me were: 'Don't you ever wash?'

'Yes', I said.

'But if you wash why is you skin so black?'

'If there was dirt on my skin I would wash and it would come off, same as yours.'

'But my skin isn't black when I've washed it.'

I took off my shoe and went to the sink and washed it. 'There you see, if you wash the dirt off your shoe it's still black.'

'But your skin isn't leather like your shoe.'

'Some skins are darker than others, but that doesn't mean they are dirty.'

My friend was angry with his niece and thought she should not ask these questions. But it seemed to me that perhaps only we ourselves can teach people who don't know, especially children. If they do not know they ask directly and you can tell them and not feel hurt. With adults it can be disguised and unexpectedly cruel.

I was having supper with an English couple and we talked all evening about politics and the way of life in the West Indies. Afterwards, when the husband took me to the bus stop he said: 'By the way, what language do you normally speak?' I felt terribly insulted. I found such little incidents very upsetting. I was becoming over-sensitive because it was happening so often. I asked myself how people could be so ignorant. That same night the bus conductor asked me what part of Africa Jamaica was in. I said: 'Just north of Egypt'. I was so angry. Surely he was being sarcastic? He couldn't be telling me he just didn't know?

I went back to camp and thought about ignorance and innocence. It was difficult to distinguish between the two. Our expectation of the English was higher than the reality. We expected them to know their own history. When they showed us they didn't, we felt disappointed in them, and angry to be asked such stupid questions. We got used to statements like: 'How can you leave your beautiful island? There's so much sunshine there. It must be wonderful.' They knew nothing about Jamaica, yet we knew so much about England. I knew the geography of every county and had some knowledge of every big town, I could recite the kings and queens of England from the beginning. But they seemed to know nothing about the Empire. They forgot there was a war on and we were in it with them because it was our war too. Years later I began to understand the difference between ignorance and innocence. With the ignorant, prejudice is a way of life. They don't like the Scots, or the Welsh, or the Irish, or the Jews. They don't like the rich or the poor and they don't like the clever. They are far more dangerous than the innocent. I learned to pick out the innocent and could deal with them apparently just as innocently. But the ignorant cause violence by the way they say things. I got into several fights with the ignorant, generally soldiers, usually Americans.

Inside myself, I searched for the reasons for the violence, for the state of the world. The ignorance of the people, being coloured, being bitter, doubtful and suspicious, these were matters that confronted me day-in day-out.

E. Ferron, *'Man, You've Mixed': A Jamaican Comes to Britain* (London: Whiting and Birch, 1995) 14–16.

Scotland

231) George Robertson travels from Glasgow to Bedford, 1771 [M.]

Born c.1734 near Edinburgh, George Robertson was an apprentice before moving to Bedford. Robertson's account was taken down during an official settlement examination in 1771.

> He on his oath saith that he is 37 years of age that he is married, his wife is named Hannah, by her he has one child named Elizabeth 4 years of age, that he was born at Corren near Edinburgh in Scotland, and served an apprenticeship of 3 years at Glasgow, but not by indenture, and that he hath done no act whatsoever to gain a settlement in England.

Settlement Examinations (Settlement Papers, Overseers of the Poor), Parish of Bedford St Paul (1771) Bedfordshire and Luton Archives, Bedford, P 1/13/4.

232) William Cameron begins his 'cadging' career, 1815 [M.]

See note on extract No.22.

> Ecclefecham in Dumfrieshire was the first place I begged in. At the first door I went to, the woman gave me a piece of bread; and at the next, the wife made me a 'bawl' (meal) bag, of which I was muckle the better, and so started briskly on the cadge. After cadging the village and going to the 'padded-ken' (lodging house), I meted my meal and found that I had eight tankerds, that stands for a jigger's peck, it would sell at 3d., this with 5d. in coppers, and plenty of bread and cheese, was my first day's cadge. The keeper of the lodging house was 'radge' (half crazy), and I had the funniest nights I ever passed in my life. Next day I travelled to Longholm, and took up in my abode in a house which kept nine 'snouses' (rough beds). They were all filled, and with difficulty I got in, on condition that I would snooze on the floor. My companions were sweeps, 'cairds', roughs, common cadgers and 'high flyers'. The town in ordinary times was worth, between

meal and money, from three to four shillings, besides 'parem' (bread), and beef.

After that I travelled by Hawick and Jedburgh, calling at each town on that south boundary of Scotland, till I reached Berwick; the town was not good, owing to a man of the name of Barney Duttie, who was detected with his wife, daughters and servant, and tried for forging 'slains' (issuing false coins). The whole five were under the sentence of death. On that account I had to cross the brig and stop in Tweedmouth. Here I met a corps of 'routers' (real or pretended widows of soldiers or sailors), on their road from London to Aberdeen. I had a night's fuddle with them, when they turned out as many schedules of marriage, discharges of their husbands, and passes of rates, as might set up a speech-crier. There were nine of them – Highland and Irish. They had an Edinburgh Almanac to help them to find out officers' names in different regiments.

They engaged me to travel with them to Aberdeen. I got a pound note of 'arles' (engagement fee), and I confess them to be the greatest sharpers and imposters I have ever met in the course of my twenty years' travel. We started next morning by Eyemouth and Ayton, having their 'routes' relieved in both parishes, and in gentleman's houses on the road. They received two 'screave'(pounds).

When we were in Cowdonham (Caldringham) Muir, we were passed by the 42nd Regiment, who had landed at Sunderland, on their return from Waterloo (1815) . . .

W. Cameron, *Hawkie: the Autobiography of a Gangrel* (Glasgow: D. Robertson, 1888) 18–19.

233) The Jewish community in Edinburgh and Glasgow, early 19th c. [I.]

A near-contemporary account of Scotland's major Jewish communities in the 1820s.

A Jew's synagogue was opened in this city in September 1823. Mr Moses Lisenheim is their priest, Hebrew teacher, killer, inspector, marker and sealer. It appears from a report of a Select Committee of the House of Commons in 1828, that in London the office of priest and killer merges in the same person, and that no Jew can use meat unless the animals are slain with a peculiar knife, and marked with Hebrew seals. The Feast of Tabernacles, which used to be celebrated by the Glasgow Jews in Edinburgh, is now being observed in this city.

Edward Davies, son of Mr David Davies, optician, was the first that was circumcised in Glasgow. The rite was performed by Mr Michael on 18th July 1824. The Jews resident in Glasgow in 1831 were 47 in number, viz. males 28, females, 19. Above twenty years of age, 28; below ditto, 19; born in the following countries, viz. in Prussian Poland, 11; in various parts of Germany, 12; in Holland, 3; in London, 5; in Sheerness, 10; in Glasgow, 6. The increase since 1831 is but trifling.

A burial ground has been made for the seed of Abraham at the north-west corner of the Necropolis. It is separated from the Christians' burying ground by an ornamental screen, on which are inscribed the beautiful and appropriate words from Byron's Hebrew Melody, beginning 'Oh! Weep for those that wept by Babel's stream.'

The community are greatly indebted to Mr James Ewing LL.D. one of the Members of Parliament for the city, for having protected the Necropolis, and to Mr. Laurence Hill, LL.B. collector to the Merchant's House, for his unwearied exertions in promoting the interests of this beautiful and romantic cemetery.

R. B. Salaman, *The New Statistical Account of Scotland*, (Glasgow: n.p., 1845) vi, 238–9.

234) P. McGeown on immigration into Craigneuk, near Glasgow, 19th c. [I.]

Born in 1897 to Irish parents in Craigneuk, P. McGeown describes here what he remembers of his pre-World War One childhood as well as earlier folklore on immigrants in the town. From his autobiography, published in 1967.

There was nothing lovely about Craigneuk. It was, and is, about twelve miles from Glasgow and a centre of heavy industry.

Steelworks, ironworks, coalmines, are not beautiful but they have their moments. I liked Craigneuk, I thought it was a grand place and I liked the name of it too. I was sure there was a history in it but I never found out. I was sure too that it had been a beautiful place before the advent of slag tips and belching stacks. Even my uncritical eye could see that.

That was before the Irish and the Poles and the Lithuanians arrived. Most of them penniless and none of them welcomed by the Scots. Only the most broad minded of heavenly beings could have welcomed that lot. I don't know about the Poles and the Lithuanians but the Irish had been coming from the eighteenth century. The first Roman Catholic church was opened in Paisley in 1808, and the first Roman Catholic school was opened in Glasgow in 1817. They were built by the pennies of the Irish immigrants. There were 120,000 Irish born residents in Scotland in 1841, and they were still packing them in, on overcrowded ships from Londonderry and Belfast. The ships *Londonderry* and *Thistle*, both less than 300 tons, often carried 1,700 people at a time. Even in good weather the journey could be uncomfortable. It was very cheap, sometimes as low as sixpence per head and there was no Avilion at the end of the journey. Most of them landed up in the disease-ridden Glasgow slums, where 60 per cent of the population lived in one-room homes, and where in 1832 more than 10,000 people had died of Asiatic Cholera.

No wonder the Scots didn't think much of the Irish, or their Roman Catholic religion. It was no consolation that many immigrants were not Catholics, but Orangemen. It only added to bloodshed and distress when the rival factions met on St. Patrick's Day and the 12th of July, the celebration of the Battle of the Boyne.

Still, they were there, and the Scots had to learn to live with them. They had even to tolerate a lot of inter-marrying. For it wasn't unnatural for a Scots Jeannie to fall in love with an Irish Paddy, even if her Paw and Maw referred to him as, 'That Irish Pig.'

Ah Well! The Scots were no' saw bad. No' sae bad ata! I liked them fine and I was an Irish Paddy too, and a Catholic to boot. To boot? That rings a bell! By jings it does, as we used to say in Craigneuk long ago.

The Irish came chiefly from Mayo and Galway, the hungry counties in the west. And from Derry and Donegal in the North, and they were hungry too. My parents came from Co. Armagh, and according to them it was the hungriest of them all . . .

P. McGeown, *Heat the Furnaces Seven Times More* (London: Hutchinson, 1967) 15–16.

235) Polish immigrants and refugees working near Glasgow, 1830s [I.]

From the Report of the Council of the Literary Association of Friends of Poland, 1837.

There are few branches of trade, art or profession in which there are not some refugees creditably occupied. . . . Mr Baxter has employed several Polish soldiers in excavating a canal in Scotland, and Mr Kirkman Finlay has five in his employ as foresters in his estate near Glasgow, and Mr Charles Tennent, also of Paisley, has two officers constantly occupied making baskets.

J. Zubrzycki, *Polish Immigrants in Britain: a Study of Adjustment* (The Hague: Nijhoff, 1956) 33–4.

236) Anti-Irish attacks in Glasgow, early 19th century [M.]

From J. E. Handley's The Irish in Modern Scotland *(1947) a description of community relations in early 19th century Glasgow.*

For many years after the commencement of Irish immigration to the city, the Glasgow mob, in addition to showing its displeasure in other ways, staged an annual demonstration against the immigrants. This was the sport of 'Hunting the Barney' – 'Barney' being the nickname bestowed by the citizens on Irishmen. The game formed the *piece de resistance* of the annual Fair. No

> Irishman was permitted to approach the Fair with impunity. If he ventured too near he was hustled by the crowd into the quadrangle formed by the booths and belaboured with bludgeons. Suspects were forced by a hastily formed committee on elocution to submit their pronunciation of such words as 'peas' and 'tea' for criticism. 'Paze' and 'tay', as phonetic interpretations, sounded the doom of the unfortunate performers. When sport lagged for lack of victims stray Irishmen were rounded up, clubbed and kicked by the bullies at the Fair. As a final episode to the hilarities of this holiday week the hooligan element, armed with clubs, rooted among the warrens of the Saltmarket, where immigrants sought uneasy shelter, and found hearty expression for their conception of rich fun by breaking doors and windows, clubbing Irishmen out of their homes and ducking them in the stream of the Molendinar, which flowed into the Clyde at this point. This annual demonstration ceased only when proper policing of the Fair was undertaken and when the number of Irishmen in the district had grown sufficiently large to lower the odds for their attackers.

B. Maan, *The New Scots: The Story of Asians in Scotland* (Edinburgh: John Donald, 1992) 12–13.

237) The Irish in Greenock, later 19th c. [M.]

An account of the late 19th century Irish community in Greenock.

> In the pattern of their distribution in Greenock, too, the Irish migrants had a distinctive experience that set them apart from other migrant groups in the town. The Irish settlers were to be found in most districts of Greenock, but there were certain areas where they tended to concentrate and which became in effect Irish communities. This situation was already evident by 1851 when the Census Enumeration Books revealed that some areas and streets had more than 50 per cent of Irish-born persons among their inhabitants, whereas in other districts fewer than 1 per cent of the residents were Irish.
>
> Two of the main zones of Irish settlement were those areas which had formed the original town of Greenock and, to the east, the neighbouring burgh of Cartsdyke. These had been small clusters of houses situated on the raised beach by the river, but towards the end of the eighteenth century they had rapidly become overcrowded as the population increased and as industries developed. Large tenement blocks were built on the higher ground to the south, while a new, and well-planned upper-class residential suburb known as the 'West End' was built to the west. As the prosperous merchants and artisans moved out to the newer parts of the town, the Irish immigrants flocked into the older areas with their overcrowded and sub-standard housing. Some parts of these areas became Irish 'Quarters' and were given such names as 'Wee Dublin' by the local populace.

Another zone of Irish settlement also appeared among the tenement flats on the higher ground to the south and close to the cotton mills and sugar refineries. This zone was centred round a certain Mill Street, 34.2 per cent of the inhabitants of which in 1891 were Irish. But as contrasted with the Irish settlers in the older part of the town who were predominantly Catholic, the Irish in this area were overwhelmingly Protestant. Here by tradition lay the strength of the Orange element in the town, and defiantly the local folk songs proclaimed their loyalties:

Come up to Mill Street, make no delay,
That's where the Mill Street Billy Boys are today.

R. D. Lobban, 'The Irish community in Greenock in the nineteenth century', *Irish Geography*, (1961) 277.

238) Chang, Roshun Khan and other 'Asiatics' in Scotland, 1873 [I.]

See note on extract No.52.

Even in Scotland Asiatics are to be found, especially in the autumn months. They have been met and spoken to at Dundee, Glasgow, Perth, Greenock, and Edinburgh, and the energising Gospel set forth before them. Chinese are often met with. The Missionary crossed the path of Chang the celebrated giant, near St. Andrew's. Chang had reason to know him, for his wife, and full-grown companion of about 2 feet 10 inches were all accommodated at the Asiatic Home on reaching England, and had been supplied while there with the words of Eternal Life in their own tongue. His interpreter, too, was a child of the Celestial Empire in reality, for he loved the Lord Jesus. Near the Waverley railway-station, at Edinburgh, he found another old acquaintance of the same nation, of whom we had lost sight for four years . . .

Not so Roshun Khan, who, with his wife and children, have always received Christian visits and teaching with every mark of pleasure. He is a well-known character, and long resident at the Scotch capital. He had returned from Musselburgh races when I first accosted him in the Hindostanee tongue, which made him smile as though he had seen a long-lost friend.

J. Salter, *The Asiatic in England: Sketches of Sixteen Years' Work Among Orientals* (London: Seeley, Jackson and Halliday, 1873) 234–5.

239) Mrs Aitken describes Jewish life in the Gorbals, 1880s [I.]

Mrs Aitken's recollections were recorded c.1980 for the BBC Radio Scotland documentary series Odyssey.

It was nearly all Jewish shops and Jewish firms in the Gorbals. There was the Fogels, the corner of Hospital Street and Cleland Street, there was the Jewish

> bakery at the corner of Dunmore Street. Gleicken, the gown people were there and the Ashers as well. The Gerbers, the Woolfsons, them that had all the jewellers, the shops in the Trongate, they came from there. There were small cabinet-making businesses and upholstery work right up to Cumberland Street. . . . Some o' them kept stock in one o' their rooms for customers to come up and see what they wanted and they could get them everything. They all opened little shops, just doing alterations and repairs to suits and everything. There was no provident checks or anything like that, everybody had a wee connection of giving credit and goin' to collect it. It was a great place the Gorbals.

M. Rodgers, 'Glasgow Jewry', in B. Kay (ed.) *The Complete Odyssey: Voices from Scotland's Recent Past* (Edinburgh: Polygon, 1996) 228.

240) N. Morrison moves from Stornoway to Glasgow, 1889 [M.]

N. Morrison was born near Shawbost, Isle of Lewis, in 1869. In this extract from his autobiography the author describes the beginnings of his career as a policeman.

> One Monday morning in January, 1889, at the age of 19, I took the proverbial plunge into the world. I boarded the steamer from Stornoway bound for Glasgow. My object in going to the city was to join the police force.
>
> I landed in Glasgow on Wednesday forenoon and made my way, or, should I say, was guided, to a friend's house. At this time recruits for the Glasgow police were enrolled every Tuesday morning, and since I had nearly a week to wait, I employed my time touring the city, gaping with open mouthed bewilderment at the huge buildings, busy thoroughfares and shop windows, and last, but not least, at the men in blue parading in their slow measured step or guiding the traffic at busy crossings with the wave of a magic hand. One building, however, was of more interest to me than all the rest and that was the old Central Police Chambers in South Albion Street . . .
>
> That night [about a week later] I accompanied a constable whose name I do not remember now. His beat was in High Street, one of the roughest districts of the city. This was my first actual lesson in real duty. Until now I had only played at being a policeman. Here I found myself in the midst of a veritable maelstrom of vehicles and pedestrians of every type, hue and variety. The vehicles ranged from horse-car, brougham and handsom to the barrow of the costamonger. The pedestrians were a mixed lot. A few in frockcoat and tall hat, but the majority, judging from their apparel and demeanour, evidently belonged to Slumland. A good percentage of the female element were hatless and clad in the usual shoulder-shawl and the loud-striped petticoat so common in some of the low quarters of Glasgow at the time of which I am writing. While gazing at this motley crowd of humanity, I was horrified to observe a large number of them, young and old, staggering and reeling

in the advanced stage of intoxication. Many were howling, yelling and cursing like a mob from the region of Bedlam let loose for the evening. So absolutely sickening and disgusting was the scene that my pride at being a member of the 'Blue Brigade' got a rude shock, and I wished myself in any garb other than that of a police uniform. Until now I had been viewing the fabric of law and order from the outside, and now this insight into its worst side came as a horrible revelation to me. 'Hey, Bridget, look at that flabbergasted, open mouthed bluebottle!' This remark was audibly made by a young woman to her companion as we passed, I being, of course, the individual referred to. Another opprobrious remark smote my ears. 'See that damned ass of a cabbage with a copper's uniform on? Wait until he runs up against Flaming Paddy and he'll make his cabbage leaves fly.'

Flushing darkly, I glanced at the speaker and saw that she was a young woman about twenty years old. She was tall and remarkably handsome, despite her environment, with a mass of jet black, waving hair and dark, flashing eyes. She was dressed in the usual gaudy petticoat and coloured shawl, but even to my unpracticed eye she scarcely looked a debauchee.

I enquired of my companion of he knew her, and he replied that she was known as 'Black Lizzie,' and had lately begun to frequent the district, mingling with its worst characters. Her antecedents, however, were unknown to the police. The 'Flaming Paddy' who was to strip my leaves was the pugilist and terror of the district. Let me remind the reader that I am describing a Saturday night scene in Glasgow High Street forty years ago. Since then, of course, a great change towards sobriety and better behaviour has come over not only the people of Glasgow but the whole country.

(N. Morrison, *My Story* (Inverness: Highland News Office, 1937) 16, 18–19.

241) Frank Dullick on Lithuanians in Lanarkshire, 1890s [I.]

Frank Dullick's father was recruited in Lithuania to work as a miner in central Scotland c.1900. These comments were recorded c.1980 for the BBC Radio Scotland documentary series Odyssey.

From what our parents told us the ironmasters in Coatbridge went to Lithuania recruiting men to dig coal. When you talk to a farm labourer of digging, what he foresees is using a spade, as if he's delving and digging ground. Now, they didn't realise that digging for coal meant going into the bowels of the earth. I'm not too sure about the name but it was the ironmasters recruited men and paid their fare over to this country only. Such that, when the men came over here they didn't know the language and they saw the conditions. Well, they had no money to leave, or even to go back to their own country. In the last decade of the century this was how it began because they were told 'You're coming to Scotland to dig coal'.

M. Rodgers, 'The Lanarkshire Lithuanians', in B. Kay (ed.) *The Complete Odyssey: Voices from Scotland's Recent Past* (Edinburgh: Polygon, 1996) 2.

242) Irish and Highland migrants in Glasgow, 1896 [M.]

P. de Rouser's contemporary observations on migrant communities in Glasgow.

> The Irish in Glasgow are not usually very amenable to the influence of environment and find it difficult to acquire the habits of self-respect and preserving energy . . . The Highlanders are more easily roused to ambition, and to the desire to better themselves, and they become modified by contact with those influences which were lacking in the solitude of their mountain or island houses . . . The Irish generally remain mere labourers, as do their children after them.

T. Gallagher, *Glasgow: The Uneasy Peace. Religious Tension in Modern Scotland* (Manchester: Manchester University Press, 1987) 61.

243) Mr Glasser describes Jewish life in the Gorbals, *c.*1900 [I.]

Mr Glasser's recollections were recorded c.1980 for the BBC Radio Scotland documentary series Odyssey.

> These loans were granted free of interest mainly to pedlars and travellers and that gave them the basis for making a living from the stock that they could buy and sell. They used to go to the outside of Glasgow, to Uddington, Baillieston, and into the mining communities like Hamilton, Coatbridge and Airdrie to sell thair wares. They were selling various things, braces, mouth-organs, games, small things that needed small money for stock. When they became a little wealthier they paid the money back. Two people out of the community, who were more affluent, would sign as guarantors so that the fund would never be depleted by loss.

M. Rodgers, 'Glasgow Jewry', in B. Kay (ed.) *The Complete Odyssey: Voices from Scotland's Recent Past* (Edinburgh: Polygon, 1996) 228.

244) A dispute between seamen, Glasgow, 1919 [I.]

A report from the Glasgow Herald *on racial tension among merchant seamen, 24 January 1919.*

> A serious disturbance extending for almost an hour and at moments of riotous description occurred . . . among seamen in Broomielaw, Glasgow. The affray began in the yard of the Mercantile Marine offices, which following upon a heated dispute was the scene of furious fighting between white and coloured sailors and firemen. In the course of the struggle a number of revolvers were fired and knives and sticks were freely used . . . A large and hostile crowd of

British seamen and white sailors of other nationalities followed the coloured men to their lodging house . . . to which they ran for refuge . . . It is understood the disturbance originated because of an alleged preference being given to British seamen in signing on the crew of a ship at Glasgow harbour.

B. Maan, *The New Scots* (Edinburgh: John Donald, 1992) 99.

245) The Irish in Greenock, 1930s onwards [M.]

See note on extract No.237.

This distinction and demarcation of areas in the town between Catholic and Protestant Irish continued well into the twentieth century, and rivalry and civil discord erupted from time to time. With the slum clearances of the 1930s, however, and the erection of several new council estates in the further suburbs of the town, the distinctions were blurred. This process was accelerated after 1945 when the older central areas were completely re-developed and when the traditionally Orange area was pulled down and re-built. The resulting transference of the town's population to new council estates beyond the old boundaries has effectively broken down the traditional zones and has created a much more balanced and integrated community. It would now be very difficult to isolate any area or street which had a distinctive character of the type that existed in former years.

R. D. Lobban, 'The Irish community in Greenock in the nineteenth century', *Irish Geography* (1961) 277–8.

246) Kartar Singh Seran describes Indian life in Glasgow, 1930s [I.]

Maan does not provide any additional biographical details to accompany his interview with Kartar Singh Seran other than to note that he was a Sikh. This account describes the relatively small Indian community in Glasgow between the wars, and supports Maan's claim that both caste and religious division dissolved among this group of Indians living abroad.

I came to Glasgow in 1932 with Mr Ali Mohammed alias Painter (a Muslim), who belonged to our village Madarpura, in the Jagraon sub-division of Ludhiana district. He had come to Scotland, probably in 1927, and went back on a visit towards the end of 1931. Ali Mohammed and my father were close friends. My father was planning to go abroad himself, but Ali Mohammed advised him to send me instead, and took it upon himself to look after me in Scotland. So I accompanied Ali Mohammed when he returned from India.

There were between 60 and 70 men from India in Glasgow then, all engaged in peddling. They were living in groups of four to eight, depending upon the size of their particular house, in the Cowcaddens/Port Dundas, Anderston and Gorbals areas. Most of them, though, were in dilapidated properties, in a state of utter disrepair, with nominal or no rents. Ali Mohammed and I stayed in Seward Street, on the South side, in the house of Mr Ghulam Mohammed. Muslims, Sikhs and Hindus all lived together. We had a common kitchen; food was cooked in turn by one member of the group for all, and all ate together at one table from one pot. There was a lot of regard, affection and concern for each other in those good old days. A newcomer was fed, clothed and looked after by the members of the community without any regard to his caste or creed until he was able to stand on his own feet.

I acquired the flat I am still living in in 1936 (in 1956 I bought this flat). My brother Hazara Singh joined me in 1949. Early in 1950 my brother and I spotted Mohammed Shafi in a warehouse in Glasgow. He had arrived only a day or two earlier, Mohammed Shafi belonged to our village, and being a Muslim he had migrated to Pakistan after the partition in 1947. Hazara Singh and Mohammed Shafi had grown up together and used to be very close friends. We therefore insisted that he come and stay with us, for old times' sake, which he kindly did until he got his own flat a year or so later.

B. Maan, *The New Scots* (Edinburgh: John Donald, 1992) 140–1.

247) The Jewish community in the Gorbals, 1934 [I.]

From L. Grassic Gibbon and H. Macdiarmid's polemical Scottish Scene, *this account by two of Scotland's leading early 20th century writers describes Glasgow's immigrant district in the mid-1930s.*

It is lovably and abominably and delightfully and hideously un-Scottish. It is not even a Scottish slum. Stout men in beards and ringlets and unseemly attire lounge and strut with pointed shoes: Ruth and Naomi go by with downcast Eastern faces . . . In the air the stench is of a different quality to Govan's or Camlachie's – a better quality. It is haunted by an ancient ghost of goodness and grossness, sun-warmed and ripened under alien suns. It is the most saving slum in Glasgow, and the most abandoned. Emerging from it, the investigator suddenly realises why he sought it in such haste from Glasgow Green: it was in order that he might assure himself that there were really and actually other races on the earth apart form the Scots.

K. E. Collins, *Second City Jewry: the Jews of Glasgow in the Age of Expansion, 1790–1919* (Glasgow: Scottish Jewish Archive, 1990) 71.

248) Mrs Taggart on Jewish Glasgow, 1940s [I.]

Mrs Taggart's recollections were originally recorded c.1980 for the BBC Radio Scotland documentary series Odyssey.

I came from Palestine as they called it then in 1944 because I had married to a Glasgow fella, he was a soldier. I went first to his parents' house in Parkhead and then we went to the Gorbals to Thistle Street. There were quite a few Jewish families but I couldnae speak to them – they couldnae speak Hebrew and I couldnae speak Yiddish! I was there about eleven years in the house, it was only a single-end, a sub-let really, but I really liked the Gorbals there, really friendly people. I used to get fruit really cheap. There was this man with a fruit barrow and 'cos I come from Palestine he used to give me oranges and all kinds of fruit cheap. One day he saw me walking along the street and stopped me and told me that there's a horse running by the name of 'Palestine' and that I should back it. I did and he won, he won the Derby! . . . It was the shopping I really liked. If I wanted any Jewish food, I went to the Jewish shops, especially the Jewish bakeries, they were really beautiful. On a Sunday morning standing in a queue to buy the cakes and muffins from the Jewish shop. We used to look forward to Sunday mornings!

M. Rodgers, 'Glasgow Jewry', in B. Kay (ed.) *The Complete Odyssey: Voices from Scotland's Recent Past* (Edinburgh: Polygon, 1996) 234.

249) Polish immigrants in Scotland, 20th c. [I.]

A recent historian's account of the World War Two generation of Poles who settled across Scotland.

At the beginning of the twentieth century the total number of Poles living in Scotland was under 100. Some authors have, however, erroneously given a figure of thousands. This is due to the mistaken Polish identity applied to Lithuanians by the local people, the local newspapers and even in the official records of those times. Lithuanians, as we have already seen, came here between 1880 and 1910. They numbered about 8,000 in 1914 and were wrongly called Poles by everybody in Scotland. The Lithuanian spokesmen always protested against this mistake, as they did not like to be referred to as Poles. The Glasgow Herald published a statement on 14 October 1914 from a Polish representative, pointing out this error and stating that there were at that time only about 60 Poles living in Scotland compared to 7–8,000 Lithuanians. Unfortunately the records have never been corrected and some researchers and authors are still being misinformed on this subject.

Few refugees or immigrants from Poland came to Scotland between the two world wars. Their numbers, therefore, remained virtually static until 1939 when Germany and then Russia invaded Poland. After the defeat and occupation of their country, a great number of Polish soldiers and civilians managed to escape. They assembled in France where they set up a Polish Government in exile and reorganised the remnants of the Polish armed forces. Soon after, France also collapsed and the Polish Government in exile, its soldiers and civilians, all sought refuge in Britain. The soldiers were sent up north to Scotland, to be trained and reformed. Huge camps were set up in 1940 along the east coast of Scotland to accommodate the Polish army. A section of that coast was allotted to this army to be patrolled and protected by them.

Scottish Polish associations were set up to promote good relations between the Polish soldiers and the Scottish people. A number of Polish soldiers married Scottish girls and a Scottish Polish Wives Society was also formed in Dundee in early 1940s. These associations succeeded in their objectives initially, and relations were good for some time between the population near the camps and the camp dwellers. However, this honeymoon did not last long.

In July 1941 an agreement was concluded between Russia and the Polish Government in exile. Under the terms of this agreement all Poles who had been deported to Siberia and other places, since the occupation of Eastern Poland by Russia in 1939, were freed and assisted to join the Polish forces under British command. This swelled the Polish ranks in Britain. The Polish army was fighting beside the allied armies on the understanding that after victory the Allies would assist the Poles in the recovery of their country. This did not materialise. On the contrary, the Allies recognised the Russian-formed communist regime in Poland at the end of the war. The Polish exiles were opposed to the Russian dominance of their motherland and would not accept or recognise that Polish Government. Animosity grew between the commissars in Poland and the Poles abroad. The expatriates, both soldiers and civilians, were thus reluctant to go back home for fear of reprisals or oppression. Realising the dilemma of the Polish refugees in Britain, the British Government allowed all those who did not wish to return to settle in Britain. Legislation and regulations were introduced to facilitate their settlement.

In Scotland, hostels were set up throughout the country to provide lodgings for Polish workers. The unskilled males among them were encouraged to take up employment with farmers, in coal mining, quarrying and brick-making industries. The females were engaged in the textile industry and hospital services. Initially the trade unions opposed the recruitment of Polish workers. In addition to the same old allegations of lowering the wages and bringing down standards, the Poles were collectively labelled as Fascists by the trade unionists. As Catholics they were also accused by some of being 'Papist spies'. So, like other refugees and immigrants, they also went through a period of prejudice, discrimination and resentment, but fortunately for the Poles this period was very short. The reasons for this are as follows.

The Poles were political and not economic refugees. They fought and laid down their lives to uphold the freedom of Britain and many other countries. The Polish community in this country was predominantly male. There were very few Polish women with them. Most of the Polish males, therefore, married Scottish girls. These mixed marriages integrated them quickly into families and through families into communities. Finally, as early as 1950, the Poles began to leave their employments and set up small businesses of their own. Once they were not competing for jobs with the local workers, hostility against them disappeared rapidly.

By the early 1950s Polish communities had penetrated nearly all the major towns of central and eastern Scotland. Between nine and ten thousand of them settled in this country. The businesses they set up included launderettes, especially in Glasgow and Edinburgh, watchmakers, jewellers, cobblers and grocers. They also formed their own associations and societies to look after the interests of their communities and to keep in touch with each other. Some of these societies are still very active, particularly in Glasgow, Edinburgh, Falkirk, Perth, Dundee, Kirkcaldy and Galashiels. Social clubs and Sunday schools are run by these societies where the Polish language, history and culture are taught to the ever-dwindling number of pupils. Naturally, not very many children of second generation mixed marriages, where the mother happens to be Scottish and the father himself a product of a mixed marriage, would have any strong persuasion to go to these Sunday Schools.

The Polish community, having already passed the integration stage, is now being fast assimilated into Scottish society. Some have even changed their Polish surnames, perhaps to lose their identity. The recent political developments in Poland, however, may change the situation. Communism is on the wane and democratic forces are emerging fast to replace it. The fears and suspicions are disappearing, and old soldiers are renewing and repairing the broken links with their families and friends in Poland. Some have already returned to pass their remaining days in the surroundings and environment in which they were born and brought up.

B. Maan, *The New Scots: The Story of Asians in Scotland* (Edinburgh: John Donald, 1992) 33–5.

250) Parvin on preserving Iranian culture in Edinburgh, *c.* 1990 [I.]

Born in Mashad (north-east Iran) in 1958, Parvin's account was recorded c.1990 as one of a series of interviews with immigrants living in Edinburgh.

I found it extremely hard in Dumfries because all the time in Riyadh we had lived in a compound with eleven other families so we led a very communal life there and one was never lonely. And suddenly we left that to live in the countryside in southern Scotland where I didn't know anybody. I even had difficulty understanding their accents. My husband had to go to London for a six-month course, so there I was, left with two children in Dumfries. The nearest shops were twenty minutes' drive and it was a very cold winter. I was snowed in for a few days, I couldn't even open the front door! We had twelve hour powercuts that winter. It wasn't a very nice start to life in Britain.

I found people didn't know how to handle me, how to approach me. There wasn't a community, just individual families living in their houses having nothing to do with each other. We lived there exactly for a year before we came to Edinburgh.

In Edinburgh there are a large number of foreigners and I'm not in such a minority. I find it easier to relate to the local population than I did in Dumfries. I like the city, I like the buildings in Edinburgh, I think it is a very beautiful city and it's full of character.

I would like to preserve my own culture but it is virtually impossible to do so. I think my way of life would have been quite different had I stayed in Iran. I would probably have been quite religious but now I'm not because the pressure isn't there. Had I lived in Iran under the present regime it would have been inescapable!

My children can't be Iranians. They know there are links with Iran but they consider themselves Scottish really, particularly my son. Living here, it's really difficult to maintain my Iranian standards as far as my children are concerned, because they go to a British school, their friends are all British, they read English books, they watch British TV. I'm particularly unhappy about my daughter, as I feel I don't want to have a teenage daughter in Britain because of the life the young girls lead. I don't want the extent of freedom they have. I don't like the social pressures here, like early pre-marital sex and alcohol. But I don't think she should be protected as I was in my teenage years. I won't approve of her going to a pub with her friends when she's 16, staying out till midnight. I don't think I could possibly allow her to do that. But then, there are so many social pressures that I will have to compromise . . .

T. Edensor and M. Kelly (eds.) *Moving Worlds: Personal Recollections of Twenty-one Immigrants to Edinburgh* (Edinburgh: Polygon, 1990) 167–8.

Wales

251) The Jewish community in Swansea, 18th c. [I.]

See note on extract No.162.

> The community of Swansea is the only one in Wales of any antiquity, its establishment going back well into the eighteenth century. Oral tradition speaks of a Solomon (?) Lyons whose business, still in existence, was established in the city in 1731: while one of the founders of Canadian Jewry, Lazarus David is reported to have been born there in 1734. A more reliable tradition tells how the first Jewish settler was David Michael, who came over from Germany as a refugee and settled in Swansea in 1741, together with Nathaniel Phillips, later a 'banker' at Haverfordwest. Later on, he was joined by two other Jews named respectively Cohen and Jewish. Before long, they began to hold regular meetings for prayer, David Michael ultimately building for this purpose a simple synagogue, holding about forty persons, at the back of his house in Wind Street. The traditional date for the foundation of the community is 1780, but this is clearly too late, as it was in 1786 that the Corporation granted Michael the plot of land used as cemetery (the first person buried there was a Jew from Caermarthon).

C. Roth, *The Rise of Provincial Jewry* (London: Jewish Monthly, 1950) 102–3.

252) Hester Thrale describes the pleasures of her country residence, *c.*1795 [M.]

See note on extract No.5.

> So you see I am better off than my Neighbours. The Three Thrales are at Brighthelmstone, refreshing from the fatigue of the Gay Winter at Sea Bathing; Sophia hinted that they should like a Country House near Town for Summer Residence, and Mr Piozzi has requested them to *accept ours*; which he could have easily let I trust for £500 o'Year, but generously – as I think – preferred the future posessors as present Inhabitants of Old Streatham Park,

which will not now look melancholy because we live in Wales – And when all Debts are paid we *may* perhaps return, but my own heart being fixed on my own Country, I shall never more wish to leave it except for a short Visit to Bath and Hot Wells – a Happiness I still keep in Sight for a Motive to go forward.

H. L. Thrale, *The Piozzi Letters: Correspondence of Hester Lynch Piozzi, 1784–1798*, ed. E. A. and L. D. Bloom (London: Associated University Press, 1991) 422–3.

253) Hester Thrale notes her affinity with the Welsh countryside *c.*1795 [M.]

See note on extract No.5.

My letter is a very short one but the Truth is I feel low and languid, and hope to amuse you better when writing from Streatham Park, whither however nothing but serious business should carry us; for we have still a great deal to do here, and I prefer this Country to any I ever lived in for Pleasure.

Farewell charming Friend! I heard from your likeness Miss Hamilton the other day; she always asks for You concluding we live close together *as both reside in Wales.*

H. L. Thrale, *The Piozzi Letters: Correspondence of Hester Lynch Piozzi, 1784–1798*, ed. E. A. and L. D. Bloom (London: Associated University Press, 1991) 466.

254) English shopkeepers in Merthyr Tydfil, 1850 [M.]

A report from the Morning Chronicle, *4 March 1850 on English occupancy in Wales.*

The better class of tradesmen have advanced a little, raising their houses to a second floor . . . A tradesman named James, who had lived in Manchester but who is opening a business here, is building a house in the High Street on the same model as good houses in English towns.

H. Carter and S. Wheatley, *Merthyr Tydfil in 1851, a Study of the Spatial Structure of a Welsh Industrial Town* (Cardiff: University of Wales Press, 1982) 22–3.

255) The anti-Irish riots in Tredegar, 1882 [M.]

See note on extract No.26.

The jealousy against the Irish which culminated in the terrible riots at Tredegar was greatly increased because many of the native population had been thrown out of employment, for in the making of rails iron was becoming superseded by steel, which was being rapidly turned out in large quantities by the Bessemer process. There being less hands required to work the new system, some one must go, and the Welsh were determined that, so far as in them lay, it was the Irish who must suffer. The correspondent of the *South Wales Daily News*, speaking of the aversion with which the Irish were regarded previous to the Tredegar riots, said, – 'The Phoenix Park and other outrages intensified this feeling, and it had been an open secret for some days that an outbreak was contemplated and inevitable.'

The impending outbreak was not entirely unknown to the Irish. Many of them, particularly the young generation, knew sufficient of the Welsh tongue to catch the muttered threats of vengeance let fall in public-houses and elsewhere by the native population, not only of Tredegar but of the other towns among the hills, were to be cleared out. Heaven knows their lives were not spent among the most cheerful surroundings, but their way of earning their daily bread was the only one known not only to the original settlers from Cork and Kerry, but to the generations of Irish parentage born here. Let us take a brief glance at their position in such places as Tredegar. Naturally there would not be a healthier locality, but the smoke and grime of the works are ever present. In Tredegar, as in other of these towns, the houses chiefly inhabited by the Irish, such as those in Iron Row, which face the works – some of which were attacked and burnt in the riots – were, and are, wretchedly poor places. They were mostly run up at slight cost by the iron masters, for the convenience of their work people, and to get out of them the greatest possible profit for the smallest possible outlay. Many of these being, as at Merthyr, actually built on the cinder-tips, the levels are irregular, so that the uneven surfaces become receptacles for refuse and stagnant water. Enter one of these dwellings – and you will occasionally find a single room on the flagged and damp floor, with a sleeping loft above, not high enough to stand up in. When added to the discomfort of these dwellings – inside and out – you have the thick, murky atmosphere engendered by the blast-furnaces, working day and night, it can well be imagined that homes like these have little attraction beyond what the light-hearted Irish nature can give to the most dreary abode. It is not surprising that some are driven to drink and to the usually brighter surroundings of where it is sold. Two generations of our people have been born and have grown up in these Welsh hill-towns. You will hear the racy Munster tongue of the original immigrant, while the accent of his children and grandchildren is undistinguishable from that of their Welsh neighbours, whose vernacular they speak; indeed you will find some who can converse in all three tongues – Irish, Welsh, and English. – It is no uncommon thing to find a man of Irish extraction born in Rhymney or Tredegar, while his wife may have been born in Merthyr, and his children in Dowlais or elsewhere; yet they are all regarded by the natives, and by themselves, as being as much Irish as the original settlers who came in the famine years or still earlier.

With the exception of a few of those of intermarriages with the native population – and some of those consider themselves good Irishmen too – they are, indeed, as a rule, as Irish in heart as though born in Cork, or Waterford, or Tipperary.

Indeed it is cheering to find, among so much that is calculated to depress you, how many of domestic virtues which are the glory of the island of saints, how many of the kindly old customs of a warm-hearted race, and how much genuine patriotism you find here.

Go among them, go to Red Lion Square or the Iron Row, where the fiercest attacks were made on the Irish, and ask the origin of the terrible riots of 1882, and you will get a far clearer view of what then took place than you can gather from the newspapers of the day. When men are bent upon hostility and outrage it is easy to make the victims appear the aggressors. In nine cases out of ten this has been so in connection with the periodical outbreaks against the Irish, whether directed against their creed nationality or both, during the last hundred and fifty years. So it was in Tredegar.

Here, as in many places in this country, there were a number of people belonging to what is known as the 'Salvation Army,' one of those hysterical religious developments of which there has been such a plentiful crop, ever since those who consider themselves such a level-headed, sensible people, left the old faith. In the early part of 1882 there came to lodge at one of the Irish houses in the Iron Row, Tredegar, an old soldier who professed to be an Irishman and a Catholic. The only sort of employment he could get in Tredegar was of a very laborious kind, and he had probably acquired in the army a taste for the lazy life. As he was a fair scholar, and had the fluent tongue of an Irishman, he saw an opening for his peculiar gifts in the 'Salvation Army,' of which he became a recruit and a shining light. He made a great display of zeal, and created bad blood among the other lodgers, who, knowing his motive, did not hesitate to express their contempt for the renegade. In one of the 'army parades,' some of the Irish children pelted the 'turncoat' with flour. This was how the Irish became the 'aggressors' – this was made the immediate excuse for the explosion which was bound to come. This was on the Tuesday night previous to the excitement, and were the cause of disorderly scenes. There is no doubt but that the Salvationists were made use of at Tredegar, as they have been at Birkenhead and other towns, where disturbances have arisen, to excite and provoke the Irish into becoming the aggressors. The special correspondent of the Freeman said: – 'On Friday night there were ominous knots of Welsh and Irish in the streets, and in the evening, when the Salvationists were holding a service in the "Paddy Quarter," as it was called, the Converted Irishman was exhibited among the proceedings. A little hooting and the throwing of some flour over the converted one gave a pretext for the next night's attack.'

It was not until the following evening, Saturday, July 8th, 1882, for the week's work was done, and men's passions were inflamed by drink, that the Civil War

– for it was no less – broke out. Hostilities commenced by the smashing of the glass in many of the Irish houses. Then a large mob proceeded to attack one of the places in which they lived – Red Lion Square. At this time there do not appear to have been many Irishmen present to defend their homes, for one who was amongst the defenders states that when the mob attempted to enter the square it was held against by but a couple of men and four women, and that these would actually have succeeded in keeping out their assailants until more help arrived, but that the police broke through, by way of affording protection to the people of the square; and let the mob in to do their work of pillage and destruction. Among the few who held the square was an old soldier named O'Meara, who, finding his dwelling attacked, armed himself with a scythe and stoutly defended himself against a host of assailants. He was eventually overpowered and severely treated. He was arrested and afterwards put upon trial for his vigorous defence of his own and his neighbours' property. At the trial of the Irish and Welsh prisoners, the prosecution counsel displayed a singular amount of ignorance, or unfairness, or both, in stating the case against O'Meara. In describing the attack on the Irish quarter; he said: – 'A number of persons assembled in a thoroughfare known as Red Lion Square.' Now this would convey the impression that, this being what he termed a 'thoroughfare,' these people might have been passing on their way to some other place where they were attacked, single-handed, by this Irishman, for he said, 'he could not but regard O'Meara as the originator of what afterwards occurred.' A brief description of the scene of the rioting will show how unjust to the old soldier was this way of putting the case against him.

Above the middle of the town of Tredegar is a large open space, called from its shape 'The Circle', where the Salvationists chiefly held forth. The Circle is crossed at right angles by two thoroughfares. The street leading southward towards the ironworks has the Iron Row, an Irish locality, crossing in at the bottom. The main thoroughfare of Tredegar cuts the Circle, running Eastwards and Westward. Leaving the Circle behind you, and going along eastward for a few hundred yards, if you turn off it to the left you will find yourself in Red Lion Square, which is not a 'thoroughfare' in the ordinary sense at all. It does not lead to or from any place in particular, and, as a rule, few would think of entering it unless led by curiosity or having some special business in the place itself. Now the mob did not 'assemble' there by accident, but actually burst violently into the place with the view to demolishing the Irish houses and turning out the inhabitants. These driven out and not daring to reappear, all the witnesses at the trial were on the one side, and the scene of savagery in Red Lion Square was afterwards all put upon the head of the unfortunate O'Meara, who, in defending himself, it is said, cut off the nose of one of his assailants.

By the time this is said to have occurred there were some five thousand Welshmen in and about Red Lion Square, and the houses of the Irish were attacked with the utmost fury.

> They made a resolute stand for their homes and their families. But what could they do against such overwhelming odds? Doors and windows were broken in, furniture and bedding were tossed out into the square and a bonfire made of them; while the unfortunate people, after being brutally treated and rendered homeless, had to fly to seek shelter wherever they could. Some found it for the night about the coal-pits or out in the bleak, open hills, where they remained huddled together under severe showers of rain; while, according to the terms of a question, based on reliable information, put in the House of Commons by Mr T. P. O'Connor, not only were these poor people left homeless and their furniture destroyed, but; owing to the robbery of their provisions and money, a number of women and children were without food for twenty-four and some for forty-eight hours. Others of the victims stayed not until they had put many miles between them and the scene of the outrage, while fathers, mothers, and children got separated in the flight, and heard nothing of each other for many days.

J. Denvir, *The Irish in Britain from the Earliest Times to the Fall and Death of Parnell* (London: Kegan Paul, Trench, Trubner, 1892) 306–8.

256) Community relations in Dowlais, 1908 [I./M.]

A report from the South Wales Daily News, *21 October 1908, on the varied migrant groups in Dowlais, Mid-Glamorgan, South Wales. The area was dominated by the coal mining, iron founding and engineering industries at this time.*

> Dowlais is far in advance of any town that I have seen, in regard to social morality and neighbourliness. It is exactly like the country. This is one reason how so few, especially of the Welsh inhabitants, apply for parish relief. Hatred of parish relief seems to be ingrained in their nature. The case is different for our Irish friends. Although they live, as a rule, very peacefully amongst their Welsh fellow citizens, yet they will not suffer much hardship, before they cry out. The Jewish population is also increasing – many Jews having come here lately from Russia. These are almost all unskilled workmen. The Spanish part of the population is different. Most of these are expert steelworkers, and many of them receive the highest wages that are paid for manual labour in these works.

C. Holmes (ed.) *Migration in European History, vol.2,* (Cheltenham: Edward Elgar, 1996) 295.

257) An Italian 'shop' in Bedlinog, *c.*1914 [I.]

Walter Haydn Davies' recollections of his pre-First World War childhood were recorded c.*1980 for Hughes' history of the Italian community in South Wales.*

> I can still visualise the warmth of the Italian shop in my home village where we congregated as boys round the roaring cast-iron store with its outlet pipe

running through the establishment as if it was a boiler house. Here we gathered to listen to those of our friends who had just started working in the colliery talking 'shop' and presenting us with somewhat idyllic pictures of conditions underground as if they had worked in a kind of treasure-yielding King Solomon's mine . . .

The amount of money spent by these young 'stags' was really very small, a matter of a few pence only, things being so cheap in those days – a packet of cigarettes, for example, could be bought for a penny, a quarter of sweets cost no more, and Fire Boys Chocolate Bars were hot favourites at that price. We were the uninitiated schoolboys at this stage 'orphans of the night' as it were, watching our more affluent companions playing the various games for chits, which would enable them to spend more freely if luck came their way, and then sometimes a few crumbs might come [our] way. 'Flushed' with their winnings the fortunate ones would be likely to stand treat 'all round', in grandiose imitation of the public house routine. In the Italian shop it was not mild and bitter that flowed freely but lime juice and sarsaparilla.

Our Italian only tolerated our presence when things were going well, for he knew that school boys more often than not had no money to spend and were merely taking up room. But if anything upset him we were there for the butt of his anger, and with his limited knowledge of the English language he would bawl from across the counter, 'Short boys, out for never!' And we the penniless had to clear out into the cold, to make for some other 'better 'ole', if entry were possible, to a billiard room maybe.

What keen, hard-working businessmen these Italians were! Every possible devise to make money was there in those shops and they were prepared to keep open all day and late into the night, indeed, they never seemed to close and even remained open all day on Sunday, to the annoyance and disgust of shopkeepers brought up in the hidebound Welsh Nonconformist tradition of the puritanical Sabbath day. On Sunday the young men patronised them for supplies of sweets to munch during the chapel service, with reserves for cajoling the young ladies they dated for after-chapel courting sessions.

C. Hughes, *Lime, Lemon and Sarsaparilla: The Italian Community in South Wales, 1881–1945* (Bridgend: Seven, 1991) 48–50.

258) Joseph Keating on the Irish community in Mountain Ash, 1916 [I./M.]

Joseph Keating was born in the South Welsh village of Mountain Ash in 1871 to Irish parents. In this opening section of his autobiography the author gives an evocative account of his family lineage and his early years in Wales.

I was born on April 16, 1871, in what, at that time, was a charming pastoral village, in South Wales, set in a wooded valley and sheltered by wonderful mountains which are still my beloved friends whom I visit on the slightest excuse. I recall mule teams picking their way down the beautifully coloured slopes on a summer evening. The mules carried packs of provisions, or wood, over the hill-ranges from valley to valley. Those were primitive and picturesque days. No coach could travel over the mountains.

The other route for commerce was a canal that glistened like a silver ribbon fringing the brilliant robes of the eastern range. A few whitewashed farms stood out distinctly from the green hillsides, and droves of cattle plodded up and down the valley road, the drovers hilariously drunk, and the sheep or cows occasionally dashing into the kitchen of a wayside cottage, and creating consternation for a housewife, and huge entertainment for the children. By the time I was going to school, railway trains had begun to run up and down the valley. One went down in the morning and another – perhaps, it was the same one – came up in the evening . . .

We lived with a little colony of Irish emigrants, a small pool formed by a trickle from the flood of emigration which had been rushing out of Ireland to every corner of the world since the famine in the middle of the last century. Iron works and mines in Wales could provide work and bread. The Irish landed at various parts of the Welsh coast; and husbands, wives and children tramped away from the ships, until the men found work. Wherever they could earn bread they settled down.

The first comers secured places near the coast. Later groups had to march farther inland amidst the valleys.

They became labourers, navvies, miners and puddlers. They worked in the dust and darkness of 'rubbish-stalls' underground, and in the scorching blaze of steel-furnaces above. They swung pick, shovel, bar and hammer, and handled drills, blasting and hewing tunnels and cutting through mountains and valleys. Destiny drove them from their beloved Irish homes and farms to build railways, sink pits, and carry the hod up to the tops of boiler-stacks that seemed to be taller than the hills of this country of strangers. The exiles landed with the power to labour as the sum total of their wealth; and as they owned nothing but their poverty and their strength, they took the poorest dwelling-places as shelters for themselves and their families.

This was a calamitous thing for a man like my father, who traced his descent from Heber the Handsome, son of Milesius, King of Spain. I am not sure, though my father could easily explain, whether Milesius conquered the Firbolgs or the Tuatha de Danann, and became, in consequence, king of all Ireland. My father was born in Cahirciveen, Co. Kerry. By that time a British Government had usurped the sovereignty of Ireland, and my father's family being dispossessed of their ancient kingdom were without any revenue. He migrated to Wales when he was about eighteen, with a Munster brogue so thick that it could have been cut with a knife. Like other emigrants, he possessed only the strength of his body and hands, whereby he might gain the means of living. He is quite sure that the Rev. Geoffrey Keating, the renowned Irish historian, is one of his distinguished ancestors. It is impossible to dispute my father's claim to descend from kings and scholars because there is no record for or against it.

Our name, Keating, is Norman. The Irish way of pronouncing it is Kaet'n. Its correct Celtic spelling is Ceitinn. The Celtic form comes from the fact that the first Normans who went to Ireland became more Irish than the Irish themselves, and intermarried with the ancient Irish families. This is the only thing that lends any colour to my father's regal origin. The rest is purely a matter of imagination.

One important distinction I willingly grant my father: There was never a man in the whole world who could dance Irish jigs and reels with his fascinating gracefulness.

In his youth he had very black, wavy, shining hair, large blue eyes, a good-humoured smile, and, as now, a courtly, fine manner which made his personality exceedingly attractive. He was short, sturdy and lively, and known as 'Kaet'n, the lady-killer.' He must have had something undeniably dashing about him to have made a handsome girl like my mother fall in love with him. In his tramps among the Welsh hills he met her at Mountain Ash. He settled down there; and one fine morning they walked down the valley road, eight miles under sunlight, between mountain ranges, to Treforest Catholic Church, got married, and walked home again the same evening. He was thirty and she sixteen.

J. Keating, *My Struggle for Life* (n.p: Simkin, Marshall, Hamilton and Kent, 1916) 1–2, 4–6.

259) Spaniards in Dowlais, 1926 [I.]

A social investigator's account of migrant communities in mid-Glamorgan, South Wales.

The Spaniards born in Spain total 176 and all are aliens. These all reside in Dowlais and in contrast to the other immigrants they are very clannish, being found together in a colony comprised of Erin's Row, Cross Street and Brecon Street, Dowlais, though this colony is not as distinct as it was. They come chiefly from the Basque Province of Spain, where there are many ironworks. During the time of the Boer War, a works manager invited a number to Dowlais because labour was short; this was in the Autumn of 1899. These were housed in different parts of the works. Some slept in the Big Mill, and others found shelter in a building in the Ivor Works. A batch who came over in the Autumn of 1900 were accommodated in a similar manner, until houses called Alfonzo Street, were erected in Penywern. All the men were skilled tradesmen. As a result there were differences between them and the Welsh, who thought they would lose their posts. The growth of trades unionism stopped the feud, and the result is that the Spaniards are ardent Trade Unionists. In spite of this it seems that they will never be absorbed into the social life of the district as are the Jews. Fears of oppression have made them embittered. The glamour of the past glory of Spain has blinded them to the realities of the present. Even the freedom of this country does not satisfy them; they feel that if they become naturalised they will in some degree be fettered – they confuse liberty and licence; temperamentally vicious, the effect of past oppression has made them desire lawlessness. In their conversation they convey the idea that the whole world is up against them; they think that they are here on sufferance. Officially, members of the Roman Catholic Church, they are frankly irreligious. There are few old Spaniards here; most of the first comers have left for Canada, France and Belgium. In spite of the surrounding squalor, the cleanliness of most houses is remarkable. Although intermarriage does take place, the value of the Spaniards to the community is negligible. The fact that they are a migratory population too, prevents their social influence being considerable.

J. R. Williams, 'The influence of foreign nationalities on the life of the people of Merthyr Tydfil', *Sociological Review*, 18 (1926) 150–1.

260) Jews in Merthyr Tydfil, 1926 [I.]

See note on extract No.259.

The Jews are an important element in local life. They have come chiefly from Poland and the Baltic States of Russia. Though many have come from Austria, Hungary and Roumania they were only temporary settlers. Their exodus from Poland and Russia was caused by the Czarist persecutions of the Jews (the 'pogroms'). Many came over during the years 1896 and 1897. The Roumanian Jews were skilled industrial workers and found employment in the steel works. These left for the United States and Canada in 1896 and 1897 under a scheme organised by the Jewish Board of Guardians. The 'Bloody Sunday' (January 22nd 1905) Massacres of Jews in Russia caused another flight abroad and many of them came to this district. The number of Jews who came from Russia and Poland can be roughly determined by the last census figures. People who stated they were of Russian birth numbered 101 and there are 48 Poles here. The Jews have never been embroiled in great conflicts with the Welsh. They have been law-abiding citizens and give great assistance to charities and all public causes. Their contribution to local life exceeds what one would expect from al small community. They own much property and are, in proportion to their numbers, the largest ratepayers in the borough. Most are engaged in business and commercial life. All the pawnbrokers here are Jews. Although they have never lived in colonies they are strongly united and have always helped those in distress so that no Jew has ever become a charge upon the local Guardians. Their local life reveals them as a race imbued with high ideals, who value education very highly and do all in their power to broaden the minds of the masses. This fact is proved by the number of Jewish children who go to our secondary schools and proceed to the Universities.

J. R. Williams, 'The influence of foreign nationalities on the life of the people of Merthyr Tydfil', *Sociological Review*, 18 (1926) 150.

261) Irish in Merthyr Tydfil, 1926 [I.]

See note on extract No.259.

The present population numbers about 10,000, of whom more than 5,000 are in Dowlas, and more that 4,000 in Merthyr. It would be difficult to say when they first came over here; it was, however, subsequent upon the opening [iron] works [in 1760/65]. Famines at various times compelled them to migrate, and since the famines of 1845–48 there have been a continuous stream of Irish immigrants to this country. Many took up the work on the land and gradually drifted into industrial life. These men, who came chiefly from southern Ireland (the counties of Cork, Kerry and Waterford) were big muscular fellows who did not know their full industrial worth. They were employed on such poorly paid jobs as the unloading of iron ore and quarrying. Even if they desired posts in the works or underground, local antipathy kept them where they were. This animosity became very pronounced during the Fenian disturbances on 1867. Largely, however, the cause of the feud was religious. Welsh nonconformity looked on Anglicanism unfavourably; their attitude towards a race composed mainly of Roman Catholics can therefore be understood. The Phoenix Park murders in Dublin brought matters to a climax. The Irish population in Tredegar had to flee from the town in the early autumn of 1882, many fled to Dowlas, but after about three months they were allowed to return. Another time of strife arose in 1880 during a Parliamentary election. Henry Richard was the Liberal Candidate and Sir W. T. Lewis the Conservative. The Irish voted for the Conservative, the Welsh sympathies were Liberal, so feeling ran very high. Saturday nights saw many fights between drunken Irish and Welsh folk. This state of affairs has now disappeared. The Irish are now able to enter into all local activities in industry, business and social life. Their industrial salvation is due to the growth of trades unionism; education has also contributed to this better feeling. Intermarriage between the Welsh and Irish is more in evidence now, too, though their allegiance to the Roman Catholic faith is as strong as ever. They have always played a big part in elections. If the Irish vote is unanimous, as it often has been, they virtually decide closely contested elections. The fact that they have never lived in distinct colonies has helped to make it more possible for them to settle down with the Welsh.

J. R. Williams, 'The influence of foreign nationalities on the life of the people of Merthyr Tydfil', *Sociological Review*, 18 (1926) 149–50.

262) Neil Sinclair's childhood in Tiger Bay, 1940s [I.]

See note on extract No.94.

On cold winter nights I didn't enjoy 'getting it' because the coal house was outside in the backyard. Sometimes Patsy Clark, 'The Coal', of North Church Street would drop his sack in the Cupboard under the stairs but most of time the coal was outside, in the back, in the dog's house. Ruff, of course, lived inside with us! He shared his place by the fire with Farrouk, our Persian cat. Anyway I'd run out and shovel up the coal and rush back to my warm stool near the fire hoping to return to the same mystical land where the fire had taken me before. Unfortunately the same path through the coals was impossible to rediscover. Nevertheless, with the magic of the fire and my innocent imagination it wasn't hard to find a new place to explore.

Meanwhile, my parents would be still engrossed in the mystery which pervaded the living room by means of another magic: the wireless. While they were there I would follow a beckoning friend into the warmth between the coals on into the glowing centre of the earth . . . 'You're not going to sleep again are you, love?' Mam's voice would ring out. 'Why don't you go to bed?' Mam always had a way of giving orders while asking questions. And Dada had a way of finalising everything she said: 'Well, you heard your mother. Off you go then!' And sadly off I'd go, up the stairs; into my cold room and bed.

But some nights by the gaslight, the mantles of which were above the fireplace, Mam would tell me a story. 'It was a dark and stormy night and the captain said to his mate, "Tell us a yarn, mate!" and the mate began, "It was a dark and stormy night . . ."' I laughed as I jumped off my mother's knee when I first ever heard that recursive sea yarn.

Many nights a story would be told sitting by the fireplace in our little Victorian terraced house, one of 26 such houses on Old Frances Street – a street now gone some 30-odd years. 19 Frances Street was where I first became aware of the world and that world was the 1940s seaport community of the already legendary Tiger Bay, known to seamen everywhere.

Frances Street could be found sandwiched between Loudoun Square and Sophia Street with Old Angelina Street as an easterly boundary. At the other end the old stone wall that ran the length of Canal Parade hid the Glamorganshire Canal from view. Victorian city planning had created quite a secluded haven from the rest of Tiger Bay for us 'Frances Street Kids' in which to play.

Mrs Sharpes' – and subsequently Ghilan Farrah's – corner shop was number 1 opposite the Westgate Public House at the Old Angelina Street end. The rest of the street consisted of family homes and everyone on the street knew everyone else quite intimately. This goes without saying for the rest of Tiger Bay. Part of its uniqueness was this fact. We were the true definition of an 'urban village'. Everybody did know who your grandfather was, mother, relatives, etc. Which one was white, which 'coloured'. Which married Catholic,

Moslem or Jew and so on. There were the Williamses in number 2, Reggie, Ivor and 'Googie' among them. In number 4 was Mrs Ali, who was white like the Williams but whose daughter Miriam was black, Somali to be exact, who, in turn, had a daughter named Lorraine. She and I were great friends. Opposite Joan Smith and her family resided the Limas, who were previously the Silvas, of number 21 – Johnnie, my best friend; his brother, Albee; and all their sisters, Valerie, Josie, Netta and Margie, to name only a few. As with most of the homes in Tiger Bay the Limas' house was furnished with old Victorian furniture. I was always fascinated by the enormous dark wood table they had in their living room practically taking up all the space they had. Something befitting the Knights of the Round Table, I thought.

N. M. C. Sinclair, *The Tiger Bay Story* (Treforest: Zenith, 1993) 5–8.

263) The Tiger Bay community, 1950s [I.]

See note on extract No.94.

On the corner of Peel Street opposite the Arab School was the home of 'Kitty Said', a Cardiff girl, who had many years before married Mr Mohammed, an Egyptian. Now Kitty's husband was called Said Mohammed but the Sinclairs were in the habit of calling Mr Mohammed Mr Said and that is how Kitty became known as Kitty Said. Mary, Farida, Said, Gaynor and Mona were their Bay born Egyptian children. Living in Peel Street they were naturally friends of the Sinclair and James families despite the Muslim and Christian difference. Religious differences never interfered in Tiger Bay life anyway and so I spent a great deal of my life in their house. Many was the day we rolled up the carpet in their front room so we could dance to all the latest Rhythm & Blues records and it was in that room that we learned to do the Cha Cha Cha to Perez Prado's 'Cherry Pink & Apple Blossom White'. Once in a while I would be 'look out' for Mr Mohammed if May or Gayneor were cooking up a bacon sandwich when desperate for a 'Christian meal'.

Also 'Up the Bay' there was a part of Bute Street along side Loudoun Square where once thrived such commercial activities and institutions as Dickie Diamond's Dairy, Corne's Seamen's Clothes, the Seamen's Mission, Moore's Jewellers, Colpstein's, Volpert's and Louis Fennig's Butcher Shop. There was also the Adelphi pub next door to which you would find the Canadian Cafe, commonly known as 'Chic Chicalos', next to where you would find a side door leading to No. 182 Bute Street, the house where Shirley Bassey was born. Such a talent as hers is the result of the West African heritage of Tiger Bay where Calabar, Kru, Igbo, Soso and Yoruba seamen met Celtic and Anglo-Saxon brides whose living descendants, with African sounding names like the Mbakwes of Old Evelyn Street and the Sangos of Old Hodges Row, can still be found, along with some with not so African sounding names, like Boston, Davids and Glasgow. Add to this the Caribbean connection and in the streets

> 'Bengal Tiger', 'King of Beasts, 'Coloured Eva' and 'Black Dolly' are some of the nicknames you would have heard. And if we go back far enough in time you would have heard Welsh speaking families on the West side of Loudoun Square who used to attend the Old Welsh Church opposite the Wesleyan Methodist Church (where, as mentioned in the previous chapter, we used to see Paul Robeson in 'Sanders of the River' and 'Proud Valley' on Thursday nights for thrupence) where now stand the Butetown Health Centre and St Paul's Church, respectively.

N. M. C. Sinclair, *The Tiger Bay Story* (Treforest: Zenith, 1993) 57–9.

Bibliography and Further Reading

Migration: primary sources

Balderstone, K. C. (ed.) *Thraliana: The Diary of Mrs Hester Lynch Thrale Later Mrs Piozzi 1776–1809* (Oxford: Clarendon, 1951).

Burnett, J. *Destiny Obscure* (London: Routledge, 1994).

Burnett, J. *Useful Toil* (London: Routledge, 1994).

Cameron, W. *Hawkie: The Autobiography of a Gangrel* (Glasgow: D. Robertson, 1888).

Craig, D. *On the Crofters' Trail: in Search of the Clearance Highlands* (London: Cape, 1990).

Dent, A. G. (ed.) *The Family Records of Benjamin Shaw Mechanic of Dent, Dolphinholme and Preston, 1772–1841* (n.p: Record Society of Lancashire and Cheshire, 1991).

Denvir, J. *The Irish in Britain from the Earliest Times to the Fall and Death of Parnell* (London: Kegan Paul, Trench, Trubner, 1892).

Heinrick, H. *A Survey of the Irish in England* (1872) ed. O'Day, A. (London: Hambledon, 1990).

Jones, M. 'Welsh immigrants in the cities of North-West England, 1880–1930: some oral testimony', *Oral History*, 9 (1981) 33–41.

Kay, J. P. *The Moral and Physical Condition of the Working Classes, Employed in the Cotton Manufacture in Manchester* (Manchester: James Ridgeway, 1832).

Keating, J. *My Struggle for Life* (n.p: Simkin, Marshall, Hamilton and Kent, 1916).

Mac Amlaigh, D. *An Irish Navvy: the Diary of an Exile* (London: Routledge, 1964).

Morrison, N. *My Story* (Inverness: Highland News Office, 1937).

Parkes, E. A. and Sanderson, J. B. *Report on the Sanitary Condition of Liverpool* (London: HMSO, 1871).

Royal Commission on the Condition of the Poorer Classes in Ireland, Appendix G; The State of the Irish Poor in Great Britain, *Parliamentary Papers* (London: HMSO, 1836).

Settlement Examinations (Settlement Papers, Overseers of the Poor), Bedfordshire County Record Office, Bedford.

Settlement Examinations (Settlement Papers, Overseers of the Poor), Bradford Record Office, Sharp Bridges.

Settlement Examinations (Settlement Papers, Overseers of the Poor), Warwickshire Record Office, Bedworth.

Tibble, J. W. and Tibble, A. (eds) *The Letters of John Clare* (London: Routledge and Kegan Paul, 1951).

Migration: secondary sources

Baines, D. *Migration in a Mature Economy: Emigration and Internal Migration in England and Wales, 1861–1900* (Cambridge: Cambridge University Press, 1985).

Clark, P. 'Migration in England during the late seventeenth and early eighteenth century', *Past and Present*, 83 (1986) 57–90.

Davey, H. *Poor Law Settlement and Removal* (London: Stevens, 1925).

Davies, N. *The Isles: A History* (London: Macmillan – now Palgrave Macmillan, 2000).

Dentith, S. *Society and Cultural Forms in Nineteenth Century England* (London: Macmillan – now Palgrave Macmillan, 1998).

Fielding, S. and Davies, A. (eds) *Workers' World: Cultures and Communities in Manchester and Salford, 1880–1939* (Manchester: Manchester University Press, 1993).

Finnegan, F. *Poverty and Prejudice, A Study of Irish Immigrants in York 1840–1875* (Cork: Cork University Press, 1982).

Flinn, M. W. (ed) *Scottish Population History from the 17th Century to the 1930s* (Cambridge: Cambridge University Press, 1977).

Friedlander, D. and Roshier, R. 'A study of internal migration in England and Wales', *Population Studies*, 19 (1966) 239–79.

Hobsbawm, E. J. 'The tramping artisan', *Economic History Review*, 3 (1951) 299–320.

Houston, R. A. and White, I. D. *Scottish Society 1500–1800* (Cambridge: Cambridge University Press, 1989).

Kearns, G. and Withers, C. (eds) *Urbanising Britain* (Cambridge: Cambridge University Press, 1991).

Kussmaul, A. *Servants in Husbandry in Early-Modern England* (Cambridge: Cambridge University Press, 1981).

Lawless, R. I. *From Ta'izz to Tyneside: An Arab Community in the North-East of England during the Early Twentieth Century* (Exeter: Exeter University Press, 1995).

Lawton, R. and Pooley, C. *Britain 1740–1950: An Historical Geography* (London: Edward Arnold, 1992).

Lobban, R. D. 'The Irish community in Greenock in the nineteenth century', *Irish Geography*, (1961) 270–281.

MacRaild, D. M. *Irish Migrants in Modern Britain, 1750–1922* (London: Macmillan – now Palgrave Macmillan, 1999).

Nicolas, S. and Shergold, R. 'Internal migration in England, 1918–39', *Journal of Historical Geography*, 13 (1987) 155–68.

Parton, A. G. 'Poor Law settlement certificates and migration to and from Birmingham, 1726–57', *Local Population Studies*, 38 (1987) 23–9.

Pooley, C. and Turnbull, J. 'Leaving home: the experience of migration from the parental home in Britain since *c.*1770', *Journal of Family History*, 22 (1997) 390–424.

Pooley, C. and Turnbull, J. *Migration and Mobility in Britain since the 18th Century* (London: UCL Press, 1998).

Pooley, C. and Whyte, I. (eds) *Migrants, Emigrants and Immigrants: a Social History of Migration* (London: Routledge, 1991).

Pope, R. *War and Society in Britain, 1894–1948* (London: Longman, 1991).

Redford, A. *Labour Migration in England, 1800–1850* (Manchester: Manchester University Press, 1926).

Saville, J. *Rural Depopulation in England and Wales, 1851–1951* (London: Routledge, 1957).

Schofield, R. 'Age specific mobility in an eighteenth-century English rural parish', in Clark, P. and Souden, D. (eds) *Migration and Society in Early Modern England* (London: Hutchinson, 1987) 261–74.

Shannon, H. A. 'Migration and the growth of London, 1841–1891', *Economic History Review*, 5 (1935) 78–86.

Stillwell, J. and Congdon, P. (eds) *Migration Models* (London: Belhaven, 1991).

Stillwell, J., Rees, P. and Boden, P. (eds) *Migration Processes and Patterns: Population Redistribution in the United Kingdom* (London: Belhaven, 1992).
Stone, C. J. *Fierce Dancing: Adventures in the Underground* (London: Faber, 1996).
Thompson, F. M. L. (ed.) *The Cambridge Social History of Britain, 1750–1950, vol. 2, People and their Environment* (Cambridge: Cambridge University Press, 1990).
Tranter, N. *British Population in the Twentieth Century* (London: Macmillan – now Palgrave Macmillan, 1996).
Withers, C. and Watson, A. 'Stepwise migration and Highland migration to Glasgow, 1852–1898', *Journal of Historical Geography*, 17 (1991) 35–55.
White, I. D. *Migration and Society in Britain* (London: Palgrave – now Palgrave Macmillan, 2000).
Woods, R. *The Population of Britain in the Nineteenth Century* (London: Macmillan – now Palgrave Macmillan, 1992).
Wrigley, E. A. and Schofield, R. S. *The Population History of England, 1541–1871: a Reconstruction* (London: Arnold, 1981).
Zelinsky, W. 'The impasse in migration theory: a sketch map for potential escapees', in Morrison, P. (ed.) *Population Movements: Their Forms and Functions in Urbanization and Development* (Brussels: Ordina, 1983) 21–49.
Zelinsky, W. 'Classics in human geography: author's response', *Human Geography*, 17 (1993) 217–19.

Immigration: primary sources

Adams, C. (ed.) *Across Seven Seas and Thirteen Rivers: Life Stories of Pioneer Sylhetti Settlers in Britain* (London: THAP, 1987).
Benedetta, M. *The Street Markets of London* (London: John Miles, 1936).
Besant, W. *East London* (London: Chatto and Windus, 1903).
Brand, W. F. *London Life Seen with German Eyes* (London: A. Siegel, 1902).
Burman, R. 'The Jewish woman as breadwinner: the changing value of women's work in a Manchester immigrant community', *Oral History*, 10 (1982) 27–39.
Cottle, T. J. *Black Testimony: The Voices of Britain's West Indians* (London: Wildwood House, 1978).
Cunningham, W. *Alien Immigrants to England* (London: Frank Cass, 1969 reprint of 1897 edition).
Darby, A. S. *A View from the Alley* (Luton: Luton Town Hall, 1974).
Dent, R. K. *The Making of Birmingham: A History of the Rise and Growth of the Midland Metropolis* (Birmingham: J. L. Allday, 1894).
Destination Bradford: A Century of Immigration (Bradford: Heritage Recording Unit, 1987).
Edensor, T. and Kelly, M. (eds) *Moving Worlds: Personal Recollections of Twenty-one Immigrants to Edinburgh* (Edinburgh: Polygon, n.d).
Edwards, P. and Dabydeen, D. (eds) *Black Writers in Britain 1760–1890* (Edinburgh: Edinburgh University Press, 1991).
Equiano, O. *The Interesting Narrative and Other Writings* (Harmondsworth: Penguin, 1995).
Faucher, M. L. *Manchester in 1844; its Present Condition and Future Prospects* (Manchester: Abel Heywood, 1844).
Ferron, E. *'Man, You've Mixed': A Jamaican Comes to Britain* (London: Whiting & Birch, 1995).

George, P. *Memories* (n.p: Commonplace Workshop, 1976).
Gershon, K. *We Came as Children: A Collective Autobiography* (London: Gollancz, 1966).
Gouldbourne, H. 'Oral history and black labour in Britain: an overview', *Oral History*, 8 (1980) 24–34.
Green, J. *Them* (London: Secker and Warburg, 1990).
Harris, S. *The History and Conversion of Samuel Harris, a Polish Jew* (Bradford: n.p., 1833).
Hughes, C. *Lime, Lemon & Sarsaparilla: The Italian Community in South Wales, 1881–1945* (Bridgend: Seven, 1991).
Hutton, W. *An History of Birmingham to the End of the Year 1780* (Birmingham: Pearson and Rollason, 1781).
Kay, B. (ed.) *The Complete Odyssey: Voices from Scotland's Recent Past* (Edinburgh: Polygon, 1996).
Latimer, J. *The Annals of Bristol in the Eighteenth Century* (n.p: Butler and Tanner, 1893).
Levinson, M. *The Trouble with Yesterday* (Bath: Cedric Chivers, 1973).
Luskačova, M. *Photographs of Spitalfields* (London: Whitechapel Art Gallery, 1991).
McGeown, P. *Heat the Furnaces Seven Times More* (London: Hutchinson, 1967).
Mayhew, H. *London Labour and the London Poor* (London: George Woodfall, 1851) (Harmondsworth: Penguin, 1985).
Mayhew, H. *The Morning Chronicle Survey of Labour and the Poor: The Metropolitan Districts* (Horsham: Caliban, 1981).
Mohanti, P. *Through Brown Eyes* (Oxford: Oxford University Press, 1985).
Ng, K. C., *The Chinese in London* (Oxford: Oxford University Press, 1968).
Osler, A. *Speaking Out: Black Girls in Britain* (London: Virago Upstarts, 1989).
Perks, R., '"You're different: you're one of us": the making of a British Asian', *Oral History*, 15 (1987) 67–74.
Phillips, C. (ed.) *Extravagant Strangers: A Literature of Belonging* (London, Faber and Faber, 1997).
Phillips, M. and Phillips, T. *Windrush: The Irresistible Rise of Multi-Racial Britain* (London: HarperCollins, 1998).
Proceedings at Sessions of Peace. City of London and County of Middlesex, 2, 1735–1740.
Report of *The Lancet* Special Sanitary Commission on 'Sweating among Tailors of Liverpool and Manchester', *The Lancet*, 21 April 1888.
Salter, J. *The Asiatic in England: Sketches of Sixteen Years' Work Among Orientals* (London: Seeley, Jackson and Halliday, 1873).
Sharma, U. *Rampal and His Family* (London: Collins, 1971).
Shinwell, M. *Lead with the Left: My First Ninety-six Years* (London: Cassell, 1981).
Sinclair, N. M. C. *The Tiger Bay Story* (Treforest: Zenith, 1993).
Singh Tatla, D. 'This is our home now: reminiscences of a Punjabi migrant in Coventry', *Oral History*, 21 (1993) 68–74.
Smith, J. T. *Mendicant Wanderers through the Streets of London* (Edinburgh: William P. Nimmo, 1883).
Smith, T and Winslow, M. *Keeping the Faith: The Polish Community in Britain* (Bradford: Heritage Recording Unit, 2000).
Thompson, J. *The Life of John Thompson, Mariner, Written by Himself* (Newcastle: J. Catnach, 1810).
Thorogood, H. *East of Aldgate* (London: George Allen and Unwin, 1935).
Tomalinson, W. *Bye-Ways of Manchester Life* (Manchester: Butterworth and Nodal, 1887).
White, A. (ed.) *The Destitute Alien in Great Britain* (London: Edward Arnold, 1892) 51.
Williams, B. 'The Jewish immigrant in Manchester: the contribution of oral history', *Oral History*, 7 (1979) 43–53.

Winters, S. *Nobody Sleeps on the Rooftops Now* (Gravesend: AIM, 1994).
Wright, L. B. and Tinling, M. *William Byrd of Virginia: the London Diary 1717–21* (Oxford: Oxford University Press, 1958).
Zubrzycki, J. *Polish Immigrants in Britain: a Study of Adjustment* (The Hague: Nijhoff, 1956).

Immigration: secondary sources

Alderman, G. *Modern British Jewry* (Oxford: Oxford University Press, 1992).
Anim-Addo, J. *Longest Journey: A History of Black Lewisham* (London: Deptford Forum, 1995).
Anwar, M. *The Myth of Return: Pakistanis in Britain* (London: Heinemann, 1979).
Bailyn, B. and Morgan, P. D. *Strangers Within the Realm: Cultural Margins of the First British Empire* (Chapel Hill: University of North Carolina, 1991).
Brown, J. *The Un-Melting Pot* (London: Macmillan – now Palgrave Macmillan, 1970).
Buckman, J. *Immigrants and the Class Struggle: the Jewish Immigration in Leeds 1880–1914* (Manchester: Manchester University Press, 1983).
Carter, H. and Wheatley, S. *Merthyr Tydfil in 1851, A Study of the Spatial Structure of a Welsh Industrial Town* (Cardiff: University of Wales Press, 1982).
Cesarini, D. (ed.) *The Making of Modern Anglo-Jewry* (Oxford: Blackwell, 1990).
Coleman, D. A. (ed.) *Demography of Immigrants and Minority Groups in the United Kingdom* (London: Academic Press, 1992).
Collins, K. E. *Second City Jewry: the Jews of Glasgow in the Age of Expansion, 1790–1919* (Glasgow: Scottish Jewish Archive, 1990).
Cowie, L. W. *Henry Newman: an American in London 1708–43* (London: SPCK, 1956).
Cox, M. *Life and Death in Spitalfields* (York: British Council for Archaeology, 1996).
Davison, R. B. *Black British* (Oxford: Oxford University Press, 1966).
Desai, R. *Indian Immigrants in Britain* (Oxford: Oxford University Press, 1963).
Foot, P. *Immigration and Race in British Politics* (Harmondsworth: Penguin, 1965).
Fryer, P. *Staying Power: The History of Black People in Britain* (London: Pluto, 1984).
Gainer, B. *The Alien Invasion: the Origins of the Aliens Act of 1905* (London: Heinemann, 1972).
Gallagher, T. *Glasgow: The Uneasy Peace. Religious Tension in Modern Scotland* (Manchester: Manchester University Press, 1987).
George, M. D. *London Life in the XVIIIth Century* (London: Kegan Paul, Trench, Trubner, 1925).
Glass, R. *Newcomers: The West Indians in London* (London: Centre for Urban Studies/George Allen & Unwin, 1960).
Gwynn, R. D. *Huguenot Heritage* (London: Routledge and Kegan Paul, 1985).
Holmes, C. *Immigrants and Minorities in British Society* (London: George Allen and Unwin, 1978).
Holmes, C. *John Bull's Island: Immigration and British Society 1871–1971* (London: Macmillan – now Palgrave Macmillan, 1988).
Holmes, C. (ed.) *Migration in European Society, vol. 2* (Cheltenham: Edward Elgar, 1996).
James, S. (ed.) *Sisters and Strangers: Women, Race and Immigration* (Bristol: Falling Wall Press, 1982).
Kay, D. and Miles, R. *Refugees or Migrant Workers? European Volunteer Workers in Britain, 1946–51* (London: Routledge, 1992).
King, D. *Making Americans: Immigration, Race, and the Origins of the Diverse Democracy* (London: Harvard University Press, 2000).

Klier, J. *Imperial Russia's Jewish Question, 1855–1881* (Cambridge: Cambridge University Press, 1995).
Krausz, E. *Leeds Jewry: Its History and Social Structure* (Cambridge: Hefer, 1964).
Lennon, M., McAdam, M. and O'Brien, J. *Across the Water: Irish Women's Lives in Britain* (London: Virago, 1988).
Levy, A. *History of the Sunderland Jewish Community* (London: Macdonald, 1956).
Lichtenstein, R. and Sinclair, I. *Rodinsky's Room* (London: Granta, 2000).
Little, K. L. *Negroes in Britain* (London: Kegan Paul, 1947).
Lunn, K. (ed.) *Hosts, Immigrants and Minorities: Historical Responses to Newcomers in British Society* (London: Dawson, 1980).
Maan, B. *The New Scots: The Story of Asians in Scotland* (Edinburgh: John Donald, 1992).
Merrimann, N. (ed.) *The Peopling of London: Fifteen Thousand Years of Settlement from Overseas* (London: Museum of London, 1994).
Myers, N. *Reconstructing the Black Past: Blacks in Britain, 1790–1930* (London: Frank Cass, 1996).
Palmer, A. *The East End: Four Centuries of London Life* (London: John Murray, 2000).
Panayi, P. *Immigration, Ethnicity and Racism in Britain: 1815–1945* (Manchester: Manchester University Press, 1994).
Ramdin, R. *Reimaging Britain: Five Hundred Years of Black and Asian History* (London: Pluto, 1999).
Robinson, V. *Transients, Settlers, and Refugees: Asians in Britain* (Oxford: Clarendon, 1986).
Roth, C. *The Rise of Provincial Jewry* (London: Jewish Monthly, 1950).
Rushdie, S. 'The location of Brazil', *Imaginary Homelands: Essays and Criticism, 1981–1991* (London: Granta, 1992) 125.
Russell, D. and Walker, G. *Trafford Park 1896–1939* (Manchester: Manchester Studies/Manchester Polytechnic, 1979).
Scouloudi, I. (ed.) *Huguenots in Britain and their French Background, 1550–1800* (London: Macmillan – now Palgrave Macmillan, 1987.
Shyllon, F. O. *Black People in Britain 1555–1833* (London: OUP/Institute of Race Relations, 1974).
Spencer, I. *British Immigration Policy Since 1939: the Making of Multi-racial Britain* (London: Routledge, 1997).
Sponza, L. *Italian Immigrants in Nineteenth-Century Britain: Realities and Images* (Leicester, Leicester University Press, 1998).
Walker, W. M. *Juteopolis* (Edinburgh: Scottish Academic Press, 1979).
Walvin, J. *Black and White: The Negro in English Society 1555–1945* (London: Allen Lane, 1973).
Walvin, J. *Passage to Britain: Immigration in British History and Politics* (Harmondsworth: Penguin, 1984).
Walvin, J. *Black Ivory: A History of British Slavery* (London: Fontana, 1993).
Watson, J. L. (ed.) *Between Two Cultures: Migrants and Minorities in Britain* (Oxford: Blackwell, 1977).
Williams, J. R. 'The influence of foreign nationalities on the life on the people of Merthyr Tydfil', *Sociological Review*, 18 (1926) 148–52.
Wilson, A. R. *Finding a Voice: Asian Women in Britain* (London: Virago, 1978).

Life story/autobiography/identity

Baddeley, A. D. *The Psychology of Memory* (New York: Basic Books, 1976).
Bakhtin, M. M. *Speech Genres and Other Late Essays* (Austin: University of Texas, 1986).

Bertaux, D. (ed.) *Biography and Society: The Life History Approach in the Social Sciences* (London: Sage, 1981).

Brockmeier, J. and Carbaugh, D. (eds) *Narrative and Identity: Studies in Autobiography, Self and Culture* (Amsterdam: John Benjamins, 2001).

Bruner, J. *Acts of Meaning* (Cambridge: Harvard University Press, 1990).

Burke, P. (ed.) *New Perspectives in Historical Writing* (Cambridge: Polity Press, 1997).

Burnett, J., Vincent, D. and Mayall, D. (eds) *The Autobiography of the Working Class: an Annotated and Critical Bibliography* (Brighton: Harvester, 1984–7).

Butler, T. (ed.) *Memory: History, Culture and the Mind* (Oxford: Blackwell, 1989).

Canary, R. and Kozicki, H. (eds) *The Writing of History: Literary Form and Historical Understanding* (Madison: University of Wisconsin, 1978).

Carrithers, M. *The Book of Memory* (Cambridge: Cambridge University Press, 1990).

Chamberlain, M. and Thompson, P. *Narrative and Genre* (London: Routledge, 1998).

Chambers, I. *Migrancy, Culture, Identity* (London: Routledge, 1993).

Conekin, B. Mort, F. and Waters, C. (eds) *Moments of Modernity: Reconstructing Britain 1945–1964* (London: Rivers Oram, 1999).

Conrad, P. *Modern Times, Modern Places: Life and Art in the 20th century* (London: Thames and Hudson, 1998).

Dunaway, D. and Baum, W. (eds.) *Oral History: An Interdisciplinary Anthology* (London: Altamira, 1996).

Eakin, P. J. *How Our Lives Become Stories: Making Selves* (London: Cornell University Press, 1999).

Ellis, C. and Flaherty, M. G. (eds) *Investigating Subjectivity: Research on Lived Experience* (Newbury Park/London: Sage, 1992).

Fortier, M. A. *Migrant Belongings: Memory, Space and Identity* (Oxford: Berg, 2000).

Ganguly, K. 'Migrant identities: personal memory and the construction of selfhood', *Cultural Studies* 11 (1) 27–50.

Gardner, K. *Age, Narrative and Migration* (Oxford: Berg, 2001).

Genette, G. *Narrative Discourse,* trans. J. E. Lewin (Oxford: Blackwell, 1980).

Giddens, A. *Modernity and Self-Identity: Self and Society in the Late Modern Age* (Cambridge: Polity Press, 1997).

Halbwachs, M. *Collective Memory* (New York: Harper and Row, 1980).

Hay, C., O'Brien, M. and Penna, S. 'Giddens, modernity and self-identity: the "hollowing out" of social theory', in Bryant, C. and Jary, D. *Anthony Giddens: Critical Assessments* (London: Routledge, 1997) 85.

Humphreys, A. *Travels into the Poor Man's Country: The Work of Henry Mayhew* (Horsham: Caliban, 1977).

Kramsch, C. *Language and Culture* (Oxford: Oxford University Press, 1998).

Matless, D. *Landscape and Englishness* (London: Reaktion, 1998).

Mitch, D. *The Rise of Popular Literacy in Victorian England* (Philadelphia: University of Pennsylvania Press, 1992).

Moretti, F. *Atlas of the European Novel 1800–1900* (London: Verso, 1999).

Moretti, F. *The Way of the World: the* Bildungsroman *in European Culture* (London: Verso, 2000).

Neisser, U. and Fivush, R. (eds) *The Remembering Self: Construction and Accuracy in the Self-Narrative* (Cambridge: Cambridge University Press, 1994).

Olney, J. (ed.) *Autobiography: Essays Theoretical and Critical* (Princeton, NJ: Princeton University Press, 1980).

Plummer, K. *Documents of Life: An Introduction to the Problems and Literature of the Humanistic Method* (London: Allen and Unwin, 1983).

Portelli, A. *The Death of Luigi Trastulli and Other Stories: Form and Meaning in Oral History* (Albany: SUNY, 1991).

Porter, R. (ed.) *Myths of the English* (Cambridge: Polity Press, 1992).

Propp, V. *The Theory and History of Folklore* (Manchester: Manchester University Press, 1984).

Radstone, S. (ed.) *Memory and Methodology* (Oxford: Berg, 2000).

Rapport, N and Dawson, A. (eds) *Migrants of Identity: Perceptions of 'Home' in a World of Movement* (Oxford: Berg, 1998).

Ricoeur, P. *Time and Narrative* (Chicago: Chicago University Press, 1984–8).

Rosenwald, G. C. and Ochberg, R. L. (eds) *Storied Selves: The Cultural Politics of Self-Understanding* (New Haven/London: Yale University Press, 1992).

Rubin, D. C. (ed.) *Remembering Our Past: Studies in Autobiographical Memory* (Cambridge: Cambridge University Press, 1996).

Sapir, J. D. and Crocker, J. C. (eds) *The Social Use of Metaphor: Essays on the Anthropology of Rhetoric* (Pennsylvania: University of Pennsylvania Press, 1977).

Samuel, R. and Thompson, P. (ed.) *Myths We Live By* (London: Routledge, 1990).

Somers, M. 'The narrative constitution of identity: a relational and network approach', *Theory and Society* 23(1994) 605–49.

Stahl, S. 'The personal narrative as folklore', *Journal of the Folklore Institute,* 14 (1977) 9–30.

Steedman, C. *Strange Dislocations: Childhood and the Idea of Human Interiority 1780–1930* (London: Virago, 1995).

Taylor, C. *Sources of the Self: the Making of the Modern Identity* (Cambridge: Cambridge University Press, 1998).

Tedlock, D. *The Spoken Word and the Work of Interpretation* (Philadelphia: University of Pennsylvania Press, 1983).

Temple, B. 'Telling tales: accounts and selves in the journeys of British Poles', *Oral History*, 23 (1995) 60–4.

Tonkin, E. *Narrating our Pasts: The Social Construction of Oral History* (Cambridge: Cambridge University Press, 1998).

Trinder, B. *The Making of the Industrial Landscape* (London: Phoenix, 1997).

Wyer, R. S. (ed.) *Knowledge and Memory: The Real Story* (Hillsdale: Erlbaum, 1995).

Yans-McLaughlin, V. (ed.) *Immigration Reconsidered: History, Sociology and Politics* (Oxford: Oxford University Press, 1990).

Index

The index is designed as a research tool which allows access to various categories of information as well as to thematic groupings of extracts which might otherwise be obscure. Individuals are listed three times: by nationality, occupation and name. Professions are listed twice: by skill as well as type of activity. Smaller towns are listed by county. Each extract is also listed according to type (oral history interview, government report etc). Bold type refers to comments in the introductory essays; all other references are to extracts.